HIDD

Arizona

HIDDEN ®
Arizona

Stephen Dolainski

SECOND EDITION

Ulysses Press ®
BERKELEY, CALIFORNIA

Published by:
ULYSSES PRESS
P.O. Box 3440
Berkeley, CA 94703-3440

ISSN 1523-5777
ISBN 1-56975-173-0

Printed in Canada by Transcontinental Printing

10 9 8 7 6 5 4 3

EDITORIAL DIRECTOR: Leslie Henriques
MANAGING EDITOR: Claire Chun
PROJECT DIRECTOR: Lily Chou
COPY EDITOR: Steven Schwartz
EDITORIAL ASSOCIATES: Deborah Brink, Natasha Lay,
    Marguerite Clipper
TYPESETTER: David Wells
CARTOGRAPHY: Stellar Cartography
COVER DESIGN: Leslie Henriques
INDEXER: Sayre Van Young
COVER PHOTOGRAPHY:
    FRONT: Markham Johnson (backroads)
    CIRCLE: Steve Cohen (Navajo Indian on horseback,
    Monument Valley Tribal Park)
    BACK: Dewitt Jones (Anasazi pottery)
ILLUSTRATOR: Glenn Kim

Distributed in the United States by Publishers Group West, in Canada by Raincoast Books, and in Great Britain and Europe by World Leisure Marketing

HIDDEN is a federally registered trademark of BookPack, Inc.

Ulysses Press 🐢 is a federally registered trademark of BookPack, Inc.

Write to us!

If in your travels you discover a spot that captures the spirit of Arizona, or if you live in the region and have a favorite place to share, or if you just feel like expressing your views, write to us and we'll pass your note along to the author.

We can't guarantee that the author will add your personal find to the next edition, but if the writer does use the suggestion, we'll acknowledge you in the credits and send you a free copy of the new edition.

ULYSSES PRESS
3286 Adeline Street, Suite 1
Berkeley, CA 94703
E-mail: readermail@ulyssespress.com

*

Ulysses Press would like to thank the following readers who took the time to write in with suggestions that were incorporated into this new edition of *Hidden Arizona*:

Betty Cheater of Wyndmoor, PA; Niki Christopher of Tulsa, OK; Sara Cornwall of Norwalk, CT; Roy and Bonnie Dern of San Antonio, TX; Wendy Disch of Oceano, CA; Michael Halpern; Robert D. Maddox; Steven and Sally Mullens of Kenya; Mary Ann Schaefer of Thornton, CO; Laurie Weakley of Chapel Hill, NC.

What's Hidden?

At different points throughout this book, you'll find special listings marked with a hidden symbol:

◄ HIDDEN

This means that you have come upon a place off the beaten tourist track, a spot that will carry you a step closer to the local people and natural environment of Arizona.

The goal of this guide is to lead you beyond the realm of everyday tourist facilities. While we include traditional sightseeing listings and popular attractions, we also offer alternative sights and adventure activities. Instead of filling this guide with reviews of standard hotels and chain restaurants, we concentrate on one-of-a-kind places and locally owned establishments.

Our authors seek out locales that are popular with residents but usually overlooked by visitors. Some are more hidden than others (and are marked accordingly), but all the listings in this book are intended to help you discover the true nature of Arizona and put you on the path of adventure.

Contents

Maps

OUTDOOR ADVENTURE SYMBOLS

The following symbols accompany national, state and regional park listings, as well as beach descriptions throughout the text.

▲	Camping		Snorkeling or Scuba Diving
	Hiking		Waterskiing
	Biking		Windsurfing
	Horseback Riding		Canoeing or Kayaking
	Downhill Skiing		Boating
	Cross-country Skiing		Boat Ramps
	Swimming		Fishing

ONE

The Grand Canyon State

 If your image of Arizona is all cowboys, ranches and hitching posts, it's time for another look. For while the flavor of the Old West is certainly still in evidence throughout the state, the trappings of the 20th century are everywhere—indeed, flourishing and growing apace. Head to the major cities—including Phoenix, Scottsdale, Tempe and Tucson—and you'll find all the culture and amenities of any cosmopolitan metropolis: vibrant arts communities, professional sports galore, shopping centers and trendy stores as far as the eye can see, fine college campuses and museums, intriguing art galleries and architecture, as well as enough golf, tennis and other activities to satisfy anyone and everyone. But if you're hankering for a taste of the great outdoors or a glimpse of the frontier life, well, they're here, too: miles of open desert, rivers to swim and sail, trails to roam and towns set more in the past than the present. So saddle up, friend, because Arizona has it all. For each cowboy, you'll find a city slicker; for each country music bar, there's a rhythm-and-blues joint; for each thirsty desert view, add a snowcapped mountain; and for each rough 'n tough dude ranch, imagine a decadently luxurious resort.

Arizona covers a 114,000-square-mile chunk of land on the southwestern corner of the United States and is bordered by Mexico on the south, California and Nevada on the west, Utah to the north and New Mexico to the east. Although it is the sixth largest state in the nation, Arizona has fewer than 5,000,000 residents. Some have called it the most geographically diverse state in the United States, a point that's hard to argue. In the north are high mountains and the Grand Canyon, as well as the Mogollon Rim, a 1500-foot-high wall of land stretching for hundreds of miles. Indian reservations cover the northeast corner, a high plateau dotted with spectacular mesas and buttes and wide open spaces known for their stark beauty. On the western border, the Colorado River is a cool, blue waterway cutting through a hot, semi-barren landscape. The Sonoran Desert, characterized by giant saguaro cacti with their wildly splayed arms and accordion pleats, spreads from Mexico to central Arizona. To the east lie the White Mountains, covered with pine trees and dotted with lakes. From low desert to snowcapped mountains to wide rivers, Arizona is proud to show off its natural jewels.

Plan to spend some time in Arizona; its greatest attractions are not seen in a blur speeding down the highway. Venture off main roads and get to know the people and land. See which of those Western myths you've seen in the movies are true, and which belong only to vivid imaginations.

But most of all, relax. The pace here is slow, the mood casual. Soak up the sun, leave your watch at home and simply enjoy. You're in Arizona.

▼▼▼▼▼▼▼▼▼
Where to Go

This book covers everything you need to know about visiting Arizona—where to sleep, shop, dine, dance, be entertained and explore the outdoors. It is divided into ten chapters. This first chapter offers practical details for planning your trip. Chapter Two explores Arizona's natural landscape, while Chapter Three delves into the region's history, including American Indian and Spanish influences. Chapter Four focuses solely on the Grand Canyon, which is worthy of a book in itself. Chapter Five heads to the northeast corner of the state and Indian Country, including the Painted Desert and Petrified Forest. Sedona, Jerome, Flagstaff and Prescott all are covered in Chapter Six, while Chapter Seven travels down the state's western edge from Kingman to Lake Havasu City and the London Bridge. Chapter Eight describes the Phoenix/Scottsdale area, while Chapter Nine ventures east into the mountains and scenic areas from Globe to Pinetop-Lakeside and the Coronado Trail. Chapter Ten moves farther south to Tucson, Tombstone and the Mexican border.

Many visitors begin a visit to Arizona by heading for the **Grand Canyon**, the largest single geological feature in the Southwest, which splits the region between north and south. The "village" on the South Rim of the Grand Canyon, just an hour's drive from interstate Route 40, is developed on a grand scale, complete with an airport. The North Rim, farther by road from major cities and main routes and closed during the winter months, is more relaxed and secluded, though still busy enough to make advance lodging or camping reservations essential. The northern area of Grand Canyon National Park adjoins Glen Canyon National Recreation Area whose focus is manmade Lake Powell. You can rent a houseboat and enjoy a leisurely trip through the region's natural beauty.

Northeastern Arizona, also known as Indian Country, includes the vast, sprawling Navajo Indian Reservation, larger than some East Coast states, as well as the remote, ancient mesa-top pueblos of the Hopi Indian Reservation, a fiercely traditional and independent region although—or perhaps because—it's completely surrounded by Navajo land. The center of the Navajo world according to legend, Canyon de Chelly is still inhabited by people who herd sheep and live without electricity. Visitors can view the hogans (traditional Navajo log homes) and pastures from high up on the canyon rim, but can only enter the labyrinth accompanied by a Navajo guide. Another national park service unit operated by the tribe, Navajo National Monument protects some of the best Anasazi ruins in the Four Corners area—the region where Arizona, Utah, Colorado and New Mexico converge. The monument's biggest Indian ruin is only accessible on horseback. The third major park on the reservation is Monument Valley Tribal Park, a landscape so familiar from the many films, television shows and advertisements filmed here that visitors may feel like they're driving through a movie as they travel the backcountry road around the valley and visit the hogans of the people who live in this, one of the most remote places in the United States. A tour of Hubbell Trading Post National Historic Site and perhaps a stop at a still-operating trading post will round out your Indian Country experience.

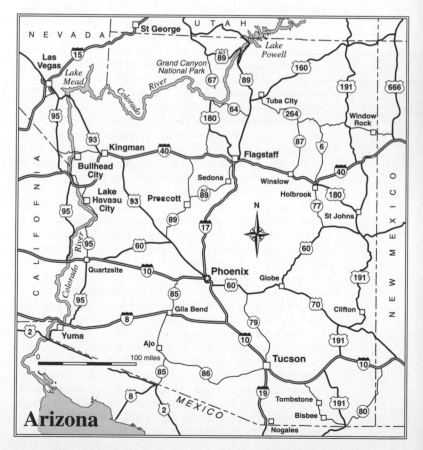

Route 40 through **North Central Arizona** will bring you to Flagstaff, a winter ski resort and college town, sitting on the edge of the dramatic San Francisco Peaks at 7000 feet and blanketed with ponderosa pine trees. Drive south through spectacular Oak Creek Canyon to Sedona, an upscale artist community with a New Age bent and an abundance of shopping. This is also the heart of scenic Red Rock Country, where red sandstone has eroded into dramatic formations of incomparable beauty. Jerome, scenically perched in the Mingus Mountains, is a former mining town that's now home to a small community of artists. Just down the road is Prescott, the original territorial capital of Arizona, which draws visitors with its numerous museums and low-key charm.

Never mind that **Western Arizona** is surrounded by parched desert. The 340-mile-long stretch of the Colorado River that establishes the state's "west coast" border has created an aquatic playground spilling over with unparalleled scenic and recreational opportunities. Kingman serves as a northern gateway to a succession of lakes, resorts and riverfront coves, as well as to the historic gold and silver mining ghost towns of Oatman and Chloride. The Lake Mead National Recreational Area extends to include Lake Mohave, where you'll find Bullhead City, the fastest growing city in Arizona. Farther south is Lake Havasu City, home to the authentic London Bridge, which was brought over from England and reassembled here. Continue down State Route 95 and you'll come to Quartzsite, which attracts more than half a million visitors every February for its annual rock and mineral extravaganza.

Phoenix, the state capital and the largest city in the Southwest, is the focus of **South Central Arizona**. It's amazing that a city of over a million people could survive at all in such a sunbaked desert valley, but a complex system of dams and aqueducts has allowed Phoenix to become the ninth-largest city in the United States. At first, this rectilinear sprawl of suburbs and shopping malls, giant retirement communities, towering office buildings, industrial parks and farmlands full of year-round citrus and cotton crops may seem to offer few charms for the vacationer. But those who take time to explore Phoenix will soon discover that this city, where it is often better to spend daytime hours indoors, has more than its share of fine museums. The winter months are the time for outdoor adventuring in the Phoenix area, and hiking, horseback riding, boating and fishing opportunities abound. Nearby Scottsdale blends the architecture of the Old West with exclusive shops, galleries, restaurants and nightclubs, while other towns within easy day-trip distance of Phoenix, such as Wickenburg, recall grittier and more authentic memories of the rough-and-rowdy mining boomtown era of turn-of-the-century Arizona.

Towering mountain peaks, sparkling streams and lakes, and dense pine forests surprise many travelers to the high country of **Eastern Arizona**. This forest primeval encompasses the mountain hamlets of Show Low, Pinetop and Lakeside, summer resorts famous for their hiking and fishing, and popular with those trying to escape the scorching temperatures on the desert floor. During winter, skiers flock to the downhill runs and cross-country trails at nearby Sunrise ski resort on the White Mountain Apache Indian Reservation. The forests deepen as you travel east to Alpine, a mountain village just a few miles from the New Mexico border. At the heart of the "Arizona Alps," Alpine is a mecca for nature buffs, who love the profusion of outdoor activities—hiking, camping, hunting and fishing. Alpine is also a northern guidepost along the Coronado Trail, which snakes south through some of the most spectacular scenery in the Southwest to the historic mining town of Clifton. Built along the banks of the San Francisco River, Clifton and its historic Chase Creek Street give a glimpse of what Arizona was like at the turn of the century. Traveling south from Clifton, juniper foothills give way to rolling grasslands and the fertile Gila River Valley, where cotton is king and the town of Safford marks Arizona's eastern anchor of the Old West Highway. This strip of Arizona, stretching 203 miles from Apache Junction to the New Mexico state line, is rich in the frontier history of the Old West. Tracing a course first charted by Coronado, Geronimo, the Dutchman, Billy the Kid, Johnny Ringo and pioneers looking for a place to call their own, you'll pass through cactus-studded valleys, pine-topped mountains, rugged and craggy canyons, lost

◆◆◆

RIDERS OF THE PURPLE SAGE

The allure of Arizona has not gone unnoticed by the publishing and film industries. Zane Grey based many of his Western novels on north central Arizona, including *Riders of the Purple Sage*. Tony Hillerman's contemporary murder mysteries are often set in the Navajo Indian Reservation and Four Corners area and include *Thief of Time* and *The Blessing Way*. Oliver LaFarge's Pulitzer prize–winning novel *Laughing Boy* describes Navajo life. Movies filmed at Old Tucson Studios include John Wayne's *Rio Bravo* and *El Dorado*; Paul Newman's *The Life and Times of Judge Roy Bean*; and *Gunfight at the O.K. Corral* with Kirk Douglas. Monument Valley was the setting for *How the West Was Won* and *The Legend of the Lone Ranger*. *Oklahoma* and *The Red Badge of Courage* were filmed in Patagonia, while *The Riders of the Purple Sage* was shot in the Sedona/Oak Creek Canyon area.

treasure and historic copper mines. Along the way you can sample the area's history in Globe's plantation-style mansions and antique shops and its pre-history at the Besh-Ba-Gowah archaeological site.

Southern Arizona in the springtime, when the desert flowers bloom, is as close as most of us will find to paradise on earth. The secret is well-kept because during the summer tourist season, when most visitors come to the Southwest, Tucson is considerably hotter than paradise—or just about anyplace else. Those who visit at any time other than summer will discover the pleasure of wandering through the stands of giant saguaro cactus that cover the foothills at the edge of town, perhaps learning more about the region by visiting the wonderful Arizona-Sonora Desert Museum and seeing the radiant 18th-century Spanish Mission San Xavier del Bac. For more desert beauty, drive west through the cactus forest of the Tohono O'Odham (Papago) Indian Reservation to Organ Pipe Cactus National Monument on the Mexican border. Many people consider the monument to be the most beautiful part of the southwestern desert. Another great side trip from the Tucson area is Cochise County to the east. National monuments in the rugged, empty mountains preserve the strongholds of Apache warlords and the cavalrymen who fought to subdue them. Old Bisbee, until recently the headquarters for one of the nation's largest open-pit copper mining operations, has been reincarnated as a picturesque, far-from-everything tourist town. Tombstone, meanwhile, enjoys its reputation as the site of a famous gunfight that occurred more than a century ago, and remains one of the most authentically preserved historic towns of the Old West.

▼▼▼▼▼▼▼▼▼▼
When to Go

SEASONS

Many people imagine Arizona to be a scorching hot place. Part of it—Tucson, Phoenix, southern and western Arizona—lives up to expectations with daytime high temperatures averaging well above the 100° mark through the summer months. Even in January, thermometers in this area generally reach the high 60s in the afternoon and rarely fall to freezing at night. The clement winter weather and practically perpetual sunshine have made the Arizona desert a haven for retired persons and seasonal residents seeking refuge from colder winters.

Yet less than 200 miles away, the North Rim of the Grand Canyon is closed in the winter because heavy snows make the road impassable. Northern Arizona has cold, dry winters with temperatures usually rising above freezing during the day, but often dropping close to zero at night. The high mountains remain snowcapped all winter and boast several popular ski areas. At lower elevations, lighter snowfalls and plenty of sunshine keep roads clear most of the time.

Where rugged mountains collide with the Sonoran Desert, small changes in elevation can mean big variations in climate. As a rule, climbing 1000 feet in elevation alters the temperature as much as going 300 miles north. For instance, the bottom of the Grand Canyon is always about 20° warmer than the top rim. In Tucson, some people bask by swimming pools during the winter, while others ski on the slopes of nearby Mount Lemmon.

Springtime is a mixed blessing. Flooding rivers, chilly winds and sandstorms sometimes await visitors in March and early April, but those who take a chance are more likely to experience mild weather and spectacular displays of desert wildflowers. Leaves do not appear on the trees until late April at moderate elevations, late May in the higher mountains.

> Umbrellas are considered an oddity in these parts. When it rains, the approved means of keeping water from running down the back of your neck is a cowboy hat.

Throughout Arizona, June is the hottest month. In the southern and western parts of the state, the thermometer can, and often does, climb above a sweltering 100°. Lizards are the most active form of life outside air-conditioned houses and buildings. People have even been known to fry eggs on the sidewalks and let popcorn pop inside closed automobiles. That's when desert dwellers vacation in northern states, or head to higher elevations, where temperatures average in the low 80s in the summer.

Much of the year's rain is dumped in what locals call the monsoon season—July, August and early September. Try to plan outdoor activities in the morning hours because during the afternoons or early evenings, winds gust and dark cumulus clouds roll in, emptying their store of water before moving on. While these thunderstorms usually cool things down on hot afternoons, the storms don't last long and the skies quickly clear. But when the rains do come, be alert to the dangers of flash floods. Water can quickly run off rocky desert surfaces and into canyons and gullies, sweeping away boulders, cars, people—anything in its path.

Autumn is the nicest time of year. Locals used to keep this fact to themselves, and until recently tourists in October were about as rare as snowflakes in Phoenix. Nowadays the secret is out, and record numbers of people are visiting during the fall "shoulder season" to experience autumn colors and bright Indian summer days.

CALENDAR OF EVENTS

Northeastern Arizona Relive a tradition of the frontier West on the **Hashknife Sheriff Posse's Pony Express Ride** from Holbrook to Scottsdale.   **JANUARY**

South Central Arizona Crowds gather in Scottsdale to watch some of the PGA Tour's best golfers at the **Phoenix Open**, one of

Arizona's largest spectator events. The **Barrett-Jackson Auction** is a huge classic and collectible car auction in Scottsdale, with some 900 vehicles ranging in price from several thousand to millions of dollars.

Eastern Arizona   **Sled Dog Races** in Alpine attract entrants from as far away as the Yukon. Rock hounds and gem collectors will like the **Gila County Gem and Mineral Show** in Globe.

FEBRUARY   **North Central Arizona**   At the **Flagstaff Winter Festival**, events include star gazing, sled-dog races, snow games, a snow softball tournament, skiing, concerts and winetasting.

Western Arizona   The **Quartzsite Gemboree** attracts several hundred thousand rock hounds and gem collectors from around the world for its festivals and flea markets in late January and early February.

South Central Arizona   **Gold Rush Days** in Wickenburg features a parade, rodeo, arts-and-crafts show, melodrama, gold mucking and drilling competitions and a beard-growing contest. More than 400 artists display their wares amidst entertainment, hot-air balloons and sky divers at the **Great Fair** in Fountain Hills. Casa Grande is the site of **O'Odham Tash—Casa Grande Indian Days,** which includes American Indian rituals and arts and crafts. Scottsdale hosts the largest **All-Arabian Horse Show** in the world.

Eastern Arizona   The **Arizona Renaissance Festival** in Apache Junction near Phoenix has music, theater, crafts, games and tournaments on weekends February through March. **Lost Dutchman Days** in Apache Junction is another community celebration full of traditional small-town events—like a Fourth of July in February.

Southern Arizona   The **Tucson Gem and Mineral Show** draws jewelers and collectors from around the world. At Tucson's **La Fiesta de los Vaqueros,** events include bareback riding, steer wrestling, barrel racing, bull riding and the world's longest nonmotorized parade. One of the oldest arts and crafts shows in Arizona, the **Tubac Festival of the Arts** features artists from all over the country, as well as entertainment. The **Tohono O'odham All-Indian Rodeo and Fair** at Sells, west of Tucson on the Indian reservation, features outstanding pottery, rug and jewelry exhibits, as well as a rodeo.

MARCH   **South Central Arizona**   An outstanding selection of Southwest arts and crafts can be found at the Phoenix **Heard Museum Guild Indian Fair and Market,** which also features American Indian food, music and dance. Explore turn-of-the-century buildings on Globe's **Historic Home & Building Tour & Antique Show.** The **Scottsdale Arts Festival,** which also takes place in November, features dance and music performances and crafts exhibitions. The unusual **Chandler Ostrich Festival** has ostrich racing for a highlight, in addition to music, a parade, art exhibits, carnival rides and an automobile show. In Tempe the huge MAMA Spring Festival of the Arts features more than 450 national artists, as well as adult and children's entertainment.

Southern Arizona Held at Tucson's **San Xavier del Bac Mission**, the Wa:k Pow Wow celebrates Tohono O'Odham traditions and features a fiddler's contest and intertribal dancing. The high point of **Tombstone Territorial Days** is a re-enactment of the events leading up to the gunfight at the O.K. Corral.

Western Arizona The **Route 66 Fun Run Weekend** in Seligman/ **APRIL**
Topock is a fundraiser that helps preserve the historic Route 66 between Chicago and Los Angeles. A street dance, car show, pageant and barbecue are all part of the festivities.

Southern Arizona Tucson is home to the **International Mariachi Contest**, a week-long celebration of mariachi music with concerts, workshops, an art exhibit and a golf tournament.

North Central Arizona Bill Williams Rendezvous Days, held on **MAY**
Memorial Day weekend in Williams, re-creates the days of the mountain men with barn dances, black-powder shoots, a pioneer costume contest and evening "whooplas." The **Prescott Off-Street Festival** transforms the downtown area with over 100 arts and craft displays, live entertainment and food booths.

Western Arizona You won't find the Nelson Riddle Orchestra, but you can get your kicks at the **Route 66 Classic Car Rally & Show** in Kingman.

Southern Arizona Tombstone's **Wyatt Earp Days** celebration fills the Memorial Day weekend with Old West costumes, staged shootouts in the streets, and arts and crafts.

Northeastern Arizona Holbrook's **Old West Day/Bucket of** **JUNE**
Blood Races features an arts and crafts show, barbecue, American Indian song and dance, a car and truck show and races.

North Central Arizona The **Heritage Program** opens at the Museum of Northern Arizona in Flagstaff, with extensive exhibits and craft demonstrations of American Indian arts continuing through early August. Also in Flagstaff is the **Wool Festival**, which features sheep shearing, weaving and spinning demonstrations as well as textile arts.

Western Arizona You won't need a seatbelt for **Parker's Inner Tube Races** down a seven-mile stretch of the Colorado River. Beat the summer heat during **Laughlin's River Days**, which include a golf tournament, fireworks display and rubber duck races along the Colorado River. Townsfolk dress up in frontier clothing to celebrate **Old Miner's Day** in Chloride.

South Central Arizona Payson's **Junior Rodeo**, the state's largest, showcases the roping and riding skills of cowboys and cowgirls aged 5 to 18.

JULY

North Central Arizona **Frontier Days and World's Oldest Rodeo** in Prescott draws cowboys from all over the country and also has fireworks, a parade and a cowboy golf tournament. The **Hopi Craftsman Exhibit** is presented at the Museum of Northern Arizona in Flagstaff in early July in connection with the Heritage Program. The **Navajo Craftsman Exhibition** opens there later in the month.

Western Arizona Step off the sidewalk and make room for solar-powered contraptions on July 4th at the **Oatman Egg-fry Contest**.

AUGUST

North Central Arizona The first weekend of August brings the **Flagstaff Summerfest**, which features more than 250 artisans, live entertainment and children's activities.

South Central Arizona The **Payson Rodeo** is the oldest continuous rodeo in the United States, well into its second century.

Southern Arizona **Fiesta de San Agustin** honors Tucson's patron saint with a Mexican-style fiesta of live music, food and street dancing.

SEPTEMBER

Grand Canyon The Shrine of the Ages Auditorium (next to the visitor center) is the setting for world-class music during the **Grand Canyon Chamber Music Festival**.

Northeastern Arizona The **Navajo Nation Fair** in Window Rock has carnival rides, a rodeo, horse races, dance competitions, a pretty-baby contest, the Miss Navajo pageant and a wonderful arts and crafts pavilion.

South Central Arizona Payson hosts the **Old-Time Fiddlers Contest and Festival** at the rodeo grounds.

Southern Arizona **Rendezvous of Gunfighters**, one of several practically identical town festivals held in Tombstone throughout the year, features a parade and a costume party on Labor Day weekend.

OCTOBER

North Central Arizona The **Sedona Arts Festival** draws artisans from all over the West to participate in one of the region's major arts and crafts fairs.

Western Arizona **London Bridge Days** commemorates the relocation of the bridge to this improbable site with a parade, live entertainment, costume contests and lots of Olde English fun. Kingman's favorite native son is remembered during **Andy Devine Days and P.R.C.A. Rodeo**.

South Central Arizona The **Arizona State Fair**, held in Phoenix, runs until early November.

Eastern Arizona Traditional dances, folk art and food are featured during **Apache (Jii) Days** in Globe.

Southern Arizona The spicy, flavorful and decorative chile takes center stage during the annual **La Fiesta de los Chiles** at the Tucson Botanical Gardens, where it features tastings of chile-accented foods from around the world, chile cooking and craft demonstrations, chile gift items, Latin jazz and salsa music, and a "Chile Rap" puppet show. **Rex Allen Days** in Willcox honors cowboy movie star Rex Allen with a golf tournament, parade, country fair, rodeo, art show and cowboy dances. Tombstone celebrates **Heldorado Days** with music, arts and crafts and gunfight re-enactments.

NOVEMBER

Western Arizona Radio-controlled model planes fill the skies during the **London Bridge Seaplane Classic** in Lake Havasu City.

South Central Arizona The **Four Corner States Bluegrass Festival** in Wickenburg presents three days of music as bands compete for thousands of dollars in prize money. The **Thunderbird Balloon Classic and Airshow** in Scottsdale has more than 150 balloons, a balloon show and street dance.

Southern Arizona The largest perimeter bicycling event in the U.S., **El Tour de Tucson** is a colorful spectator sport and a charity fundraiser.

DECEMBER

Western Arizona Christmas lights sparkle during Lake Mead Marina's **Harbor Parade of Lights**.

South Central Arizona The annual **Indian Market at the Pueblo Grande Museum** in Phoenix draws over 700 artisans and also features tribal singers, dancers and Southwestern food booths.

▼▼▼▼▼▼▼▼▼▼
Before You Go

For free visitor information packets including maps and current details on special events, accommodations and camping, contact the **Arizona Office of Tourism.** ~ 2702 North 3rd Street, Suite 4015, Phoenix, AZ 85003; 602-230-7733. In addition, most towns have a chamber of commerce or visitor information center. As a general rule, these tourist information centers are not open on weekends.

VISITORS CENTERS

PACKING

Arizonians are casual in their dress and expect the same of visitors. Restaurants with dress codes are few and far between. Even if you attend a fancy $100-a-plate fundraiser or go out for a night at the opera, you'll find that a coat and tie or evening gown and heels instantly brand you as a tourist. Chic apparel in these parts is more likely to mean a Western-cut suit, ostrich-hide boots and a bolo tie with a flashy turquoise-and-silver slide, or, for women, a fiesta dress with a concho belt, long-fringed moccasins and a squash blossom necklace—all fairly expensive items that you may never have occasion to wear back home. Relax. Sporty, comfortable clothing will pass practically anywhere.

When packing clothes, plan to dress in layers. Temperatures can turn hot or cold in a flash at any time of year. During the course of a single vacation day, you can often expect to start by wearing a heavy jacket, a sweater or flannel shirt and a pair of slacks or jeans, peeling down to a T-shirt and shorts as the day warms up, then putting the extra layers back on soon after the sun goes down.

Other essentials to pack or buy along the way include a good sunscreen and high-quality sunglasses. Bear in mind that in many areas off the beaten path, you'll be unlikely to find a store selling anything more substantial than curios and beef jerky. If you are planning to camp in the mountains during the summer, you'll be glad you brought mosquito repellent.

For outdoor activities, tough-soled hiking boots are more comfortable than running shoes on rocky terrain. Even RV travelers and those who prefer to spend most nights in motels may want to take along a backpacking tent and sleeping bag for irresistible urges to stay out under star-spangled skies. A canteen, first-aid kit, flashlight and other routine camping gear are also likely to come in handy. Cycling enthusiasts should bring their own bikes. Especially when it comes to mountain biking, there are a lot more great places to ride than there are towns where you can find bicycles for rent. The same goes for boating, golf and other activities that call for special equipment.

A camera is essential for capturing your travel experience; of equal importance is a good pair of binoculars, which let you explore distant landscapes from scenic overlooks. And don't, for heaven's sake, forget your copy of *Hidden Arizona*.

LODGING   In Arizona, lodgings run the gamut from tiny one-room mountain cabins to luxurious hotels that blend Indian pueblo architecture with contemporary elegance. Bed and breakfasts can be found not only in chic destinations like Sedona but also in such unlikely locales as former ghost towns and the outskirts of Indian reservations. They come in all types, sizes and price ranges. Typical of the genre are lovingly restored old mansions comfortably furnished with period decor, usually with fewer than a dozen rooms. Some bed and breakfasts, however, are guest cottages or rooms in nice suburban homes, while others are larger establishments, approaching hotel size, of the type sometimes referred to as country inns.

Both rims of the Grand Canyon have classic, rustic-elegant lodges built during the early years of the 20th century. Though considerably more expensive than budget motel rooms, the national park lodges are moderate in price and well worth it in terms of ambience and location. Reservations should be made far in advance.

The abundance of motels in towns along all major highway routes presents a range of choices, from name-brand motor inns to traditional mom-and-pop establishments that have endured for the half-century since motels were invented. Older motels along main truck routes, especially interstate Route 40, offer some of the lowest room rates in the United States today.

At the other end of the price spectrum, the height of self-indulgent vacationing is to be found at upscale resorts in destinations such as Tucson and Sedona. These resorts offer riding stables, golf courses, tennis courts, fine dining, live entertainment nightly and exclusive shops right on the premises so that guests can spend their entire holidays without leaving the grounds—a boon for celebrities seeking a few days' rest and relaxation away from the public eye, but a way to miss out on the real Arizona.

Other lodgings throughout the state offer a different kind of personality. Many towns—preserved historic districts like Tombstone, as well as larger communities like Flagstaff—have historic hotels dating back before the turn of the century. Some of them have been lavishly restored to far surpass their original Victorian elegance. Others may lack the polished antique decor and sophisticated ambience, but make up for it in their authentic feel. These places give visitors a chance to spice up their vacation experience by spending the night at a place where they can look out their window onto a Main Street that has changed surprisingly little since the days of the Old West.

ANCIENT INDIAN RUINS

Some of the best of the Indian ruins to see in Arizona include the Anasazi ruins of Betatakin and Keet Seel at the Navajo National Monument 18 miles northwest of Kayenta off Route 160; Montezuma Castle National Monument which are cliffside dwellings built by the Sinagua people in Camp Verde; the four-story Hohokam ruins at the Casa Grande Ruins National Monument, 20 miles east of Casa Grande off Route 87; the pueblos of the Hopi ancestors at Homolovi Ruins State Park on Route 87 three miles east of Winslow; the ruins of the apartment-style dwellings of the Salado people at Tonto National Monument on Arizona 88 in Roosevelt; the volcanic rock Mogollon ruins at Casa Malpais Pueblo in Springerville; and the Besh-Ba-Gowah Archaeological Park with the pueblo ruins of the Salado people in Globe.

Whatever your preference and budget, you can find something in this book to suit your taste. Remember, rooms can be scarce and prices may rise during the peak season, which is summer throughout most of the region and winter in low-lying desert communities such as Phoenix, Scottsdale and Tucson. Travelers planning to visit a place in peak season should either make advance reservations or arrive early in the day, before the "No Vacancy" signs start lighting up. Those who plan to stay in Sedona or Grand Canyon National Park at any time of year are wise to make lodging reservations well ahead of time.

Accommodations in this book are organized by region and classified according to price. Rates referred to are high-season rates, so if you are looking for off-season bargains, it's good to inquire. *Budget* lodgings generally run less than $70 per night for two people and are satisfactory and clean, but modest. *Moderate* hotels range from $70 to $110; what they have to offer in the way of luxury will depend on where they are located, but they generally offer larger rooms and more attractive surroundings. At a *deluxe* hotel or resort you can expect to spend between $110 and $180 for a double; you'll generally find spacious rooms, a fashionable lobby, a restaurant and often a group of shops. *Ultra-deluxe* facilities, priced above $180, are a region's finest, offering all the amenities of a deluxe hotel plus plenty of extras.

Room rates vary as much with locale as with quality. Some of the trendier destinations have no rooms at all in the budget price range. In other communities—especially those along interstate highways where rates are set with truck drivers in mind—every motel falls into the budget category, even though accommodations may range from $19.95 at run-down, spartan places to $45 or so at the classiest motor inn in town. The price categories listed in this book are relative, designed to show you where to get the most out of your travel budget, however large or small it may be.

DINING   Within a particular chapter, restaurants are categorized by region, with each restaurant entry describing the establishment according to price. Dinner entrées at *budget* restaurants usually cost $8 or less. The ambience is informal, service usually speedy and the crowd often a local one. *Moderately* priced restaurants range between $8 and $16 at dinner; surroundings are casual but pleasant, the menu offers more variety and the pace is usually slower. *Deluxe* establishments tab their entrées from $16 to $24; the cuisine may be simple or sophisticated, depending on the location, but the decor is more plush and the service more personalized. *Ultra-deluxe* dining rooms, where entrées begin at $24, are often the gourmet places; here, cooking has become a fine art and the service should be impeccable.

The Cactus League

Each year, eight major league baseball teams migrate to the sunny Arizona desert during the months of February and March for their Cactus League spring training schedule. And where there's baseball, the fans aren't far behind.

It's become an increasingly popular way to spend a vacation as more and more fans take the opportunity to enjoy a little welcome sunshine, root for their favorite teams, and get a close-up look at some of professional baseball's super stars, all at the same time. If you can't wait for the first ball of the regular season to be thrown out in April, catch the preseason action at Arizona's Cactus League.

National League fans root for the following teams at their practice fields: **San Francisco Giants** (Scottsdale Stadium, 7408 East Osborn Road, Scottsdale; 602-990-7972); **Chicago Cubs** (Hohokam Park, 1235 Center Street, Mesa; 602-964-4467); **Colorado Rockies** (Hi Corbett Field in Reid Park, 22nd Street and Randolph Way, Tucson; 520-327-9467, 303-292-0200); and the **San Diego Padres** (Peoria Municipal Stadium, 16101 North 83rd Drive, Peoria; 602-486-7000, 619-881-6500).

If the American League teams are your favorites, take a seat in the bleachers to watch the **Milwaukee Brewers** (Maryvale Sports Complex, 51st Avenue and Indian School Road, Maryvale; 602-245-5500); **Oakland A's** (Phoenix Municipal Stadium, 5999 East Van Buren Boulevard, Phoenix; 602-392-0217); **Seattle Mariners** (Peoria Municipal Stadium, 16101 North 83rd Drive, Peoria; 602-878-4337); and the **Anaheim Angels** (Diablo Stadium, 2200 West Alameda Street, Tempe; 602-438-9300).

Adding to the excitement is the intimacy and informality of the small-town ballparks, where stadium bleachers are much closer to the action, and ticket prices are substantially less than regular season prices, although tickets to some games—like the Chicago Cubs'—can be surprisingly hard to come by.

To save on the cost of the tickets, look into package deals offered by many local hotels and tour companies. For general information about all the Cactus League teams, call the **Mesa Convention and Visitors Bureau**. ~ 120 North Center Street; 602-827-4700, 800-283-6372. Contact your local travel agency for information on hotel and ticket prices for other teams.

Some restaurants change hands often and are occasionally closed in low seasons. Efforts have been made in this book to include places with established reputations for good eating. Breakfast and lunch menus vary less in price from restaurant to restaurant than do dinner offerings.

DRIVING NOTES

The canyons, mountains and deserts of Arizona are clearly the major sightseeing attractions for many visitors. This is a rugged area and there are some important things to remember when driving on the side roads throughout the region. First and foremost, believe it if you see a sign indicating four-wheel drive only. These roads can be very dangerous in a car without high ground clearance and the extra traction afforded by a four-wheel drive—and there may be no safe place to turn around if you get stuck. During rainy periods, dirt roads may become impassable muck. And in winter, heavy snows often necessitate the use of snow tires or chains on main roads, while side roads may or may not be maintained at all.

Some side roads will take you far from civilization, so be sure to have a full radiator and tank of gas. Carry spare fuel, water and food. In winter, it is always wise to travel with a shovel and blankets in your car. Should you become stuck, local people are usually quite helpful about offering assistance to stranded vehicles or in case no one else is around, for extended backcountry driving, a CB radio or a car phone would not be a bad idea.

TRAVELING WITH CHILDREN

Any place that has cowboys and Indians, rocks to climb and limitless room to run is bound to be a hit with youngsters. Plenty of family adventures are available during a stay in Arizona, from manmade attractions to wilderness experiences. A few guidelines will help make travel with children a pleasure.

Book reservations in advance, making sure that the places you stay accept children. Many bed and breakfasts do not. If you need a crib or extra cot, arrange for it ahead of time. A travel agent can be of help here, as well as with most other travel plans.

If you are traveling by air, try to reserve bulkhead seats where there is plenty of room. Take along extras you may need, such as diapers, changes of clothing, snacks and toys or small games. When traveling by car, be sure to take along the extras, too. Make sure you have plenty of water and juices to drink; dehydration can be a subtle but serious problem. Most towns, as well as some national parks, have stores that carry diapers, baby food, snacks and other essentials, though they usually close early. Larger towns often have all-night grocery or convenience stores.

A first-aid kit is a must for any trip. Along with adhesive bandages, antiseptic cream and something to stop itching, include any medicines your pediatrician might recommend to treat allergies, colds, diarrhea or any chronic problems your child may have.

Arizona sunshine is intense. Take extra care for the first few days. Children's skin is usually more tender than adult skin and severe sunburn can happen before you realize it. A hat is a good idea, along with a reliable sunblock.

Many national parks and monuments offer special activities designed just for children. Visitor-center film presentations and rangers' campfire slide shows can help teach children about the natural history of Arizona and head off some questions. However, kids tend to find a lot more things to wonder about than adults have answers for. To be as prepared as possible, seize every opportunity to learn more—particularly about American Indian history and culture, a constant curiosity for young minds.

GAY & LESBIAN TRAVELERS

The unique beauty of the Southwest is appealing to many: the wide open spaces stretching for miles and miles invite people who are looking to get away from it all. It's a region that gives people a lot of space, literally, and encourages you to do your own thing, which allows gay or lesbian travelers to feel comfortable here. Whether you're interested in exploring the area's magnificent scenery, sightseeing in the cosmopolitan cities, or just relaxing by the pool, the Southwest has much to offer.

Arizona boasts the gay and lesbian hot spot of Phoenix, to which this book has dedicated a special "gay-specific" section. Phoenix is home to a large gay and lesbian community and there's a growing number of gay-friendly bars, nightclubs and restaurants.

You'll find news and entertainment listings for Phoenix in *Echo Magazine*, a free biweekly that is distributed in cafés, bookstores and bars. ~ P.O. Box 16630, Phoenix, AZ 85011; 602-266 0550; www.echomag.com.

For information on virtually anything from lodging to HIV/AIDS resources in Phoenix, call or drop by **The Valley of the Sun Gay and Lesbian Community Center** between 10 a.m. and 10 p.m. seven days a week. ~ 24 West Camelback Road, Suite C; 602-265-7283; www.phxcenter.org.

WOMEN TRAVELING ALONE

Traveling solo grants an independence and freedom different from that of traveling with a partner, but single travelers are more vulnerable to crime and must take additional precautions.

It's unwise to hitchhike and probably best to avoid inexpensive accommodations on the outskirts of town; the money saved does not outweigh the risk. Bed and breakfasts, youth hostels and YWCAs are generally your safest bet for lodging, and they also foster an environment ideal for bonding with fellow travelers.

Keep all valuables well-hidden and clutch cameras and purses tightly. Avoid late-night treks or strolls through undesirable parts of town, but if you find yourself in this situation, continue walking with a confident air until you reach a safe haven. A fierce scowl never hurts.

These hints should by no means deter you from seeking out adventure. Wherever you go, stay alert, use your common sense and trust your instincts.

If you are hassled or threatened in some way, never be afraid to scream for assistance. It's a good idea to carry change for a phone call and to know the number to call in case of emergency. Most areas have 24-hour hotlines for victims of rape and violent crime. The **Rape Crisis Hotline** serves the Phoenix area. ~ 2333 North Central Avenue, Phoenix, AZ 85004; 602-254-9000. In Tucson, call the **Rape Crisis Center**. ~ 1632 North Country Club Drive, Tucson, AZ 85016; 520-327-1171, 24-hour hotline 520-327-7273, 800-400-1001.

For more helpful hints, get a copy of *Safety and Security for Women Who Travel* (Travelers' Tales, 1998).

DISABLED TRAVELERS   Arizona is striving to make public areas fully accessible to disabled persons. Parking spaces and restroom facilities for the handicapped are provided according to both state law and national park regulations. National parks and monuments also post signs that tell which trails are wheelchair accessible.

There are many organizations offering information for travelers with disabilities, including the **Society for the Advancement of Travellers with Handicaps**. ~ 347 5th Avenue, Suite 610, New York, NY 10016; 212-447-7284. Also try the **Travel Information Service**. ~ 1200 West Tabor Road, Philadelphia, PA 19141; 215-456-9600. For general travel advice, contact **Travelin' Talk**, a networking organization. ~ P.O. Box 3534, Clarksville, TN 37043; 931-552-6670.

SENIOR TRAVELERS   Arizona is a hospitable place for older vacationers, many of whom turn into part-time or full-time residents thanks to the dry, pleasant climate and the friendly senior-citizen communities that have developed in southern Arizona and, on a smaller scale, in other parts of the state. The large number of national parks and monuments in the region means that persons age 62 and older can save considerable money with a Golden Age Passport, which allows free admission. Apply for one in person at any national park unit that charges an entrance fee. Many private sightseeing attractions also offer significant discounts for seniors.

The **AARP** offers membership to anyone over 50. AARP's benefits include travel discounts with a number of firms. ~ 601 E Street NW, Washington, D.C. 20049; 800-424-3410.

Elderhostel offers educational courses as part of all-inclusive packages at colleges and universities. In Arizona, Elderhostel courses are available in numerous locations including Flagstaff, Nogales, Phoenix, Prescott, Scottsdale, Tempe and Tucson. ~ 75 Federal Street, Boston, MA 02110; 617-426-7788, 877-426-8056.

Be extra careful about health matters. In Arizona's changeable climate, seniors are more at risk of suffering hypothermia. High altitudes may present a risk to persons with heart or respiratory conditions; ask your physician for advice when planning your trip. Many tourist destinations in the state are a long way from any hospital or other health care facility.

"Snowbirds" are seasonal residents who come from colder climes to bask in the southern Arizona sun. When summer's 100-plus temperatures arrive, the snowbirds return home and southern Arizonians head for cooler parts of the state.

In addition to the medications you ordinarily use, it's a good idea to bring along written prescriptions from your doctor for obtaining more if needed. Consider carrying a medical record with you, including your history and current medical status, as well as your doctor's name, phone number and address. Make sure that your insurance covers you while you are away from home.

Passports and Visas   Most foreign visitors need a passport and tourist visa to enter the United States. Contact your nearest United States Embassy or Consulate well in advance to obtain a visa and to check on any other entry requirements.

Customs Requirements   Foreign travelers are allowed to carry in the following: 200 cigarettes (1 carton), 50 cigars, or 2 kilograms (4.4 pounds) of smoking tobacco; one liter of alcohol for personal use only (you must be 21 years of age to bring in alcohol); and US$100 worth of duty-free gifts that can include an additional quantity of 100 cigars. You may bring in any amount of currency, but must fill out a form if you bring in over US$10,000. Carry any prescription drugs in clearly marked containers. (You may have to produce a written prescription or doctor's statement for the custom's officer.) Meat or meat products, seeds, plants, fruits and narcotics are not allowed to be brought into the United States. Contact the **United States Customs Service** for further information. ~ 1300 Pennsylvania Avenue NW, Washington, DC 20229; 202-927-6724.

Driving   If you plan to rent a car, an international driver's license should be obtained before arriving in the United States. Some car rental agencies require both a foreign license and an international driver's license. Many also require a lessee to be at least 25 years of age; all require a major credit card. Seat belts are mandatory for the driver and all passengers. Children under the age of five or

FOREIGN TRAVELERS

under 40 pounds should be in the back seat in approved child-safety restraints.

Currency   United States money is based on the dollar. Bills come in denominations of $1, $5, $10, $20, $50 and $100. Every dollar is divided into 100 cents. Coins are the penny (1 cent), nickel (5 cents), dime (10 cents) and quarter (25 cents). Half-dollar and dollar coins are rarely used. You may not use foreign currency to purchase goods and services in the United States. Consider buying traveler's checks in dollar amounts. You may also use credit cards affiliated with an American company such as Interbank, Barclay Card, VISA and American Express.

Electricity and Electronics   Electric outlets use currents of 110 volts, 60 cycles. To operate appliances made for other electrical systems, you need a transformer or other adapter. Travelers who use laptop computers for telecommunication should be aware that modem configurations for U.S. telephone systems may be different from their European counterparts. Similarly, the U.S. format for videotapes is different from that in Europe; National Park Service visitors centers and other stores that sell souvenir videos often have them available in European format.

Weights and Measures   The United States uses the English system of weights and measures. American units and their metric equivalents are: 1 inch = 2.5 centimeters; 1 foot (12 inches) = 0.3 meter; 1 yard (3 feet) = 0.9 meter; 1 mile (5280 feet) = 1.6 kilometers; 1 ounce = 28 grams; 1 pound (16 ounces) = 0.45 kilogram; 1 quart (liquid) = 0.9 liter.

▼▼▼▼▼▼▼▼▼▼▼▼▼▼
Outdoor Adventures

CAMPING

Tent or RV camping is a great way to tour Arizona. Besides saving money, campers enjoy the freedom of watching sunsets from beautiful places, spending nights under spectacularly starry skies and waking up in lovely surroundings that few hotels can match.

Most towns have commercial RV parks of some sort, and long-term mobile-home parks often rent spaces to RVs by the night. But unless you absolutely need cable television, none of these places can compete with the wide array of public campgrounds available in national and state parks, monuments and forests. Federal campground sites are typically less developed and only the biggest ones have electrical hookups. National forest campgrounds don't have hookups, while state park campgrounds just about always do. The largest public campgrounds offer tent camping loops separate from RV loops, while backcountry camping areas offer the option of spending the night far from the crowds.

With the exception of both rims of the Grand Canyon, where campsite reservations are booked through the **National Park Reservation Service** (800-365-2267, credit cards only), you won't find much in the way of sophisticated reservation systems. The general rule in public campgrounds is still first-come, first-served, even though they fill up practically every night in peak season. For campers, this means traveling in the morning and reaching your intended campground by early afternoon. In many areas, campers may find it more convenient to keep a single location for as much as a week and explore surrounding areas on day trips.

For listings of state parks with camping facilities and reservation information, contact the **Arizona State Parks.** ~ 1300 West Washington Street, Phoenix, AZ 85007; 602-542-4174. Information on camping in the national forests in Arizona is available from **National Forest Service—Southwestern Region.** ~ Public Affairs Office, 517 Gold Avenue Southwest, Albuquerque, NM 87102; 505-842-3292. Camping and reservation information for national parks and monuments is available from **National Park Service—Southwest System Support Office** or from the individual parks and monuments listed in this book. ~ 1100 Old Santa Fe Trail, Santa Fe, NM 87504; 505-988-6100.

Many Indian lands have public campgrounds, which usually don't appear in campground directories. For information, contact: **Navajo Parks and Recreation.** ~ P.O. Box 9000, Window Rock, AZ 86515; 520-871-6647. **Hopi Tribal Headquarters.** ~ P.O. Box 123, Kykotsmovi, AZ 86039; 520-734-2441. **Havasupai Tourist Enterprise.** ~ P.O. Box 160, Supai, AZ 86435; 520-448-2141. The **White Mountain Apache Game and Fish Department.** ~ P.O. Box 220, Whiteriver, AZ 85941; 520-338-4385. **Zuni Pueblo.** ~ P.O. Box 339, Zuni, NM 87327; 505-782-4481.

Also see the "Parks" sections in each chapter to discover where camping is available.

PERMITS

Tent camping is allowed in the backcountry of all national forests here except in the few areas where signs are posted prohibiting it. You no longer need a permit to hike or camp in national forest wilderness areas, but plan to stop at a ranger station anyway for trail maps and advice on current conditions and fire regulations. In dry seasons, emergency rules may prohibit campfires and sometimes ban cigarette smoking, with stiff enforcement penalties.

For backcountry hiking in national parks and monuments, you must first obtain a permit from the ranger at the visitor center. The permit procedure is simple and free. It helps park administrators measure the impact on sensitive ecosystems and distribute use evenly among major trails to prevent overcrowding.

BOATING & RAFTING

Most of the large desert lakes along the Colorado and other major rivers are administered as National Recreation Areas and supervised by the U.S. Army Corps of Engineers. Federal boating safety regulations that apply to these lakes may vary slightly from state regulations. Indian reservations have separate rules for boating on tribal lakes. More significant than any differences between federal, state and tribal regulations are the local rules in force for any particular lake.

Ask for applicable boating regulations at a local marina or fishing supply store or use the addresses and phone numbers listed in "Parks" or other sections of each chapter in this book to contact the headquarters for lakes you plan to visit.

Boats, from small power boats to houseboats, can be rented for 24 hours or longer at marinas on several of the larger lakes. At most marinas, you can get a boat on short notice if you arrive on a weekday, since much of their business comes from local weekend recreation. The exception is Lake Powell, where houseboats and other craft are booked far in advance. Take a look at Chapter Four for details on how to arrange for a Lake Powell boat trip.

River rafting is a very popular sport and the ultimate whitewater rafting experience, of course, is a trip through the Grand Canyon. Independent rafters are welcome, but because of the bulky equipment and specialized knowledge of river hazards involved, most adventurous souls stick with group trips offered by any of the many rafting companies located in Flagstaff, Page and towns farther upriver. Rafters, as well as people using canoes, kayaks, windsurfers or inner tubes, are required by state and federal regulations to wear life jackets.

FISHING   Many Arizona residents seem to have an irresistible fascination with water. During the warm months, lakeshores and readily accessible portions of streams are often packed with anglers, especially on weekends. Vacationers can beat the crowds to some extent by planning their fishing days during the week.

Fish hatcheries keep busy stocking streams with trout, particularly rainbows, the most popular game fish throughout the region. Catch-and-release fly fishing is the rule in some popular areas, allowing more anglers a chance at bigger fish. Be sure to inquire locally about eating the fish you catch, since some seemingly remote streams and rivers have contamination problems from old mines and mills.

The larger reservoirs offer an assortment of sport fish, including crappie, carp, white bass, smallmouth bass, largemouth bass and walleye pike. Striped bass, an ocean import, can run as large as 40 pounds, while catfish in the depths of dammed desert canyons sometimes attain mammoth proportions.

For copies of state fishing regulations, inquire at a local fishing supply store or marina, or contact the **Arizona Game and Fish Department**. ~ 2222 West Greenway Road, Phoenix, AZ 85023; 602-942-3000. State fishing licenses are required for fishing in national parks and national recreation areas, but not on Indian reservations, where daily permits are sold by the tribal governments. For more information about fishing on Indian lands, contact the tribal agencies listed in "Camping" above.

TWO

The Arizona Landscape

GEOLOGY   Arizona's geology can be summed up in one word —diverse. Its treasures include everything from spectacular canyons to high mountain peaks, from arid deserts to lush forests, from sparse volcanic fields to abundant alpine meadows.

Arizona's riches lie not only in grand overviews, but also in a myriad of unique details. Dinosaur tracks. Petrified wood. Pure white gypsum sand dunes. Huge underground caverns. Salt domes, arches, natural bridges, hoodoos and goblins fancifully shaped by water and weather.

Some of the state's greatest assets are its mountains, creatively dubbed "sky islands" by biologists. Humphrey's Peak, part of the San Francisco Peaks north of Flagstaff, soars up 12,670 feet to make it the highest point in Arizona. Other high mountain ranges are the White Mountains in the east, and the Santa Catalina and Santa Rita mountains around Tucson.

While the grandeur of Arizona's mountains are hard to miss, its desert beauty is much more subtle. It's a rugged, prickly area that welcomes with wide open vistas, cactus blooms and a profusion of texture and color.

Four deserts sprawl across Arizona. The granddaddy of them all is the Sonoran Desert, which gets more rain than any other desert in North America. Residents of Phoenix and Tucson call it home, as do more than 300 species of birds. The Chihuahuan Desert occupies just a fraction of land in southeastern Arizona, but offers some unusual geological features. One is Texas Canyon, a mountain range made of giant boulders. Another is the Willcox Playa, where what at first appears to be a lake proves instead to be a mirage—an empty, 50-mile-wide basin of glimmering sand. The Mohave Desert in northwestern Arizona is a dry, stark region of sand dunes, but manmade Lake Havasu lends some refreshing contrast. Finally, there's the Great Basin Desert in the Colorado Plateau, a majestic land of mesas, buttes, spires, cliffs and canyons.

Of course, Arizona's most famous geological formation is the Grand Canyon, sculpted by nature over the last five million years. Geological shifting slowly lifted the plateau up to higher elevations as the rushing waters of the Colorado River sliced it in half. The dark rocks at river level, which contain no fossils, are some of the oldest matter on the face of the earth. The different layers of color and texture seen in the cliffs attest to times when the area was sea floor, forest and swamp. Tiny fossilized sea creatures from the Paleozoic era, long before dinosaurs, trace the development of some of the first life on the planet up through strata of shale, limestone and sandstone.

A lesser known, miniature version of the Grand Canyon also inspires awe— Salt River Canyon in eastern Arizona. Spectacular views await at every corner as you drive down Route 60 between Show Low and Globe. At the Salt Banks, where a series of salt springs deposited travertine formations, visitors find colorful minerals and algae, as well as petroglyphs dating from the 13th century.

You can also trace the past with a visit to the Petrified Forest National Park, which includes the Painted Desert. The barren hills here contain a fossil record of life as far back as 225 million years ago, including fish, reptiles and amphibians. The surrounding hills, mainly devoid of vegetation, have been called the Painted Desert because the sun reflects the iron, manganese and other minerals contained in the rocks, tinting them with shades of red, gray, white and orange.

There are two explanations of how the trees in the Petrified Forest National Park turned to stone—one colorful, one scientific. The more riveting explanation is the Indian legend. They say that a goddess came into the area hungry and tired. She killed a rabbit and tried to make a fire to cook it, but the logs were wet and would not burn. Angrily, she put a curse on the area, turning the logs to stone.

The scientific explanation is that the forest was formed about 170 million years ago while part of a large valley. Over time, the valley filled with sediment, until large trees floated into the lowlands and were buried 3000 feet below the earth's surface. Before the trees could decay, water rich with silica, iron, manganese, copper and other minerals seeped into the trees, eventually turning them into "stone."

South of the Petrified Forest, you'll come eventually to the Mogollon Rim, which slices across east central Arizona like a sheer wall 200 miles long and up to 1500 feet high, dividing eastern Arizona into two halves—the mesalands to the north and the southern deserts.

Yet another unique feature of the Arizona landscape is Sunset Crater, a national monument in the San Francisco Volcanic Fields outside Flagstaff. The highlight here is a 1000-foot-tall volcanic cone that sprayed molten rock and ash when it first erupted in the winter of 1064–65. You can see the cinder and lava fields and climb nearby O'Leary Crater for a closer view. The fields of pumice gravel prevent vegetation from growing, but make hiking easy at the foot of these picture-perfect volcanic cones.

The geological features of Arizona are so spectacular that it is certainly possible to appreciate the various landscapes for their beauty without knowing how they were formed. But travelers who take a little time to learn about the region's geology by visiting the many natural history museums and park visitors centers along the way develop a different perspective. A closer look lets a visitor see how the many different colors and kinds of surface rock connect in a wonderfully complex formation hundreds of miles across. For example, Kaibab limestone (the

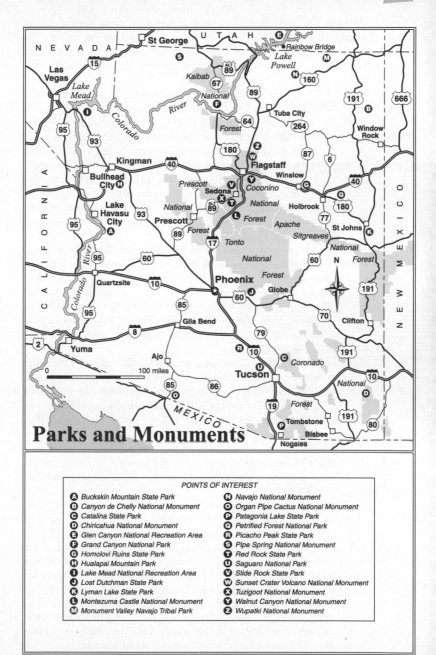

Parks and Monuments

POINTS OF INTEREST

Ⓐ Buckskin Mountain State Park
Ⓑ Canyon de Chelly National Monument
Ⓒ Catalina State Park
Ⓓ Chiricahua National Monument
Ⓔ Glen Canyon National Recreation Area
Ⓕ Grand Canyon National Park
Ⓖ Homolovi Ruins State Park
Ⓗ Hualapai Mountain Park
Ⓘ Lake Mead National Recreation Area
Ⓙ Lost Dutchman State Park
Ⓚ Lyman Lake State Park
Ⓛ Montezuma Castle National Monument
Ⓜ Monument Valley Navajo Tribal Park

Ⓝ Navajo National Monument
Ⓞ Organ Pipe Cactus National Monument
Ⓟ Patagonia Lake State Park
Ⓠ Petrified Forest National Park
Ⓡ Picacho Peak State Park
Ⓢ Pipe Spring National Monument
Ⓣ Red Rock State Park
Ⓤ Saguaro National Park
Ⓥ Slide Rock State Park
Ⓦ Sunset Crater Volcano National Monument
Ⓧ Tuzigoot National Monument
Ⓨ Walnut Canyon National Monument
Ⓩ Wupatki National Monument

250,000,000-year-old, 300-foot thick, grayish-white layer along the top rim of the Grand Canyon) is also visible at Lee's Ferry, a half-day's drive to the east. By stopping to explore the panorama in three dimensions, not just two, you'll gain a greater appreciation of the geological wonders that form the Arizona landscape.

▼▼▼▼▼▼▼▼▼▼▼▼
Flora and Fauna

FLORA

Different kinds of plants thrive within Arizona's wide range of altitudes. Arid deserts below 4500 feet stretch over about a third of the state, including Phoenix and Tucson. This is home for saguaro, mesquite and paloverde trees, prickly pear, cholla and barrel cactus and creosote bushes. Climb from 4500 to 6500 feet, and tall grasses, agave plants, evergreen shrubs, oak, piñon and juniper trees will appear. This zone lies in central Arizona and a few other areas scattered throughout the state. In the fragrant ponderosa pine forests found at the 7000- to 9000-foot-level, mainly in northern Arizona and near Payson, pine trees grow up to 125 feet high.

And from the 7500- to 10,000-foot-level, Douglas and white fir and quaking aspen create thick forests. In some areas, accessible only by hiking trails, fir trees stand that are 100 feet tall and bigger around than a man's reach. This zone includes the Kaibab Plateau of the Grand Canyon North Rim, the San Francisco Peaks, the White Mountains and other high peaks. From desert cacti to mountaintop aspens, studying the flora of Arizona can be endlessly fascinating.

Built in the 1920s as an educational facility, **Boyce Thompson Southwestern Arboretum** with its large cactus gardens is a good place to study desert plants. A creek and pond area showcases plants that need more water, but the arboretum generally features drought-tolerant plants. Don't miss the boojum trees from Baja California with their thick trunks and sparse leaves, or a stop at the visitors center, a building on the National Register of Historic Places. There are also potted plants for sale if you want to take a bit of Arizona with you. Admission. ~ Route 60 near Superior; 602-689-2811.

One downright odd-looking plant is the elephant tree. Its massive, contorted papery trunk most closely resembles the roots of a tree turned upside down.

One of the oldest living things on earth makes its home in the Arizona desert—the creosote bush. Some of these humble shrubs have been alive for 11,000 years, which makes the 500-year life span of the Joshua tree look like nothing. And then there's the organ pipe cactus and the saguaro. They may not live as long as the creosote, but they're so rare and interesting that whole monuments have been set up for them—the Organ Pipe Cactus National Monument and Saguaro National Monument.

The senita cactus is found only in Organ Pipe National Monument. Similar to the organ pipe cactus, the senita is called "whisker cactus" because of its long gray hair-like spines. Both it and the organ pipe cactus are night blooming, with flowers closing soon after sunrise. The fruit of the organ pipe cactus was harvested by the Papago Indians.

The most famous of Arizona's plants is the saguaro, the giant, multi-armed cactus that poses for thousands of tourist snapshots and travels through the mail on slick postcards. The saguaro is found in the Sonoran Desert, the most diverse of Arizona's four deserts. In part, this is because the Sonoran averages seven and a half to ten inches of rain annually, a lot of rain for the desert, and there is rarely a hard freeze. The saguaro reaches a ripe old age of 75 before even sprouting its arms. Most are pockmarked with holes. These are not decay; they're natural houses. The Gila woodpecker drills holes in mature saguaro trunks in order to nest in a cool, humid environment safe from predators. After they leave this "house," other species move in, anything from owls to purple martins. And the saguaro continues to give by providing nectar for bats via its white flowers.

> Once every seven years in the fall, piñon trees produce pine nuts, which many consider a delicacy.

In order to live in the desert, the saguaro cactus has had to be very inventive. The green weight in a mature saguaro is from 75 to 95 percent water. When the weather is so dry that the roots can no longer get water from the soil, there is enough water in the saguaro tissue to stay alive. During dry months, the saguaro's diameters shrink and fold in like an accordion and their ribs become more angled. Even with an 80 percent water loss from their stems, a young saguaro can live. (A human can't live with even a 12 percent water deficit.) The saguaro's roots are shallow—usually not more than three feet below the surface, but extend as much as 100 feet laterally from the plant to eke every bit of moisture from the earth.

There is a fascinating biological association between the yucca plant and the tiny yucca moth. Each is completely dependent on the other to perpetuate its species. The female moths collect pollen from yucca flowers, fly to other yucca blossoms, then lay their eggs and deposit fertilizing pollen. Some of the plant's seeds become food for the moth larvae, while others mature and reproduce. The new larvae fall to the ground, burrow into it and remain there until spring when they become moths and repeat the cycle.

When spring rains come, which may be only once every few years, the desert bursts forth for a few weeks with a fantastic display of wildflowers. But there can be a downside to desert flora, as well. Many of the desert's plants have a special thorny sting for those who dare to touch them. In addition, it is against the law to destroy or even collect most desert plants and cacti. As one Phoenix man found out, it's not worth the trouble to harass a cactus—after he fired a gun at it, the saguaro cactus toppled and killed him.

Instead, it's better just to enjoy from a distance the beauty of the desert's botanical offerings, especially in spring when they're in bloom. Some of the more colorful you're likely to see are the yellow flowers of the brittlebush, the yellow to orange Mexican poppy, the blue desert lupines that dot roadsides and hills, and the brilliant orange blooms on the whiplike stems of the ocotillo. If you're lucky enough to arrive at the right time, you'll find this wildly colorful mix a truly memorable sight.

FAUNA

Many animals of Western legend still roam free in the forests and canyons of Arizona. Mountain lions, rarely seen because they inhabit remote areas and hunt in the dark, sometimes flash past late-night drivers' headlight beams. Black bears live deep in the mountains—in times of drought, when food is short, they may stray into towns to raid trash cans.

Coyotes, the most commonly seen southwestern predators, have been dubbed "urban coyotes" by wildlife management officials because of their adaptability to the urban landscape. They will eat almost anything, often feasting on rodents, rabbits, garbage can leftovers or, to the owner's dismay, household pets. Intelligence is another of their attributes; they'll look both ways before safely crossing busy highways. Even if you don't see them, it's not uncommon to hear their high-pitched yipping and howling on a desert night or at dawn.

Often found foraging in groups, the javelina is another common Arizona animal. It resembles a pig with its oversized head, short, muscular legs and canine teeth.

Some of the strangest animals are spadefoot toads, who spend most of their life alone in a sealed burrow three feet under the ground. When the ground shakes from thunder during summer storms, they come to the surface to feed and mate.

It's a stunning sight to watch bighorn sheep leaping and climbing on the rocky ranges that jut up from low desert plains. A ram usually weighs in at anywhere from 250 to 300 pounds, with a stocky body and massive, curved horns. They eat thistles, grasses and flowers, and even open barrel cacti with their horns to get to the succulent pulp.

One of the most distinctive regional birds is the magpie, a longtailed, exotic-looking, iridescent cousin of Asian mynah birds. Another is the roadrunner, with its bristle-tipped topknot and long tail. Named because of their penchant for sprinting along roadways, you'll see them out dodging cars while hunting for lizards.

Large birds often seen by motorists or hikers include turkey vultures, ravens and many different kinds of hawks. Both golden and bald eagles live throughout Arizona and are occasionally spotted soaring in the distance. Eagles and vultures are about the same size, and the easiest way to tell them apart is to remember that eagles glide with their wings horizontal, while vultures' wings sweep upward in a V-shape.

Dozens of hummingbird species fly from Mexico to southwestern Arizona for the summer, while Canadian geese and other northern waterfowl warm up for the winter on rivers and lakes in the desert area.

Many visitors come to Arizona with some trepidation about the area's less attractive species. Sharing the land with humans are 11 species of rattlesnakes, 30 species of scorpions, 30 kinds of tarantulas, as well as Gila monsters with their black and yellow bead-like skin. But these creatures would rather retreat than attack, and even people who live in Arizona rarely see them. Just remember to walk loudly and don't put your hand or foot where you can't see it—like most insects and mammals, these creatures would be just as happy without an introduction.

THREE

History

 At one time, nearly 25,000 Indians were the exclusive residents of what is now Arizona. The earliest were the Hohokam, who thrived from 30 A.D. until about 1450 A.D. Signs of their settlements remain intact to this day. Two other major tribal groups followed: the Anasazi (a Navajo word meaning ancient ones) in the state's northern plateau highlands, and the Mogollon People, in the northeastern and eastern mountain belt.

Their hunting/gathering lifestyle changed around 300 B.C., partly because of droughts that drove the antelope and mammoths away. People began cultivating food and shifting their focus to farming. Freed from having to constantly search for food, they developed complex societies and built large pueblos on mesas, in valleys and in the steep cliff walls of canyons.

By 200 A.D., the Anasazi began living in Canyon de Chelly, building spectacular cliff dwellings and living in harmony with nature. Remains of their works can be seen at Keet Seel and Betatakin at Navajo National Monument, and in ruins in Canyon de Chelly. These ruins reveal the dark, tiny, claustrophobic rooms that served as home, but afforded no luxuries. Possibly because of drought, the cliff dwellings were abandoned by 1300.

During this time, the Sinagua culture was developing northeast of what is now Flagstaff and farther south in the Verde River Valley. Settling in arid regions, they were named Sinagua, or "without water" in Spanish. Remnants of the Sinagua stone pueblos remain in Tuzigoot and Wupatki national monuments, and their cliff dwellings are at Walnut Canyon and Montezuma Castle.

By 450 A.D., the Hohokam culture had begun to farm the Gila and Salt River valleys between Phoenix and Casa Grande. Eventually, they spread out across a third of the state and built an impressive 600-mile network of irrigation canals, planting corn, beans and squash. They vanished by 1450. Although few of the Hohokam dwellings remain, one prime example is the four-story-high pueblo at the Casa Grande Ruins National Monument about 20 miles east of Casa Grande.

The Pima, desert farmers who next occupied this region, were the ones who named their predecessors Hohokam, meaning "all used up." No one knows the real reason the Hohokam disappeared, but possible explanations have included a long drought, disease and the arrival of more aggressive tribes.

Some 600 years ago, during the century just before Columbus' ships reached American shores, a new group of people arrived in the region. They were Athabascans, nomads from the far north (from an area that is now Canada) who had gradually wandered down the front range of the Rocky Mountains in small groups. They were to become the Apache and Navajo, warlike hunters who eventually settled down as farmers—but only after another kind of stranger had come to change the character of the Southwest forever.

THE SPANISH

In the mid-1500s, the Spaniards were the first Europeans to explore what is now Arizona. Lured by a Moorish legend about treasures in the Seven Cities of Cibola, the viceroy of New Spain sent explorers from Mexico City to search for the riches. Upon seeing pueblos glittering in the sun, the explorers returned home and reported their finding of a golden city. Francisco Vasquez de Coronado arrived a year later with great hopes, but discovered with disappointment that the "glitter" was only mica embedded in the adobe walls.

The conquistadors were looking not only for gold, but seeking souls to save. They found more souls than gold and in the process introduced the native peoples to cattle, horse raising and new farming methods, augmenting their crops of beans, squash and maize with new grains, fruits and vegetables. The Franciscans made forays into the area in the 1670s, founding missions among

BIRTH OF THE NAVAJO NATION

The Pueblo Revolt created the Navajo nation. To persuade their Athabascan neighbors to help chase away the Spanish, the Pueblo leaders agreed that the Athabascans could keep the livestock driven off from ranches they attacked. In that way, the tribe came to own sheep and horses, which would profoundly change their culture. When the Spanish colonists returned, many Pueblos who had participated in the revolt fled to avoid retaliation and went to live with the nomads, bringing with them such advanced technologies as weaving cloth and growing corn. The Athabascan descendants who herded sheep and farmed became known as the Navajo people, while those who held to the old way of life came to be called Apache.

the Hopi and converting many of them to Christianity. In 1687, Jesuit priest Eusebio Francisco Kino began establishing missions in Arizona. He taught the American Indians European farming techniques, planted fruit trees and gave them animals to raise. Kino visited the Pima village of Tumacacori in 1691, and in 1700 laid the foundation for the church at Mission of San Xavier del Bac.

Although the Spaniards brought some positive improvements, there was also a downside. The Spanish imported European diseases such as measles and smallpox and invaded Indian territory. As a result, the American Indians staged several battles, including the violent revolt of 1680. And in 1751, the normally peaceful Pima people rebelled, killing more than a hundred Spaniards, while the Apache continued their hit-and-run raids and ambushes on both the Spaniards and the Pima.

In response, the Spanish government built a presidio at Tubac. But after Mexico won its independence from Spain in 1821 and Spanish soldiers were withdrawn, the Indians again attacked. Settlers finally moved to the safety of walled cities such as Tucson.

STATEHOOD In 1848, most of Arizona became part of the United States as a result of the Mexican-American war. The only exceptions were Tucson and part of southern Arizona. This was soon to change. Having this area in Mexican hands became inconvenient during California's Forty-niner Gold Rush—the route to the gold went through what was Mexico. So the U.S. government negotiated the Gadsden Purchase in 1853, acquiring the remainder of southern Arizona and some additional land for a mere ten million dollars.

Still, the American Indians were a problem. Until about the mid-1860s, they accepted the few white miners, traders and farmers who came west, but as the number of settlers grew, friction arose and fighting resulted. The Navajo and Apache especially resented the white settlers. In the minds of many, a final solution had to be found.

The cavalry was called in and one of the most brutal chapters in the history of the Southwest followed. Black troops of the Tenth Cavalry, known as Buffalo Soldiers because of their dark skin and curly black hair, came in large numbers to protect settlers of the Arizona land where Geronimo, Cochise, Mangus, Alchise and other chieftains had dotted the terrain with the graves of thousands of emigrants and prospectors. Numerous sites still exist throughout the state that bring those days of conflict into vivid focus—Cochise Stronghold in the Dragoon Mountains south of Willcox, hideout of the notorious Apache chief; Fort Bowie National Historic Site, an adobe ruin that was a key military outpost during the Indian wars, and nearby Fort Huachuca, an important territorial outpost that's still in operation today as a communications base for the U.S. Army; and Fort Verde State Historic Park, in Camp Verde on Route 17 between Phoenix and Flagstaff, yet another military base that played a key role in subduing the Apache in the 1870s.

In 1864, under the leadership of Colonel Kit Carson, the Navajo were forced to surrender and were shipped to an internment camp in New Mexico. Although they returned to Arizona within five years, the Navajo were required to live on reservations. The longest and most violent army campaign against the American Indians was the Apache Wars. Though never numerous, the Apache were so fierce and elusive that the wars lasted for 19 bloody years. The Apache fell when leader Cochise died in the Chiricahua Mountains and Geronimo was forced to surrender in 1886. Only then could settlers from the United States establish the first towns in Arizona.

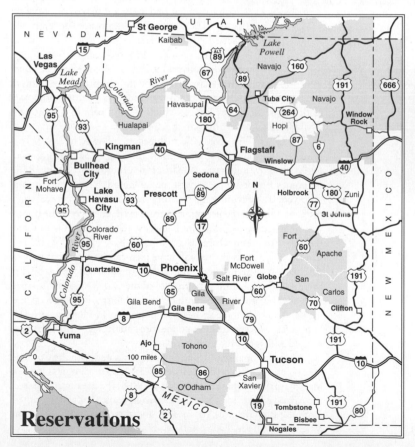

Reservations

During the 1860s and 1870s, the Arizona Territory was symbolic of the Wild West. Saloons did a bang-up business, literally, as shootouts and boisterous behavior were common events. Outlaws who were caught and tried were sent to Yuma, known for its strict Territorial Prison.

Soon the territorial sources of income began to shift toward grazing, farming and mining. Cattlemen established herds in the high desert grasslands of southeastern Arizona and the meadows of north central Arizona. But they created a modern environmental disaster. In 1870, about 5000 cattle grazed in Arizona; by 1891, this number had jumped to 1.5 million. The land simply could not support them. About 50 to 75 percent of the cattle died in the drought of 1892 and 1893. By the time the rains returned, thousands of square miles had been destroyed by hungry cows. The grasslands disappeared forever, replaced by raw desert.

The first English-speaking settlers in the region were Mormons, who escaped persecution in the empty desert. From the 1840s on, they settled throughout northern Arizona, often in places that are still remote today.

Around this time, Mormons came to colonize farmlands, convert Indians and find refuges isolated enough to discourage the government from harassing the polygamists among them. They settled along the Little Colorado River and in Mesa, leaving behind a legacy of fertile farmland and top public schools.

In 1857, a short-lived gold rush began, followed by silver. The most famous lode was discovered in 1877 by Ed Schieffelin, who found silver ore and named the first stake Tombstone. But in 1886, the mines flooded and Tombstone collapsed. The copper boom followed, transforming the territory from a frontier to a real cash economy. Since large investments were needed, much of the boom was financed by corporations back east. They brought with them their style of architecture; as a result, the boom towns of Jerome, Clifton, Globe and Bisbee still have picturesque Victorian homes perched on their hillsides. But it was the gold prospector who eventually became the very symbol of the Old West—an old man with a white beard, alone with his trusted burro, looking to strike it rich. You only have to head 30 miles east of Phoenix into the Superstition Mountains to find the lore and the legend and the lure of gold still very much alive today.

When the Civil War broke out, Arizona sided with the Confederacy. One reason was that citizens were mad at Congress for not making theirs a separate territory. In 1863, the area was declared the Arizona Territory. Over the following years, the capital jumped from the Prescott area to Tucson, and then finally Phoenix. On Valentine's Day in 1912, Arizona became the 48th state.

Arizona didn't boom in the years immediately after statehood and the reason was obvious—a lack of water. Providing water to the desert was quite a task. All that changed in 1911 when the Theodore Roosevelt Dam was completed on the Salt River. Not only did it curb the occasional river flooding, but it also provided irrigation water to Phoenix and the surrounding area. In 1936, the Hoover Dam was completed, forming Lake Mead, the largest artificial lake in North America. Once the water became plentiful, large-scale industry and agriculture followed.

The economy was based on the three C's: cattle, cotton and copper. Copper mining boomed in the 1920s and 1930s and copper was really sought during World War II when it was used for military munitions. Towns that rose with the copper boom and died after the war include Jerome and Bisbee, which have had renaissances as artist communities.

During the postwar years, Arizona moved away from its agricultural economic base; today, electronics, aerospace engineering and other high-tech industries are large employers. In addition, the tourism industry is an important part of the Arizona economy, with people arriving daily to explore the natural and man-made attractions in the state. It has been a winter retreat for the wealthy since the 1920s with its warm climate and healthy, dry air that helped people suffering from allergies. Unfortunately, this is no longer the case. Today, imported plants irritate those with allergies and levels of smog during parts of the year have grown to alarmingly high levels.

As for the American Indians, today there are 23 reservations in Arizona, more than any other state, with an estimated 190,091 Indians from 17 different tribes living in sad testimony to the white settlers' land grabs. The tribes speak 18 languages, and are spread across 31,000 square miles—about a quarter of Arizona. Some 150 miles east of Phoenix in the White Mountain region of eastern Arizona is the Fort Apache Indian Reservation with a million and a half acres of land. Bordering it, with another two million acres, is the San Carlos Apache Indian Reservation. The largest reservation in North America, Navajoland, home to over 200,000 Navajos, begins 76 miles north of Flagstaff and extends into northwestern New Mexico and southeastern Utah. Located almost in the center of the Navajo Indian Reservation is the Hopi Indian Reservation, 10,000 members strong, who have lived on the same site without interruption for more than 1000 years, retaining more of their ancient traditions and cultures than any other indigenous group.

The Spanish-Mexican influence is strongly evident throughout the area. About 18 percent of the state's population is Hispanic, and that number is growing daily. The Hispanic culture permeates much of Arizona. Mexican restaurants are in almost every neigh-borhood, boasting thick enchiladas and mouthwatering burritos. Some are frequented by strolling mariachi bands, whose music goes back to a ribald Spanish song and dance form of the 18th century. Boisterous celebrations such as Cinco de Mayo liven up the cultural climate, and Hispanic artwork hangs in museums across the state. All this is just part of that unique cultural mix that is Arizona today.

FOUR

The Grand Canyon

Awesome. Magnificent. Breathtaking. It's easy to slip into hyperbole when trying to describe the Grand Canyon, but it's understandable. No matter how many spectacular landscapes you have seen in your lifetime, none can compare with this mighty chasm stretching across the northwest corner of Arizona.

The Grand Canyon comes as a surprise. Whether you approach the South Rim or the North Rim, the landscape gives no hint that the canyon is there until suddenly you find yourself on the rim looking into the chasm ten miles wide from rim to rim and a mile down to the Colorado River, winding silver through the canyon's inner depths. From anywhere along the rim, you can feel the vast, silent emptiness of the canyon and wonder at the sheer mass of the walls, striated into layer upon colorful layer of sandstone, limestone and shale.

More than five million years ago, the Colorado River began carving out this canyon that offers a panoramic look at the geologic history of the Southwest. Sweeping away sandstones and sediments, limestones and fossils, the river cut its way through Paleozoic and Precambrian formations. The layers of rock exposed by erosion on the walls of the Grand Canyon range from 250 million to more than two billion years in age, the oldest exposed rock on Earth. By the time mankind arrived, the canyon extended nearly all the way down to schist, a basement formation.

The Grand Canyon is aptly named—being, perhaps, the grandest geological marvel of them all. It is as long as any mountain range in the Rockies and as deep as the highest of the Rocky Mountains are tall. For centuries, it posed the most formidable of all natural barriers to travel in the West, and to this day no road has ever penetrated the wilderness below the rim. No matter how many photographs you take, paintings you make or postcards you buy, the view from anywhere along the Grand Canyon rim can never be truly captured in two dimensions. Nor can the mind fully comprehend it; no matter how many times you have visited the Grand Canyon before, the view will always inspire the same awe as it did the first time you stood and gazed in wonder at the canyon's immensity and the silent grandeur of its massive cliffs.

The Grand Canyon extends east to west for some 277 miles, from the western boundary of the Navajo Indian Reservation to the vicinity of Lake Mead and the Nevada border. Only the highest section of each rim of the Grand Canyon is accessible by motor vehicle. Most of Grand Canyon National Park, both above and below the rim, is a designated wilderness area that can only be explored on foot or by river raft.

The South Rim and the North Rim are essentially separate destinations, more than 200 miles apart by road. For this reason, we've divided this chapter into three sections covering the developed national park areas on both rims as will as "The Arizona Strip." For the adventuresome, we've also included hiking possibilities in the canyon, as well as two lesser-known areas of the Grand Canyon that are challenging to reach—Toroweap Point in the Arizona Strip on the North Rim and the scenic area below the Indian village of Supai on the South Rim.

With more than five million visitors a year, the Grand Canyon is one of the most popular national parks in the United States. While many come to enjoy the panoramic vistas, others come to tackle the most challenging hiking trails in the country or to explore the narrow canyons and gorges by pack mule. Whatever reason you choose to visit the Grand Canyon, it will be worth it.

▼▼▼▼▼▼▼▼▼▼
The South Rim

The South Rim is the most accessible area of the Grand Canyon. It's no wonder that you'll find most of the facilities here. The many trailheads leading into the canyon and along the rim make this a good place to start your Grand Canyon tour.

SIGHTS

If you enter Grand Canyon National Park via the south entrance from Williams or Flagstaff, as most visitors do, you'll drive through **Tusayan**, about a mile south of the park entrance. The IMAX Theater in Tusayan shows films about the Grand Canyon on a seven-story, 82-foot-wide wraparound screen with six-track Dolby sound. These films can add an extra dimension to a Grand Canyon visit because they present river-rafting footage, aerial photography and closeup looks at places in the canyon that are hard to reach on foot. Admission. ~ Route 64; 520-638-2203.

Once inside the park's boundary, follow the road and signs to the visitors center. You'll pass **Mather Point** lookout and **Yavapai Observation Station;** both offer spectacular views of the canyon. There's a ranger on duty at Yavapai, and from this spot you can see Phantom Ranch, nearly a mile below, the Colorado River and the Suspension Bridge used by hikers of the Kaibab Trail to cross the river.

Stop at the **visitors center** as you enter **Grand Canyon Village**. Parking at the visitors center may be difficult in the summer, so you may want to park your car in the large lot near Yavapai Lodge

Text continued on page 42.

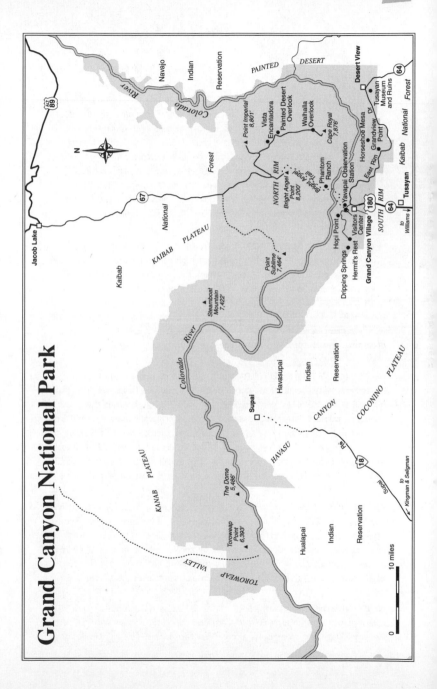

Grand Canyon National Park

South Rim Information

WHEN TO VISIT   The South Rim of Grand Canyon National Park is open all year. Most park visitors go to the South Rim, making it crowded even during the off-season, but the heaviest crowds can be expected during the spring, summer and fall months. Day visitors can expect traffic congestion and even some delays entering the park, especially during the summer. Overnight visitors must plan well in advance. Accommodations within the park are extremely limited and often are booked more than a year in advance. (See "Lodging" listings.)

WEATHER AND ELEVATION   The South Rim of the Grand Canyon is 7000 feet above sea level in a high-desert region. Temperatures during the summer are generally pleasant on the rim, ranging between 50° and 80°. Since the canyon floor lies some 5000 feet below the rim, daytime temperatures there are quite a bit higher, often climbing past 100°. Winter can bring snow, icy roads and clouds that can obscure canyon views. Spring and fall weather can change quickly in the canyon. The park's elevation can affect breathing, and it can take several days to become acclimated.

GETTING TO THE SOUTH RIM   The South Rim of Grand Canyon National Park is about 60 miles north of Williams (via Route 64 from Route 40) and about 80 miles from Flagstaff (via Route 180). Besides the south entrance, through which most visitors enter, the park can be entered from the east near Cameron, off Route 89. Grand Canyon Railway operates daily steam train service from Williams. ~ 520-773-1976, 800-843-8724. **Grayline Nava-Hopi Tours** provides public bus service from Flagstaff. ~ 520-774-5003. Limited air service is available to Grand Canyon Airport.

ENTRANCE FEES   The tariff for private vehicles is $20, for pedestrians and bicyclists, $10. The fee is nonrefundable, but admission is good for seven consecutive days for both the South and North rims. U.S. seniors over 62 and permanently disabled U.S. citizens may obtain specially priced passes; frequent national-park visitors should inquire about the Golden Eagle Passport. An annual Grand Canyon passport is also available.

GETTING AROUND THE PARK   A free Village shuttle bus system operates from mid-March to mid-October and makes stops within Grand Canyon Village and viewpoints along West Rim Drive. The eight-mile-long

West Rim Drive is closed to private vehicles during the same months. The East Rim Drive, however, follows the canyon rim for 25 miles and is open year-round. A hikers shuttle is available to South Kaibab Trail (at Yaki Point). ~ 520-638-3283. Shuttle transportation between the South and North rims (a four- to-five hour trip) operates seasonally, for a fee. Reservations required. ~ 520-638-2820.

POSTAL, MEDICAL AND OTHER SERVICES   The South Rim has its own post office, located in the shopping center next to Yavapai Lodge. A bank and a general store are also located in the center. Emergency medical service is available 24 hours (dial 911). The South Rim has its own medical clinic (520-638-2551), pharmacy (520-638-2460) and dental office (520-638-2395), all operating on limited hours. There's only one service station in the park on the South Rim, so if you drive to the Grand Canyon, make sure your car is in good working order. If something goes wrong, it could take days to get parts to repair your vehicle.

SERVICES FOR PERSONS WITH PHYSICAL DISABILITIES   Many buildings in the park are historic and do not meet accessibility standards. However, some structures are accessible with assistance. The Grand Canyon Accessibility Guide is available at the visitors center and the Yavapai Observation Station. Free wheelchairs are available at the visitors center, as are special vehicle permits allowing access to the West Rim Drive during summer months. Wheelchair accessible bus tours are available by prior arrangement (the Village shuttle bus is not wheelchair accessible). ~ 520-638-2631.

PETS   Pets are permitted in the park, but must be leashed, and, with the exception of certified service dogs, they're not allowed in lodgings, on park buses or below the rim. There is a kennel on the South Rim. ~ 520-638-2631.

BIKES   There are no bike rentals in the park. Bikes are not allowed on park trails. Mountain bikes are allowed only on those roads open to automobile traffic.

AND DON'T FORGET: Bring moleskin for potential blisters if you plan to go hiking, and a good pair of binoculars.

or at one of the other lots in the village and walk over to the center. The following phone numbers provide information: 520-638-7888 (taped recording), 520-638-7771 (live operator) and 520-638-2631 (switchboard for lodging, dining and other services). Or you can check out the website at www.thecanyon.com

Park rangers are on duty at the visitors center to answer questions, and maps and brochures about the park are available at the information desk. Books about the Grand Canyon, American Indian cultures and related topics are for sale at the small bookstore. You can arrange mule rides, view an exhibit about the natural and cultural history of the Grand Canyon and find out about ranger programs and audio-visual presentations. If you haven't already received a copy of the park newspaper, *The Grand Canyon Guide*, pick up a copy here. It's full of helpful information, including seasonal events, activities and park services. The visitors center is open daily, from 8 a.m. to 5 p.m.

The **Rim Trail** is a paved pathway that extends along the edge of the canyon from Yavapai Station, which is three-fourths of a mile east of the visitors center, to Maricopa Point, about three miles west of the center. Beyond Maricopa Point, the Rim Trail continues unpaved to Hermit's Rest. Night and day, the Rim Trail is a busy, at times crowded, walkway leading past all the major historical structures on the South Rim. You can sit on a bench and gaze out over the canyon or, at night, gaze up at a blue-black sky glittering with a zillion stars.

Native stone and Oregon pine were the materials used by architect Charles Whittlesey to build the sprawling **El Tovar Hotel** in 1905. Named for an officer in the expedition led by the Spanish explorer Coronado, the rustic lodge was operated by the Fred Harvey Company. It's still considered to be one of the nation's great historic hotels.

Several of the historic buildings set along the canyon rim were built by Mary Colter, an architect hired by the Fred Harvey Company. **Hopi House**, Colter's first effort for Harvey, was built of

✔ CHECK THESE OUT

- Wax nostalgic when you chug through the Kaibab National Forest on the turn-of-the-century **Grand Canyon Railway**. *page 53*
- Retreat at the **Phantom Ranch**, which sits at the bottom of the canyon and is reached by foot, mule and river raft only. *page 45*
- Reserve a table at the **Grand Canyon Lodge Dining Room** and feast on the stunning views of the canyon. *page 60*
- Boat out to Utah's **Rainbow Bridge National Monument**, the world's largest stone arch spanning 275 feet. *page 65*

THE SOUTH RIM SIGHTS 43

stone and adobe to resemble a pueblo building. Inside, ceilings are thatched, and there are niches and corner fireplaces, elements that are typical of Hopi pueblo dwellings. Completed on New Year's Day, 1905, Hopi House was originally used as living quarters for Hopi who danced for guests in the evening.

Bright Angel Lodge is another Colter building, dating to 1935. Built on the site of Bright Angel Camp of tents and cabins, the lodge was intended to provide moderately priced accommodations for tourists. Colter incorporated a stone fireplace that represents the rock layers of the canyon. Colter's **Lookout Studio** was completed in 1914. Perched on the edge of the canyon, the studio was built of native stone profile to make it seem an extension of the canyon wall. It offers exceptional views of the canyon.

Kolb Studio was started in 1904 by photographers Ellsworth L. Kolb and Emery C. Kolb who took pictures of mule passengers descending Bright Angel Trail. They built their studio at the trailhead. The brothers were the first to film a Grand Canyon river run.

WEST RIM DRIVE   West Rim Drive is closed to private vehicles during the summer months, reopening again to private vehicles in October. But a free shuttle bus (brown and tan) departs from West Rim Interchange, near Bright Angel Lodge. The drive clings to the rim of the canyon as it brings you to a series of overlooks, each more spectacular than the last. **Pima Point** offers one of the best canyon views, and from **Mohave Point** one of longest stretches of river is visible. (Mohave also serves as a good sunset-viewing spot.) The road ends at **Hermit's Rest**, the most popular spot to watch the sunset (it gets very crowded). Shuttle buses run about every 15 minutes between 7:30 a.m. and sunset; it takes about 90 minutes to travel the entire loop, if you don't get off the bus.

EAST RIM DRIVE   From Grand Canyon Village, East Rim Drive extends 25 miles east along the rim to the park's east entrance at Desert View. There are several overlooks along the way—**Yaki Point** (a favorite for viewing sunrise), **Grandview**, **Moran** (named for landscape painter Thomas Moran) and **Lipan** (with views of the river and Unkar Rapids).

The turnoff for the **Tusayan Museum and Ruins** comes up between Moran and Lipan points. Hopi ancestors inhabited the region, and this ruin, believed to be about 800 years old, is what remains of a hamlet of about 30 people who lived at the site for about 20 years. In the Hopi belief system, the canyon is said to be the *sipapu*, the hole through which the Earth's first people climbed from the mountaintop of their previous world into this one. Visitors can tour the site by themselves or join a ranger-led walk. Signage along the path explains specific features of the construction and uses of the site. The small museum displays artifacts of ancient life along the rim.

From **Desert View**, the last stop before exiting the park (or the first if you enter at the east entrance), the Painted Desert is visible as is Navajo Mountain, some 90 miles away. Mary Colter built a multilevel observation **Watchtower** here, her interpretation of prehistoric storage towers scattered over portions of the Southwest. Hopi wall decorations depict ceremonial paintings and designs. An observation room on the fourth level provides an incredible panorama of the surrounding landscape. Visitor information, restrooms and a general store are operated at Desert View, as is a service station (open seasonally).

HIDDEN ►

For the adventuresome, an intriguing Grand Canyon experience that is only accessible by foot is found far downriver near the west end of the canyon. The **Havasu Trail** (10 miles), entirely within the Havasupai Indian Reservation, is reached by leaving the interstate at Seligman (westbound) or Kingman (eastbound) and driving to the Supai turnoff near Peach Springs. From there, the Supai Road (Indian Road 18) goes for 63 miles before it dead-ends and a foot trail descends 2000 feet in eight miles to the Indian village of **Supai** where about 500 people live. All hikers must check in at tribal headquarters. From there, the main trail continues for about two more miles into Havasu Canyon, a side canyon from the Grand Canyon, which includes a series of three high waterfalls—75-foot **Navajo Falls**, 100-foot **Havasu Falls** and 200-foot **Mooney Falls**—with large pools that are ideal for swimming. There is a campground near Mooney Falls, and from there the trail continues down to the Colorado River in the bottom of the Grand Canyon. Whether you plan to stay in the campground or the modern lodge at Supai, advance reservations are essential. For camping, write Havasupai Tourist Enterprise, P.O. Box 160, Supai, AZ 86435 or call 520-448-2141. For accommodations, see "Lodging" below.

LODGING

The South Rim offers many lodging choices. To make same-day reservations or for information about South Rim accommodations, call 520-638-2631. Reservations at any of them can be made up to 23 months in advance by writing to the **AmFac Parks and Resorts, Grand Canyon National Park Lodges**. ~ 14001 East Iliff Avenue, Suite 600, Aurora, CO 80014; 303-297-2757, fax 303-297-3175; www.amfac.com.

Top of the line is the **El Tovar Hotel**. Designed after European hunting lodges, El Tovar was built by the Fred Harvey Company in 1905 and some staff members still wear the traditional black-and-white uniforms of the famous "Harvey Girls" of that era. The lobby retains its original backwoods elegance, with a big fireplace, massive wood ceiling beams and dark-stained pine decor throughout. All have full baths, color televisions and telephones. ~ DELUXE TO ULTRA-DELUXE.

More affordable historic lodging is available nearby at **Bright Angel Lodge**. The main log and stone lodge was built in 1935 on the site of Bright Angel Camp, the first tourist facility in the park. Its lobby features Indian motifs and a huge fireplace. Rooms are clean and modest. Most have televisions and phones; some have shared baths. Besides rooms in the main building, the lodge also rents several historic cabins, a few with fireplaces. Budget for rooms in the main lodge and budget to ultra-deluxe for historic cabins. ~ BUDGET TO ULTRA-DELUXE.

Also in Grand Canyon Village, on the rim between El Tovar and Bright Angel Lodge, are the modern twin stone lodges, **Thunderbird Lodge** and **Kachina Lodge**. Located on the rim trail, these caravansaries are within easy walking distance of the restaurants at the older lodges. All have televisions and phones. ~ MODERATE TO DELUXE.

The largest lodging facility in the park, **Yavapai Lodge** is situated in a wooded setting about one mile from the canyon rim, near the general store, across the road from the visitors center and about one mile from Grand Canyon Village. The contemporary guest rooms are equivalent in quality to what you would expect for the same price at a national chain motor inn. Closed January through March. ~ MODERATE.

Maswik Lodge is a half mile from the canyon rim at the southwest end of Grand Canyon Village. It presents a variety of motel-style rooms as well as cabins. All the rooms have TVs and phones. The cabins are available mid-May through mid-October only. ~ BUDGET TO MODERATE.

An elegant modern-rustic building with the look of a ski lodge and a lobby with multistory picture windows, **Moqui Lodge** is managed as part of the national park lodge system although it is located in Kaibab National Forest just outside the park's Southgate entrance. Rates include breakfast. Closed November through March. ~ 520-638-2424. MODERATE.

No survey of lodgings at the Grand Canyon would be complete without mentioning **Phantom Ranch**. Located at the bottom of the canyon, this 1922 lodge and cabins is at the lower end of

◀ HIDDEN

• •

FRED HARVEY TO THE RESCUE

In 1876, Fred Harvey (with the permission of the railroad) opened a restaurant in the Santa Fe station in Topeka, Kansas, to rescue diners from the rather tasteless food being served on the train. As years went by, a string of Fred "Harvey Houses" (hotels and restaurants) followed the tracks of the Santa Fe line. When the railroad built a spurline to the Grand Canyon in 1901, the Fred Harvey Company was not far behind.

the North Kaibab Trail from the North Rim and the Bright Angel and South Kaibab trails from the South Rim. It can only be reached by foot, mule or river raft. Cabins are normally reserved for guests on overnight mule trips, but hikers with plenty of advance notice can also arrange lodging. The prices for overnight mule trips include all meals and lodging. Bunk beds are available by reservation only in four ten-person dormitories for hikers. There is no television at the ranch, and only one pay phone. Food service is provided in the dining room. Do not arrive at Phantom Ranch without reservations! Contact AmFac Parks and Resorts, Grand Canyon National Park Lodges. ~ BUDGET.

HIDDEN ▶   Located in a remote red rock canyon on the Supai Indian Reservation, the 24 motel-style units at **Havasupai Lodge** is a truly hidden destination. There's a café next door, swimming in the nearby creek and a convenient barbecue pit. Just two miles away are Navajo, Havasu and Mooney falls. You can also enjoy American Indian–led horseback and hiking tours of this scenic region. ~ Supai; 520-448-2111, fax 520-448-2551. MODERATE.

Just outside the South Rim entrance gate, the community of Tusayan has several motels and motor inns that are not affiliated with the national park. If you cannot get reservations at one of the national park lodges, try one of the typical chain motels, such as the **Red Feather Lodge**. ~ 520-638-2414, 800-228-2000, fax 520-638-9216. MODERATE TO DELUXE. The **Best Western Grand Canyon Squire Inn** is another such establishment. ~ 520-638-2681, 800-622-6966, fax 520-638-0162. DELUXE. Or try the **Grand Canyon Quality Inn & Suites**. ~ 520-638-2673, 800-221-2222, fax 520-638-9537. DELUXE TO ULTRA-DELUXE.

DINING   The phone number for all South Rim Grand Canyon restaurants is 520-638-2631 and reservations are not required.

The most elegant (and the *only* elegant) South Rim restaurant is **El Tovar Dining Room**. Entrées such as filet mignon with crab legs béarnaise are served on fine china by candlelight. Prices are high, the ambience is classy, but casual dress is perfectly acceptable. Three meals are served; dinner reservations required. ~ MODERATE TO ULTRA-DELUXE.

More informal surroundings and lower prices are to be found at the **Bright Angel Coffee Shop** in the Bright Angel Lodge, which serves three meals daily. Menu selections include chicken piccata, grilled rainbow trout and fajitas. Cocktails and wine are available. BUDGET TO MODERATE.

Adjoining the Bright Angel Lodge, the **Arizona Steakhouse** specializes in steaks and seafood. The open kitchen lets you watch the chefs cook while you eat. Dinner only. Closed January through mid-February. ~ MODERATE TO DELUXE.

In the Yavapai Lodge, located across the highway from the visitors center, the **Yavapai Cafeteria** serves fast food—burgers and fries, pizza and fried chicken—for breakfast, lunch and dinner. Nearby in the general store, **Babbitt's Delicatessen** features sandwiches, salads and fried-chicken box lunches to go or eat on the premises. ~ 520-638-2262. BUDGET.

There are two other cafeterias in the park. The first is **Maswik Cafeteria** at Maswik Lodge, which serves breakfast, lunch and dinner. ~ Located at the west end of Grand Canyon Village. BUDGET. The **Desert View Snack Shop** serves a changing selection of hot meals. ~ Located 23 miles east of the village along the East Rim Drive. BUDGET.

Ice cream, sandwiches and soft drinks are available at the **Hermit's Rest Snack Bar** at the end of the West Rim Drive as well as at the **Bright Angel Fountain**, near the trailhead for the Bright Angel Trail. ~ BUDGET.

Mail sent from Phantom Ranch bears the postmark, "Mailed by Mule from the Bottom of the Canyon."

Outside the park entrance, the town of Tusayan has nearly a dozen eating establishments ranging from McDonald's to the beautiful **Moqui Lodge Dining Room**, which specializes in steak, chicken and seafood with a Southwestern flair. Breakfast and dinner only. Closed November through March. ~ Tusayan; 520-638-2424. MODERATE TO DELUXE.

Other options include the **Coronado Restaurant** at the Best Western Grand Canyon Squire Inn, which serves prime rib, steak and daily specials in a Southwestern-style dining room. Dinner only. ~ Route 64; 520-638-2681. MODERATE TO ULTRA-DELUXE.

For standard coffee shop fare check out the **Canyon Room** at the Grand Canyon Squire Inn, which is open for breakfast and lunch. ~ Route 64; 602-638-2681. BUDGET TO MODERATE.

SHOPPING

Of several national park concession tourist stores on the South Rim, the best are **Hopi House**, the large Indian pueblo replica across from El Tovar Hotel, and the adjacent **Verkamp's Curios** (520-638-2242). Both have been in continuous operation for almost a century and specialize in authentic American Indian handicrafts, with high standards of quality and some genuinely old pieces.

Other Grand Canyon shops, at least as interesting for their historic architecture as their wares, include the old **Kolb Studio**, originally a 1904 photographic studio and now a bookstore, and the **Lookout Studio**, which has rock specimens and conventional curios. Both are in Grand Canyon Village. Another souvenir shop is the **Hermit's Rest Gift Shop**. ~ End of West Rim Drive. With more of the same is the **Desert View Watchtower**. ~ East Rim Drive.

Text continued on page 50.

Touring the Grand Canyon

It seems like there are more ways to explore the Grand Canyon than there are routes down its walls. Hikers, mule riders, aviators and even whitewater enthusiasts have all discovered its sporting opportunities.

Of course the most rigorous way to tour the famous chasm is by *hiking*. If you have the time, making your way by foot down to the bottom is an amazing experience. Be forewarned—it is impossible to complete the journey in a day; people are often airlifted out for trying. Rest stops with shade and refreshing cold water are scattered intermittently along the trails. Plan ahead and camp or stay at the Phantom Ranch. (Do not arrive at the Phantom Ranch without reservations!)

For a taste of the Old West, mules are a classic mode of transport. *Mule trips* range from one-day excursions that venture as far as Plateau Point to two- and three-day trips to the bottom of the canyon. The cost is several hundred dollars per person, including meals and accommodations at the Phantom Ranch. Mule trips depart from both the North and South rims. Reservations must be made well ahead of time—as much as a year in advance for weekends, holidays and the summer months. For South Rim departures, contact **Grand Canyon National Park Lodges**. ~ 14001 East Iliff Avenue, Suite 600, Aurora, CO 80014; 303-297-2757, fax 303-297-3175. For North Rim departures, call **Grand Canyon Trail Rides**. Closed mid-October to mid-May. ~ P.O. Box 128, Tropic, UT 84776; 435-679-8665.

Many *"flightseeing"* tours offer spectacular eagle-eye views of the Grand Canyon. **Grand Canyon Airlines**' fully narrated tour circles the canyon starting at the South Rim and offers views of the Painted Desert and the confluence of the Colorado and Little Colorado rivers. ~ P.O. Box 3038, Grand Canyon, AZ 86023; 520-638-2407, 800-528-2413. With **Air Grand Canyon** you can choose from three different trips ranging from a 50-minute tour of the Eastern Gorge and the confluence of the Colorado and Little Colorado rivers to a 105-minute flight that visits all the major canyon sights. ~ P.O. Box 3399, Grand Canyon, AZ 86023; 520-638-2686, 800-247-4726. Both of these companies operate from Grand Canyon Airport near Tusayan.

Even more thrilling—and more expensive—are *helicopter tours*. Helicopters can fly considerably lower than airplanes, affording an even closer look at the magnificent canyon. Neither helicopters nor planes are allowed to fly beneath the rim, however, keeping the canyon peaceful for hikers and riders. The 45-minute Imperial Flight offered by **Papillon Grand Canyon Helicopters** affords views of the Painted Desert, Marble Canyon and Dragon's Corridor. The shorter North Canyon flight explores the Central Corridor. ~ P.O. Box 455, Grand Canyon, AZ 86023; 520-638-2419, 800-528-2418. **Kenai Helicopters**' 30-minute and 50-minute tours start at the South Rim and cross the canyon to visit the major sights. ~ P.O. Box 1429, Grand Canyon, AZ 86023; 520-638-2412, 800-541-4537. With **AirStar Helicopters** you can choose the 30-minute Central Corridor tour, the 45-minute Eastern Canyon tour or a 60-minute tour combining the two. ~ P.O. Box 3379, Grand Canyon, AZ 86023; 520-638-2622, 800-962-3869.

If simply looking at the bottom of the canyon isn't enough, water adventurers might consider a *rafting trip* down the Colorado River. Raft trips operate from April through September. Most start at Lee's Ferry, northeast of the national park boundary near Page, Arizona, and just below Glen Canyon Dam. The rafts are motorized, with pontoons, and provide seating for about 14 people.

More exciting are the smaller oar-operated dories that ride closer to the water and occasionally tip over in the rough rapids. Rafting the full length of the canyon, 280 miles from Lee's Ferry to Lake Mead, takes a leisurely eight days, providing plenty of time to hike and explore remote parts of the canyon inaccessible by other means. Many rafting companies also offer shorter trips that involve being picked up or dropped off by helicopter part way through the canyon.

One of the leading raft tour companies is **Grand Canyon Expeditions**, offering eight-day motorized expeditions and fourteen-day rowing trips. Transportation, camping gear and all meals are provided. ~ P.O. Box O, Kanab, UT 84741; 435-644-2691, 800-544-2691. Another good organization is **Arizona River Runners** for multiday motorized or oar-powered trips. Meals and equipment are included. ~ P.O. Box 47788, Phoenix, AZ 85068; 602-867-4866, 800-477-7238. A complete list of river trip outfitters is available from **Rivers and Oceans**. ~ 520-526-4575, 800-473-4576. Private parties can take the river route through the Grand Canyon. Contact the South Rim visitors center for additional information.

NIGHTLIFE   Bright Angel Lodge offers live weekly entertainment—usually a folk guitarist—and El Tovar Lounge has a piano bar. In general, though, Grand Canyon National Park does not have much in the way of hot nightlife. We suggest taking in one of the ranger-produced slide shows presented in the amphitheater or simply sitting in the dark along the canyon rim and listening to the vast, deep silence.

▼▼▼▼▼▼▼▼▼▼▼▼▼
Outdoor Adventures

RIDING STABLES   At the Grand Canyon, the **Apache Stable** at Moqui Lodge in Tusayan, near the park's south entrance, offers a selection of guided rides to various points along the South Rim, lasting from one to four hours. Groups can range from 2 to 40 people depending on the season. Most popular is the four-hour East Rim ride, which winds through the ponderosa forest of the Kaibab Plateau to Long Jim Canyon and a viewpoint overlooking the Grand Canyon. One- and two-hour rides are also available. Horseback rides do not go below the canyon rim. Call for reservations. ~ 520-638-2891.

For information on mule trips into the canyon, see "Touring the Grand Canyon" in this chapter.

BIKING   Although trails within the national park are closed to bicycles, Kaibab National Forest surrounding the park on both the North and South Rims offers a wealth of mountain-biking possibilities. The forest areas adjoining Grand Canyon National Park are laced with old logging roads and the relatively flat terrain makes for low-stress riding.

Located at the South Rim of the Grand Canyon, the **West Rim Drive** is closed to most private motor vehicles during the summer months but open to bicycles. This fairly level route (eight miles one way) makes for a spectacular cycling tour. Watch out for bus traffic during the summer months. One ride the National Forest Service recommends in the vicinity of the South Rim is the **Coconino Rim Trail** (9.1 miles), a loop trail, which starts near Grandview Point and travels southeast through ponderosa forests.

For other suggestions, stop in at the Tusayan Ranger Station just outside the South Rim entrance (520-638-2443) or contact Kaibab National Forest Headquarters. ~ 800 South 6th Street, Williams, AZ 86046; 520-635-8200.

HIKING   The ultimate hiking experience in Grand Canyon National Park —and perhaps in the entire Southwest—is an expedition from either rim to the bottom of the canyon and back. With an elevation change of 4800 feet from the South Rim to the river, or 5800 feet from the North Rim, the hike is as ambitious as an ascent of a major Rocky Mountain peak, except that the greatest effort is required in the last miles of the climb out, when leg muscles may already be sore from the long downhill trek. Strenuous as it may be, hiking the Grand Canyon is an experience sure to stay vivid for a lifetime.

Though some people claim to have done it, hiking round-trip from the rim to river level and back in a single day is a monumental feat that takes from 16 to 18 hours. Most hikers who plan to go the whole way will want to allow at least two, preferably three, days for the trip. The park service does not recommend attempting to hike from the rim to the canyon bottom during the summer months *unless* starting the trek before 7 a.m. or after 4 p.m. (Though it might be 85° on the rim, it could be 115° at the bottom.) A wilderness permit, required for any overnight trip into the park back country, can be obtained free of charge at the backcountry office on either rim.

The **Bright Angel Trail** (7.8 miles to the river or 9.3 miles to Phantom Ranch), the most popular trail in the canyon, starts at Grand Canyon Village on the South Rim, near the mule corral. It has the most developed facilities, including resthouses with emergency phones along the upper part of the trail and a ranger station, water and a campground midway down at Indian Garden where the Havasupai people used to grow crops. The one-day round-trip hike will take you along a ridgeline to Plateau Point, overlooking the Colorado River from 1300 feet above, just before the final steep descent. Allow about five hours to hike from the rim down to the river and about ten hours to climb back up. It is therefore advisable to camp and make the return trip the following day. Remember, a permit is required for overnight trips. A lot of hikers use this trail, as do daily mule riders—not the route to take if you seek solitude.

Another major trail from the South Rim is the **South Kaibab Trail** (7.3 miles to Phantom Ranch), which starts from the trailhead on East Rim Drive, four and a half miles from Grand Canyon Village. A free shuttle bus takes hikers to the trailhead. The shortest of the main trails into the canyon, it is also the steepest, and due to lack of water and shade along the route, it is not recommended during the summer months.

Several less-used trails also descend from the South Rim. All of them intersect the **Tonto Trail** (95 miles), which runs along the edge of the inner gorge about 1300 feet above river level. The **Grandview Trail** (3 miles), an old mine access route that starts at Grandview Point on East Rim Drive, goes down to Horseshoe Mesa where it joins a loop of the Tonto Trail that circles the mesa, passing ruins of an old copper mine. There is a primitive campground without water on the mesa. All camping in the canyon requires a free backcountry permit.

The **Hermit Trail** (8.5 miles) begins at Hermit's Rest at the end of West Rim Drive and descends to join the Tonto Trail. Branching off from the Dripping Springs Trail, which also starts at Hermit's Rest, the **Boucher Trail** (11 miles) also goes down to join the Tonto Trail and is considered one of the more difficult hiking trails in the park. Ask for details at the rangers' counter in the South Rim visitors center.

The paved, handicapped-accessible **Rim Trail** (1.5 miles) goes between the Kolb Studio at the west side of Grand Canyon Village and the Yavapai Observation Station. A one-third-mile spur links the Rim Trail with the visitors center. At each end of the designated Rim Trail, the pavement ends but unofficial trails continue for several more miles, ending at Hopi Point near the Powell Memorial on West Rim Drive and at Yaki Point, the trailhead for the South Kaibab Trail, on East Rim Drive.

Williams

This historic mountain town, tucked away in the ponderosa pine forest of northern Arizona, is still somewhat undiscovered. But it's only 60 miles southeast from the Grand Canyon and, working hard to get its name on more visitors maps, has adopted (and legally registered) the moniker "Gateway to the Grand Canyon." Founded in 1882, long before it had a savvy chamber of commerce, Williams was known as a tough, bawdy railroad and logging center. Across the street from the railroad yards, brothels and opium dens sprung up to serve the loggers, Chinese laborers, railroad workers and cowboys. At that time, a muddy roadway through town was part of the network of trails known as Old Trails Highway. By the 1920s, the roadway became part of the U.S. highway system and entered cultural lore as Route 66. As the interstate highway system replaced the old Route 66, Williams held out until 1984, when it became the last town along the old route to be bypassed by the interstate.

Today, many of the buildings along Bill Williams and Railroad avenues (the old Route 66 roadways) are listed on the National Register of Historic Places and now house American Indian and Western arts-and-crafts galleries, antique stores and restaurants, as well as a few saloons.

With at least a dozen motels that hark back to the old Route 66 days, this small town (pop. 2700) is something of a quaint, living museum of a bygone era in American culture. Quaint, however, does not mean out of touch: The chamber of commerce in Williams has a web site (www.thegrandcanyon.com).

SIGHTS The first place to stop in Williams is the **Williams Forest Service Visitors Center**, located in the old Santa Fe railroad freight depot, to pick up brochures about attractions or obtain information about lodging, dining or visiting the Grand Canyon. ~ 200 West Railroad Avenue; 520-635-4061; www.thegrandcanyon.com.

From the visitors center, a walk around downtown Williams is quite manageable. The **historical core** extends no more than four blocks in either direction along Bill Williams and Railroad avenues. Most of the shops and galleries of interest to visitors are on Bill Williams Avenue, which is only two blocks from the visitors center. Sidewalks have been brick-paved, and most turn-of-the-century buildings have been restored and now house galleries of Western and American Indian art, jewelry and crafts, collectibles, restaurants and a couple of authentic Route 66 saloons.

The Grand Canyon Railway is just across the tracks from the visitors center, in the historic 1908 Williams Depot. Using either turn-of-the-century steam engines (summer months) or 1950s-diesel engines (winter), the train leaves Williams in the morning for a two-and-a-half-hour trip through Kaibab National Forest to the Grand Canyon, tracing the route that brought early tourists to the park. The return trip to Williams departs from the Grand Canyon in midafternoon. Trains run daily year-round. The depot building also houses a small but well-done historical and railroad museum. ~ Williams Depot, Railroad Avenue and Grand Canyon Boulevard, Williams; 520-773-1976, 800-843-8724.

A drive south about 12 miles on **Perkinsville Road** (referred   ◀ HIDDEN
to locally as the South Road) will bring you to open meadows, where, at dusk, it's not uncommon to spot deer and elk emerging from the forest to graze. Early October, when the aspen trees have turned golden and flame, is an especially lovely time to make the drive during the day to see the fall colors.

The summer months, June through August, are a good time to visit **Grand Canyon Deer Farm Petting Zoo**. That's when the fawns are born at the small, walk-through park. Although most of the animals, including pronghorn antelope, buffalo, potbellied pigs, turkeys, wallabies and reindeer, are enclosed, several types of deer and some of the goats have free reign and will demand to eat right out of your hand. If you buy some feed before entering the park grounds, you'll be guaranteed an upclose visit. Open year-round, weather permitting in winter. Admission. ~ Eight miles east of Williams, 6752 East Deer Farm Road on Route 40, Exit 171; 520-635-4073, 800-926-3337.

Aviation history buffs might want to stop at **Planes of Fame Air Museum** on Route 64 in Valle, about halfway between Williams and the Grand Canyon. The historic aircraft on display, many of them restored to flying condition, represent a spectrum of aviation history from World War I through the supersonic jet age. Besides a 1928 Ford Trimotor, America's first airliner, there are several fighter craft, as well as General Douglas MacArthur's Lockheed Constellation transport called "Bataan." (There's an extra charge to tour this craft.) Admission. ~ Grand Canyon-Valle Airport, junction of Routes 64 and 180, Valle; 520-635-1000.

Just down the road from the Planes of Fame Air Museum is an odd sight: **Bedrock City**, a cartoon-colored, life-size theme park of sorts where you can walk into the Flintstones' and Rubbles' homes, as well as the jail and the schoolhouse. But there's not much of the fun and wild antics of the Hanna-Barbera cartoons: no costumed Fred and Barney wandering around, no animated Dino or Pebbles. The cinder pathways are hard to walk on. A campground, coffee shop and souvenir store are on the premises. Admission. ~ Junction of Routes 64 and 180, Valle; 520-635-2600.

LODGING

Williams has several choices for motel accommodations located along historic Route 66, many offering low prices as well as nostalgia. The chamber of commerce can provide a list. ~ 520-635-4061; www.thegrandcanyon.com.

HIDDEN ►

Visitors looking for a historical connection to Williams' rowdy railroad and mining past might consider booking a room at the **Red Garter Bed and Bakery**. Innkeeper John Holst has completely restored and renovated an 1897 Victorian Romanesque building that was used as a saloon and a bordello. The original eight cribs on the second floor have been remodeled into four guest rooms and furnished with antiques. Each room has a private three-quarter bath. Of course, the rooms tend be smaller than standard hotel or motel rooms, and two of the rooms don't have windows; but 12-foot ceilings, over-the-door transoms, skylights and ceiling fans keep things cheerful, bright and airy. The "best" girl's room is a small bedroom–sitting room suite in the front of the building. An extended continental breakfast is served each morning in the bakery downstairs. Innkeeper Holst has lived in Arizona for many years and is extremely knowledgeable about Williams and the region. He's glad to help out with suggestions for itineraries, day trips and activities in the area. Closed January. ~ 137 West Railroad Avenue; 520-635-1484, 800-328-1484; e-mail redgarter@thegrandcanyon.com. BUDGET TO MODERATE.

YOU CAN'T BE TOO EARLY

If you're planning a trip to the Grand Canyon it's important to make reservations for lodging early—at least a year in advance! The first thing to do is to write or call for a free Trip Planner offered by the National Park Service. It has information about accommodations, activities, itineraries and do's and don'ts. Write to Trip Planner, Grand Canyon National Park, P.O. Box 129, Grand Canyon, AZ 86023; 520-638-7888. If you're on-line you can also get the Trip Planner and a parcel of other information at www.thecanyon.com.

Adjacent to the Grand Canyon Railway depot is the 89-room **Fray Marcos Hotel**, built in the same architectural style as the Williams Depot. The large, comfortable rooms have two queen-size beds; smoking and nonsmoking rooms are available. Newspapers and coffee are available in the lobby in the morning. ~ Williams Depot, 235 Grand Canyon Boulevard; 520-635-4010, 800-843-8724, fax 520-635-2180; www.thetrain.com. DELUXE.

The area's only AAA four-diamond rated motel is the **Best Western Inn of Williams**. Perched on a hillside just off Route 40, the inn features an outdoor pool and spa and provides hairdryers, phones and laundry facilities. ~ 2600 West Route 66, Route 40 Business Loop, Exit 161; 520-635-4400, 800-635-4445, fax 520-635-4488. MODERATE TO DELUXE.

The only hostel located on the highway to the Grand Canyon, **Grand Canyon Red Lake Hostel** has a total of 32 beds; private rooms are available. Facilities include a common room (equipped with TV and VCR) and a kitchen area (with microwave, toaster and mini-refrigerators); showers are coin-operated. ~ Route 64, eight miles north of Williams; 520-635-9122, 800-581-4753, fax 520-635-5321; www.amdest.com/az/williams/redlake.html. BUDGET.

DINING

This is still cowboy country when it comes to food, and steak and ribs are popular on local menus. You can't miss the big neon cow in front of **Rod's Steak House**, a Route 66 landmark that's been around for 50 years. A casual, no frills place, Rod's keeps the menu straightforward: steaks are prepared eight different ways; four cuts of prime rib are served plus a few fish and chicken dishes. There's a children's menu available. ~ 301 East Route 66; 520-635-2671. MODERATE TO ULTRA-DELUXE.

Besides platters of steak, barbecued ribs or prime rib, **Miss Kitty's Steakhouse and Saloon** offers up live country music each evening during tourist season. It's a big place, with lots of wood and brick and high beamed ceilings. A balcony rings two sides of the room and a stage and dancefloor occupy one end of the room. It's fast, efficient and fun. Breakfast, lunch and dinner are served. ~ In the Ramada Inn Canyon Gateway, 642 East Route 66; 520-635-9161. MODERATE TO DELUXE.

Pancho McGillicuddy's Mexican Cantina is located in the downtown Williams historic district, next to the Red Garter Bed and Bakery. The atmosphere is cheerful and friendly, and the food is fresh tasting and generously portioned. Call ahead for winter schedule. ~ 141 Railroad Avenue; 520-635-4150. BUDGET TO MODERATE.

Set in a renovated gas station, **Cruiser's Cafe 66** generates the spirit of Route 66 with antiques and memorabilia galore. Sidle up to gas pumps, neon signs, old photographs and road signs for a closer look at those magical motoring days. Grab a drink at the horseshoe bar before ordering burgers, pizza, ribs, steaks or chicken. ~ 233 West Route 66; 520-635-2445. MODERATE.

SHOPPING Get your kicks—or at least Navajo, Hopi and Zuni jewelry and Route 66 souvenirs—at the **Turquoise Teepee**. ~ 114 West Route 66; 520-635-4709.

NIGHTLIFE If hanging out in a Route 66 saloon or motel lounge isn't your idea of a fun evening, there isn't too much to do in Williams after dark. But on most Saturday evenings you can head over to the
HIDDEN ► **Red Garter Bed and Bakery** and peek into the bakery where you'll probably find a group of local musicians playing and singing. Come in, have a cup of coffee and observe the proceedings or, perhaps, join in them. The friendly, informal gathering is a great way to meet local people. Closed January. ~ 137 West Railroad Avenue; 520-635-1484.

▼▼▼▼▼▼▼▼▼▼▼▼▼▼
Outdoor Adventures

The nine-hole **Elephant Rocks at Williams**, surrounded by ponderosa forest, may be a short course, but it's fairly difficult. The ninth hole,

GOLF for instance, starts at an elevation of 7000 feet and drops some 80 feet to the cup. Besides that, it has a distractingly enjoyable
HIDDEN ► view of the surrounding countryside and Bill Williams Mountain a few miles away. Open March through November, weather permitting. Putting green, driving range and club and cart rentals. ~ Country Club Road, Williams; 520-635-4936.

SKIING The family-oriented **Williams Ski Area**, atop 9264-foot Bill Williams Mountain, offers beginners and intermediate skiers especially a variety of groomed slopes and trails on which to practice. Snowboarding is allowed here. Downhill and cross-country rentals, as well as downhill lessons, are available. Closed Monday through Wednesday. ~ 520-635-9330 or the chamber of commerce at 520-635-4061.

RIDING STABLES **Stable in the Pines** offers easy guided trail rides through the countryside just outside Williams. The emphasis is on enjoying the outdoors, with trail guides pointing out flora and fauna. Rides last from a half hour to all day. Children must be six and older; there are pony rides for the younger kids. Special rides can be set up to explore Bill Williams Mountain. Stables are open from April through September. ~ Circle Pines KOA Campground, Route 40, Exit 167, Williams; 520-635-2626, 800-562-9379.

HIKING **Bill Williams Mountain** also offers two especially pleasant short day hikes lasting no more than six hours roundtrip. The trailhead for **Benham Trail** (4.5 miles) is about a 15-minute trek from Williams, on frontage road 140 off Perkinsville Road. The trail starts at the 7200-foot level, in ponderosa pine and oak thickets, and climbs up moderately difficult slopes to about 9200 feet into the mixed conifer forest on the mountain. At several places along the trail, hikers have good views of the valley below and distant peaks.

Bill Williams Mountain Trail #21 (4 miles) also starts out in ponderosa pine and oak thickets, near the Williams Ranger Station at Clover Hill. The trail then leads hikers through stands of aspen and fir. The ancestors of the Hopi people inhabited this land at one time, and the area is still considered sacred. Trail guides are available at the Williams Visitors Center and at the ranger station.

The North Rim of the Grand Canyon receives only about one-tenth of the number of visitors the South Rim gets. Snowbound during the winter because it is

▼▼▼▼▼▼▼▼▼▼
The North Rim

1200 feet higher in elevation, the North Rim is only open from mid-May through October, while the South Rim is open year-round. The South Rim is much more convenient for more travelers since it is much closer to a major interstate highway route and to the large population centers of southern Arizona and California. But if your tour of the Southwest includes destinations such as the Navajo Indian Reservation, Lake Powell, Page, Bryce Canyon and Zion national parks, or even Las Vegas, then your route will take you closer to the North Rim, giving you an opportunity to explore the cooler, quieter side of the canyon.

Before starting the drive into the park from Jacob Lake, stop at the **National Forest Visitors Center**. A small exhibit details information on human habitation and wildlife on the plateau, and a ranger is on duty to answer questions. Closed from late October through April. ~ 520-643-7298.

SIGHTS

The drive across the **Kaibab Plateau** into the park on Route 67 (also called the Kaibab Plateau North Rim Parkway) winds through a forest of ponderosa pine, quaking aspen, blue spruce and Douglas fir, and large open mountain meadows. Mule-deer and other wildlife can be seen occasionally in the meadows (early morning and early evening are the best times to spot them grazing). In the fall, stands of aspen trees set the landscape ashimmer in a trembling glow of yellow and flame orange.

Several miles into the park, a turnoff at Fuller Canyon Road leads to the scenic drives on **Point Imperial Road** and **Cape Royal Road**. At 8801 feet, **Point Imperial** is the highest point on either rim and commands a stunning view of Mt. Hayden, a huge carved sandstone spire, and the sprawling vistas of the eastern canyon. Cape Royal Road leads to **Vista Encantadora, Painted Desert Overlook** and **Walhalla Overlook**. There's an ancient Anasazi ruin across the road from Walhalla. The drive ends at **Cape Royal**, where you can take a self-guided nature walk, and get a look at the Colorado River and the large natural arch called **Angels Window**. Cape Royal is also a popular spot to watch the sun rise or set. (Narrated tours to both Cape Royal and Point Imperial are available. Check at the information desk in the lobby of Grand Canyon Lodge.)

Route 67 dead-ends at the **Grand Canyon Lodge**, built of native stone and timber and perched right on the edge of the rim. Verandas on either side of the lodge offer sunny, open spots to view the canyon. At night, the lights of Grand Canyon Village, 11 miles away on the South Rim, are visible.

From the lodge, to the east, a path leads out to **Bright Angel Point**. Though paved, the quarter-mile path clings precipitously to the canyon rim, and rises and falls in some spots. A pamphlet to a self-guided walking tour to Bright Angel Point is available for a quarter. It points out places to look for fossils and where to see **Roaring Springs**, some 3800 feet below and the North Rim's source of water. From Bright Angel Point, which is at an elevation of 8200 feet, there are good views of the South Rim and the San Francisco Peaks near Flagstaff, some 50 miles away. The high elevation, however, can make breathing difficult for some people. Other viewpoints on the North Rim are reached by foot trails. (See "Hiking" under "Outdoor Adventures.")

Extremely adventuresome motorists can visit a separate area along the North Rim of the Grand Canyon, Toroweap Point, by leaving Route 89A at Fredonia, about 75 miles north of the North Rim entrance. Don't forget to fill up the gas tank in Fredonia, because you won't see another gas station for nearly 200 miles. Next, proceed west from Fredonia for 14 miles on Route 389 to **Pipe Spring National Monument**. Take time to see the monument. The remote, fortresslike old Mormon ranching outpost, which had the only telegraph station in the Arizona Territory north of the Grand Canyon, was home to the Winsor family and their employees, thus its historical nickname, Winsor Castle. The ranch buildings and equipment are well preserved, and the duck pond provides a cool oasis. Park rangers costumed in period dress recreate the pioneer lifestyle during the summer months. Admission. ~ Route 389; 520-643-7105.

Backtracking, nine miles from the Fredonia turnoff and six miles before you reach Pipe Springs, an unpaved road turns off to the south. It goes 67 miles to the most remote point that can be reached by motor vehicle on the Grand Canyon rim. The road is wide and well maintained, easily passable by passenger car, but very isolated. You will not find a telephone or any other sign of habitation anywhere along the way. You may not see another car all day. Several other dirt roads branch off along the way, but if

North Rim Information

WHEN TO VISIT   Although the park remains open for day use until December (or until heavy snow closes the road), visitor facilities on the North Rim of the Grand Canyon are open only from May 15 to October 15.

WEATHER AND ELEVATION   The North Rim's elevation is 8200 feet. Summers are temperate, with warm days and mild evenings. Winter snow can accumulate to over 12 feet.

GETTING TO THE NORTH RIM   The distance across the canyon from the South Rim to the North Rim is only about ten miles as the crow flies. But the distance in road miles is about 200. Access is on Route 67, from Routes 89 and 89A. From Jacob Lake to the Grand Canyon Lodge, the distance is 45 miles. Page and Lake Powell are about 120 miles to the east. Shuttle transportation between the rims is available daily from May 15 to October 15 for a fee. ~ 520-638-2820.

ENTRANCE FEES   The tariff for private vehicles is $20, for pedestrians and bicyclists, $10. The fee is nonrefundable, but admission is good for seven consecutive days for both the North and South rims. U.S. seniors over 62 and physically disabled U.S. citizens may obtain specially priced passes; frequent national park visitors should inquire about the Golden Eagle Passport. An annual Grand Canyon passport is also available.

GETTING AROUND THE PARK   The main road into the park dead-ends at the Grand Canyon Lodge. From there you can walk along a paved but precipitous path to one of the park's most popular overlooks, Bright Angel Point. Before reaching the lodge, a turnoff leads to Cape Royal Scenic Drive, a 20-mile drive to several other lookouts. Van tours are also available; a schedule is posted in the lobby of the lodge.

POSTAL, MEDICAL AND OTHER SERVICES   A general store and a service station are located near the campground. The post office is located in the lodge complex. Dial 911 for emergency medical service; a medical clinic is staffed by a nurse practitioner. ~ 520-638-2611 ext. 222.

SERVICES FOR PERSONS WITH PHYSICAL DISABILITIES   The Accessibility Guide is available at the information desk in the lodge lobby. Many of the viewpoints and other facilities are wheelchair accessible or accessible with assistance.

you keep to the road that goes straight ahead and looks well used, following the "Toroweap" and "Grand Canyon National Monument" signs whenever you see them, it's hard to get lost. Have fun experiencing this wide-open countryside as empty as all of Arizona used to be long ago.

HIDDEN ►   There is a small, primitive campground at **Toroweap Point** but no water. As likely as not, you may find that you have the place all to yourself. The elevation is 2000 feet lower than at the main North Rim visitor area, so instead of pine forest the vegetation around Toroweap Point is desert scrub. Being closer to the river, still some 3000 feet below, you can watch the parade of river rafts drifting past and even eavesdrop on passengers' conversations.

LODGING   On the North Rim, the only lodging within the park is the **Grand Canyon Lodge**, which consists of a beautiful 1930s-vintage main lodge building overlooking the canyon and a number of cabins—some rustic, others modern, a few with canyon views. Clean and homelike, both rooms and cabins have an old-fashioned feel, though they can be a little noisy. North Rim accommodations are in very high demand, so reservations should be made far ahead. They are accepted up to 23 months in advance. Reservations for the lodge are booked through AmFac, which also handles reservations for the lodges at Bryce Canyon and Zion national parks. The lodge is closed from mid-October to mid-May. ~ Lodge: 520-638-2611, fax 520-638-2554. Reservations: 14001 East Iliff Avenue, Suite 600, Aurora, CO 80014; 303-297-2757, fax 303-297-3175; www.amfac.com. BUDGET TO MODERATE.

Just five miles from the entrance to the park, the **Kaibab Lodge** offers basic sleeping accommodations—26 small rooms with private bathroom in cabin-style buildings set around the main lodge building. There are no televisions or phones in the rooms (you'll find them in the lobby of the main lodge). Reserve rooms well in advance. ~ Grand Canyon North Rim Parkway (Route 67); 520-638-2389 (May to mid-October only), 520-526-0924, 800-525-0924; www.canyoneers.com. MODERATE.

Forty-four miles from the North Rim is the **Jacob Lake Inn**. This small, rustic resort complex surrounded by national forest offers motel rooms and cabins, both smoking and nonsmoking, including some two-bedroom units. All cabins have decks and forest views (cabins 28 and 29 front the edge of the forest). Reservations should be made well in advance. ~ Junction of Routes 89 and 67, Jacob Lake; 520-643-7232; www.jacoblake.com. MODERATE.

DINING   The **Grand Canyon Lodge Dining Room** offers breakfast, lunch and dinner at affordable prices. The food is good, conventional meat-and-potatoes fare and the atmosphere—a spacious, rustic

THE NORTH RIM HIKING

log-beamed dining room with huge picture windows overlooking the canyon—is simply incomparable. Reservations are required for dinner. The lodge also operates a budget-priced snack shop serving breakfast, lunch and dinner in plain, simple surroundings, as well as a saloon offering pizza and sandwiches. Nearby, the camper store sells pizza sandwiches. Closed mid-October to mid-May. ~ 520-638-2611. MODERATE TO DELUXE.

KAIBAB NATIONAL FOREST  This 1,500,000-acre   **PARKS**
expanse of pine, fir, spruce and aspen forest includes both sides of the Grand Canyon outside the park boundaries. Most recreational facilities are located near the North Rim, where they supplement the park's limited camping facilities. Wildlife in the forest includes mule deer, wild turkeys, several other bird species and even a few bison. There are picnic areas, restrooms and a visitors center. The facilities in the forest close from about November to March. ~ The national forest visitors center is at Jacob Lake, the intersection of Routes 89A and 67; 520-643-7298 (North Rim visitors center), 520-635-4061 (South Rim). Jacob Lake Campground is at the same location, while Demotte Campground is 23 miles south on Route 67, about five miles from the national park entrance.

▲ Demotte Campground has 23 sites, $12 per night, and Jacob Lake Campground has 53 sites, $12 per night; information, 520-643-7395. RV hookups are available at the privately owned Kaibab Camper Village, $12 for tent sites, $22 for motor homes. ~ 520-643-7804, 520-526-0924 (from October to May).

Although trails within the national park are closed to bicycles, Kaibab National Forest surrounding the park on the North Rim offers a

▼▼▼▼▼▼▼▼▼▼▼▼▼▼
Outdoor Adventures

wealth of mountain biking possibilities. The forest areas adjoining Grand Canyon National Park are laced with old logging roads and the relatively flat terrain makes for low-stress riding.   **BIKING**

Toward the west end of the Grand Canyon on its North Rim, visitors to **Toroweap Point** will find endless mountain biking opportunities along the hundreds of miles of remote, unpaved roads in the Arizona Strip.

The main trail into the canyon from the North Rim is the **North   HIKING
Kaibab Trail** (14.2 miles). The trail starts from the trailhead two miles north of Grand Canyon Lodge and descends abruptly down Roaring Springs Canyon for almost five miles to Bright Angel Creek. This is the steepest part of the trip. Where the trail reaches the creek, there are several swimming holes, a good destination for a one-day round trip. The trail then follows the creek all the way to Phantom Ranch at the bottom of the canyon. Park rangers

recommend that hikers allow a full day to hike from the rim to the ranch and two days to climb back to the rim, stopping overnight at Cottonwood Camp, the midway point. Because of heavy snows on the rim, this trail is not recommended during the winter months.

Without descending below the canyon rim, hikers can choose from a variety of trails ranging from short scenic walks to all-day hikes. The easy, paved, handicapped-accessible **Transept Trail** (2 miles) runs between the campground and the lodge, then continues gradually downward to Bright Angel Point, which affords the best view of the Bright Angel Trail down into the canyon.

The **Uncle Jim Trail** (2.5 miles) starts at the same trailhead as the Roaring Springs Canyon fork of the Bright Angel Trail, two miles north of the lodge. It circles through the ponderosa woods to an overlook, Uncle Jim Point.

The **Ken Patrick Trail** (10 miles) runs from Point Imperial to the Kaibab Trail parking lot.

A quiet North Rim trail that leads through the forest to a remote canyon viewpoint is the **Widforss Trail** (5 miles), named after artist Gunnar Widforss, who painted landscapes in the national parks during the 1920s. The trail winds along the lip of the plateau through scrubby oak, piñon pines, ponderosa pines and juniper. The viewpoint overlooks a side canyon known as Haunted Canyon.

HIDDEN ▶

Visitors to remote Toroweap Point may wish to try the **Lava Falls Route** (1.5 miles), which begins as a jeep road midway between the old ranger station and the point. Although this trail is not long, it is recommended for experienced hikers only, as it is rocky, edgy, very steep and marked only by cairns, descending 3000 feet to the Colorado River and the "falls"—actually a furious stretch of white water formed when lava spilled into the river. Allow all day for the round-trip hike and do not attempt it during the hot months.

▼▼▼▼▼▼▼▼▼▼
Arizona Strip

The rectangular-shaped stretch of Arizona sandwiched between the Colorado River and the borders of Utah and Nevada is referred to as the Arizona Strip. Most of the area is remote, with few paved roads and, aside from Colorado City, Fredonia and Jacob Lake, few towns or settlements for visitors. Along the eastern edge of the Arizona Strip, on the Colorado River, however, the manmade Lake Powell is an increasingly popular resort, especially well known for houseboat vacations. The nearby town of Page offers ample accommodations and dining options. Page is about 120 miles from the North Rim of the Grand Canyon. Glen Canyon Dam, Lee's Ferry (a prized spot for trophy trout), Marble Canyon, and Vermillion Cliffs are along the route to the North Rim from Page.

Like life, **Lake Powell** is grand, awesome and filled with contra- **SIGHTS**
dictions. Conservationists considered it a disaster when Glen Canyon Dam was built in Page, flooding beautiful Glen Canyon and
creating a 186-mile-long reservoir that extended deep into the
heart of Utah. Today, the lake is part of the Glen Canyon National
Recreation Area and covers one and a quarter *million* acres. It
is an enormously popular recreation area, and the desert canyon
landscape of multihued sandstone mesas, buttes and spires is spectacular. The shoreline of Lake Powell exceeds 1900 miles, more
than the length of the west coast of the United States.

The depth of Lake Powell's turquoise waters varies from year
to year depending on mountain runoff and releases from Glen
Canyon Dam. An interesting cave discovered on one trip may well
be under water the next season. The same holds true for favorite
sandy beaches, coves and waterfalls. But part of the fun of exploring this multi-armed body of water is finding new hidden treasures and hideaways around the next curve.

Arizona Strip

0   25 miles

POINTS OF INTEREST
Ⓐ Bullfrog Marina
Ⓑ Dangling Rope Marina
Ⓒ Glen Canyon Dam
Ⓓ Hall's Crossing Marina
Ⓔ Lee's Ferry
Ⓕ Navajo Bridge
Ⓖ Wahweap Marina

Page started out as a construction camp for the workers building the Glen Canyon Dam in 1956. The U.S. government had to trade land with the Navajo tribe to acquire the 17-square-mile site, and a road was cut into the remote region from Route 89. The town incorporated in 1975, and today, Page has a population of 8200 residents and an annual visitor count over three million.

The Page–Lake Powell Chamber of Commerce Visitor Bureau can provide you with information. Closed Saturday and Sunday. ~ 644 North Navajo Drive, Page; 520-645-2741, 888-261-7243; e-mail chamber@page-lakepowell.com.

Wedged into a sandstone gorge, **Glen Canyon Dam** took ten years to construct, starting in 1956. Over 400,000 buckets of concrete (a "bucket" holds 24 tons) were poured to build the dam, which holds back the Colorado River and by flooding Glen Canyon, created Lake Powell, the nation's second-largest manmade lake. The powerplant at the toe of the dam produces nearly 1.3 million kilowatts of power, which is sold to municipalities, government agencies and public utilities in seven Western states.

Each year, about a million visitors begin their visit to the dam at the **Carl Hayden Visitor Center**. Exhibits explain the dam's construction, the benefits of the dam, and the story of John Wesley Powell and his nine companions who charted the waters of the Colorado by rowboat in 1869 and 1871. If you join a free guided tour, you'll find yourself descending in a large elevator to a depth of more than 500 feet below the crest of the dam. At one point on the tour, over 100 feet of concrete separates you from the waters of Lake Powell. ~ Route 89, Page; 520-608-6404.

Lake Powell's waters usually warm to a comfortable temperature for swimming by May or early June. During the summer months, when the majority of the three million-plus annual visitors come, the surrounding temperatures can exceed a sizzling 100°. Vacationers seek cool relief and a relaxing getaway in this stark desert ocean. Even at peak periods like July 4th and Labor Day weekends, when all the rental boats are checked out and hotel rooms booked, Lake Powell still manages to provide ample shoreline for docking and camping and, as always, clear, blue-green water for aquatic pursuits.

You can become acquainted with Powell from atop its sky-high buttes and adjacent byways, but those truly interested in getting to know the complex personality, curves and quirks must travel by vessel to the quiet box canyons and deep, gleaming pools for an experience akin to spiritual cleansing. Aficionados claim the best season to visit is early fall when rates and temperatures drop to a comfortable level.

Speed boats and houseboats are most popular for exploring, but a smaller water vehicle like a skiff or canoe will give access to outlying areas where you can just pitch a tent or throw down a sleeping bag on the shore.

Groups of friends and family typically rent a fuel-inefficient houseboat, fully equipped with bunks, bathroom and kitchen, as their mobile base and pull along a smaller boat for exploring nooks not easily charted with the lumbering mother ship. Sole concessionaire for Lake Powell is **Lake Powell Resort & Marinas**, which rents boats at Wahweap, Bullfrog, Hall's Crossing and Hite marinas. The marina has houseboats equipped for travelers with disabilities. ~ On Lakeshore Drive off Route 89, near Glen Canyon Dam; 520-645-2433, 800-528-6154.

Another way to explore Lake Powell is to take a **boat tour**, either a half-day tour to Rainbow Bridge, a full-day tour that enters many of the lake's high-walled canyons and includes a box lunch, or a sunset or dinner cruise aboard a paddle-wheeler. The boat tours and paddle-wheel cruises depart from Wahweap Marina. ~ Lakeshore Drive; 800-528-6154; 520-645-2433.

The highlight of the Lake Powell boat tours is **Rainbow Bridge National Monument**, the world's largest stone arch located about 50 miles from Wahweap. "Nonnezoshi"—or rainbow turned to stone, as it's called by the Navajos—spans 275 feet. Declared a national monument in 1910, it wasn't until Glen Canyon Dam was completed 53 years later, and the lake started to fill, that the site became a favorite destination. Well touristed and commercialized on countless posters and cards, the stone arch with its awesome girth and prisms of color never ceases to amaze. Rainbow Bridge is reached only by boat or on foot.

Before you reach the awesome bridge, between Warm Creek and Wahweap bays, is **Antelope Island**, site of the first known expedition of whites to the area. Franciscan priests Francisco Dominguez and Silvestre Velez de Escalante trekked across a low point in the river (before it became a lake) and established camp on the

---

TREAT WITH RESPECT

Rainbow Bridge is considered sacred by many American Indians, and the site has religious significance. To the Navajo, Rainbow represents guardians of the Universe. Boat tour passengers approach the bridge on a quarter-mile walkway that's part pontoon. The bridge may be photographed from a viewing area, but visitors are not permitted to walk under the bridge. Although signs that advise of the site's sacred status are clearly posted, many visitors tend to ignore the request to remain in the viewing area and must be called back by tour guides or boat crew members.

island. Nearby **Padre Bay** was also named for the priests. Within these waters is the rock fortress called **Cookie Jar Butte**.

A landmark visible from the Wahweap section of the lake is the hump-backed, 10,388-foot **Navajo Mountain** and the striking **Tower Butte**, both located on the Navajo Indian Reservation. They are good landmarks to keep in mind when your directional sense gets churned in the water.

A primitive Indian "art gallery" is located approximately ten miles east of the Rainbow Bridge Canyon up the San Juan River arm in **Cha Canyon**. You must motor past what are termed the Bob Hope Rock (check out the profile) and Music Temple Canyon to reach Cha.

For more extensive history and sightseeing tips on Lake Powell, Stan Jones' *Boating and Exploring Map* is essential to your enjoyment and is available at any Lake Powell shop.

The name John Wesley Powell pops up everywhere in this area. Major Powell, a Civil War veteran, led two expeditions down the Colorado River through the Grand Canyon, in 1869 and 1871. Powell mapped and kept journals of the 1000-mile journey through the largest uncharted section of the United States. A small museum in Page, the **John Wesley Powell Museum**, chronicles his expeditions and presents a small exhibition of American Indian basketry. Call for schedule. ~ Lake Powell Boulevard and North Navajo Drive, Page; 520-645-9496.

One of the most extraordinary sights of this high-desert region around Page is a **slot canyon**, a narrow passage cut by flash-flood water and wind into the sandstone. The erosion cuts striated patterns into the rock walls, like ripples of water, and as sunlight drifts down from the opening 120 feet above, rock shapes and forms seem to undulate in the light and shadow. Quartz crystals in the rock reflect the light, while magnesium and iron create the dark, reddish colors and calcium and lime give the lighter tones. Photographers, of course, love slot canyons. **Roger Ekis,** a professional photographer who lives in Page, conducts **photographic and sightseeing tours** to the most impressive and accessible slot canyon in the area. It's located on a Navajo land, so it's not otherwise accessible to the public. ~ 520-645-8579 (mobile), 801-675-9109 (toll-free from Page).

LODGING   Even those who don't enjoy roughing it in a tent and sleeping bag will take to the great outdoors experience on a **houseboat**. Under Lake Powell's silent, starry skies, waves gently rock the boat, providing the perfect tonic for deep sleep. During the day, is there a more relaxing pastime than reclining on the boat's flat-topped roof with book or drink in hand? The mobile floating homes come equipped with all-weather cabins, bunk beds, showers, toilets and kitchens. Three sizes of boats sleep up to 12 people.

Lake Powell Resort & Marinas rents houseboats at the Wahweap Marina (520-645-2433). To make reservations more than a week ahead of time, contact Lake Powell Resort & Marinas. Otherwise, call the marina directly. Prices vary depending on the season and the number in the party. ~ 800-528-6154. ULTRADELUXE.

Accommodations on the Arizona side of Lake Powell are limited to **Wahweap Lodge & Marina**, which is set on the lake's westernmost bay. Rooms are bright and airy; those facing the lake have especially lovely views of the marina, blue waters and rugged lakeshore. Wahweap gets bonus points for its two swimming pools, spa and manicured grounds. ~ 100 Lakeshore Drive; 520-645-2433, 800-528-6154. DELUXE.

Courtyard by Marriott occupies a prime spot where the local business loop of Route 89 starts to swing up the mesa into Page. The property has fine views of Glen Canyon and is surrounded by a golf course. The Southwest adobe-style design fits into the sandstone butte landscape. Each of the 153 rooms are comfortably furnished with two double beds and have a balcony. There is room service, a pool and a spa and exercise room. ~ 600 Clubhouse Drive, Page; 520-645-5000, 800-851-3855, fax 520-645-5004. DELUXE.

Several motels are located along Lake Powell Boulevard, the main drag in Page, including three Best Westerns. The 103-room **Best Western Arizona Inn** has a pool and spa. ~ 716 Rimview Drive, 520-645-2466, 800-826-2718, fax 520-645-2053. MODERATE. Somewhat bigger, the **Best Western Lake Powell**, with 132 rooms offers similar amenities (pool and spa). ~ 208 North Lake Powell Boulevard; 520-645-5988, 800-528-1234, fax 520-645-2578. DELUXE. The smaller, 100-room **Best Western Weston Inn and Suites** also has a pool. ~ 207 North Lake Powell Boulevard; 520-645-2451, 800-637-9183, fax 520-645-9552. BUDGET TO MODERATE.

The city of Page has licensed and approved several **bed and breakfast** accommodations; the chamber of commerce will provide a list. ~ 520-645-2741. BUDGET TO MODERATE.

DINING

Aside from having dinner on your rented houseboat or at a campsite along the shore, dining on Lake Powell is limited to the **Rainbow Room** at Wahweap Lodge & Marina. Considering the volume of traffic handled in the round, large, two-tiered dining room, the food—prime rib, seafood, chicken, salads and a few American Indian dishes—isn't bad, and it's served in generous proportions. Service is friendly and efficient. Three meals are served. There's also a budget-priced pizza café on the Wahweap launch dock, open May through September. ~ Wahweap Lodge & Marina, 100 Lakeshore Drive, Lake Powell; 520-645-2433. MODERATE TO DELUXE.

HIDDEN ►   In Page, the **Dam Bar & Grill** is an unexpected upscale and kind of hip restaurant and bar. The dam theme may be a bit overdone—a "transformer" at the entrance shoots off neon bolts of electricity, one wall of concrete is sculpted like the dam, and heavy wire mesh used to hold back sandstone walls of the gorge becomes decorative partitions between booths. But other touches—a huge etched glass panel separating the bar and the dining room, generous use of wood, linen napkins—and the surprisingly good food show that someone is paying attention. Steak and prime rib are the main events here, but fish also receives excellent attention in the kitchen. Pasta, chicken, sandwiches, burgers and salads round out the menu. Closed Sunday from mid-November through April. ~ 644 North Navajo Drive, Page; 520-645-2161. MODERATE TO DELUXE.

Even just a slice of pizza (it's huge) at **Strombolli's Restaurant and Pizzeria** is enough to fill you up if you're not too hungry. Otherwise you can order from a menu of traditional Italian dishes, calzones and salads. There's an outdoor covered patio, if the weather's nice, but the view of the commercial strip doesn't offer much to look at. Closed November through January. ~ 711 North Navajo Drive, Page; 520-645-2605. BUDGET TO MODERATE.

For a quick sandwich to eat on the run or for a picnic, try the **Sandwich Place**, where you can also get hot subs and burgers. ~ 662 Elm Street, next to Safeway, Page; 520-645-5267. BUDGET.

SHOPPING   Michael Fatali has been photographing the Arizona and Utah landscapes for a dozen years. His work has been published in *Arizona Highways* and other magazines. He specializes in fine art Cibachrome prints that capture the extraordinary, luminous beauty of these landscapes. His **Fatali Gallery** in Page contains a large photographic archive of original Cibachrome prints. While the cost of a fine-art photograph can run into several hundred or thousands of dollars, Fatali has produced a series of limited-edition posters of several of his most popular images. The posters are very affordable and make terrific souvenirs. Closed mid-November through mid-March. ~ 40 North Lake Powell Boulevard, Page; 520-645-3553, 800-206-0602.

HIDDEN ►

NIGHTLIFE   At Lake Powell, enjoy a sunset cruise with dinner on the **Canyon King Paddlewheeler** from Wahweap. This is a favorite time of day to be on the lake because natural-rock amphitheaters appear to change colors before your very eyes as the late afternoon sun makes its curtain call. If you prefer not to dine on the water, sunset cruises are also available on other boats. ~ 520-645-2433.

GLEN CANYON NATIONAL RECREATION AREA 🚶⛵🚤

PARKS

🚤⛵ Glen Canyon Dam confines the waters of the Colorado River forming Lake Powell, the second-largest manmade reservoir in the world. The 1869-square-mile area harbors countless inlets, caves and coves sheltering Pueblo Indian sites that are ever-changing because of the water level. Marinas are found at five separate locations on the lake (some in Utah): Hite, Bullfrog, Hall's Crossing, Dangling Rope and Wahweap. All kinds of water sports, from skiing to windsurfing, kayaking to inner tubing, have their place at Powell. You'll also find hotels, restaurants, groceries, visitors centers, picnic areas and restrooms. Day-use fee, $5 for a seven-day pass. ~ Both Routes 95 and 89 lead to Lake Powell; 520-608-6404.

▲ There are over 800 sites at five campgrounds: Bullfrog, Hall's Crossing, Lee's Ferry and Wahweap; $10 to $13.50 per night. Primitive campsites are available at Bullfrog and Hite; $6. RV hookups are available ($23) through a private concessionaire (520-645-2433) at Wahweap, Bullfrog and Hall's Crossing only. There is free backcountry camping with a permit. Camping is not allowed within one mile of marinas and at Rainbow Bridge National Monument.

RAINBOW BRIDGE NATIONAL MONUMENT 🚶🏇🚤 The
greatest of the world's known natural bridges, this symmetrical, salmon-pink sandstone span rises 290 feet above the floor of Bridge Canyon. Rainbow Bridge sits on 160 acres within Glen Canyon National Recreation Area. Tours of the monument leave regularly in the summer season from Wahweap marina; during the rest of the year there is sporadic service. Facilities are limited to restrooms. ~ Accessible by boat or on foot. To go the land route means traversing mostly unmarked trails through Navajo Indian Reservation land and requires a permit (520-871-6436, 520-871-7371); the number at the monument is 520-608-6404.

When Europeans began exploring this part of the country in the late 18th century, there were very few places that the Colorado River could be crossed from both sides. Lee's Ferry was one of them. But not since the Anasazi had inhabited the area centuries before had there been any permanent residents. Around 1872, John Doyle Lee and one of his 17 wives, Emma, arrived to set up a ferry across the river. Lee, a Mormon, had been sent by church leaders to establish the ferry as a way to help the Mormons settle in Northern Arizona. Some years before, Lee had been involved in an incident known as Mountain Meadow Massacre, an attack on a wagon train involving Piaute Indians, Lee and other Mormons. Lee was eventually apprehended by authorities and executed. Today, Lee's Ferry is part of the Glen Canyon National Recreation Area.

▼▼▼▼▼▼▼▼▼
Lee's Ferry

SIGHTS   There are only seven land crossings of the Colorado River within 750 miles. **Navajo Bridge**, which spans Marble Canyon Gorge, is one of them. There are actually two bridges: a newer structure for vehicles traveling on Route 89A and the older bridge, which pedestrians may walk across to get a look at the 470-foot gorge. Pick up area maps and general books at the visitors center, which also has a permanent exhibit covering geological and historical facts about Lee's Ferry. ~ Route 89A at the western side of the new bridge; 520-355-2320.

Just to the west of Navajo Bridge, a turnoff to **Lee's Ferry** winds back to the spot where the Colorado and Paria rivers join. At the **ranger station** you can pick up maps and limited information about hiking and fishing in the area. ~ Located five miles north of Marble Canyon, at the top of the hill below the water tower; 520-355-2234.

A few historical structures still stand at the **old ferry crossing** and at the settlement site known as **Lonely Dell**, so called because Emma Lee is reported to have said "Oh, what a lonely dell" when she first saw the site of her new home. Parking is available at the launch ramp, and from there you can set off on one of several hikes along the river or into the cliffs above. A self-guided walking tour booklet and a hiking map are available at the ranger station.

Back on Route 89A, heading toward Jacob Lake, **Vermillion Cliffs** dominate the landscape to the north. The Navajo sandstone cliffs are clearly reddish even during the bright light of the day but at sunset they take on a more brilliant color. A pullout on the flatlands (about 20 miles east of Jacob Lake) as well as in the foothills (about 11 miles east of Jacob Lake) as the road climbs up the plateau toward Jacob Lake both provide good viewing.

LODGING   **Marble Canyon Lodge** is at the turnoff to Lee's Ferry on Route 89A, just west of Navajo Bridge. Motel accommodations are basic, but clean. No in-room phones. The lodge also has a restaurant serving breakfast, lunch and dinner, and a general store. ~ Route 89A at Lee's Ferry turnoff, Marble Canyon; 520-355-2225, 800-726-1789, fax 520-355-2227. BUDGET.

About three miles west of Marble Canyon, **Lee's Ferry Lodge** offers quainter (read knotty pine) motel accommodations at the base of the Vermillion Cliffs. The lodge is particularly popular with anglers and has an angler's shop (520-355-2261) offering complete guide services. Reservations required. ~ Route 89A at Vermillion Cliffs; 520-355-2231. BUDGET.

DINING   In these parts, there's not much to choose from in the way of restaurants. The restaurant at **Marble Canyon Lodge**, which serves an American-style menu for breakfast, lunch and dinner, is per-

The Grand
Canyon
Railway

A century ago, the first tourists to see the Grand Canyon had to endure a long, bumpy, dusty ride on horseback or in a stagecoach. No wonder there wasn't much interest in the the canyon as a tourist attraction. Mining, logging and ranching interests had spurred early partial development of a rail line into the canyon area. But it wasn't until 1901, when the Grand Canyon was made part of a national forest preserve, that the Atchison, Topeka and Santa Fe Railroad completed a spur from Williams to the South Rim. The railroad, along with the Fred Harvey Company, developed the Grand Canyon into a major tourist attraction. Twice a day, steam trains left the Williams Depot for the South Rim. Over the years, until 1968, when the last train pulled out of Williams for the Grand Canyon, millions of visitors, including Theodore Roosevelt, FDR, John Muir and Jimmy Durante, had ridden the Grand Canyon Railway.

In 1989, Arizona businessman Max Biegert and his wife, Thelma, bought the railway. They had steam locomotives and coach cars rebuilt or restored, and on September 17, 1989—88 years after the inauguration of the first passenger service began—they renewed daily steam locomotive passenger service from Williams to the South Rim. About 130,000 passengers ride the railway each year now, which keeps about 50,000 vehicles a year out the South Rim part of the Grand Canyon (an important benefit considering the congestion and pollution generated by monumental automobile traffic).

The railway operates year-round, with trains leaving from Williams Depot at 9:30 a.m. for the two-and-a-half-hour, 65-mile journey to the South Rim. Before boarding restored 1923 Harriman coaches, passengers are entertained in the depot plaza by cowboy skits and gunfights. Onboard, musicians perform and move from coach to coach. Snacks and beverages are available. Meanwhile, as the train rounds a bend, the landscape of the Arizona high country changes from ponderosa pine to open plain. Once in the park, there's time for one of four bus tours (three of which include a cafeteria lunch) of the South Rim before reboarding at 3 p.m. for the return trip to Williams. And if chatting with fellow passengers about your Grand Canyon experience isn't enough to keep you occupied, the musicians are along to keep you entertained. It's also been reported that occasionally on the return trip, masked train robbers have held up the train.

Roundtrip fares are about $50 for adults, $25 for children (3–16). Upgrades to Club and Chief classes are available, as are one-way options and overnights at the South Rim. Call 800-843-8724 for information and reservations.

fectly suitable but not especially cheerful. ~ Marble Canyon Lodge, Route 89A at Lee's Ferry turnoff, Marble Canyon; 520-355-2225. MODERATE TO DELUXE.

About the only other choice is **Vermillion Cliffs Bar & Grill** at Lee's Ferry Lodge, which, happily, serves good food—steaks, chops, sandwiches and pasta—in a pleasantly rustic and friendly atmosphere. Besides that, it stocks 150 different kinds of beer. Three meals are served. ~ Route 89A at Vermillion Cliffs; 520-355-2231. BUDGET TO MODERATE.

PARKS

LEE'S FERRY, GLEN CANYON NATIONAL RECREATION AREA
Halfway along the most direct route between the North Rim and South Rim of the Grand Canyon, this beach area on the river below Glen Canyon Dam makes a good picnic or camping spot. It is situated at the confluence of the Colorado and Paria rivers, which often have distinctly different colors, giving the water a strange two-toned appearance.

Today, Lee's Ferry is the departure point for raft trips into the Grand Canyon. Shaded picnic tables and restrooms; groceries are 55 miles away in Page. Day-use fee, $5 for a seven-day pass. ~ Located in Marble Canyon about five miles off Route 89A, 85 miles from the North Rim entrance to Grand Canyon National Park and 104 miles from the east entrance to the South Rim; 520-355-2234. To reach Lee's Ferry Campground, take Lee's Ferry Road north about three miles from Marble Canyon. Wahweap Campground and Wahweap RV Park are located off Route 89, one mile north of Page. Page Lake Powell Campground is located half a mile outside of Page on Route 98.

▲ Within Glen Canyon National Recreation Area, **Lee's Ferry Campground** (520-355-2234) has 52 tent/RV sites (no hookups); $10 per night. **Wahweap Campground** has 708 sites, $13.50 per night, and **Wahweap RV Park** has 123 sites, $23 per night. ~ 520-645-2433. The privately owned **Page Lake Powell Campground** has 12 tent sites and 112 RV sites; $15 per night for tents and $17 to $20 per night for hookups. ~ 520-645-3374.

▼▼▼▼▼▼▼▼▼▼▼
Transportation

CAR

The Grand Canyon's North Rim is at the end of **Route 67**, which forks off of **Route 89A** at the resort village of Jacob Lake. It is more than 150 miles from the nearest interstate highway—**Route 15**, taking Exit 15 north of St. George, Utah—but is within an easy morning's drive of either Zion National Park or Bryce Canyon National Park or Lake Powell.

Although only 12 miles of straight-line distance separate them, the shortest driving distance between the North Rim and South Rim visitors areas of the Grand Canyon is 216 miles around the eastern end of the canyon via Route 67, Route 89A, **Route 89** and **Route 64**, crossing the Colorado River at Navajo Bridge. The only other alternative for driving from rim to rim is to go by way of Las Vegas, Nevada—a trip of more than 500 miles.

From Route 40, eastbound motorists can reach Grand Canyon Village on the South Rim by exiting at Williams and driving 60 miles north on Route 64. Westbound travelers, leaving the interstate at Flagstaff, have a choice between the more direct way to Grand Canyon Village, 80 miles via Route 180, or the longer way, 105 miles via Route 89 and Route 64, which parallels the canyon rim for 25 miles. These routes combine perfectly into a spectacular loop trip from Flagstaff.

AIR

Flights can be booked from most major cities to **Grand Canyon Airport**, which is located near Tusayan just outside the south entrance to the national park. Airlines that fly there include Air Vegas, Argosy Airlines, Arizona Pacific, Eagle Canyon, Scenic Airlines, Sunshine Airlines and Vision Airlines. A shuttle service runs hourly between the airport and Grand Canyon Village. ~ 520-638-2446.

BUS

Grayline Nava-Hopi Tours provides bus service to the Grand Canyon South Rim, as well as Flagstaff, Williams and Phoenix. ~ 114 Route 66, Flagstaff; 520-774-5003, 800-892-8687. **Trans Canyon Shuttle** operates a daily shuttle bus service between the two rims of Grand Canyon National Park. ~ Tusayan; 520-638-2820.

CAR RENTALS

The only car-rental agency at the Grand Canyon Airport is **Enterprise Rent A Car**. ~ 800-736-8222.

FIVE

Northeastern Arizona

East of the Grand Canyon stretches a land of sandstone monuments and steep-walled canyons that turns vermilion by dawn or dusk, a land of foreign languages and ancient traditions, of sculptured mesas and broad rocky plateaus, of pine forests and high deserts. This is the heart of the Southwest's Indian Country.

It is home to the Navajos, the biggest American Indian tribe, and the Hopis, one of the most traditional. To them belongs the top northeastern third of Arizona, 150 miles in length and 200 miles across the state. In addition to this impressive expanse, Navajoland spills into New Mexico, Utah and Colorado.

Here, by horseback or jeep, on foot or in cars, visitors can explore the stark beauty of the land, delve into its uninterrupted centuries of history, then dine on mutton stew and crispy blue-corn piki bread. You can watch dances little changed in centuries or shop for a stunning array of crafts in American Indian homes, galleries and trading posts dating back to the end of the Civil War. And here, in the pit houses, pueblos and cliff dwellings of people who have occupied this land for 12,000 years, are more remnants of prehistoric American Indian life than anywhere else in the United States.

Five generations of archaeologists have sifted through ruins left by the region's dominant prehistoric culture, the Anasazi—Navajo for "ancient enemy." None are more beautiful or haunting than Betatakin and Keet Seel at Navajo National Monument, 45 miles due north of today's Hopi mesas.

Hopi traditions today offer insights about life in those older cities. Traditional and independent, most villages are run by their religious chiefs. Each maintains an ancient, complex, year-long dance cycle tied to the renewal and fertility of the land they regard with reverence. As one Hopi leader put it, the land is "the Hopi's social security." Their multistoried architecture, built on mesa tops, has influenced many 20th-century architects.

Surrounding the Hopis is Navajoland, the largest Indian reservation in the United States. At 26,000 square miles, it is twice the size of Israel. Unlike the village-dwelling Hopis, most of the more than 200,000 Navajos still live in far-flung family compounds—a house, a hogan, a trailer or two, near their corrals and fields. (Some clans still follow their livestock to suitable grazing lands as seasons change.)

This is both an arid, sun-baked desert and verdant forested land, all of it situated on the southeastern quarter of the Colorado Plateau. At elevations of 4500 to 8000 feet above sea level, summer temperatures average in the 80s. July through September is monsoon season, when clear skies suddenly fill with clouds that turn a thunderous lightning-streaked black. These localized, brief, intense summer rains bearing wondrous smells have been courted by Hopi rituals for centuries and are crucial to the survival of their farms.

For the modern adventurer, September and October can be the most alluring months to visit—uncrowded, less expensive, sunny, crisp, with splashes of fall color.

The Colorado Plateau is famous for its rainbow-colored canyons and monuments that have been cut by rivers and eroded by weather. Erosion's jewels here are Monument Valley on the Arizona–Utah border, a stunning pocket of towering red spires, bluffs and sand dunes, and Canyon de Chelly, a trio of red-rock canyons that form the heart of Navajo country.

At Navajoland's southernmost boundary, the world's densest, most colorful petrified logs dot Petrified Forest National Park. They're located amid bare hills that look like they were spray painted by a giant artist and aptly named the Painted Desert.

This mesmerizing geography serves as a backdrop to the region's riveting history. Navajos probably began arriving from the north a century or two before the Spaniards rode in from the south in the 1540s. The conquistadors brought horses, sheep, peaches, melons, guns and silversmithing—all of which would dramatically change the lives of the indigenous Indians. The Navajos had arrived in small groups, nomadic hunters, primitive compared to their Pueblo neighbors.

Cultural anthropologists now believe the turning point in Navajo history followed the Pueblo Indian Revolt of 1680 when all the village-dwelling Indians of the Southwest united to push the much-hated Spanish out of what is now New Mexico. When the Spaniards returned a dozen years later, heavily armed and promising slavery for unyielding villagers, many Pueblo people from the Rio Grande fled west to the canyons of Navajo country, intermarrying and living as neighbors for three-quarters of a century.

During that time the Navajos grew in wealth due to their legendary raiding parties—helping themselves to Indian- or Anglo-owned sheep, horses and slaves. By the late 1700s, a much-changed race of part Athabascan and part Pueblo blood —the Dineh, Navajo for "the people"—had emerged. Powerful horsemen, wealthy sheepherders and farmers, they had developed a complex mythology and had surpassed their Pueblo teachers at the craft of weaving.

Navajo "shopping spree" raids continued along the Spanish, Mexican and Anglo frontiers. The United States army built Fort Defiance, near present-day Window Rock, and dispatched Colonel Kit Carson to end the incursions. Carson's tactic was to starve the Navajos out of Canyon de Chelly and neighboring areas by killing their livestock and burning their fields. On March 14, 1864, the first of some 8000 Navajos began what is known as their "long walk"—300 miles at 15 miles a day—to Fort Sumner, New Mexico. Here a 40-square-mile government compound became home to the Navajo for four of their bitterest years. They were plagued by crop failures, hunger, sickness, death and gross government mismanagement. Finally, on June 1, 1868, a treaty was signed, and some 7000 survivors moved back home.

Trading posts became the Indians' new supply source and conduit to the white man's world. While modern shopping centers, crafts galleries and convenience stores have replaced most of them, a few originals remain. The most famous is the rural, creek-side Hubbell Trading Post, a National Historic Site at Ganado. Others worth seeking out include Oljato near Monument Valley and posts at Cameron, Tuba City and Keams Canyon.

During the 20th century the Navajos and the Hopis have moved from a subsistence to a cash economy. The Indian Reorganization Act of 1934 ended overt repressive government policies toward American Indians and launched an era of increased self-government. Since 1961, when oil and coal reserves were found on reservation lands, both tribes have parlayed millions of resulting dollars into paved roads, schools, hospitals, civic centers, low-cost housing, expanded electrical services and running water for more homes. Three mines, three power plants, a 60,000-acre farming project, forest industries and scattered electronic assembly plants are gradually providing jobs for Navajos. But the most widespread employment is the cottage industry—creation of their own arts and crafts.

Today in every village and town you will find the rich and wonderfully evolving legacy of American Indian arts and crafts. From the Navajo—weavings respected worldwide, sandpaintings and silver and turquoise jewelry. From the Hopis—some of the finest pottery in the Southwest, superb carvings of wooden kachinas, woven basketry and plaques and masterful incised silver jewelry. You will hear Indian languages and see rich spiritual traditions carried on by new generations. You will experience the history of this Western region, the blend of Indian, Spanish and Anglo cultures. All this in a setting of striking geography.

▼▼▼▼▼▼▼▼▼▼▼▼▼▼▼▼▼▼
Southern Navajo Country

Indian Country is a concept that barely does justice to the astonishing diversity of the southern Navajo realm. There is so much to see and do in this region, which also embraces the pastel realm of the Painted Desert, that you may be tempted to extend your stay. Ancient Anasazi ruins and colorful badlands are just a few of the highlights.

SIGHTS   On the southwest corner of the Navajo Indian Reservation, during spring runoff—usually March and April—a detour off Route 40 brings you to the thundering, muddy **Grand Falls** of the Little Colorado River—plummeting 185 feet into the canyon of the Little Colorado River. A lava flow from Merriam Crater ten miles to the southwest created the falls about 100,000 years ago. Some

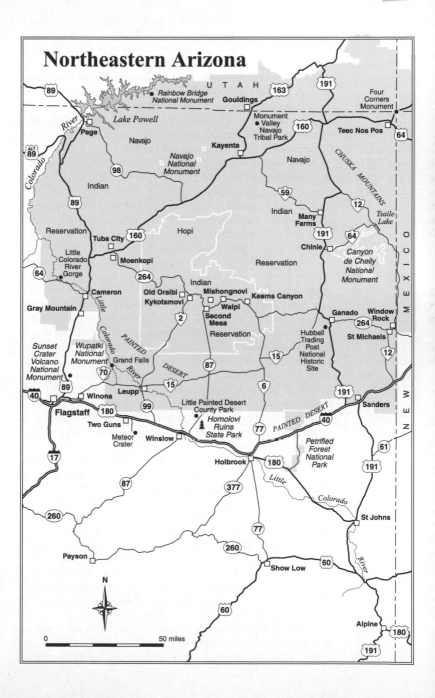

Northeastern Arizona

years the falls are only a trickle, and even during the best years they dry up by May, resuming again briefly during abundant summer monsoons. It is wise to inquire in Winslow or Flagstaff about the level of the Little Colorado River before making the trip. To get there, turn off Route 40 either at Winona, 17 miles northeast of Flagstaff to Route 15, or at the Leupp Junction (Route 99), ten miles west of Winslow to Route 15. Either way, ask at the turnoff for exact directions. The Winona route is the shortest from the highway—about 20 miles, the last eight unpaved. *Note:* Do not try to drive on this road after local rainfall.

HIDDEN ▶ Many locals contend the most colorful and dramatic concentration of Painted Desert hills in central Arizona is at **Little Painted Desert County Park**, 15 miles north of Winslow. A one-mile hiking trail and picnic tables overlook this vast basin where clay and silt deposited by ancient rivers have eroded into gray, red, purple, ochre and white striped badlands—300 feet to 400 feet tall. Colors are most vivid at dawn and dusk. ~ Route 87; 520-524-4250.

The scattered broken pottery, rock drawings and crumbling walls speak with quiet eloquence of an ancient past at **Homolovi Ruins State Park** three miles east of Winslow. The park contains four major 14th-century pueblos of 40 to 2000 rooms, with over 300 identified archaeological sites, a visitors center and museum where interpretive programs are presented. Nine miles of paved roads and a mile of hiking trails lead to the two largest village ruins, inhabited between 1150 and 1450 A.D. The park also includes petroglyphs and a pithouse village dating from 600 to 900 A.D. Hopis believe this was home to their ancestors just before they migrated north to today's mesas. They still consider the ruins—located on both sides of the Little Colorado River—sacred and leave *pahos* (prayer feathers) for the spirits. Admission. ~ Route 87; 520-289-4106.

Winslow, the hub of Northeastern Arizona, is a railroad town and was an early trade center. Its current history goes back to Mormon pioneers who arrived in 1876 and built a small rock fort known as Brigham City, as well as a few other small settlements. The town grew, and soon a water system, stores and an opera house appeared, along with a school, saloons and, that harbinger of all frontier civilizations, sidewalks. The Aztec Land and Cattle Company purchased a million acres of land from the railroad in the late 1800s and thousands of head of cattle were brought in to be handled by local cowboys. The town was incorporated in 1900. For information contact the **Winslow Chamber of Commerce**. ~ 300 West North Road; 520-289-2434.

The **Old Trails Museum** houses changing exhibits related to Winslow's history, including American Indian and pioneering artifacts, and a collection of railroad and Route 66 memorabilia.

Closed Sunday and Monday. ~ 212 Kinsley Avenue, Winslow; 520-289-5861.

To the east of Winslow on Route 40, you'll come to **Holbrook**. Headquarters for the Apache-Sitgreaves National Forest, Holbrook was named for H. R. Holbrook, first engineer of the Atlantic and Pacific Railroad, forerunner of the Santa Fe Line. Built along the Little Colorado River and set at the edge of the Navajo Indian Reservation, Holbrook consists of a string of motels and restaurants, along with a half-dozen good souvenir shops specializing in petrified wood and other rocks and gems, as well as American Indian arts, crafts and jewelry.

Each January, members of the present-day Hashknife Posse carry the mail Pony Express–style from Holbrook to Scottsdale—the only mail run on horseback authorized by the U.S. Postal Service.

Founded in the 1880s as a railroad station and ranching center, Holbrook exists today as the gateway to the Petrified Forest. Once among the largest cattle ranches in the country with its 60,000 head of cattle, Holbrook was one of Arizona's toughest cowboy towns—ranch hands from the Aztec Ranch were a rough-and-tumble bunch who often shot up everything and earned the nickname the "Hashknife Posse." There are probably more people still wearing ten-gallon hats and cowboy boots here than in any other small town in the West.

The **Historic Navajo Courthouse Museum** is located in the County Courthouse, which flourished from 1898 until 1976. It's now a museum focusing on Holbrook's past, including the town's original one-piece iron jail. The museum is like a musty attic, stuffed with old photos, pioneer utensils and tortoise-shell combs, and even features an old parlor. There's a turn-of-the-century apothecary complete with snake oil and other wonder tonics. It also houses the Holbrook Tourism Information Center, where you can pick up maps and brochures, as well as a historic downtown tour map. Closed Saturday and Sunday. ~ 100 East Arizona Street, Holbrook; 520-524-6558.

The signs advertising sale of "gems" and "petrified wood" on every other block in Holbrook offer a good clue that **Petrified Forest National Park** can't be far away. Entrances at the northern and southern gateways to this park are located 22 miles east of Holbrook—the northern entrance on Route 40, the southern one on Route 180. Visitors centers at the north and south entrances provide maps, brochures, books and posters, as well as exhibits of the park's geology and history. Either entrance launches you on the 28-mile scenic drive, the best way to see the park. Admission. ~ 520-524-6228.

Eons ago, trees fell into an ancient swamp and were converted over time to rainbow-colored rock—much of it still in massive logs. These colorful rare stone trees lie scattered throughout the 100,000-acre park, which may be the largest forest of petrified wood in the world. There are also many other types of fossils, both plant and animal, as well as evidence of the American Indians who once lived here.

The national monument was established in 1906, in response to the large number of logs and fossils that were being poached. It became a national park in 1962. Despite the barren desert environment, the park is dotted with prickly pear, cholla cacti and other natural vegetation. Look closely and you may find evening primrose, Indian paintbrush, mariposa lily and other plants.

The most frequently visited area of the park is the southern section, which holds the greatest concentration of petrified wood. Here, you'll find a wide variety of specimens—from giant logs to small agatized chunks. Farther north are ancestral Pueblo sites and petroglyphs. The northern end of the park penetrates the Painted Desert, an eerie landscape of colorful, heavily eroded mudstone and siltstone that resembles the moon's surface, except for the brightly hued formations.

Taking the scenic drive from the Route 40 (north) entrance brings you to the **Painted Desert Visitors Center**. Here you'll see a 20-minute film on the mysteries of the making of the forest—silica crystals replacing wood cells in the cone-bearing trees—aricarioxylon pine. Adjacent to the center is a cafeteria and gift-shop amenities.

The **Painted Desert Inn National Historic Site** is a 1930s pueblo-style building, originally a trading post, restaurant and inn. Detailed hand-carved wood and tin furnishings were made by the CCC. Murals painted by the late Hopi artist Fred Kabotie depict scenes of Hopi life: a winter buffalo dance to ensure return of buffalo each spring, the journey of two Hopis to Zuni lands to gather salt. ~ Three miles north of the visitors center, at Kachina Point on the scenic drive; 520-524-6228.

✔ CHECK THESE OUT—UNIQUE SIGHTS

- Marvel at the Hopi murals and the hand-carved wood furnishings inside the **Painted Desert Inn National Historic Site**, a 1930s pueblo-style building that was once a Fred Harvey Hotel. *page 80*
- Give the locals a small tip and you will be escorted to the impressions left by a 20-foot-long *Diloposaurus* at **Dinosaur Tracks**. *page 87*
- Appreciate how Window Rock got its name when you see **Tseghahodzani**, "the rock with a hole in it." *page 98*
- Cruise by the natural roadside attraction, **Elephant Feet**, a sandstone formation resembling the legs and feet of elephants. *page 106*

The overlooks at the north end of the park provide good views of the Painted Desert. If you're ready for a rest stop, there are sheltered tables, seasonal water and restrooms (closed in the winter) at the **Chinde Point Picnic Area**. At the **Nizhoni Point Overlook**, the hills below appear to sparkle with crystals. The minerals are actually selenite gypsum. From the **Whipple Point Overlook** and the **Lacey Point Overlook** you'll see bands of red, white and pink—the effect of the sun reflecting on mudstone and siltstone stained by iron, manganese and other minerals. Colors are the most intense at sunrise and sunset or on cloudy days.

South of Route 40 on the scenic drive, the park's midsection contains ancestral sites of ancient American Indian cultures dating from 300 A.D. to 1400 A.D. Scientists have discovered petroglyphs here used as solar calendars. A trail at **Puerco Pueblo**, the first pullout south of Route 40, leads through the pueblo. Built of stone and masonry walls, the pueblo was home to about 75 people from 1100–1300 A.D. The ruin has been partially excavated and restored.

Although named **The Tepees**, these giant cone-shaped mounds look more like ant hills, wrinkled through erosion and colored blue and gray by iron, manganese and other mineral deposits. Nearby, **Newspaper Rock**, a huge sandstone block, is covered with a fine collection of petroglyphs. You'll need binoculars to get a good look, or you can use the coin-operated telescopes.

The petrified wood occurs at **Blue Mesa**, where a trail leads through dramatic towering hills, is a favorite of photographers because of its blue, gray and white cone-shaped hills with chunks of agatized wood scattered about. The eroded sandstone formations suggest a mini Grand Canyon. This is also one of the best overlooks of the Painted Desert, whose strange multicolored buttes seem to glow in the distance.

The southern third of the park holds the greatest concentration of petrified logs. **Jasper Forest Overlook** provides a panorama of the area and includes barren hills sprinkled with petrified logs. Notice how the softer clay-like soil has eroded from around the heavier petrified wood, creating a mosaic on the desert floor. Some logs are complete with root systems indicating they had grown nearby.

A trail at **Crystal Forest** leads you close to dense pockets of logs, many over 100 feet long and a foot or two in diameter. In 1886, on a $10 bet, a daring cowboy rode his steed across a treacherous divide spanned by a petrified long log, now shored up with cement. The large concentration of petrified wood here is mostly chunks scattered about like the remains of an ancient woodpile. Look closely at the logs and you'll see hollows and cracks where early souvenir hunters and gem collectors chipped away clear quartz and amethyst crystals. In fact, fossil destruction and poaching in this area prompted the Arizona Territory to petition Congress to preserve the petrified wood sites.

At **Rainbow Forest Museum**, photographs, drawings and samples tell the story of the area's geologic and human history. Outside, the half-mile-long Giant Logs trail leads past enormous rainbow-hued trees. Many of the longest petrified logs (up to 170 feet) are found across the road at the **Long Logs** spur. A side trail leads to **Agate House**, a small eight-room pueblo-style structure built nearly 900 years ago entirely from chunks of petrified wood. Two of the rooms have been partially restored. The scenic drive ends two miles farther south at Route 180. ~ Two miles in from Route 180, near the park's southern entrance; 520-524-6228.

HIDDEN ▶   Outside of the park, check in at **Petrified Forest Gift Shop** to pick up sample minerals and geodes (cut on the premises). A variety of natural and polished petrified wood is for sale, from tiny $2 chunks to massive coffee-table slabs costing thousands of dollars. ~ Route 180, 19 miles southeast of Holbrook; 520-524-3470.

LODGING   The top two hotels in Winslow are both Best Westerns. The two-story **Adobe Inn** has 72 rooms, each decorated in typical motel fashion. You'll find a café and an indoor pool on the premises. ~ 1701 North Park Drive, Winslow; 520-289-4638, 800-528-1234, fax 520-289-5514. BUDGET.

On the western edge of town, the **Town House Lodge** has 68 rooms with modern furnishings all on the first floor. Amenities include a laundry, an outdoor pool and a restaurant. ~ 1914 West 3rd Street, Winslow; phone/fax 520-289-4611, 800-528-1234. BUDGET.

Fifteen dazzling white stucco wigwams, the sort of kitsch old Route 66 was famous for, are found in Holbrook. They make up one of the world's most novel motels, and affordable yet! **Wigwam Motel and Curios** "is the funnest place I've ever slept," insisted our three-year-old neighbor. We couldn't argue. Built in 1950 by Chester Lewis (six other cities had wigwam motels of similar design; only one other survives), the wigwams were restored by his children and grandchildren who still operate them. Inside each, matching red-plaid curtains and bedspreads adorn original hand-made hickory furniture. Scenes from Tony Hillerman's *Dark Wind* were filmed here in 1990. There's no extra charge for lulling vibrations as trains rumble by in the night. ~ 811 West Hopi Drive, Holbrook; 520-524-3048. BUDGET.

For a more traditional resting spot there's the **Adobe Inn**, a two-story, 54-room Best Western that has typical motel furnishings and a pool. ~ 615 West Hopi Drive, Holbrook; 520-524-3948, 800-528-1234, fax 520-524-3612. BUDGET.

Another Best Western motel is the **Arizonian Inn** with 70 guest rooms, contemporary furnishings and a pool. ~ 2508 East Navajo Boulevard, Holbrook; phone/fax 520-524-2611, 800-528-1234. BUDGET.

With 40 rooms, the **Rainbow Inn** falls into the small, no-frills category. But all of the modern, well-maintained rooms have refrigerators and Southwest paintings on the walls. ~ 2211 East Navajo Boulevard, Holbrook; phone/fax 520-524-2654, 800-551-1923. BUDGET.

Dining out in the Southern Navajo Indian Reservation area is not a very exciting experience. You can take a counter seat on one of the swivel stools or settle into a booth at **Falcon Restaurant** where the menu includes steaks, chicken, roast turkey and seafood. This brown stucco establishment also features the only Greek mural we found in Navajo country. ~ 1113 East 3rd Street, Winslow; 520-289-2342. BUDGET TO MODERATE.

DINING

Celebrated by locals and in newspapers from New York to San Francisco, the **Casa Blanca Cafe** is known for its tacos, chimichangas, cheese crisps and burgers. Choose between booth and table seating at this ceramic-tiled establishment where cactus baskets grace the walls. The dining room is cooled by Casablanca fans but, alas, there's no trace of Bogie. ~ 1201 East 2nd Street, Winslow; 520-289-4191. BUDGET.

At **Gabrielle's Pancake and Steak House,** Navajo sandpaintings line the wall, adding a decorative touch. Inside this shake-shingle coffee shop you can enjoy burgundy booth or counter seating and dine on steaks, Chinese food, seafood and homemade pies. Closed Sunday. ~ 918 East 2nd Street, Winslow; 520-289-2508. BUDGET.

In Holbrook, the best spot for Mexican cuisine is **Romo's Cafe,** which has been serving tasty South-of-the-Border dishes since the 1960s. The decor isn't fancy in this storefront café, but the rear dining room with its used-brick walls and hanging plants is a more private setting than the bustling area out front for enjoying green-chile chimichangas or traditional enchilada dinners, as well as American food. In your world travels, don't be surprised to see a Romo sweatshirt—they've turned up as far away as Munich, Germany. ~ 121 West Hopi Drive, Holbrook; 520-524-2153. BUDGET TO MODERATE.

For a taste of the Old West, saddle up and head for the **Butterfield Stage Company Restaurant**. The specialty here is sizzling porterhouse steak served with all the fixin's, as well as barbecue beef and prime rib. In addition to the cowboy tack and memorabilia on the walls, there's a stagecoach on display. ~ 609 West Hopi Drive, Holbrook; 520-524-3447. MODERATE TO ULTRA-DELUXE.

In Holbrook, **Aguilera's Restaurant** serves authentic Mexican cuisine in a casual, café-style room with pictures of comical love stories from Mexico. Breakfast, lunch and dinner Monday through Friday, breakfast and lunch on Saturday and Sunday. ~ 200 Navajo Boulevard, Holbrook; 520-524-3806. BUDGET TO MODERATE.

Navajo ceramics are simple, unadorned brown pieces glazed with hot pitch. The pieces look wonderful when made by a master.

Rock walls add an earthy note to **The Plainsman**. For casual dining try the coffee shop where there's booth seating. Enjoy meals such as liver and onions, veal cutlet and turkey sandwiches. The dining room is a favorite of the local Chamber of Commerce which meets here monthly. Popular items include châteaubriand, prime rib, frogs' legs and grilled trout. ~ 1001 West Hopi Drive, Holbrook; 520-524-3345. BUDGET TO ULTRA-DELUXE.

The **Roadrunner Cafe** offers everything from grilled-cheese sandwiches to pot roast and steaks. The carpeted dining room has table and booth seating. Plants and wildflower photos bring the Southwest indoors. ~ 1501 East Navajo Boulevard, Holbrook; 520-524-2787. BUDGET TO MODERATE.

SHOPPING Most of the souvenir and gift shops in Holbrook contain a blend of American Indian handiwork and Old Route 66 memorabilia. One of the best is **Julien's Roadrunner** on Old Route 66. The well-stocked shop sells everything from railroad and Route 66 memorabilia to nostalgic signs. The proprietor, Ted Julien, is a long-time resident of Holbrook and a veritable expert on the area's history and attractions. Feel free to ask him anything (even about his competition), but be prepared for thorough and unabbreviated answers. ~ 109 West Hopi Drive, Holbrook; 520-524-2388.

Linda's Indian Arts and Crafts is a small shop, but it offers a good selection of American Indian jewelry and Navajo skirts, as well as porcelain dolls and Route 66 memorabilia. ~ 405 Navajo Boulevard, Holbrook; 520-524-2500.

For the biggest selection of top-of-the-line American Indian arts and crafts, **McGee's Beyond Native Tradition** sells everything from Hopi jewelry and kachinas to Navajo blankets. ~ 2114 East Navajo Boulevard, Holbrook; 520-524-1977.

Nakai Indian Cultural Trade Center, in business for over 27 years, also features top-quality American Indian products as well as jewelry made on the premises. ~ 357 Navajo Boulevard, Holbrook; 520-524-2329.

Painted Desert Visitors Center Gift Shop sells books, postcards and music. ~ Route 40 entrance to the Petrified Forest National Park; 520-524-6228, ext. 236.

You can find natural and polished petrified wood, from tiny stones to great slabs, along with American Indian jewelry, crafts and curios at **Fred Harvey Curios and Fountain**. ~ On Route 180 at the entrance to the Petrified Forest National Park; 520-524-3756.

At **R. B. Burnham & Co. Trading Post** is a room lined with naturally dyed yarns. Behind that room is a shrine to Hopi and Navajo crafts. Assembled with much care, and for sale, are carved furniture upholstered in Navajo weavings, gallery-quality Navajo rugs, plus the whole array of American Indian arts and crafts. It's worth a stop just to look! ~ Route 191 at Route 40, Sanders; 520-688-2777.

It's pretty quiet out this way. For nightlife the choices are limited.   **NIGHTLIFE**

The **Tumbleweed Lounge and Patio**, one of the hottest nightspots in Winslow, draws the biggest crowds. There is live music some weekends. ~ 1500 East 3rd Street, Winslow; 520-289-5213.

All the action happens at **Young's Corral Bar**, where some weekends are filled with the sounds of live country-and-western music. ~ 865 East Navajo Boulevard, Holbrook; 520-524-1875.

LITTLE PAINTED DESERT COUNTY PARK 🏃 One of the nicest,   **PARKS**
most colorful chunks of the 40-mile-long Painted Desert is concentrated in this 900-acre park, at 5500-foot elevation near the southern boundary of the Navajo Indian Reservation north of Winslow. In fact, many locals contend that the most colorful and dramatic concentration of Painted Desert hills is located right here. Large 300- to 400-foot-tall fragile mounds of mud slate in grays, reds, purples and yellows tend to change in color intensity throughout the day. Colors are most vivid at dawn and dusk. There's an overlook, two picnic ramadas and restrooms. ~ Located 15 miles north of Winslow on Route 87; 520-524-4250.

MCHOOD PARK CLEAR CREEK RESERVOIR 🚤🚤🛥️
Once an important water source for Winslow, the deep canyon five miles from town is now a favorite boating, swimming and picnic area. Fishing is good for trout, bass and catfish. You'll find a picnic area and restrooms. Day-use fee, $3. ~ Take Route 87 south to Route 99, and turn left; 520-289-5714.

▲ There are 11 campsites; $6 per night, $7 for hookups.

CHOLLA LAKE COUNTY PARK 🏃🚤🛶🚤🛥️ One of the larger bodies of water in northeastern Arizona, the park is adjacent to a power station. This manmade lake offers swimming, boating, fishing (for bass, catfish, bluegill and carp) and picnicking. Facilities include a playground, picnic tables, restrooms and showers; groceries and restaurants are two miles away in Joseph City. Day-use fee, $2. ~ Take Route 40 east from Winslow for about 20 miles to Exit 277, then follow the power plant road to the park; 520-288-3717.

▲ There are 20 sites (8 with RV hookups); $8 per night for standard sites, $12 for hookups.

PETRIFIED FOREST NATIONAL PARK 🚶🚴 Straddling Route 40 and abutting the southern boundary of the Navajo Indian Reservation, this 28-mile-long (north to south) park features rolling badlands of the Painted Desert—mainly red-hued hills—north of Route 40. South of Route 40 lies the densest concentration of petrified prehistoric forests in the world. Each section has a wilderness area. At each entrance is a visitors center with restaurant, restrooms and museum. A 27-mile road leads visitors past nine Painted Desert vistas and 13 Petrified Forest stops. Day-use fee, $10. ~ Both park entrances are 18 miles east of Holbrook: the northernmost on Route 40, the southern one on Route 180; 520-524-6228.

▲ Backcountry only; a wilderness permit is required; they're free at the visitors center.

Western Navajo Country

▼▼▼▼▼▼▼▼▼▼▼▼▼▼▼▼▼▼ The Western Navajo Indian Reservation, bordering such wonders as the Grand Canyon National Park and Lake Powell National Recreation Area, is a land of great beauty and ancient sights. President William McKinley signed an order January 8, 1900, deeding these one and a half million acres of land to the Navajos who had migrated westward 32 years earlier after outgrowing their original reserve.

SIGHTS   Where Routes 89 and 64 meet, the Navajos operate **Cameron Visitors Center**, offering advice and brochures on tribal attractions. ~ 520-679-2303.

Follow Route 64 west ten miles to an unpaved spur road and walk a few hundred feet to a dramatic overlook. At the bottom of hundreds of feet of sheer canyon walls is a muddy ribbon of the Little Colorado River. Upper limestone cliffs, layered like flapjack stacks, contrast with massive sandstone slabs below, evidence of a shallow sea 250 million years ago. This **Grand Canyon of the Little Colorado Gorge Tribal Park** is owned by the Navajos. From Memorial Day through Labor Day a festive air reigns as Indians set up their flag and banner-bedecked crafts booths in the parking area.

A mile north of the visitors center is **Cameron Trading Post, Motel and Restaurant**, a stone pueblo-style complex built in 1916 by Hopis and Navajos, and recently restored. Long known as an oasis of hospitality, it's located by Tanner's Crossing, the last place wagons could cross the Little Colorado before the river enters gorges too deep to navigate. Quicksand pockets made this one especially treacherous. ~ Route 89, Cameron; 520-679-2231.

Today this mini-city is a great place to people watch: old Navajo women in traditional velvet blouses, men in tall, black reservation hats and turquoise jewelry accompanied by youngsters in mod T-shirts and tennies. Inside the post, packed with curios and quality crafts, you'll often see a weaver at work. Next door, don't miss **Cameron Collector's Gallery** offering antique Indian crafts and outstanding works of contemporary American Indian art— rare chief's blankets, pottery, dolls, weaponry and ceremonial garb. Behind the gallery, **Mrs. Richardson's Terraced Garden**, recently revived, is a garden spot of vegetables and flowers.

◀ HIDDEN

North of Cameron, continuing on Route 89 to The Gap, lies the northernmost extension of the **Painted Desert**, an ancient land of silt and volcanic ash hills barren of vegetation. The Painted Desert draws it name from the undulating mounds of multihued sediments that grace the strange landscape. Red sphynx shapes astride crumbling pyramids of eroded solidified sand, these badlands are red and white along some miles; gray and white along others. They're part of the Chinle Formation beloved by geologists for its dinosaur-era fossils.

At **Dinosaur Tracks**, jewelry shacks mark the spot where scientists believe a 20-foot-long carnivorous *Diloposaurus* left tracks. For a small tip locals escort you to the several impressions— three-toed footprints twice as big as adult hands. (Look for the reconstructed skeleton of this dinosaur in Window Rock at the Navajo Tribal Museum.) ~ The turnoff is seven miles west of Tuba City on Route 160, then north one-eighth mile along a dirt road.

Worth a stop in Tuba City, named for a 19th-century Hopi leader, is the hogan-shaped, two-story native stone **Tuba Trading Post**. Built in 1905 during a tourism boom, its door faces east to the rising sun; crafts, groceries and sundries are for sale. Next door, you can enter a built-for-tourists hogan replica. Now administrative and trade center for western Navajos, Tuba City was founded by Mormons in 1877. ~ Main Street and Moenave Avenue, Tuba City; 520-283-5441.

Lodging in Navajo and Hopi country can be summed up in one word: scarce. In an area about the size of Massachusetts, barely 720 rooms are available, so it's no wonder reservation motels claim 100 percent occupancy most nights from Memorial Day through Labor Day. If you get stuck, reservation border towns (Holbrook, Winslow and Flagstaff) usually have vacancies, though they too can sell out, especially on weekends of special events.

LODGING

Padded headboards and brown Santa Fe–style bedspreads and drapes cozy up 112 simple, cementblock rooms in the **Anasazi Inn**, located 42 miles north of Flagstaff. It boasts the Western Navajo Indian Reservation's only swimming pool. ~ Route 89, Gray Mountain; 520-679-2214, 800-678-2214, fax 520-679-2334. BUDGET.

Cameron Trading Post and Motel, 40 miles east of the Grand Canyon's east entrance, and 54 miles north of Flagstaff, is a favorite overnight stop in Indian Country. This tiny, self-contained, 112-acre, privately owned outpost sits on a bluff overlooking the eastern prelude to the Grand Canyon of the Colorado. From 6 a.m. until 10 p.m. or later, the trading post is a beehive of tourists and Navajos mingling to shop, dine or pick up everything from mail and tack to baled hay. It's mainly the tourists who stay overnight in 62 rooms. Built in 1916, the motel rooms are of native stone and wood architecture (variously called Pueblo style or Victorian territorial) as is the rest of the compound. The rooms tend to be a little funkier here than elsewhere on the reservation. ~ Route 89, Cameron; 520-679-2231, 800-338-7385, fax 520-679-2350. MODERATE.

Adjacent to the historic octagonal-shaped Tuba Trading Post is the pleasant, lawn-studded **Quality Inn**, furnished with tan rugs and furniture of Southwestern hand-carved fashion. It has 80 rooms. ~ Main Street at Moenave Street, Tuba City; 520-283-4545, 800-644-8383, fax 520-283-4144. MODERATE.

Students at Tuba City's Greyhills High School are learning the hotel management business by operating the 32-room **Greyhills Inn**. Open year-round to all ages, rooms are comfy and carpeted, with modern interiors. Guests share bathrooms, and for a modest fee can share meals with Navajo students in their cafeteria during the school year. ~ 160 Warrior Drive, northeast of Bashas off Route 160, near Tuba City; 520-283-6271, fax 520-283-4432. BUDGET.

DINING

If you're not on a cholesterol-free diet, you'll find Indian country food, as with everything else here, an adventure. Fry bread appears at lunch and dinner with taco trimmings as an Navajo taco, or as bread for a sandwich, or as dessert dripping with honey. Other favorites include mutton stew, usually served with parched corn, chili, Mexican food, burgers, steaks, and for breakfast, biscuits with gravy.

◆◆◆

✔ CHECK THESE OUT—UNIQUE LODGING

- *Budget:* Re-live '50s kitsch at **Wigwam Motel and Curios**, where the wigwams feature red-plaid curtains and handmade hickory furniture. *page 82*
- *Moderate:* Immerse yourself in the daily activities of Indian Country when you stay over at the **Cameron Trading Post and Motel**. *page 87*
- *Moderate:* Experience rural Navajo life by sleeping in an authentic dirt-floor hogan and using the old-fashioned outhouses at the **Coyote Pass Hospitality: Hogan Bed and Breakfast**. *page 101*
- *Deluxe:* Check into **Gouldings Lodge** for front-row views of Monument Valley's red and orange sandstone buttes. *page 107*

Budget: under $70   Moderate: $70–$110   Deluxe: $110–$180   Ultra-deluxe: over $180

Anasazi Gray Mountain Restaurant fills its walls with Southwestern kitsch. Entrées (hamburgers, chicken-fried steak, halibut, pepper steak) come with soup or salad, hot rolls, baked potato, cowboy beans or french fries and salsa. ~ Route 89, Gray Mountain; 520-679-2203. MODERATE TO DELUXE.

A nice surprise is the **Cameron Trading Post Restaurant.** After walking through the typically low, open-beam ceiling trading post, you enter a lofty room lined with windows looking out onto the Little Colorado River. Tables and chairs are of carved oak and the ceiling glimmers silver from its patterned pressed tin squares. Forty-one breakfast choices include Navajo taco with egg, *huevos rancheros* and hot cakes; for dinner, try the deep-fried fish and chicken or steak entrées. ~ Route 89, Cameron; 520-679-2231. BUDGET TO MODERATE.

Hogan Restaurant, amid open-beam and wood decor, offers dinners of steak and shrimp, chicken-fried steak, Navajo taco and a variety of Mexican entrées. Look for the large historic photos of Charles H. Algert, pioneer Indian trader and founder of Tuba Trading Post, shown on horseback in 1898, and an 1872 photo of the Hopi leader Tuba, standing with arms folded. ~ Main Street, Tuba City; 520-283-5260. BUDGET TO MODERATE.

SHOPPING

In business for more than half a century, **Sacred Mountain Trading Post** is often a good outlet for museum-quality Navajo pitch-glazed pottery; also available are glass beads and bead-making materials, Hopi pottery, kachinas and Navajo and Paiute baskets. Closed Sunday and Monday. ~ Located 23 miles north of Flagstaff on Route 89; 520-679-2255.

The 1916 stone **Cameron Trading Post** is like a department store of Indian crafts, crammed with a good selection of nearly everything—lots of Navajo rugs, cases of jewelry from all Southwestern tribes, kachinas, sandpaintings, baskets and pottery. The adjoining Cameron Gallery offers the most expensive crafts including antique Indian weavings, Apache baskets, Plains beadwork, weaponry and ceremonial garb. ~ Route 89, Cameron; 520-679-2231.

Tuba Trading Post emphasizes Navajo rugs, usually including large pictorials. Also for sale are kachinas, jewelry and the Pendleton blankets Indians like to give one another for births, graduations and other celebrations. ~ Main Street and Moenave Avenue, Tuba City; 520-283-5441.

▼▼▼▼▼▼▼▼▼▼▼▼▼▼
Hopi Indian Country

Three sand-colored mesas stacked and surrounded by a dozen ancient villages form the core of the Hopi Indian Reservation. Completely surrounded by the Navajo Indian Reservation, the villages are strung along 90 miles of Route 264. Home for several centuries to the Hopi, some structures standing today have been used by the same families for 900 years. This fascinating high-desert place (about 4000-foot elevation) is a study in contrasts: it looks stark and poor one minute, then ancient and noble the next.

SIGHTS

Looking for crafts to buy at the homes of Hopi craftsmakers or attending dances are good reasons to visit the villages. **Hopi Indian Dances**, nearly all of them involving prayers for rain for their dry-farm plots, occur year-round. Dates are rarely announced more than two weeks in advance. Whether or not you can attend will vary with the dance and the village. To ask, call the **Hopi Tribal Council Office of Public Relations** (520-734-2441). Don't miss a chance to attend one. Instructions for visitors will be posted outside most villages. In all cases, leave cameras, tape recorders and sketching pads in the car. Photography is not permitted in the villages or along Hopi roads.

Two miles southeast of Tuba City at **Moenkopi** ("the place of running water"), a village founded in the 1870s by a Hopi chief from Oraibi, note the rich assortment of farm plots. This is the only Hopi village that irrigates its farmland—water comes from a nearby spring. Elsewhere farmers tend small plots in several locations, enhancing their chance of catching random summer thundershowers. It's also the only one of 12 Hopi villages not situated on or just below one of the three mesas.

It's some 40 miles to the next two villages. **Bacavi**, consisting mostly of prefab homes, was built in 1909 following a political upheaval at Old Oraibi. **Hotevilla**, also a relatively new (built in 1906) village, with its mix of adobe and cinderblock homes at the edge of a mesa, is nonetheless a traditional village known for its dances and crafts. A few miles down the road, on the edge of Third Mesa, **Old Oraibi** is one of the oldest continuously inhabited villages in the United States. Hopis lived here as early as 1150. Try the ten-minute walk from the south edge of the village to ruins of a church built in 1901 by H. R. Voth, a Mennonite minister. It was destroyed by lightning. At **Kykotsmovi**, "mound of ruined houses," two miles east, then south one mile on Route 2, the Hopi Tribal Council Office of Public Relations provides visitor information. ~ Route 2; 520-734-2441.

Continue east on Route 264 a half dozen miles to **Shungopavi**, Second Mesa's largest village, built at a cliff's edge. It's two more miles to the **Hopi Cultural Center**, the biggest social center for Indians and visitors. Hopi staffers of this white, pueblo-style museum-restaurant-motel-gift shop complex always know when and where dances are scheduled; ask at the motel desk. ~ At Second Mesa on Route 264; 520-734-2401.

At the **Hopi Arts and Crafts Cooperative Guild**, silversmiths work amid the biggest assortment of Hopi-made crafts on the reservation. Closed Sunday. ~ 520-734-2463.

East of the Cultural Center, the two weathered villages of **Sipaulovi** and **Mishongnovi** are strikingly placed above the desert floor on Second Mesa, many of their dwellings carved from stone. It's a steep climb north to both up an unnamed road from Route 264. Founded in the 1680s, both are known for their dances and are worth a visit for the views. ~ Information: 520-737-2570.

> Note that prohibition is still observed throughout the Hopi and Navajo country. It is illegal to bring or drink alcoholic beverages here.

If you have time to make only one stop, visit the trio of villages on First Mesa—**Hano**, **Sichomovi** and **Walpi**. Perched atop the flat oblong mesa, its sides dropping precipitously 1000 feet to the desert below, the village locations help you understand why the Hopis believe they live at the center of the universe. Accessible only by a thrilling curvy drive up a narrow road with no guardrails (signs off Route 264 point the way), all three villages seem to grow out of the mesa's beige-colored stone. Vistas are uninterrupted for miles amid an eerie stillness. ~ Six miles east of the Secakuku Trading Post; 520-737-2262.

Most awesome is Walpi. Built some 300 years ago on a promontory with panoramas in all directions, Walpi's houses stack atop one another like children's blocks, connected with wooden ladders. From the parking lot (no cars are permitted in Walpi) the village resembles a great stone ship suspended on a sea of blue sky. Leaders keep the village traditional so that neither electricity nor running water is permitted. During the summer, shy schoolgirls lead **tours of Walpi** daily. Sign up at Ponsi Hall. ~ 520-737-2262.

Here, as in the other villages, kivas or ceremonial chambers dug into the earth, serve as they have since Hisatsinom days, a refuge where clan dancers fast and observe rituals for days prior to dances. Then on dance days, no longer farmers in denims, the Hopis slowly emerge through ladders on kiva roofs to the hypnotic rhythm of drums and rattles. Transformed in feathers, bells and pine boughs, they appear as sacred beings.

Everyday activities include women baking bread out of doors in beehive ovens or tending clay firings. These are excellent pottery villages. Crude signs in windows invite you into homes of kachina and pottery makers, a wonderful chance to get acquainted with these hospitable people.

Hano resembles its neighboring Hopi villages, but in language and custom it remains a Tewa settlement of Pueblo Indians who fled Spanish oppression in the Rio Grande region in the late 1690s.

Continuing east on Route 264, Hopi Indian Country ends at Keams Canyon, the federal government administrative center, with tourist facilities (restaurant, motel, grocery) clustered around **Keams Canyon Trading Post**. Well-chosen crafts are for sale; the finest art is in a side room. ~ Route 264; 520-738-2294.

Text continued on page 94.

The Fine Craft of Shopping

While shopping for arts and crafts in Indian Country we've been invited into Hopi homes to eat corn fresh from the field, have discussed tribal politics with college-educated shopkeepers and met traditional basketmakers who spoke no English. At the same time we've longingly admired contemporary Indian-crafted jewelry that would dazzle New York's Fifth Avenue crowd.

Shopping can occur anywhere in Indian Country. Once we bought sandpaintings from the trunk of an Indian artist's car while camping in the Chuskas. But Indian Country's main shopping avenue is Route 264, from Tuba City to Window Rock where you'll find two fine old trading posts. **Tuba Trading Post** offers an assortment of Indian-crafted merchandise. ~ Main Street and Moenave Avenue, Tuba City; 520-283-5441. Expect more of the same at **Hubbell Trading Post**, including the best selection of Navajo rugs along this route. ~ Route 264, Ganado; 520-755-3254.

Throughout Hopi country, shopping is the best way to get to know the locals. Shops line entrances to all three mesas and most villages have at least a few signs in home windows inviting visitors in to look at family-made crafts. (*Note:* Tribal officials caution against making a deposit on any craft you can't take with you unless you know the craftsmaker or have a reliable personal reference.)

What should you be you looking for when shopping? Both Hopi and Navajo offer crafts unique to their tribes.

HOPI CRAFTS

Baskets   Hopi wedding and other ceremonial baskets are still woven by Hopi women. Third Mesa villages are also known for their wicker plaques of colorfully dyed sumac and rabbit brush. Coiled yucca plaques are preferred at Second Mesa. Trays of plaited yucca over a willow ring serve as sifters and are made at First and Second Mesa villages.

Jewelry   The favorite Hopi jewelry form is overlay—designs cut from silver sheets, then soldered onto a second silver piece. Cut-out areas are oxidized black.

Kachinas   The Hopi believe that kachinas are ancestral spirits who periodically visit the pueblo. Elaborately costumed dancers dressed up as kachinas during important ceremonies. Kachinas are often carved in dancers' poses, then painted or dressed in cloth, feathers and bright acrylics. The newer trends feature stylized, intricately detailed figures carved from one piece of cottonwood root, then stained. (Navajos now make imitation kachinas too, to the irritation of Hopi carvers.)

Pottery   Nampeyo, a First Mesa woman inspired by ancient pottery shards, started the revival of yellow-to-orange Sikyatki pottery a century ago. First Mesa remains a major producer of pottery decorated with black thin-curved-line motifs.

Weaving   Traditionally, Hopi men do the weaving in this tribe—mostly ceremonial belts, wedding clothes and some rugs.

NAVAJO CRAFTS

Baskets   The most popular basketry of the Navajos is the coiled wedding basket, with its bold-red, zigzag pattern. Other baskets found in Navajo trading posts are likely to be made by Paiutes who also live in the area. During the 1980s, a renaissance resulted in some large, intricately designed coil baskets—both plate and jug-shaped.

Jewelry   Since the 1860s, Navajos have engaged in the art of silver-smithing, shaping silver to fit turquoise stones. Other popular items are stoneless silver rings, bolos, earrings, necklaces—especially the squash blossom—made by handwrought or sand-cast methods.

Pottery   Navajo ceramics are simple, unadorned brown pieces glazed with hot pitch. The pieces look wonderful when made by a master; clunky and amateurish otherwise.

Sandpaintings   Medicine men sing curing ceremonies while assistants create elaborate pictures on the ground with sands and crushed minerals in an astonishing assortment of colors. Each is destroyed at the ceremony's end. Similar designs glued onto wood are sold as sandpaintings. Widely available, these are made mainly in the Shiprock, New Mexico area.

Weaving   Thousands of Navajo women and a few dozen Navajo men weave rugs today on the reservation, but only a small percentage are considered master-weavers, commanding the highest prices. Still, even a saddle blanket can be a treasured memento.

HIDDEN ►

Follow the canyon northeast into the woods. About two miles in, on the left, near a ramada and a small dam, you'll find **Inscription Rock** where Kit Carson signed his name on the tall sandstone wall about the time he was trying to end Navajo raiding parties.

LODGING

Designed by Arizona's award-winning architect Benny Gonzales, Second Mesa offers the only Hopi-owned tourist complex. Here are 33 rooms of the **Hopi Cultural Center Motel** with their white walls, blonde furniture, television, desk, vanity, dusty rose rug and Indian print-wall decor. Check to make sure your room has a door lock; things can be a little casual here. This is a non-smoking establishment. ~ Route 264 at Second Mesa; 520-734-2401, fax 520-734-6651. MODERATE.

DINING

HIDDEN ►

Hopi's primary meeting place, the **Hopi Cultural Center Restaurant** with open-beam ceiling and sturdy, wood-carved furniture, offers Hopi options at all meals. Breakfasts include blue-corn pancakes, blue-corn cornflakes with milk and fry bread. For lunch or dinner, Nok Qui Vi—traditional stew with corn and lamb, served with fresh-baked green chiles and fry bread—as well as steak, chicken and shrimp entrées round out the menu. For dessert there's strawberry shortcake. ~ Route 264 at Second Mesa; 520-734-2401 ext. 306. BUDGET TO MODERATE.

Murals depicting Hopi mesa life decorate the exterior at **Keams Canyon Cafe**. This simple eatery has such entrées as T-bone steak, roast beef, barbecued ribs and enchiladas, all served on formica tables. ~ Route 264 in Keams Canyon; 520-738-2296. MODERATE.

SHOPPING

The number of roadside Hopi galleries and shops doubled in the early '90s. Owned by individual families, groups of artists or by craftsmakers with national reputations, all these Hopi crafts enterprises are located on or near Route 264.

Third Mesa's **Monongya Gallery** has large rooms filled with Indian jewelry, some pottery and kachina doll sculptures. ~ Third Mesa; 520-734-2344.

Driving east a half-mile, follow the Old Oraibi signs south to **Old Oraibi Crafts** specializing in Hopi *dawas*—wall plaques made of yarn. This tiny shop with a beam ceiling also sells stuffed Hopi clown dolls.

Eastbound on 264, **Calnimptewa's Gallery** looks like a house. Spacious, white-walled rooms are lined with gallery-quality rugs, pots and jewelry made primarily by Hopi and Navajo people. Many of the crafts have a sleek contemporary look. ~ Route 264; 520-734-2406.

In Second Mesa, by the Hopi Cultural Center, the pueblo-style **Hopi Arts and Crafts Cooperative Guild Shop** sells work by more than 350 Hopi craftsmakers, often introducing new artists. You'll see fine, reasonably priced samples of all Hopi crafts—coil baskets, wicker plaques, kachina dolls—from traditional to the contemporary baroque and even the older-style flat dolls, plus silver jewelry, woven sashes and gourd rattles. Prices are good. Staff members are knowledgeable about who the best craftsmakers are in any specialty and where to find them. In the shop you'll occasionally see Hopi silversmiths at work. ~ Second Mesa; 520-734-2463.

East of the Hopi Cultural Center one and a half miles, on the left, stop at an unassuming-looking **Tsakurshovi** to find the funkiest shop en route, the only place you can buy sweetgrass, bundled sage, cottonwood root, fox skins, elk toes, warrior paint, dance fans, the oldest-style kachina dolls and the largest selection of Hopi baskets on the reservation, amid a delightful hodgepodge of crafts and trade items adored by Hopi dancers. (Owners invented the "Don't Worry, Be Hopi" T-shirts.) ~ Second Mesa; 520-734-2478.

◀ HIDDEN

Honani Crafts Gallery, with its stained-glass windows of Hopi dancer designs, sells jewelry made by 16 silversmiths from all three mesas plus kachinas, pottery, books and concho belts. ~ Five and a half miles east of the Hopi Cultural Center, Route 264; 520-737-2238.

It's seven more miles to First Mesa, where Walpi residents welcome you to see pottery and kachinas they've made in Hopi's most picturesque village.

Thirteen miles east, visit **McGee's Indian Art Gallery** at Keams Canyon Shopping Center, distinctive for its Hopi village murals. For sale are a variety of Hopi and Navajo crafts—concho belts, silver jewelry, wicker plaques, kachinas, sandpaintings, moccasins and rugs. Be sure to look in the room housing their finest award-winning crafts. ~ Route 264, Keams Canyon; 520-738-2295.

HOPI CEREMONIAL DANCES

Although some Hopi dances are held in plazas and are open to the public, others are held privately in underground kivas. Many of their dances are appeals for rain or to improve harmony with nature. Starting times are determined by Hopi elders according to the position of the moon, sun and vibrations. The **Powamu Ceremony** or **Bean Dance** in late February is a fertility ritual to help enhance the summer harvest, while the **Snake Dance** is done near the end of August. Live rattlesnakes are used during the ceremony as a form of communication with the Underworld. If you attend a ceremony, remember to respect the proceedings and not take pictures or use tape recorders.

▼▼▼▼▼▼▼▼▼▼▼▼▼▼▼▼▼
Central Navajo Country

This is the heart, soul and capital of Navajoland—a strikingly beautiful land of canyons, red rocks, forests and mountains where the Navajos have recorded their proudest victories and most bitter defeats. The longer you stay and explore, the more you'll appreciate the ever-evolving culture that is the Navajo Way.

The ruins of ancient cities you'll see also remind us that long before the Navajo arrived this too was homeland to ancestors of the Hopis—the Anasazi.

SIGHTS

Forty miles east of Keams Canyon, near the small village of Ganado, follow a shaded road a half mile west along a creek to **Hubbell Trading Post National Historic Site**, which still operates as it did when Lorenzo Hubbell, dean of Navajo traders, set up shop here last century. Now owned by the National Park Service and operated by South West Parks and Monuments Associations, Hubbell's remains one of only a few trading posts with the traditional "bullpen" design—shoppers stand outside a wooden arena asking for canned goods, yards of velvet, tack and such. Built in the 1870s, part museum and part gallery, these three stone rooms smell and look their age—the floors uneven from years of wear. Walls are jammed to their open-beam ceilings with baskets, pottery, books, rugs, historical photos, jewelry, postcards, dry goods and grocery items. Tack and tools still dangle from the rafters. ~ Route 264, Ganado; 520-755-3254.

Self-guiding tours of the 160-acre complex and exhibits in the **Visitors Center** explain how trading posts once linked the Navajo with the outside world, and how Hubbell was not just a trader but a valued friend of the Indian community until his death in 1930. The Hubbell family continued to operate the post until it was given to the National Park Service in 1967. Also in the Visitors Center is a good selection of Indian-related books. And for a tip, Navajo weavers and silversmiths demonstrating their crafts will pose for photos—but be sure to ask first. (Please obtain consent before snapping pictures on Navajo land.) ~ Ganado; 520-755-3475.

Half-hour-long tours of the **Hubbell House**, with his excellent collection of crafts, give further insights into frontier life and the remarkable trader who lies buried on a knoll nearby.

Navajo-owned ponderosa pine forest lands comprise part of the 30-mile drive to Window Rock, eastward along Route 264. Picnickers may wish to stop a while at **Summit Campground**, where the elevation reaches 7750 feet. ~ Located 20 miles east of Ganado.

Seven miles east of Summit Campground, before entering Window Rock, stop in St. Michaels, on your right, at trailers labeled **Navajo Nation Tourism**. Here you'll be able to obtain Central

Navajo Country maps and tourism information. ~ 520-871-6436 or 520-871-7371.

Also here is **St. Michaels Mission Museum** in the white, hand-hewn native stone building that in the late 1890s was four-bedroom living quarters and chapel for Franciscan friars from Cincinnati. (Sleeping must have been tough on such thin mattresses atop box crates!) Other displays—everything from uncomfortable-looking wooden saddles to vintage typewriters—include old photographs that depict their work and life. You'll see pages of the first phonetic systems they made to help create the written Navajo language. Outside, towering cottonwoods and a friar's three-quarter-acre flower garden create a parklike oasis. Closed from Labor Day to Memorial Day. ~ Three miles west of Window Rock off Route 264, St. Michaels; 520-871-4171.

Next door, the **St. Michaels Prayer Chapel** houses a 16-foot wood carving entitled "The Redemption of Mankind," created by German artist Ludwig Schumacher as a gift to Americans Indians.

East on Route 264 three miles, a rare Indian Country traffic light (at Route 12) marks "downtown" **Window Rock**, a growing, modern Navajo Nation capital. East of the Navajo Nation Inn, the **Navajo Nation Museum** leads visitors through an overview of historic and contemporary Navajo life and traditions with rotating exhibits. **Navajo Arts & Crafts Enterprise**, located west of the inn, encourages innovation among its members and guarantees the quality of everything it sells. ~ At the intersection of Route 264 and Loop Road, Window Rock; Navajo Nation Museum: 520-871-6675; Navajo Arts & Crafts Enterprise: at the intersection of Routes 12 and 264, 520-871-4095.

The natural setting of **Navajo Nation Zoological and Botanical Park** serves as the stomping ground for domestic and wild

JOHN LORENZO HUBBELL—HERO

To American Indians at the turn of the century, John Lorenzo Hubbell was a local hero. He operated a trading post at Ganado, giving the Indians important contact with the outside world. They traded silver work, wool, sheep and rugs for essentials such as flour, coffee, sugar, tobacco and clothing. To smooth the trading process, Hubbell spoke English, Spanish, Navajo and Hopi. He was also a sheriff and a member of the territorial legislature. Hubbell tried improving the lot of American Indians by bringing in a silversmith from Mexico to teach them silver working. But he really gained their respect during a smallpox epidemic. Having had smallpox, he had developed an immunity to it. So he was able to treat the Navajo without getting the disease himself.

animals that figure in Navajo culture and folklore—everything from coyote, wolves, cougars, bears, deer, elk, bobcats, rattlesnakes and prairie dogs to goats. In all, 53 species live here. Look for the Navajo-churro sheep, brought by the Spanish. Herds are being increased because of their proven resistance to disease and the excellent weaving quality of their wool. Displays here include fork-stick and crib-log examples of hogan architecture. A modest botanical garden labels typical high-desert plants: Indian rice grass, Navajo tea, lupine, asters and junipers. ~ Route 264, Window Rock; 520-871-6573.

A row of towering red-sandstone pinnacles resembling **Haystacks,** for which they are named, forms the zoo's western border.

When you arrive at the street light at the town of Window Rock, follow Route 12 north past Window Rock's shopping center, then drive right a mile to **Tseghahodzani**—"the rock with the hole in it." Here you'll find a sweeping wall, several stories tall, of vermilion-colored sandstone. Almost dead center is an almost perfectly circular "window" 130 feet in diameter eroded in it, offering views to the mountains beyond. John Collier, Commissioner of Indian Affairs in the 1930s, was so stirred by it, he declared it the site for the Navajo administrative center. Visitors can picnic and walk here.

Nearby, visit the octagonal stone **Council Chambers,** designed as a great ceremonial hogan. Murals painted by the late Gerald Nailor depict tribal history. It is here the 88-member Tribal Council meets four times a year to set policy. You'll hear Navajo and English spoken at all proceedings. ~ Window Rock; 520-871-6417.

The prettiest route in Indian Country is **Route 12** from Route 40 through Window Rock and north another 65 miles. The road hugs red-rock bluffs while skirting pine forests, lakes, and Navajo homes and hogans surrounded by pasture, orchards and cornfields.

NATIVE ARCHITECTURE

The first talented architects of Arizona were the local tribes, with their handiwork ranging from cliff dwellings to pit houses. The Anasazi specialized in pueblos on cliff walls in northern Arizona. They mortared together cut stones for walls, while using logs and earth for the ceiling. Considering that rooms were small and without windows, they spent much time on their flat roofs, a perfect surface for chores. The Anasazi also built pit houses, flat-roofed stone houses partially dug into the ground. The Sinagua built pueblos similar to the Anasazi, but they preferred hills rather than canyons. And the Navajo people favored six-sided hogans made of logs and earth.

Follow signs to the pine-clad Navajo Community College's **Tsaile Campus** and its tall glass hogan-shaped Ned Hatathli Cultural Center with two floors devoted to the **Hatathli Museum and Gallery**. From prehistoric times to the present—dioramas, murals, photographs, pottery, weaponry and other artifacts interpret Indian cultures including the Navajo. Wonderfully detailed murals tell the Navajo story of Creation, but you'll need to find someone to interpret it for you as there's little text. Visitors are also welcome in the college's library and dining hall. Closed Saturday and Sunday. ~ Route 12, about 60 miles north of Window Rock; college: 520-724-3311, museum and gallery: 520724-6653.

Route 64, to the left off of Route 12, leads to a favorite spot of tourists from around the world, **Canyon de Chelly National Monument** (access is also available three miles east off Route 191 on Route 7). By the time the Spanish arrived in the 1540s the Navajos already occupied this trio of slick, towering red-walled canyons that converge in a Y. The canyons and rims are still home to Navajo families, their sheep and horses grazing. Water near the surface moistens corn, squash and melon crops, apple and peach orchards.

It's hard to decide if Canyon de Chelly is most impressive from the rim drives, with their bird's-eye views of the hogan-dotted rural scenes, or astride a horse or an open-air jeep, sloshing (during spring runoff) through Chinle Wash. The best introduction for any adventure is the **Visitors Center**. Chinle, the shopping and administrative center for this part of the reservation, is as plain as its famed canyons are spectacular. ~ Along the main road through Chinle; 520-674-5500.

Be sure to stop at the visitors center museum where exhibits on 2000 years of canyon history, plus cultural demonstrations, local artists' exhibits and a ranger-staffed information desk will enlighten you about the area. Next door is a typical Navajo hogan. The center is also the place to hire Navajo guides—required if you hike, camp, or drive your own four-wheel-drive vehicle into the canyons.

Proud tales of the Navajos' most daring victories are retold daily by guides who also point out bullet holes in the walls from brutal massacres. Thousands of much older ruins leave haunting clues to a people who lived and died here from about 200 A.D. until the late 1300s when prolonged drought throughout the Four Corners region probably caused them to move to the Rio Grande and other regions of Arizona and New Mexico. Each bend in the canyon reveals ever-taller canyon walls, more pictographs and petroglyphs (historic and prehistoric art drawn on rock walls). Each turn showcases vivid red walls and the yellow-green of leafy cottonwoods thriving along the canyon floor.

North and South Rim drives, each approximately 16 miles one way, take about two hours each to complete. (It's a good idea to bring along brochures that point out geological, botanical and historical sites for both overlooks.) **South Rim Drive** follows the Canyon de Chelly, which gives the monument its name. Highlights include: **White House Overlook** (located at 5.7 miles; the only nonguided hike into the canyon begins here), to view remains of a multistory masonry village where about 100 persons lived about 800 years ago; **Old Hogan and Sliding Rock Overlook** (at 11 miles), where you will see ruins of a hogan; and **shallow basins** (at 12.9 miles) eroded out of sandstone. The Navajo still sometimes gather fresh water from these basins. On a narrow ledge across the canyon, ancients built retaining walls to try to keep their homes from sliding off the sloping floor into the canyon.

Spider Rock Overlook (at 16 miles) is a vista of the steepest canyon walls, about a 1000-foot vertical drop. Look right to see Monument Canyon; left to see Canyon de Chelly. The 800-foot-tall spire at their junction is **Spider Rock**, where Spider Woman is said to carry naughty Navajo boys and girls. Those white specks at the top of her rock, Navajo parents say, are the bleached bones of boys and girls who did not listen to mother and dad. According to the Navajo creation story, Spider Woman wove the world then taught the Navajo to weave.

North Rim Drive explores the **Canyon del Muerto** ("Canyon of the Dead") named in 1882 by Smithsonian Institution expedition leader James Stevenson after finding remains of prehistoric Indian burials below Mummy Cave. Highlights include:

Antelope House Overlook (at 8.5 miles), which is named for paintings of antelope, probably made in the 1830s, on the canyon wall left of this four-story, 91-room ruin. Prehistoric residents contributed hand outlines and figures in white paint. Viewers from the overlook will see circular structures (kivas, or ceremonial chambers) and rectangular ones (storage or living quarters). Across the wash in an alcove 50 feet above the canyon floor is where 1920s archaeologists found the well-preserved body of an old man wrapped in a blanket of golden eagle feathers; under it was a white cotton blanket in such good shape it appeared brand new. It is believed he was a neighborhood weaver. Also here, at Navajo Fortress Viewpoint, the isolated high redstone butte across the canyon was once an important Navajo hideout from Spanish, American and perhaps other Indian raiders.

Mummy Cave Overlook (at 15.2 miles) is site of the largest, most beautiful ruins in Canyon del Muerto. The 1880s discovery of two mummies in cists found in the talus slope below the caves inspired this canyon's name.

Massacre Cave Overlook (at 16 miles) is site of the first documented Spanish contact with Canyon de Chelly Navajos. In the winter of 1805 a bloody battle is believed to have occurred at the rock-strewn ledge to your left, under a canyon rim overhang. Hoping to end persistent Navajo raiding on Spanish and Pueblo Indian villages, Antonio de Narbona led an expedition here and claimed his forces killed up to 115 Navajos, another 33 taken captive.

The Navajo Nation's only tribally owned motel, **Navajo Nation Inn** bustles with a mix of Navajo politicians and business people in suits and cowboys in black "reservation hats." The 56 rooms are pleasantly decorated with turquoise carpet, Southwest-style wood furniture and matching bedspreads and curtains with traditional Navajo rural scenes. ~ 48 West Route 264, Window Rock; 520-871-4108, 800-662-6189, fax 520-871-5466. BUDGET.

LODGING

A parklike scene is the setting for the historic stone and pueblo-style **Thunderbird Lodge.** All 72 adobe-style rooms handsomely blend Navajo and Southwestern architectural traditions. Each features American Indian prints and is an easy walk to the canyon entrance. There's a gift shop and cafeteria. ~ A quarter-mile southeast of Canyon de Chelly National Monument Visitors Center, Chinle; 520-674-5841, 800-679-2473, fax 520-674-5844. MODERATE.

Best Western Canyon de Chelly Motel makes up for its sterile architecture by providing one of Chinle's two swimming pools (indoor, for guests only); 102 rooms, some for nonsmokers. ~ A block east of Route 191 on Navajo Route 7, Chinle; 520-674-5875, 800-327-0354, fax 520-674-3715. MODERATE.

The only enterprise on the entire Navajo Indian Reservation letting you experience life with a rural Navajo extended family is **Coyote Pass Hospitality: Hogan Bed and Breakfast.** Accommodations are primitive: Guests sleep in an authentic dirt-floor log hogan and use old-fashioned outhouses. Scholars, artists and folks eager for a rest from the more predictable conveniences have found the Coyote Pass Hospitality a refuge. Special tours (520-724-3383) to favorite backcountry haunts can be arranged. There is a special presentation of Navajo life and traditions in the evening and a traditional Navajo breakfast in the morning. ~ Near Tsaile, very close to Canyon de Chelly; 520-724-3383. MODERATE.

◀ HIDDEN

Cafe Sage, located in a two-story, brown stucco building, once the former Presbyterian College campus, welcomes tourists to dine in the Navajo Nation Health Foundation cafeteria where daily dinner specials might include tortellini and chicken with vegetables and garlic toast. Breakfast, lunch and dinner are served. Closed Saturday and Sunday. ~ Turn right a half-mile east of Hub-

DINING

bell's on Route 264; in the Sage Memorial Hospital, Ganado; 520-755-3411 ext. 292 or 294. BUDGET.

A trailer wide enough for two rows of sky-blue booths makes up **Tuller Cafe**. Here they dish up meat loaf, pork chops, Navajo sandwiches (tortilla or fried bread with roast beef), Navajo stew (mutton, vegetable stew) and Homer's goulash (macaroni, meat, green pepper, tomatoes) with garlic toast. Closed Sunday. ~ Located on the south side of Route 264, St. Michaels; 520-871-4687. BUDGET TO MODERATE.

Navajo Nation Inn Dining Room in a modern, spacious room is the Navajo capital's biggest restaurant. Seating 250 and decorated with Navajo art, the menu includes chicken, steak, Navajo sandwiches, Navajo burgers, beef stew, vegetable stew and sometimes a mutton buffet. Lunch is always busy, the restaurant filled with politicians from nearby tribal headquarters offices. ~ 48 West Route 264, Window Rock; 520-871-4108. MODERATE.

Junction Restaurant is one of only two sit-down (nonbuffet) restaurants in Chinle. A mix of peach and blue booths and blonde-wood tables and chairs seat patrons dining on everything from *huevos rancheros* for breakfast to hot sandwiches for lunch to American and Navajo specialties for dinner. ~ Adjacent to Canyon de Chelly Motel, a block east of Route 191 on Navajo Route 7, Chinle; 520-674-8443. MODERATE.

Thunderbird Restaurant, in the original 1902 trading post built by Samuel Day, serves up half a dozen entrées cafeteria-style for each meal. The menu offers a good variety, and changes some each day. You sit in a choice of booths or tables surrounded by walls with top-quality, for-sale Navajo crafts. ~ Thunderbird Lodge, a quarter-mile southeast of Canyon de Chelly National Monument Visitors Center, Chinle; 520-674-5841. BUDGET TO MODERATE.

▲▲▲

✔ CHECK THESE OUT—UNIQUE DINING

- *Budget:* Satisfy your cravings for *chile rellenos* at **Casa Blanca Cafe**, a quaint spot that's been celebrated in papers from coast to coast. *page 83*
- *Budget to moderate:* Squeeze into the trailer housing the **Tuller Cafe**— you won't be disappointed with the Navajo sandwiches or Homer's goulash. *page 102*
- *Moderate:* Contemplate the Hopi way of life as you fill up on steak, ribs or enchiladas at **Keams Canyon Cafe**. *page 94*
- *Moderate to deluxe:* Take in panoramic vistas from the tri-level **Stage Coach Dining Room**, where a dinner favorite is roast leg of lamb. *page 107*

Budget: under $8　Moderate: $8–$16　Deluxe: $16–$24　Ultra-deluxe: over $24

Be sure to stop at the **Hubbell Trading Post**, whose low stone walls, little changed in 90 years, contain the best Navajo rug selection en route, plus several rooms crammed with jewelry, dolls, books, baskets and historic postcards. ~ Route 264, Ganado; 520-755-3254.

SHOPPING

Navajo Arts & Crafts Enterprise sells the work of some 500 Navajo craftsmakers. Selection is excellent and quantity is large —rugs of all styles, Navajo jewelry of all kinds, stuffed Navajo-style dolls. ~ At the intersection of Route 12 and Route 264, Window Rock; 520-871-4095.

The **Thunderbird Lodge Gift Shop** provides a good selection of rugs, many of them made in the Chinle area, as well as kachinas, jewelry, baskets and souvenirs. Some of the fine-quality arts and crafts decorating the neighboring cafeteria walls are also for sale. ~ Thunderbird Lodge, a quarter-mile southeast of Canyon de Chelly National Monument Visitors Center, Chinle; 520-674-5841.

LAKE ASAAYI BOWL CANYON RECREATION AREA 𝅘 ⤶ One of the prettiest of the Navajo fishing lakes, located in the Chuska Mountains known as the "Navajo Alps," Asaayi Lake (elevation 7600 feet) is popular for fishing (rainbow trout), picnicking and primitive camping. The 36-acre lake and creek are fishable year-round (icefishing in the winter). Facilities include picnic areas, barbecue grills and pit toilets. Fishing permits are available from the Navajo Fish and Wildlife Department (520-871-6451), in Window Rock. ~ From Window Rock, take Route 12 to Route 134. Drive northeast four miles then south seven miles on a graded dirt road to the lake; 520-871-6647.

PARKS

▲ Allowed; the $2 permit is available at the recreation area or at the Navajo Parks and Recreation, in Window Rock; 520-871-6647.

CANYON DE CHELLY NATIONAL MONUMENT 𝅘 🚲 🐎 The most famous and popular Navajo Indian Reservation attraction is this 130-acre land of piñon and juniper forests cut by a trio of red-walled sandstone canyons. Extending eastward from Chinle to Tsaile, the canyon's rim elevations range from 5500 to 7000 feet while the canyon bottoms drop from 30 feet nearest Chinle to 1000 feet farther east. Cottonwood trees and other vegetation shade farms connected by miles of sandy wash along the canyon bottom. Two major gorges, 27 and 34 miles long, dramatically unveil walls of 250-million-year-old solidified sand dunes in a strata geologists call the Defiance Plateau. There is a motel, restaurant, bookstore, visitors center, museum, crib-log hogan, restrooms, jeep and horse tours and guided hikes. ~ Located in Chinle, via Route 191; 520-674-5500. Spider Rock Campground is eight miles east of the visitors center on South Rim Canyon Drive.

▲ There are two campgrounds available. Cottonwood Campground has 96 sites (no hookups); no fee. Spider Rock Campground, run by a private concessionaire, offers 30 sites (no hookups); $10 per night. ~ 520-674-8261.

▼▼▼▼▼▼▼▼▼▼▼▼▼▼▼▼▼▼▼▼▼

Northern Navajo Country

There's something both silly and irresistible about driving to Four Corners to stick each foot in a different state (Colorado and Utah) and each hand in still two others (Arizona and New Mexico) while someone takes your picture from a scaffolding. But then, this is the only place in the United States where you can simultaneously "be" in four different states. The inevitable Navajo crafts booths offer up necklaces, bracelets, earrings, T-shirts, paintings, sandpaintings, fry bread and lemonade—a splendid way to make something festive out of two intersecting lines on a map.

SIGHTS
To get to Northern Navajo Country from the south, you'll have to pass by **Teec Nos Pos Arts and Crafts Center**, the usual roadside gallery of Southwest Indian crafts, with an emphasis on area sandpaintings and Navajo rugs. Closed Sunday. ~ Routes 160 and 64; 520-656-3228.

Heading westbound on Route 160, even before travelers reach Kayenta, amazing eroded shapes emerge on the horizon—like the cathedral-sized and -shaped **Church Rock**. Kayenta, originally a small town that grew up around John Wetherill's trading post at 5564-feet elevation, today is both Arizona's gateway to Monument Valley and a coal-mining center.

The 24 miles north to Monument Valley on Route 163 is a prelude to the main event, huge red-rock pillars. **Half Dome** and **Owl Rock** on your left form the eastern edge of the broad Tyende Mesa. On your right rise **Burnt Foot Butte** and **El Capitan**, also called Agathla Peak—roots of ancient volcanoes whose dark rock contrasts with pale-yellow sandstone formations.

A half-mile north of the Utah state line on Route 163 is a crossroads; go left two miles to Gouldings Trading Post and Lodge, or right two miles to **Monument Valley Navajo Tribal Park Headquarters** and Monument Valley Visitors Center. Inside you can see excellent views from a glass-walled observatory. This was the first Navajo Tribal Park, set aside in 1958. Within you'll see more than 40 named and dozens more unnamed red and orange monolithic sandstone buttes and rock skyscrapers jutting hundreds of feet. It is here that you can arrange Navajo-owned jeep tours into the Valley Drive. Admission. ~ P.O. Box 360289, Monument Valley, UT 84536; 435-727-3287.

For a small fee, you can explore the **17-mile Loop Drive** over a dirt road, badly rutted in places, to view a number of famous landmarks with names that describe their shapes, such as **Rain God Mesa, Three Sisters** and **Totem Pole**. At **John Ford's Point**, an Indian on horseback often poses for photographs, then rides out to chat and collect a tip. A 15-minute round-trip walk from **North Window** rewards you with panoramic views.

The Navajos and this land seem to belong together. A dozen Navajo families still live in the park, and several open their hogans to guided tours. For a small fee, they'll pose for your pictures. A number of today's residents are descendants of Navajos who arrived here in the mid-1860s with Headman Hoskinini, fleeing Kit Carson and his round-up of Navajos in the Canyon de Chelly area. Hoskinini lived here until his death in 1909.

The ultimate cowboy-Indian Western landscape, Monument Valley has been the setting for many movies—*How the West Was Won*, *Stagecoach*, *Billy the Kid*, *She Wore a Yellow Ribbon*, *The Trial of Billy Jack* to name just a few films. In all, seven John Ford Westerns were filmed in Monument Valley between 1938 and 1963.

Gouldings Trading Post, Lodge and Museum, a sleek, watermelon-colored complex on a hillside, blends in with enormous sandstone boulders stacked above it. The original Goulding two-story stone home and trading post, now a museum, includes a room devoted to movies made here. Daily showings can be seen in a small adjacent theater. ~ Two miles west of Route 163, Monument Valley; 435-727-3231.

From Gouldings it's nearly 11 miles northwest on paved Oljato Road to the single-story stone **Oljato Trading Post**, its Depression-era gas pumps and scabby turquoise door visible reminders of its

◄ **HIDDEN**

NAVAJO CEREMONIAL DANCES

Three popular Navajo dances, which you may be lucky enough to see, are the Corral Dance, the Night-Way Dance and the Enemy-Way Dance. The **Corral Dance** seeks divine help to avoid dangerous lightning and snakebites; it's so named because part of the ceremony takes place within a corral of branches around a bonfire. The nine-day-long **Night-Way Dance** supposedly helps people suffering from nervousness or insanity. And the **Enemy-Way Dance** performed during the summer is a purifying ceremony to help people suffering from nightmares and other "enemies of the mind." Activities are held in a different place for each of the three nights of the ceremony and, at the conclusion, a sheep is slaughtered for breakfast.

age. Inside ask to see a dusty museum room filled with a variety of American Indian crafts hidden behind the turquoise bullpen-style mercantile. Often you can buy a fine used Navajo wedding basket for a good price. ~ Oljato; 435-727-3210.

Back to Kayenta and Route 160, it's a scenic 18-mile drive northwest to the turnoff for the **Navajo National Monument**, which encompasses some of the Southwest's finest Anasazi ruins (open only from Memorial Day to Labor Day). This stunning region showcases the architectural genius of the area's early inhabitants.

To gain an overview of the monument, stop by the **Visitors Center and Museum** featuring films and exhibits of the treasures tucked away beneath the sandstone cliffs, including a replica of an Anasazi ruin. You'll be impressed by pottery, jewelry, textiles and tools created by the Kayenta Anasazi who lived in these exquisite canyons. There's also a craft gallery selling Zuni, Navajo and Hopi artwork. ~ Nine and a half miles north of Route 160 on Route 564, or 27 miles west of Kayenta; 520-672-2366.

From the visitors center you can hike an undemanding forest trail to **Betatakin Point Overlook**. Here you'll get an overview of Betatakin Ruin and Tsegi Canyon. One of the ruins here, **Inscription House**, is closed to protect it for posterity. However, it is possible to make the strenuous but rewarding hike to **Betatakin Ruin**, located in a dramatic alcove 700 feet below the canyon's rim. On this trip back in time, you'll see a 135-room ledge house that rivals the best of Mesa Verde. Also well worth a visit is remote **Keet Seel**. Even some of the roofs remain intact at this 160-room, five-kiva ruin. You can only reach this gem with a permit obtained at the visitors center. For more information on the ranger-led walks to these two well-preserved ruins, see "Hiking" at the end of the chapter.

Back on Route 160, it's about 28 miles southwest to **Elephant Feet**, roadside geologic formations that resemble legs and feet of a gigantic sandstone elephant.

RIDE 'EM COWBOY!

Statisticians claim Navajos host more rodeos per year than all other United States tribes combined. Rarely does a summer weekend pass without Navajo cowboys and cowgirls of all ages gathering somewhere on the reservation. To find one when you visit, call *The Navajo Times*, a weekly, in Window Rock (520-871-6641), the Navajo Tourism Office (520-871-6659) or Navajo Radio Station KTNN (520-871-2666).

Wetherill Inn has 54 spacious rooms sporting dark-brown furniture, upholstered chairs, multicolored spreads and matching curtains in Southwest style. ~ Route 163, a mile north of Route 160,
Kayenta; 520-697-3231, fax 520-697-3233. MODERATE.

Tour buses full of French, German, Italian and Japanese guests
frequent the 162-room **Holiday Inn Monument Valley**. All guest
rooms in the two-story adobe brick buildings offer floral carpets
in hallways, cherry-wood furniture, upholstered chairs and spacious bathrooms. There's also an outdoor pool. ~ At the junction
of Routes 160 and 163, Kayenta; 520-697-3221, fax 520-697-
3349. DELUXE.

The only lodging right at Monument Valley, open since the
1920s, takes brilliant advantage of the views. Sliding glass doors
lead to balconies for each of the 62 guest rooms at **Gouldings
Lodge** so guests can enjoy the eroded Mitten Buttes. The indoor
pool is for guests only. ~ Four miles east of the tribal park, Monument Valley, UT; 435-727-3231, 800-874-0902, fax 435-727-
3344. DELUXE.

Anasazi Inn at Tsegi Canyon, with 57 rooms and a view of
the canyon, is the closest lodging to Navajo National Monument.
~ Ten miles west of Kayenta on Route 160; 520-697-3793, fax
520-697-8249. MODERATE.

An American Indian theme prevails at the **Holiday Inn Restau-**
rant, complete with Anasazi-style walls and sandpainting room
dividers. Tables for four and matching chairs are decorated in
Southwest style. There's a continental breakfast buffet for diners
in a hurry; a salad bar and burgers, sandwiches, Navajo tacos for
lunch or dinner; meat and fish entrées for dinner. ~ At the junction of Routes 160 and 163, Kayenta; 520-697-3221. BUDGET TO
DELUXE.

Old West saloon architecture signals Kayenta's **Golden Sands
Cafe**. Inside, the walls are lined with photographs of old movies
and commercials shot in Monument Valley. Breakfast specials include omelettes or blueberry pancakes; dinner entrées include rib
steak, chicken-fried steak and Navajo tacos. ~ Adjacent to the
Wetherill Inn on Route 163, a mile north of Route 160, Kayenta;
520-697-3684. BUDGET TO MODERATE.

Lively, crowded and cheery, **Amigo Cafe** serves fresh (nothing
served here comes out of a can) Mexican, American and Navajo
entrées. Popular with locals. ~ On the east side of Route 163, a
mile north of Route 160, Kayenta; 520-697-8448. BUDGET TO
MODERATE.

Three levels of dining stairstep a bluff so that the **Stage Coach
Dining Room** patrons can enjoy the panoramas of Monument
Valley. Part of a late 1980s major expansion and remodel, this

former cafeteria now offers sit-down service. The peach and burnt umber booths and tables compliment the stunning sandstone bluffs and views outside. A dinner favorite is the roast leg of lamb. Desserts worth a splurge include blueberry pie and cherry pie with ice cream. There's a salad bar, and nonalcoholic wine and beer are offered. ~ At Gouldings Lodge, Monument Valley; 435-727-3231 ext. 404. MODERATE TO DELUXE.

An all-American menu at **Anasazi Inn Café** offers burgers, steak, chicken and a few Navajo dishes and is open 24 hours a day during the summer. ~ On Route 160, ten miles west of Kayenta; 520-697-3793. MODERATE.

SHOPPING

HIDDEN ►

Ask to see the crafts room at the 1921 **Oljato Trading Post**, 11 miles northwest of Gouldings near Monument Valley, and you'll be led into a dusty museum-like space. The room is crammed with crafts, some for sale, some for admiring. Best buys here are Navajo wedding baskets popular with today's local brides and grooms. Simple, brown-pitch Navajo pottery made in this area is also sold here as well as cedar cradleboards, popular on the "res" as a baby's safety seat. ~ Oljato; 435-727-3210.

Yellow Ribbon Gift Shop provides Southwestern tribal crafts and souvenirs for all budgets. ~ Part of Gouldings complex, Monument Valley; 435-727-3231.

PARKS

MONUMENT VALLEY NAVAJO TRIBAL PARK 🏃 🚲 🐎 Straddling the Arizona–Utah border is the jewel of tribally run Navajo Nation parks. With its 29,816 acres of monoliths, spires, buttes, mesas, canyons and sand dunes—all masterpieces of red-rock erosion—it is a stunning destination. With dozens of families still living here, it is also a sort of Williamsburg of Navajoland. There's a visitors center with shops, showers, restrooms and picnic tables. You must arrange for a guide if you want to explore the park. ~ On Route 163, 24 miles northeast of Kayenta. The visitors center is east another four miles. The Gouldings complex is west three miles; 435-727-3353, 435-727-3287.

▲ Mitten View has 99 sites; $10 per night up to six people.

NAVAJO NATIONAL MONUMENT 🏃 🐎 Three of the Southwest's most beautiful Anasazi pueblo ruins are protected in the canyons of this 360-acre park, swathed in piñon and juniper forests at a 7300-foot elevation. Inscription House Ruin is so fragile it is closed. Betatakin Ruin, handsomely set in a cave high up a canyon wall, is visible from an overlook. But close looks at Betatakin and the largest site, Keet Seel, require fairly strenuous hikes permitted between Memorial Day and Labor Day. You'll find a visitors center, museum, gift shop, restrooms, picnic areas and barbecue grills. ~ Take Route 160 west of Kayenta, turn right at Route 564 and continue nine miles; 520-672-2366.

▲ There are 30 sites in the campground, plus a handful of overflow sites; no hookups, no running water; no fee.

Fishing is permitted year-round in Indian Country with a one-day to one-year Navajo tribal license required at all lakes, streams and rivers in the Navajo Nation. No fishing tackle or boats are for rent on the reservation. Boats are permitted on many of the lakes; most require electric motors only.

▼▼▼▼▼▼▼▼▼▼▼▼▼
Outdoor Adventures

FISHING

WESTERN NAVAJO COUNTRY Get fishing licenses and boating permits from CSWTA Inc. Environmental Consultant. ~ Tuba City; 520-283-4323.

CENTRAL NAVAJO COUNTRY Whiskey Lake and Long Lake are known for their trophy-size trout, located in the Chuska Mountains, a dozen miles south of Route 134 via logging routes 8000 and 8090. Their season is May 1 through November 30.

Popular all-year lakes stocked with rainbow trout each spring include Wheatfields Lake (44 miles north of Window Rock on Route 12) and Tsaile Lake (half-mile south of Navajo Community College in Tsaile). Tsaile Lake is also popular for catfish.

Good for largemouth bass and channel catfishing is Many Farms Lake (three miles via dirt road east of Route 191 in Many Farms). You can get licenses and permits from Navajo Fish & Wildlife. ~ Window Rock; 520-871-6451. Wilkinson's Tsaile Trading Post also has licenses and a few supplies. ~ Tsaile; 520-724-3484.

NORTHERN NAVAJO COUNTRY The Kayenta Trading Post has fishing licenses and boating permits. ~ Kayenta; 520-697-3541.

JOGGING

Navajos and Hopis, who pride themselves on their long-distance-running traditions that date back to first contact with whites in the 1540s, host races at every tribal fair. Races are open to non-Indians as well. And it is common to see American Indian joggers daily along virtually any route, so bring your togs and run too.

CENTRAL NAVAJO COUNTRY At Canyon de Chelly, try the White House Ruins trail or either of the rim trails.

NORTHERN NAVAJO COUNTRY The four-mile road leading into Monument Valley or roads to Oljato and around Gouldings Lodge are good places for a jog.

JEEP TOURS

Jeeps, either with tops down or with air conditioning on (not all jeeps have air conditioning, so ask operators before you pay money) are a popular way to see Navajo Indian Reservation attractions noted for occasional sand bogs and even quicksand pockets. Navajo guides often live in the region and can share area lore and American Indian humor.

At Canyon de Chelly, **Thunderbird Lodge Tours** takes visitors on outings in large, noisy, converted all-terrain army vehicles. There are eight-hour trips that cover both Canyon de Chelly and Canyon del Muerto, as well as three-and-a-half-hour trips to either canyon. ~ Thunderbird Lodge, Chinle; 520-674-5841.

Monument Valley tour operators all offer half-day and all-day tours of Monument and adjoining Mystery Valley. It's the only way visitors can see the stunning back country. Most tours include visits to an inhabited hogan. Some offer lunch or dinner.

Gouldings Monument Valley Tours takes visitors on morning and all-day tours in 20-passenger open-air vehicles. ~ At Gouldings Lodge near Monument Valley; 435-727-3231. **Tom K. Bennett Tours** transports guests via four-wheel-drive sports utility vehicles; a visit to a hogan includes a rug-weaving demonstration. ~ 435-727-3283. Depending on the group's size, **Bill Crawley Monument Valley Tours** uses vehicles ranging from a seven-passenger Suburban to a 30-person bus. By arrangement native guides serenade you with traditional songs. ~ Kayenta; 520-697-3463. Information on **Frank and Betty Jackson's Dineh Guided Tours** and **Navajo Guided Tour Service** can be obtained at the Monument Valley Visitors Center. ~ 435-727-3287.

GOLF

In Holbrook you can tee up at **Hidden Cove Golf Course**, a nine-hole course carved out of the high desert grasslands and surrounded by scenic mountains and hillsides. Club and cart rentals available. ~ Exit 283, two miles west of Route 40; 520-524-3097.

RIDING STABLES

Horses have been an important icon of Navajo culture since the Spanish introduced them in the mid-16th century. They're a grand way to connect with a Navajo guide while seeing awesome country through his eyes. Most offer one-hour to overnight or longer options; there's flexibility on where you go and how long you stay.

CENTRAL NAVAJO COUNTRY   In Canyon de Chelly, **Justin Stables**, located right at the entrance of the reservation, offers two-hour, half-day and all-day guided tours to White House Ruins and elsewhere in and beyond the canyon. Groups range from 1 to 25 people. ~ 520-674-5678. **Twin Trails Tours** leads trips ranging from a two-hour rim ride to an all-day horseback tour of the canyon, departing from the North Rim of Canyon de Chelly, about one mile past Antelope House turnoff. ~ 520-6748425.

NORTHERN NAVAJO COUNTRY   In Monument Valley, **Ed Black's Horse Riding Tours** can be an hour around The Mittens, or all day or longer into the valley. Groups range from two to ten. ~ Located via a dirt road north from the visitors center a quarter-mile; 435-739-4285.

Biking is permitted on any paved roads in Navajo Country, but only on the main paved highways on the Hopi Indian Reservation.

BIKING

SOUTHERN NAVAJO COUNTRY   Petrified Forest National Park routes will often be too hot for daytime summer riding but offer a splendid way to sightsee in cooler spring and fall seasons.

CENTRAL NAVAJO COUNTRY   While you'll find no designated bike paths or trails within the reservation, bicycles are well suited to both rim roads at Canyon de Chelly. Cyclists from around the world are attracted to the uphill challenges of the Chuska Mountain Routes 134 (paved), 68 and 13 (partially paved).

NORTHERN NAVAJO COUNTRY   Bicycling is popular along the paved, pine-clad nine miles of Route 564 into Navajo National Monument. Mountain bikes are particularly suited to the 17-mile rutted dirt loop open to visitors in Monument Valley.

Because most of the land covered in this chapter is tribally owned or in national parks and monuments, hiking trail options are limited. Hopi back country is not open to visitors; it is, however, on the Navajo Indian Reservation. For the mountains, ask for suggestions from area trading posts, or hire an Indian guide by the hour or overnight or longer. Guides know the way and can share stories about the area.

HIKING

A hat, sunglasses and drinking water are recommended for all hikes; add a raincoat during the July and August monsoon season. All distances for hiking are one way unless otherwise noted.

SOUTHERN NAVAJO COUNTRY   Little Painted Desert County Park has a strenuous one-mile hiking trail descending 500 feet into some of the most colorful hills in all the Painted Desert. Colors are most intense early and late in the day.

Petrified Forest National Park's summertime temperatures often soar in the 90s and 100s. Hiking is best early or late in the day. Water is available only at the visitors center at the north and south end of the park, so you're wise to carry extra with you.

✔ **CHECK THESE OUT—UNIQUE OUTDOOR ADVENTURES**

- Head to Whiskey and Long lakes in the Chuska Mountains and try for the trophy-size trout. *page 109*
- Join the long-distance-running tradition of the Hopis and Navajos and jog the White House Ruins trail. *page 109*
- Gallup through Canyon de Chelly and view the area through the eyes of your Navajo guide. *page 110*
- Descend 500 feet into the technicolor hills on a strenuous hike in Little Painted Desert County Park. *page 111*

A loop that begins and ends at the Crystal Forest stop on the park's 28-mile scenic loop, **Crystal Forest Interpretive Trail** (.5 mile) leads past the park's most concentrated petrified wood stands. You can see how tall these ancient trees were (up to 170 feet), and the variety of colors that formed after crystal replaced wood cells.

An introduction to the Chinle Formation, **Blue Mesa Hike** (1 mile) is a loop interpretive trail that leads past a wonderland of blue, gray and white layered hills. Signs en route explain how the hills formed and are now eroding.

The Flattops (unlimited miles) trailhead descends off sandstone-relic mesas several hundred feet into Puerco Ridge and other areas of the 10,000-acre Rainbow Forest Wilderness at the park's southeastern end. A quarter-mile trail leads into the area, and then you are on your own, exploring a vast gray-and-brown mudstone and siltstone badlands with wide vistas around every hill. The backcountry permits required to visit this remote portion of the park are free from the visitors center; you can stay up to 14 days.

Painted Desert Wilderness Area (unlimited miles) trailhead begins at Kachina Point at the park's north end. A brief trail descends some 400 feet, then leaves you on your own to explore cross-country some 35,000 acres of red-and-white-banded badlands of mudstone and siltstone, bald of vegetation. The going is sticky when wet. Get free backcountry permits at either visitors center.

CENTRAL NAVAJO COUNTRY   Canyon de Chelly's only hike open to visitors without a guide is **White House Ruin Trail** (2.5 miles roundtrip), beginning at the 6.4-mile marker on the South Rim Drive. The trail switchback is down red sandstone swirls, crosses a sandy wash (rainy seasons you will do some wading in Chinle Creek; bring dry socks) to a cottonwood-shaded masonry village with 60 rooms surviving at ground level and an additional ten rooms perched in a cliff's alcove above.

Four-hour, four-and-a-half-mile Navajo-led hikes up the canyon to White House Ruin start at the visitors center at 9 a.m. and noon. Navajo guides can be hired at the **Canyon de Chelly National Monument Visitors Center** to take you on short or overnight hikes into the canyon. The maximum group size for both ranger-led and private guided hikes is 15 people. ~ 520-674-5500.

Hiking is not permitted in **Monument Valley** without a Navajo guide. Hire one at the visitors center (435-727-3287) for an hour, overnight or longer. Fred Cly (435-739-4294, or ask at the visitors center) is a knowledgeable guide especially good for photo angles and best times of day. Reservations cannot be made in advance of arrival; as soon as you pull into Monument Valley, go to the visitors center parking lot and make tour arrangements for the following day.

Navajo National Monument trails include **Sandal Trail** (.5 mile), a fairly level self-guided trail to Betatakin Ruin overlook;

bring binoculars. The ranger-led hike to **Betatakin Ruin**, or "ledge house" in Navajo (2.5 miles), is strenuous, requiring a return climb up 700 steps. But it's worth the effort for the walk through the floor of Tsegi Canyon. National Park Service guides lead one tour of no more than 25 hikers each day, May through September. Tokens are awarded on a first-come, first-served basis at the visitors center. The hike to **Keet Seel** (8 miles), the biggest Anasazi ruin in Arizona (160 rooms dating from 950 A.D. to 1300 A.D.) is open to hikers for long weekends, May through September. Much of the trail is sandy, making the trek fairly tiresome, and hikers must wade through cold, shallow water along the way. You can stay only one night; 20 people a day may hike in. A free backcountry permit is required. Reservations are made 60 days in advance; call 520-672-2367. Or take your chances and ask about cancellations when you get there.

▼▼▼▼▼▼▼▼▼▼

Transportation

This is a land of wide-open spaces, but don't despair. Roads have vastly improved in the last decade, easing the way for travelers. Bounded on the south by **Route 40**, two parallel routes farther north lead east and west through Indian Country: the southern **Route 264** travels alongside the three Hopi mesas and Window Rock; the northern **Route 160**, en route to Colorado, is gateway to all the northern reservation attractions. **Route 89**, the main north–south artery, connects Flagstaff with Lake Powell, traversing the Western Indian Reservation. Five other good, paved north–south routes connect Route 40 travelers with Indian Country. **Route 99/2** and **Route 87** connect the Winslow area with Hopi villages. **Route 191** leads to Ganado, Canyon de Chelly and Utah. **Route 12**, arguably the prettiest of all, connects Route 264 with Window Rock and the back side of Canyon de Chelly. This is desert driving; be sure to buy gas when it is available.

CAR

There is no regularly scheduled commuter air service to Hopi or Navajo lands. The nearest airports are Gallup, New Mexico; Flagstaff, Arizona; and Cortez, Colorado.

AIR

Navajo Transit System offers weekday bus service between Fort Defiance and Window Rock in the east and Tuba City in the west. The system also heads north from Window Rock to Kayenta on weekdays with stops including Navajo Community College at Tsaile. ~ Based in Fort Defiance; 520-729-4002.

BUS

Amtrak's daily "Southwest Chief" connects Los Angeles with Chicago stops at three Indianland gateway cities: Flagstaff, Winslow and Gallup. ~ 800-872-7245. **Grayline Nava-Hopi Tours** out of Flagstaff offers people arriving on Amtrak bus tours to Indian Country. ~ 520-774-5003.

TRAIN

SIX

North Central Arizona

When it comes to north central Arizona, visitors soon discover that it's a region of vivid contrasts. The many unusual places to be found in this area vary dramatically in everything from altitude to attitude, from climate to culture. Here, you'll find communities that range from Old West to New Age, from college town to artist colony, along with lava cones and red rock spires, American Indian ruins and vast pine forests, even a meteor crater, all just waiting to be explored.

Set at the edge of a huge volcano field, Flagstaff grew up as a railroad town in the midst of the world's largest ponderosa pine forest. Its name came about when a local pine tree was used as a flagstaff for the 1876 Fourth of July festivities. The flagstaff later became a landmark for passing wagon trains. The town was founded in 1882, less than a year before the first steam train clattered through, and thrived first on timber and later on tourism. Today, both freight and passenger trains still pass through Flagstaff. The largest community (population 56,000) between Albuquerque and the greater Los Angeles area on Route 40, one of the nation's busiest truck routes, Flagstaff's huge restaurant and lodging industry prospers year-round. In fact, casual visitors detouring from the interstate to fill up the gas tank and buy burgers and fries along the commercial strip that is Flagstaff's Route 40 business loop can easily form the misimpression that the town is one long row of motels and fast-food joints. A closer look will reveal it as a lively college town with considerable historic charm. A short drive outside of town takes you to fascinating ancient Indian ruins as well as Arizona's highest mountains and strange volcanic landscapes.

Less than an hour's drive south of Flagstaff via magnificent Oak Creek Canyon, Sedona is a strange blend of spectacular scenery, chic resorts, Western art in abundance and New Age notions. You can go jeeping or hiking in the incomparable Red Rock Country, play some of the country's most beautiful golf courses, shop for paintings until you run out of wall space or just sit by Oak Creek and feel the vibes. People either love Sedona or hate it. Often both.

You'll also have the chance to visit one of the state's best-preserved ghost towns. Jerome, a booming copper town a century ago, was abandoned in the 1950s and then repopulated in the 1960s by artists and hippies to become a tourist favorite today.

Prescott is a quiet little town with a healthy regard for its own history. Long before Phoenix, Flagstaff or Sedona came into existence, Prescott was the capital of the Arizona Territory. Today, it is a city of museums, stately 19th-century architecture and century-old saloons. Change seems to happen slowly and cautiously here. As you stroll the streets of town, you may feel that you've slipped back through time into the 1950s, into the sort of all-American community you don't often find any more.

▼▼▼▼▼▼▼▼▼▼

Flagstaff Area

Flagstaff has been called "The City of Seven Wonders" because of its proximity to the Grand Canyon, Oak Creek Canyon, Walnut Canyon, Wupatki National Monument, Sunset Crater, Meteor Crater and the San Francisco Peaks.

Visitors who view Flagstaff from the heights of the San Francisco Peaks to the north will see this community's most striking characteristic: It is an island in an ocean of ponderosa pine forest stretching as far as the eye can see. At an elevation of 7000 feet, Flagstaff has the coolest climate of any city in Arizona. Because of its proximity to slopes on 12,000-foot Agassin Peak, Flagstaff is the state's leading winter ski resort town. It is also a lively college town, with students accounting for 10 to 20 percent of the population.

SIGHTS

A good place to start exploring Flagstaff is downtown, toward the west end of Santa Fe Avenue, which is also known as both Historic Route 66 and the business loop of Route 40. The **Flagstaff Visitors Center**, located in the Amtrak train depot, provides ample information about the area and sells a building-by-building **walking tour brochure** of historic Flagstaff. ~ 1 East Route 66; between San Francisco and Beaver streets; 520-774-9541, 800-842-7293; www.flagstaff.az.us.

San Francisco Street is the main thoroughfare through the historic downtown district. Neither rundown nor yuppified, the district retains much of its turn-of-the-century frontier architecture. The **Hotel Weatherford** was built partially of locally quarried sandstone and opened in 1899. It was the first structure in Flagstaff to be listed on the National Register of Historic Places, and is still operated as a hotel and a youth hostel. The present owners restored the structure by uncovering original fireplaces and rebuilding balconies that overlook downtown. ~ 23 North Leroux Street, Flagstaff; 520-774-2731.

The 1888 **McMillan Building** now houses an art gallery. ~ 2 West Route 66 at Leroux Street, Flagstaff. The **Hotel Monte Vista**, also listed on the register, dates from the 1920s and was popular with movie stars in the 1930s and 1940s. ~ 100 North San Francisco Street, Flagstaff.

Take time to stroll through the old residential area just north of the downtown business district. Attractive Victorian houses, many of them handmade from volcanic lava rock, give the neighborhood its unique character.

South of downtown, on the other side of the interstate and across the railroad tracks, is **Northern Arizona University**. The original structure, Old Main, was built in 1894 and now houses administrative offices and an art gallery. Campus tours are available. ~ Butler Avenue and South Beaver Street, Flagstaff; 520-523-9607.

Another sightseeing highlight in the university area is **Riordan Mansion State Historic Park**, a block off Milton Road north of the intersection of Route 40 and Route 17. The biggest Territorial-day mansion in Flagstaff, it was built in 1904 by two brothers who were the region's leading timber barons. Constructed duplex-style with over 40 rooms and 13,300 square feet of living space, the mansion blends rustic log-slab and volcanic rock construction with turn-of-the-century opulence and plenty of creative imagination. Tour guides escort visitors through the home to see its original furnishings and family mementos. Reservations are required. Admission. ~ 1300 Riordan Ranch Road, Flagstaff; 520-779-4395.

On a hilltop just a mile west of downtown is **Lowell Observatory**. The observatory was built by wealthy astronomer Percival Lowell in 1894 to take advantage of the exceptional visibility created by Flagstaff's clean air and high altitude. His most famous achievement during the 22 years he spent here was the "discovery" of canals on the planet Mars, which he submitted to the scientific community as "proof" of extraterrestrial life. The planet Pluto was discovered by astronomers at Lowell Observatory 14 years after Dr. Lowell's death, and the facility continues to be one of the most important centers for studying the solar system. Take a guided tour of the observatory during the day and see Dr. Lowell's original Victorian-era telescope, which is now 100 years old. The Steel Visitor Center presents interactive, hands-on exhibits about astronomers' tools. On some summer evenings, astronomers hold star talks and help visitors stargaze through one of the center's smaller telescopes. Call for hours. Admission. ~ 1400 West Mars Hill Road, Flagstaff; 520-774-3358; recorded schedule information, 520-774-2096; www.lowell.edu.

HIDDEN ► Overshadowed by Lowell Observatory, the **Northern Arizona University Campus Observatory** actually offers visitors a better chance to look through a larger telescope. Public viewing sessions are held on Friday evenings from 7:30 to 10 p.m. when the sky is clear. The campus observatory specializes in studying eclipsing binary stars and pulsating stars. Closed Saturday and Sunday. ~ Northeast corner of San Francisco Street and University Drive on campus, Flagstaff; 520-523-7170.

If you travel four miles south of Old Route 66 (Business Loop 40), Woody Mountain Road leads back into the ponderosa pine forest to **The Arboretum at Flagstaff**. The nearly four-mile road is ◄ *HIDDEN* unpaved most of the way, but well maintained and easily passable for all vehicles. Set on 200 acres, the arboretum specializes in plants of the Colorado Plateau and maintains a collection of over 700 native and apt plants appropriate for survival in this high-elevation, arid region. The arboretum is a horticultural resource for area residents with gardening and landscaping questions. For visitors, the attractions are the herb garden, where a tour guide will encourage you to pinch a leaf of this or that; the Butterfly

North Central Arizona

Garden, which is laid out in the shape of a butterfly and, when blooming, attracts over a dozen species throughout the summer (the view of Humphrey's Peak from the garden is the best in Flagstaff); and the nature trail, a one-and-a-half-mile stroll on a cinder path through ponderosa pine and mountain meadows. Guided tours, bird walks and other programs are offered. Closed December 24 through March 14. Admission. ~ South of Old Route 66 on Woody Mountain Road, Flagstaff; 520-774-1442.

In the same vicinity, the **Arizona Historical Society–Pioneer Museum** presents a regular program of changing exhibits. Themes are drawn from the history of northern Arizona, including logging, livestock raising and social life. Highlights are a stuffed bear, Percival Lowell's 1912 mechanical computer and early-day photos of the Grand Canyon. The museum is housed in the historic Coconino County Hospital, also known as the "poor farm." Closed Sunday. ~ 2340 North Fort Valley Road, Flagstaff; 520-774-6272.

The **Museum of Northern Arizona**, which is known worldwide for its exhibits about the Colorado Plateau, is just three miles north of downtown, on Route 180 (Fort Valley Road), and is one of the best museums in the Southwest. The permanent anthropology exhibit, "Native Peoples of the Colorado Plateau," documents 12,000 years of human occupation in the region. This exhibit in the archaeology gallery charts the history and characteristics (such as foodstuffs) of the plateau's human inhabitants since prehistoric times. A life-size, skeletal model of *Diloposaurus*, a carnivorous dinosaur once found in northern Arizona, dominates the geology gallery. In the Branigar/Chase Discovery Center, an exhibit of fine arts, part of the museum's five-million-plus collection of objects, now has a regular home. A reception room in this wing has been furnished with Mission-style furniture and a fireplace and is a cozy, comfortable spot to relax. Outside the museum is a half-mile nature trail, which follows along a canyon

▶ ◀ **CHECK THESE OUT—UNIQUE SIGHTS**

- Stargaze through one of the **Lowell Observatory** telescopes when you visit Flagstaff during the summer. *page 116*
- Look in awe at the 800-year-old cliff dwellings built by the Sinagua and now protected in the **Montezuma Castle National Monument.** *page 127*
- Take time to stroll the streets of historic **Jerome** (population 500), a ghost town that was once a thriving silver-mining district. *page 139*
- Visit **Arcosanti**, the meeting place of architecture and ecology that will be home to 5000 people some day. *page 143*

rim and creek. The gift shop has an excellent collection of American Indian artworks. Admission. ~ 3101 North Fort Valley Road, Flagstaff; 520-774-5213.

From Memorial Day through mid-October, the Agassiz chair lift at **Arizona Snowbowl** in Flagstaff operates a scenic **skyride**, taking visitors to an elevation of 11,500 feet. The panoramic views at the top of Agassiz Peak extend some 70 miles. Dress warmly. There is no hiking access from the top of the chair lift. The lift operates every day between Memorial Day and Labor Day, then on Friday, Saturday and Sunday only until mid-October. Admission. ~ Off Route 180 on Snowbowl Road, Flagstaff; 520-779-1951, 520-526-0866.

Not far beyond the Museum of Arizona on Route 180 is the turnoff for **Schultz Pass Road**. The unpaved road is rough and dusty, but as a drive it offers glimpses of the spectacular San Francisco Peaks, which tower above Flagstaff. About 14 miles long, the road comes out on Route 89 a short distance south of the turnoff to Sunset Crater National Monument.

◄ *HIDDEN*

North of Flagstaff, off Route 89, are Wupataki National Monument and Sunset Crater Volcano National Monument. A paved 36-mile loop road connects both monuments and links up with Route 89 at both ends.

Sunset Crater Volcano National Monument, a bright-colored 1000-foot-tall volcanic cone in the San Francisco Volcano Field, is of recent (in geologic time) origin. It first erupted in the winter of 1064–65 and kept spraying out molten rock and ash until about 1200. A one-mile self-guided nature trail, which starts one and a half miles away from the visitors center, leads through cinder and lava fields. The ice cave along the trail has been closed because of unstable conditions since a 1984 cave-in. Hiking is no longer permitted on the slopes of Sunset Crater, either, since footprints create streaks and erosion visible from a great distance and mar the beauty of the perfect cone, but several other volcanic craters in the national forest are open to hikers and off-road vehicles. Admission. ~ Forest Service Road 545; 520-526-0502.

North of Sunset Crater, **Wupatki National Monument** preserves numerous pueblo ruins on the fringes of the volcano field. These settlements were inhabited in the 12th and 13th centuries, at the same time the volcanic activity was at its peak. Repeatedly, fiery eruptions would drive the Sinagua Indians out of the area and volcanic ash would fertilize the land and lure them back. As a result, Wupatki's communities were small, architecturally dissimilar, often designed for defense as different groups competed for use of the rich farmland. Park at the visitors center and then take the self-guided walk around the Wupatki Pueblo, a remarkably intact 700-year-old structure made of native materials, such as sandstone and clay-based mortars, that were suitable for free-standing masonry dwellings. Admission. ~ Forest Service Road 545; 520-679-2365.

Sinagua Indians (the name is Spanish for "without water," referring to their farming methods) lived from the Grand Canyon southward throughout central Arizona and are thought to be the ancestors of the Hopi people. One of the most interesting Sinagua sites is at **Walnut Canyon National Monument.** Here, the Sinaguas built more than 300 cliff dwellings in the walls of a 400-foot-deep gorge. A paved trail takes visitors around an "island in the sky" for a close-up look at the largest concentration of cliff dwellings, while a second trail follows the rim of this beautiful canyon. Admission. ~ Take Exit 204 from Route 40 just east of Flagstaff; 520-526-3367.

The Apollo astronauts trained at Meteor Crater before their moon landings in the late 1960s.

Another fascinating bit of north central Arizona's flamboyant geology is **Meteor Crater.** A shooting star 80 feet in diameter and traveling 133,000 miles per hour struck the earth here 49,000 years ago. The impact blasted a crater 570 feet deep and a mile across. All life within a 100-mile radius was destroyed. A century ago geologist Daniel Barringer theorized that this was a meteor impact crater. Experts scoffed at the idea, especially since volcanic craters, so common east of Flagstaff, suggested a rational explanation for the phenomenon. He staked a mining claim to search for the huge, valuable mass of iron and nickel which, he was convinced, lay buried beneath the crater. An ambitious drilling operation did not strike a mother lode from outer space but did come up with fragments proving the theory and the geologist's family has been operating the claim as a tourist attraction ever since. The visit is worth the fairly steep admission fee if you take time to go on a guided tour along the main trail. Admission. ~ About 30 miles east of Flagstaff, five miles off Route 40 at Exit 233; 520-289-2362.

LODGING   For a directory of bed and breakfasts throughout Arizona, call or write to the **Arizona Association of Bed & Breakfast Inns.** ~ P.O. Box 36656, Tucson, AZ 85740; 800-284-2589.

Flagstaff offers a good selection of bed-and-breakfast accommodations. The large, rather elegant modern **Radisson Woodlands Hotel** has spacious and modern rooms, with pastel color schemes and king-size beds. Facilities for guests include indoor and outdoor whirlpool spas, a steam room, sauna, fitness center and heated swimming pool. Room service, valet service and complimentary shuttle service are also among the hotel's amenities. ~ 1175 West Route 66, Flagstaff; 520-773-8888, 800-528-1234, fax 520-773-0597; www.radisson.com. DELUXE.

Among the antique-furnished vintage lodgings available in the downtown area is **The Inn at Four Ten**, a 1907 home extensively restored and remodeled in 1996. The nine guest suites are individually decorated in various themes including Victorian, Santa Fe and cowboy. Most have fireplaces. ~ 410 North Leroux Street, Flagstaff; 520-774-0088, 800-774-2008, fax 520-774-6354. DELUXE.

Another bed and breakfast located in the historic district is the homelike **Birch Tree Inn**. It has five rooms (three with private baths), air conditioning and a whirlpool spa. ~ 824 West Birch Avenue, Flagstaff; 520-774-1042, 888-774-1042, fax 520-774-8462. BUDGET TO MODERATE.

There is also the **Dierker House**, where two of the three guest rooms have king-size beds (the other has a queen). All have down comforters and share a common sitting room and bath. Two-night minimum on weekends. ~ 423 West Cherry Street, Flagstaff; phone/fax 520-774-3249. BUDGET.

Downtown, the **Hotel Monte Vista**, a 1927 hotel listed on the National Register of Historic Places, has spacious rooms that feature oak furniture, brass beds, velvet wall coverings and gold-tone bathroom fittings—a touch of old-time elegance. During the hotel's glory days, movie stars used to stay here and some rooms bear plaques naming the most famous person who ever slept in them: Humphrey Bogart, Cornell Wilde and Walter Brennan, to name a few. ~ 100 North San Francisco Street, Flagstaff; 520-779-6971, 800-545-3068, fax 520-779-2904; www.hotelmontevista.com. BUDGET.

Flagstaff has three youth hostels. Especially in the summer months, all three of these affordable accommodations host backpack travelers of all ages from all parts of the world, and solitary travelers are sure to make instant friends. Theodore Roosevelt and William Randolph Hearst once slept at the **Hotel Weatherford**, now refurbished to show off original fireplaces and turn-of-the-century style. See if the door Wyatt Earp shot through still stands in the ballroom, which features an antique bar and stained-glass windows. Dorm-style and private rooms are available at this hostel/hotel in a historic building downtown. ~ 23 North Leroux Street, Flagstaff; 520-774-2731, fax 520-773-8951; www.weatherfordhotel.com. BUDGET.

You can also try the **Grand Canyon Downtowner Independent Youth Hostel**, which has private and dormitory accommodations. The hostel offers free pick-up service from both the Amtrak and Greyhound stations. ~ 19 South San Francisco Street, Flagstaff; 520-779-9421, fax 520-774-6047; www.grandcanyonhostel.com. BUDGET.

Also with private and four-person dormitory rooms is the third hostel, **Du Beau International Hostel**. Tours of the Grand Canyon are offered daily in the summer and less frequently during the rest of the year. Rates include a continental breakfast. ~ 19 West Phoenix Avenue, Flagstaff; 520-774-6731, 800-398-7112, fax 520-774-4060; www.dubeau.net. BUDGET.

If you get your kicks on Route 66, there are still wigwam motels to pull into for a night's stay. There are no wigwams or other relics of kitsch at **Five Flags Inn**, a rather large motel that's horseshoed around a wide lawn where there's a small playground for the kids. Most of the rooms, which are large, clean and cheerful, face the lawn and are far enough off the highway to afford a peaceful night's sleep (rooms 149, 150 and 230 are the ones to avoid). Besides that, many of the bathrooms have windows. ~ 2610 East Route 66, Flagstaff; 520-526-1399, 800-535-2466, fax 520-527-8626. BUDGET.

The **Marriott Residence Inn** offers beautifully maintained apartment-like accommodations near the Flagstaff Mall. Granted, there's a generic "this could be anywhere" feel to the setup, but the privacy, fireplaces, fully equipped kitchens and pool make up for any lack of local character. "Extras," like grocery-shopping service, complimentary newspapers and complimentary continental breakfast, also make life a bit easier. If you've been traveling for several days, you'll appreciate the laundry facilities. ~ 3440 North Country Club Road, off Route 40, Flagstaff; 520-526-5555, 800-331-3131, fax 520-527-0328; www.marriott.com. DELUXE TO ULTRA-DELUXE.

In the pines just five minutes south of town, the **Arizona Mountain Inn** offers bed-and-breakfast rooms in the main inn (rates include a continental breakfast) and one- to five-bedroom cottages with fireplaces and cooking facilities. Amenities include volleyball, horseshoe and basketball areas as well as hiking and cross-country skiing trails. ~ 4200 Lake Mary Road, Flagstaff; 520-774-8959, 800-239-5236, fax 520-774-8837. MODERATE.

DINING

In the mood for a romantic dinner? Try the **Woodlands Café**. There's booth and table seating at this spacious yet intimate dining room with atrium windows and forest views. White walls are decorated with photographs of local scenery; the chandelier is crafted from deer racks. You can select from such entrées as firecracker shrimp, lobster stuffed chicken breast and salmon florentine. Reservations recommended. **Sakura**, a popular Japanese restaurant, shares the premises and has the same address and phone number. ~ 1175 West Route 66, Flagstaff; 520-773-9118. MODERATE TO DELUXE.

For fine dining, one good bet is the small, homey-feeling **Cottage Place Restaurant**. Specialties include châteaubriand and duet of duckling with raspberry demiglaze, as well as *vermicelli e* *pomodori.* Reservations recommended. Dinner only. Closed Monday. ~ 126 West Cottage Avenue, Flagstaff; 520-774-8431. MODERATE TO DELUXE.

One contemporary restaurant in Flagstaff's downtown area emphasizes creative Southwestern dining. Stop in at **Charly's Pub and Grill** on the ground floor of the Hotel Weatherford. Lunch, dinner and weekend brunch are served. ~ 23 North Leroux Street, Flagstaff; 520-779-1919. BUDGET TO MODERATE.

Just down the block from Chez Marc Bistro is **Tea & Sympathy**, a cozy, three-room cottage serving tea and scones, small sandwiches, pâté, fruit and desserts. You can also buy packaged teas and small gifts. ~ 409 North Humphreys Street, Flagstaff; 520-779-2171. BUDGET TO MODERATE.

Yet another of Flagstaff's finest dining establishments is **Chez Marc Bistro**, a small, intimate restaurant in a house listed on the National Register of Historic Places. The menu is decidedly French, with some modern touches. A typical dinner might consist of duck pâté, baby greens with dijon vinaigrette and warm goat cheese, sea scallops on spinach fettuccine, and berry crème brûlée. No lunch Sunday through Wednesday. ~ 503 North Humphreys Street, Flagstaff; 520-774-1343. DELUXE TO ULTRA-DELUXE.

Or you can try **Café Espress**, which specializes in vegetarian, poultry and fish selections. Changing exhibits by local artists adorn the walls. ~ 16 North San Francisco Street, Flagstaff; 520-774-0541. BUDGET TO MODERATE.

Down Under New Zealand Restaurant is located in an old carriage house near the downtown historical center. It's a small, cozy spot that's popular with local theater and arts organizers for lunch and dinner. Lamb, of course, is the specialty; and it's prepared in several ways: grilled rack, kabobs, stews and casseroles. The vegetarian samosas, frittata, spinach turnover and quiche are nicely done too. ~ Carriage House Antique Mall, 413 North San Francisco Street, Flagstaff; 520-774-6677. MODERATE TO DELUXE.

The **Main Street Catering**, located directly behind the Flagstaff   ◄ HIDDEN
Brewing Company, is a favorite among locals. Dishes include Philly cheesesteaks, fresh soups, stuffed sandwiches on homemade bread, barbecued ribs and daily specials. ~ 16 East Route 66, Suite 103, Flagstaff; 520-774-1519. BUDGET TO MODERATE.

A bit of Old West burlesque lives on at **Black Bart's Steak House, Saloon, and Musical Revue**, just east of downtown off Interstate 40, where local college students not only serve your steak, prime rib or chicken but also entertain you with show songs and a bit of choreography. Children (and the young at heart) should enjoy the lively proceedings as well as the Old West decor. ~ 2760 East Butler Avenue, Flagstaff; 520-779-3142. MODERATE TO DELUXE.

HIDDEN ▶ For an unusual dining environment, head out of town to the **Mormon Lake Lodge Steak House & Saloon**, which has been in operation since 1924 and is reputed to be one of the West's finest steak houses. The restaurant also features ribs, chicken and trout, all cooked over a bed of mountain oak embers. The authentic brands from ranches all across Arizona that have been seared into the wood paneling of the restaurant's walls are said to be the result of one of the wildest branding parties ever. ~ Located 25 miles southeast of Flagstaff on Mormon Lake Road, Mormon Lake Village; 520-354-2227. MODERATE TO ULTRA-DELUXE.

SHOPPING Flagstaff has quite a few regional arts-and-crafts shops, most of them featuring traditional and contemporary Navajo and Hopi work. One of the largest is **Four Winds Traders**. Closed Sunday and Monday. ~ 118 West Route 66, Flagstaff; 520-774-1067.

Wander around the downtown area and you will inevitably find a number of "trading posts." East of downtown is **Jay's Indian Arts**. In operation since 1953, the store sells rugs, jewelry, pottery, kachinas and the like direct from artists on the Navajo, Hopi, Tohono O'odham, Apache and Pueblo reservations. ~ 2227 East 7th Avenue, Flagstaff; 520-526-2439.

The **Museum of Northern Arizona**'s gift shop is the best place in town to buy authentic Native works. You'll find an excellent collection of American Indian kachina dolls, rugs, sandpaintings, as well as other arts and crafts. ~ 3101 North Fort Valley Road, Flagstaff; 520-774-5213.

The **Art Barn**, located in Fort Valley Historical Park, offers works of local and reservation artists for sale, emphasizing Navajo and Hopi art. A nonprofit, member-supported organization, the Art Barn provides artist facilities including exhibition space, a bronze foundry and sometimes classes. ~ 2330 North Fort Valley Road, Flagstaff; 520-774-0822.

NIGHTLIFE Because of the university, Flagstaff boasts both a busy cultural events calendar and a lively nightclub scene. On the cultural side, the performing arts roster includes the **Flagstaff Symphony Orchestra**. ~ 520-774-5107. Classical fans may also want to attend a performance of the **Master Chorale of Flagstaff**. ~ 520-779-9987. The **Flagstaff Oratorio Chorus** holds performances in Flagstaff as well. ~ 520-523-1856. Also found in town is the NAU **Choir Office**. ~ 520-523-2642. Some are held at the **Northern Arizona University School of Performing Arts**. ~ Corner of Riordan Road and Knoles Drive; 520-523-3731.

The **Theatrikos Community Theatre Group** performs at the Flagstaff Playhouse. ~ 11 West Cherry Street, Flagstaff; 520-774-1662.

For current performance information, inquire at the Flagstaff Visitors Center or tune to the university's National Public Radio station, KNAU, at 88.7 on your FM dial. ~ Visitors center: 1 East Route 66, Flagstaff; 520-774-9541.

Bluesman Tommy Dukes has been packing 'em in at Monday Blues Night at **Charly's** in the Hotel Weatherford for years. Dukes and his band perform between 9 and closing time. He occasionally appears other nights as well, so check the schedule. Tuesday is open-mike night; other jazz and blues performers fill out the week's schedule. Occasional cover. ~ 23 North Leroux Street, Flagstaff; 520-779-1919.

A college crowd likes the happy hour and big-screen TV at **Granny's Closet**, where a DJ spins mellow dance music on weeknights. Saturday is karaoke night. ~ 218 South Milton Road, Flagstaff; 520-774-8331.

A microbrewery located in a landmark building with exposed brick walls and Old West antiques, the **Flagstaff Brewing Company** serves a changing selection of house-brewed beers, ranging from pale ales to stout, on tap every night. Live acoustic, blues and bluegrass music is featured on weekend nights. ~ 16 East Route 66, Flagstaff; 520-773-1442.

Prefer your music performed live? Head over to **Monsoons**, where you can enjoy world beat, R&B, classical, jazz and other styles several nights a week. Occasional cover. ~ 22 East Route 66, Flagstaff; 520-774-7929.

"Take me to the Zoo." That's what locals say when they want to go to **The Museum Club**, one of the West's best examples of a cowboy roadhouse. Oftentimes rowdy, but always fun, the Zoo began as a trading post and taxidermy shop in 1931. It has operated as a nightclub since 1936, and is now listed on the National Register of Historic Places. The huge log cabin–style building is decorated with an ornate 1880 mahogany bar and an astonishing number of big-game trophies mounted on the walls. The dancefloor was built around five ponderosa pine tree trunks. A forked trunk forms the entryway into the club. Legendary country artists who have performed here include Willie Nelson, Bob Wills and the Texas Playboys, Commander Cody and the Lost Planet Airmen. The owners have arranged with a local cab company to provide free taxi service from the club. ~ 3404 East Route 66, Flagstaff; 520-526-9434.

LAKE MARY 🏃 🚵 ⚓ 🚤 ⛵ 🦆 🛶 🛥️ 🐟 ⛏️ Actually two long reservoirs, Upper and Lower Lake Mary provide the primary water supply for Flagstaff. They were created by damming Walnut Creek, which explains why there is no longer any water flowing through Walnut Canyon National Monument. The National For-

PARKS

est Service operates picnic areas on the wooded lakeshore and the small Lakeview Campground overlooks the upper lake. Both lakes are popular places to fish for northern pike, walleye pike and catfish. The upper lake is also used for powerboating and water-skiing. ~ Located eight miles south of Flagstaff on Lake Mary Road. From Route 40, take Exit 195-B and follow the signs; 520-774-1182.

▲ Lakeview Campground has 30 sites; $8 per night. Pinegrove Campground has 46 sites; $10 per night. Campgrounds are closed from mid-October to May.

MORMON LAKE 🏃 🚲 🐎 🛶 ⛵ 🚣 🛥️ 🛶 The largest natural lake in Arizona, covering over 2000 acres when full, is very shallow, averaging only ten feet in depth and can shrink to practically nothing during spells of dry weather. Several hiking trails run along the lakeshore and into the surrounding forest. Nature trail, lodge, restaurant, groceries, winter sports. ~ It's 26 miles southeast of Flagstaff via Lake Mary Road. For information, contact the forest service at 520-774-1182.

▲ There are 27 sites at Dairy Springs and 16 sites at Double Springs; $8 per night. Campgrounds are closed mid-September to Memorial Day.

▼▼▼▼▼▼▼▼▼
Sedona Area

Sedona. The creative and the mystical have always been intrigued by the place. Indians once came here to worship, New Agers to feel the "vibrations," artists to capture the beauty. But no matter the number of its devotees, no one knows exactly why this place has such appeal. Its essence remains elusive. Perhaps part of the seduction is the colors—red rock mountains that rise from the earth to nestle in brilliant blue sky. The landscape is a dreamy mix of fancifully shaped hoodoos, buttes and spires rising above green piñon and juniper trees, low shrubs and stark patches of reddish rock. Adjacent to Sedona is the spectacular Oak Creek Canyon, named after the creek that formed it by carving into the southern edge of the Colorado Plateau. All of these natural elements are highlighted by an intense sunlight that brings out contrast and color.

Sedona is located about halfway between Phoenix and the Grand Canyon. The first to discover this special spot were the Sinaguas. About 800 years ago, the Southern Sinagua tribe settled here, leaving behind a 600-room cliff dwelling ruin called Honaki, which is now on the National Register of Historic Places.

More settlers came at the turn of the century. At the time, the economic base of the economy was ranching and farming, and apple orchards dotted the area. Writer Zane Grey was also charmed by the area, drawing attention to it in the book *Call of the Canyon* in the 1920s and publicizing it even more in the film version, which was shot on location.

With all this attention, it was only a matter of time before tourism became the main attraction. Today about four million people visit the town annually to shop at the numerous art galleries, to nurture their spirits, and to relax amidst a red-rock fantasy.

SIGHTS

Oak Creek Canyon is the most accessible of several magnificent canyons that plunge from the high forests of northern Arizona down toward the low deserts of southern Arizona. A major highway—Route 89A from Flagstaff—runs the length of Oak Creek Canyon, making for a wonderful, though often crowded, scenic drive. After a long, thrilling descent from Flagstaff to the bottom of the canyon, where the creek banks are lined with lush riparian vegetation, the highway passes a number of picnicking, camping and fishing areas.

Midway down the canyon is one of Arizona's most popular state parks, **Slide Rock State Park** (see "Parks" below). At the lower end of the canyon, travelers emerge into the spectacular Red Rock Country, the labyrinth of sandstone buttes and mesas and verdant side canyons surrounding Sedona.

> Sedona is named after the wife of the town's first postmaster, Sedona Schnebly.

Sedona is a town for shopping, for sports, for luxuriating in spectacular surroundings. It is not the kind of place where you will find tourist attractions in the usual sense. A good place to get your bearings, pick up brochures and have your questions answered is the visitors center at the **Sedona-Oak Creek Chamber of Commerce**. ~ Corner of Forest Road at Route 89A, just above the Y; 520-282-7722.

Other than Oak Creek Canyon, Sedona's most popular tourist spots are spiritual in nature. The **Chapel of the Holy Cross**, south of town is a Catholic "sculpture church" built between two towering red sandstone rock formations. A long spiral ramp leads up to the chapel. It is open to visitors daily from 9 a.m. to 5 p.m. Parking is very limited. ~ Chapel Road off Route 179, Sedona; 520-282-4069.

The **Shrine of the Red Rocks**, on Table Top Mesa two miles off Route 89A on Airport Road, features a large wooden cross and a great view of the Red Rock Country.

And then there are Sedona's "**Vortexes.**" The Vortex idea was "channeled" through members of the town's highly visible New Age community several years ago and keeps evolving. For more information, see "Capture the Energy" in this chapter.

A half-hour's drive south of Sedona via Route 179 and Route 17, **Montezuma Castle National Monument** protects 800-year-old cliff dwellings built by the Sinagua people, ancestors of the Hopi. The ruins got their name from early explorers' mistaken belief that Aztecs fled here and built the structures after the Spanish conquest of Mexico. Though there is no truth to the old theory, archaeologists now know that several centuries before the Spanish arrived, Toltec traders used to visit the Southwest, bringing with them architectural methods from central Mexico. The main "castle" is a five-story, 20-room residential structure set high on the cliff. Although visitors cannot climb up to the ruin, the view from the nature trail below will tingle the imagination. The visitors center displays artifacts of the Sinagua and Hohokam cultures. Admission. ~ 2800 Montezuma Castle Highway, Camp Verde; 520-567-3322.

South of Montezuma's Castle via Route 17, in the small town of Camp Verde, portions of an old cavalry fort from the Apache Wars in the 1870s and early 1880s are preserved as **Fort Verde State Historic Park**. Visitors can walk through the former surgeons' and officers' quarters, and there is a museum of Arizona military history. The fort formed the start of the **General Crook Trail**, the major patrol and supply route during the Apache Wars, which followed the Mogollon Rim west for more than 100 miles to Fort Apache. Today the trail is used for hiking and horseback riding. Admission. ~ 125 Hollamon Street, Camp Verde; 520-567-3275.

Near the little town of Cottonwood, en route from Sedona to Prescott, is **Tuzigoot National Monument**, an uncharacteristically large Sinagua Indian pueblo ruin. Once home to about 225 people, the fieldstone pueblo stood two stories high and had 110 rooms. Today its white walls still stand on the hilltop and command an expansive view of the valley. Although the vista is marred by slag fields from a refinery that used to process Jerome's copper ore, the museum at the national monument offers a good look at the prehistoric culture of the Sinagua people. Admission. ~ Off of Route 89A between Cottonwood and Clarkdale; 520-634-5564.

One of the most beautiful canyons in the area is remote and rugged **Sycamore Canyon**, which parallels Oak Creek Canyon. Sycamore Canyon is a designated wilderness area, meaning that no wheeled or motorized vehicles are allowed. The Parsons Trail takes you up the wild, lushly wooded canyon bottom, along Sycamore Creek, for most of its four-mile length, passing several small cliff dwellings resting high above. Camping is not permitted in the lower part of Sycamore Canyon. For additional information, call the Sedona Rangers Station. ~ Turn off at Tuzigoot National Monument and follow the rough and rarely maintained dirt road for about 12 miles to the trailhead at the end of the road; 520-282-4119.

For Sedona visitors who wish to explore the surrounding Red Rock Country, there are numerous companies offering jeep tours. They'll usually pick you up at any Sedona lodging. For more information see "Jeep Tours" in Outdoor Adventures.

Capture
the Energy

For years, Sedona has received attention as a place with an unusual energy. Long considered sacred ground by American Indian tribes, the Sedona area has become a haven for New Age followers who are drawn to unique energy points termed "Vortexes."

There are various theories underlying the Vortexes' existence. Some say they are focal points in the earth's "natural energy grid," places where energy, both negative and positive, enter and leave the earth. Others explain the phenomena as electric and magnetic forces or yin/yang energy.

While it's believed there are many such places in the world, this area has become well known within the New Age community. It is commonly claimed that psychic powers, emotions and talents are stronger here, and people say it's a place where you are forced to face yourself—for better or worse. Indeed, some people move to the area expecting to enjoy the heightened energy and, finding Sedona too intense a place, move on.

Before either accepting the Vortexes as real or dismissing them, why not go there yourself and see whether you can feel the power that draws thousands of people to Sedona every year. It is as good an excuse as any to explore deeper into this stunning Red Rock Country.

While some local visionaries claim to have identified as many as 13 Vortexes, only four are generally recognized. The **Airport Mesa Vortex** is a little more than a mile south of Route 89A on Airport Road. (There's also a great spot to watch the sunset on the way up. Just as Airport Road sharply ascends to the right, look for a pullout on the left where you can park. Climb up the west-facing rocks for a spectacular vantage point.) The **Boynton Canyon Vortex**, one of the area's most popular hiking areas, is several miles north of West Sedona via Dry Creek Road and Boynton Pass Road (for more information see "Hiking" at the end of the chapter).

The **Cathedral Rock Vortex** is by a lovely picnic area alongside Oak Creek, reached from Route 89A in West Sedona via Red Rock Loop Road and Chavez Ranch Road; the rock itself is one of the most photographed places in the area. The **Bell Rock Vortex**, a popular spot for UFO watchers, is just off Route 179 south of Sedona near the Village of Oak Creek. Each vortex reportedly has a radius of ten miles, so you don't need to be standing on one particular spot to feel the force.

See "Jeep Tours" for information on companies that offer tours to Sedona's vortexes.

LODGING   As you drive down Oak Creek Canyon from Flagstaff to Sedona, you will notice several privately owned lodges and cabin complexes in the midst of this spectacular national forest area. You can reserve accommodations at these places and enjoy the canyon in the cool of the evening and early morning, avoiding the midday throngs and traffic of peak season and weekends. Several places are located near Slide Rock State Park.

Top of the line, **Junipine Resort** offers modern suites and one- and two-bedroom "creekhouses." These individually decorated one- and two-story units are all crafted from wood and stone. Offering mountain, forest or creek views, each 1300 to 1500 square foot unit comes with a kitchen and redwood deck overlooking the canyon. ~ 8351 North Route 89A, Sedona; 520-282-3375, 800-742-7463, fax 520-282-7402; e-mail chrisb@sedona.net. DELUXE TO ULTRA-DELUXE.

Canyon Wren Cabins consists of one old-fashioned log cabin and three chalets with loft bedrooms, kitchens, fireplaces, whirlpool bathtubs and patios, all within walking distance of swimming holes, fishing spots and hiking trails. Rates include continental breakfast. No phones, no smoking indoors or out. ~ 6425 North Route 89A, Sedona; 520-282-6900, 800-437-9736, fax 520-282-6978; www.canyonwrencabins.com. DELUXE.

In the same part of the canyon, there are more simple accommodations at **Don Hoel's Cabins**. Cabins are being remodeled one at a time, and the ones that have been fixed up cost more. Closed January and February. ~ Route 89A, Oak Creek Canyon; 520-282-3560, 800-292-4635, fax 520-282-3654; www.sedona.net/resorts/hoel. MODERATE TO DELUXE.

Houses, all with fireplaces and fully equipped kitchens, are available at **Forest Houses**. Closed January through early March. ~ Route 89A, Oak Creek Canyon; 520-282-2999. MODERATE TO DELUXE.

Farther down canyon, **Oak Creek Terrace** offers resort accommodations ranging from motel-style rooms with king-size beds, color TV and fireplaces to one- and two-bedroom suites with jacuzzis. ~ Route 89A, Oak Creek Canyon; 520-282-3562, 800-224-2229, fax 520-282-6061; www.sedona.net/resort/oct. MODERATE TO DELUXE.

Charming, affordable lodging in Sedona can be found at the **Rose Tree Inn**, which strives for an "English garden environment" and has patios and a jacuzzi. There are five rooms, four with kitchens and two with fireplaces. All have king-size beds. This small inn is close to uptown. ~ 376 Cedar Street, Sedona; 520-282-2065, 888-282-2065, fax 520-282-0083. MODERATE TO DELUXE.

Near Uptown Sedona, the **Star Motel** offers standard rooms with telephones, cable TV and refrigerators, plus one deluxe-priced apartment unit with a fireplace. ~ 295 Jordan Road, Sedona; 520-282-3641. BUDGET.

A Touch of Sedona Bed and Breakfast, uphill from Uptown, offers panoramic views from five individually decorated theme rooms with corresponding motifs—the "Eagle," "Hummingbird," "Kachina," "Roadrunner" and "Wolf's Den." Close to hiking, shopping and restaurants. Full breakfast comes with the room. ~ 595 Jordan Road, Sedona; 520-282-6462, 800-600-6462, fax 520-282-1534; www.touchsedona.com. MODERATE TO DELUXE.

Sedona specializes in upscale resorts. A top-of-the-line Sedona lodging is **L'Auberge de Sedona**. Individually designed guest rooms and cottages are decorated with furnishings imported from Provence, France, in order to re-create the atmosphere of a French country inn on ten acres of creekside grounds within walking distance of uptown Sedona. ~ 301 L'Auberge Lane, Sedona; 520-282-1661, 800-272-6777, fax 520-282-1064; www.lauberge.com. DELUXE TO ULTRA-DELUXE.

Also among the poshest accommodations in town is **Los Abrigados**. Situated next to the atmospheric Tlaquepaque shopping area, Los Abrigados features fanciful Mexican-inspired modern architecture throughout and elegantly stylish suites with kitchens, fireplaces and patios or balconies. Guest facilities include tennis courts, swimming pool, weight room and spa. ~ 160 Portal Lane, Sedona; 520-282-1777, 800-521-3131, fax 520-282-2614; www.ilxinc.com. ULTRA-DELUXE.

Enchantment Resort, secluded five miles west of town in Boynton Canyon, sits in the shadow of magnificent red rocks. Over 60 adobe-style casitas, which convert from studio to two- and three-bedroom accommodations, are well appointed with Southwest-style furnishing, fireplaces, kitchenettes, skylights and private patios. Resort facilities include pools, spas and tennis courts, as well as massages, aromatherapy and other spa treatments. Continen-

✔ **CHECK THESE OUT—UNIQUE LODGING**

- *Budget:* Retire to the room Humphrey Bogart slept in at **Hotel Monte Vista,** once a popular place among movie stars. *page 121*
- *Moderate:* Gallup your way to the **Greyfire Farm,** where people *and* horses are welcome to stay overnight. *page 133*
- *Deluxe:* Warm yourself in front of the fireplace of your cozy chalet at **Canyon Wren Cabins** after a day's fishing. *page 130*
- *Ultra-deluxe:* Treat yourself to the luxury of **Los Abrigados,** a lavish Sedona resort with stylish suites and endless amenities. *page 131*

Budget: under $70   Moderate: $70–$110   Deluxe: $110–$180   Ultra-deluxe: over $180

tal and regional Southwest dishes are served in the restaurant. ~ 525 Boynton Canyon Road, Boynton Canyon; 520-282-2900, 800-826-4180, fax 520-282-9249; www.arizonaguide.com/enchantment. ULTRA-DELUXE.

South of the Y, on Route 179, **Poco Diablo Resort** is built around a private nine-hole golf course. A major renovation of the property recently added 28 new deluxe executive rooms that are quite large (480 square feet) and luxurious with fireplaces, wet bar and refrigerators, whirlpool bathtubs and private patios that look out over the golf course to the red rocks beyond. ~ 1752 South Route 179, Sedona; 520-282-7333, 800-528-4275, fax 520-282-2090; www.pocodiablo.com. MODERATE TO ULTRA-DELUXE.

Surrounded by spruce, piñon and juniper trees is the aptly named **Apple Orchard Inn**, built on the site of the old Jordan Apple Farm. Despite its wooded location, this bed and breakfast is just a hop, skip and a jump away from Uptown. Luxuriate in seven, plush unique rooms, many sporting whirlpool tubs, fireplaces and patios. For added pampering, summon the on-call massage therapist for a session. In the morning, drink in majestic mountain views while enjoying breakfast in the cozy dining room. Reservations suggested. ~ 656 Jordan Road, Sedona; 520-282-5328, 800-663-6968, fax 520-204-0044; www.appleorchardbb.com. DELUXE TO ULTRA-DELUXE.

For basic motel rooms in Sedona, the **White House Inn** in West Sedona, located just before the Dry Creek Road turnoff, provides lodging with phone and cable television. ~ 2986 West Route 89A, Sedona; 520-282-6680. BUDGET.

HIDDEN ►

Visitors seeking to change their lives in Sedona might want to consider staying at the **Healing Center of Arizona**. Rates for accommodations in this dome complex are mid-range, and inexpensive gourmet vegetarian meals are served to groups only. Amenities, offered for reasonable fees, include a sauna and steambath and an indoor and outdoor spa. Holistic therapies available to

GETTING AROUND SEDONA

Sedona is divided into three areas: Uptown, the Y and West Sedona. Uptown is the stretch of Route 89A north of the junction with Route 179 from Phoenix. Many of the boutiques, galleries, tourist-oriented services like jeep tours are located Uptown. The junction of 89A and 179 is called the Y. "At the Y" and "below the Y" are commonly-used directionals. The shopping center Tlaquepaque, for example, is "below the Y." West Sedona is the portion of Route 89A west of the Y junction. Here's where you'll find supermarkets, gas stations, and banks.

guests at the center include massage, acupressure treatments, herbology, rebirthing, crystal healing, psychic channeling and more. ~ 25 Wilson Canyon Road, Sedona; phone/fax 520-282-7710; www.inlancom.com/center. BUDGET TO MODERATE.

A comfortable ranch-style home bordering a national forest, the **Cozy Cactus** is a bed-and-breakfast inn that has sitting areas with fireplaces and kitchens shared by each pair of rooms. All rooms are decorated with personal touches from the owners' collections of antique memorabilia; a particular favorite is the Nutcracker Room which is embellished by over 50 vintage nutcrackers and an 1890s high-back bed and dresser from Sweden. Some guest rooms have great views of Sedona's stunning red rock formations. Gay-friendly ~ 80 Canyon Circle Drive, Sedona; 520-284-0082, 800-788-2082, fax 520-284-4210. MODERATE TO DELUXE.

It may not be historic, but the sleek, contemporary **Canyon Villa** bed-and-breakfast inn has other charms. A cozy library. Eleven guest rooms with themes ranging from Victorian to Santa Fe–style. French doors leading to balconies. And, of course, views of the red rocks. ~ 125 Canyon Circle Drive, Sedona; 520-284-1226, 800-453-1166, fax 520-284-2114; www.canyonvilla.com. DELUXE TO ULTRA-DELUXE.

Another inn is **The Adobe Village and the Graham Inn**, where each individually decorated room has views of Sedona's famous red rocks. Features found in some of the seven guest rooms in the Graham Inn are king-sized beds, marble showers, private balconies, fireplaces and jacuzzis. Adobe Village's four casitas include waterfall showers and private decks. Additional amenities are the outdoor pool and hot tub. Breakfast is included. ~ 150 Canyon Circle Drive, Sedona; 520-284-1425, 800-228-1425, fax 520-284-0767; www.sedonasfinest.com. DELUXE TO ULTRA-DELUXE.

Greyfire Farm is one of the area's more unusual bed and breakfasts. Nestled among the pines in a rural canyon between the Red Rock Country and Wild Horse Mesa, near hiking and horseback riding trails in the national forest, the "farm" can accommodate two guest horses. It also provides bed and breakfast lodgings for two-footed guests that include bright rooms with quilts and private baths. ~ 1240 Jacks Canyon Road, Sedona; 520-284-2340, 800-579-2340, fax 520-284-1907; www.greyfire farm.com. MODERATE.

◀ HIDDEN

L'Auberge de Sedona has an outstanding French restaurant with a view on Oak Creek and memorable prix-fixe dinners. The six-course menu, which changes nightly, typically features pâté, soup, a small baby green salad and entrées such as poached salmon, grilled lamb, venison, quail or chicken. ~ 301 L'Auberge Lane, Sedona; 520-282-1661. ULTRA-DELUXE.

DINING

Another outstanding Continental restaurant is **Rene at Tlaque-paque**, which specializes in rack of lamb carved tableside and tableside flambé. The most elaborate French Provincial decor in the Southwest makes this restaurant extra special. Open-air patio dining is available. ~ Route 179 at Tlaquepaque, Sedona; 520-282-9225. DELUXE.

Italian cuisine is featured at the **Hideaway**, with tables on a balcony over the creek, surrounded by a stand of sycamore trees. ~ Route 179 near Route 89A, Sedona; 520-282-4204. MODERATE.

Amidst Aegean blue walls and artistic tablecloths topped with fresh flowers, diners enjoy Greek and Continental food at **Fournos Restaurant**. Watch the chef cook in the open kitchen, whipping up such specialties as flaming shrimp Santorini flambéed in *ouzo* and baked with feta cheese and Santorini sauce, or fish baked in a sauce of yogurt, steamed onions and olive oil. Closed Monday through Wednesday. Dinner only Thursday through Saturday. Sunday brunch. ~ 3000 West Route 89A, Sedona; 520-282-3331. MODERATE.

For health-conscious Thai food, made with all natural, organic ingredients, try **Thai Spices Natural**, a restaurant located in the White House Inn motel in West Sedona. Closed Sunday. ~ 2986 West Route 89A, Sedona; 520-282-0599. BUDGET TO MODERATE.

HIDDEN ▶ A choice of 101 omelettes is the main attraction at the **Coffee Pot Restaurant**, a local dining spot since the 1950s. Although the brass rails and sautillo tile floors add charm, the brown plastic booths give away the casual atmosphere. On the wall hangs artwork by White Bear, a former Hopi Indian chief who's now in his 80s. A nice touch is the outdoor patio. ~ 2050 West Route 89A, Sedona; 520-282-6626. BUDGET TO MODERATE.

Another good spot is the **Red Planet Diner**, offering everything from burgers and fries, Cajun and Italian fare to seafood and steaks in an entertaining "intergalactic" environment. Check out

◆◆◆

✔ CHECK THESE OUT—UNIQUE DINING

- *Budget:* Join the other folks who go back time and again to the **Dinner Bell Café** for the delicious home-style cooking. *page 145*
- *Moderate:* Sit back as the shrimp Santorini is served flaming from **Fournos Restaurant**'s open kitchen to your table. *page 134*
- *Deluxe to ultra-deluxe:* Savor the lamb and poultry served in the **House of Joy**, an elegant restaurant that was once a bordello. *page 140*
- *Ultra-deluxe:* Indulge in fine French dinners at **L'Auberge de Sedona**, where there's a gorgeous view of Oak Creek. *page 133*

Budget: under $8   Moderate: $8–$16   Deluxe: $16–$24   Ultra-deluxe: over $24

the spaceship fountain and sci-fi scenes. ~ 1655 West Route 89A, Sedona; 520-282-6070. BUDGET TO MODERATE.

To experience an eclectic synthesis of cuisines from all over the world, head for the **Heartline Cafe,** where you can enjoy dishes such as mesquite-roasted rack of lamb with garlic-scented mashed potatoes and pecan-crusted local trout with Dijon cream sauce. ~ 1610 West Route 89A, Sedona; 520-282-0785. MODERATE TO ULTRA-DELUXE.

More views and an elegant setting await diners at the **Yavapai Dining Room** at Enchantment Resort. Typical of the Southwest cuisine served here is the rack of Colorado lamb roasted with an herb and pistachio nut crust along with sage and sun-dried tomatoes. And don't miss the Sunday jazz champagne brunch. ~ 525 Boynton Canyon Road, Sedona; 520-282-2900. DELUXE TO ULTRA-DELUXE.

Contemporary furnishings adorn the long, narrow balcony where diners can enjoy seafood and steak at the **T. Carl's Restaurant** at the Poco Diablo Resort. The well-prepared cuisine has a Continental flair. ~ 1752 South Route 179, Sedona; 520-282-7333. MODERATE TO DELUXE.

Sedona's shopping district is one of the three or four best in Arizona. Many of the galleries, boutiques and specialty shops are labors of love, the personal creations of people who spent years past daydreaming about opening a cute little store in Sedona. The town has more than 60 art galleries, most of them specializing in traditional and contemporary American Indian art, "cowboy" art and landscape paintings. Quality is relatively high in this very competitive art market. You can easily spend a whole day shopping your way up and down the main street of town, leaving your feet sore and your credit cards limp.

SHOPPING

Uptown Sedona has an abundance of fine little galleries. One that's easily overlooked but worth checking out is the gallery at the **Sedona Arts Center.** The paintings, ceramics, art glass and jewelry of local artists are featured; quality is high and prices are reasonable. ~ Located at the north end of the Uptown commercial core on Route 89A at Art Barn Road, Sedona; 520-282-3809.

The most relaxing and enjoyable place in Sedona to browse is **Tlaquepaque,** a picturesque complex of two-story Mexican-style buildings that house specialty shops, galleries and restaurants below the Y on Route 179. Built with old-looking stone walls, courtyards, tile roofs and flowers in profusion, the Spanish Colonial–style Tlaquepaque looks more like Old Mexico than the real thing. **Aguajito del Sol** features cement and bronze animal sculptures, as well as watercolors, glass pieces and baskets. ~ 520-282-5258. **Mother Nature's Trading Company** carries educational toys and games in addition to rocks and minerals. ~ 520-282-5932.

Across the highway from Tlaquepaque is the **Crystal Castle**, one of the larger New Age stores in this town which, according to many, is the New Age capital of the known cosmos. It carries unusual books, incense, jewelry, runes, visionary art and, of course, crystals. In front of the store, a "networking" bulletin board lets you scan the array of alternative professional services in town—channelers, psychic surgeons, clairvoyants, kinesiologists, numerologists and many more. ~ 313 Route 179, Sedona; 520-282-5910.

There are many other stores in the same vein in Sedona, such as **Angels, Art & Crystals**. ~ 2445 West Route 89A; 520-282-7089. The **Golden Word Book Centre** offers New Age literature. ~ 3150 West Route 89A; 520-282-2688. Get your chakras aligned at **Crystal Magic**. ~ 2978 West Route 89A; 520-282-1622. Can't get enough? The **Center for the New Age** has Vortex information, networking for New Age activities, psychic readings daily and a "Psychic Faire" every Saturday. ~ 341 Route 179; 520-282-1949.

Garland's Navajo Rugs has one of the largest collections of Navajo rugs in the world with a selection of more than 5000. They hang on rafters, grouped according to subjects ranging from people to storm patterns. There are also about 500 kachina dolls in stock. ~ 411 Route 179, Sedona; 520-282-4070.

There are a variety of specialty shops and galleries at **Hozho** shopping center including the **Lanning Gallery** with contemporary artwork made by people from Arizona, Colorado, New Mexico and California, including ceramic American Indian folklore characters by Susan Wagoda-Bergquist. ~ 431 Route 179, Sedona; 520-282-6865.

The **Hillside** is a two-level center with about 25 shops, galleries and restaurants set amidst waterfalls and sculptures. **Agni-siuh** (520-282-5622), a sanskrit word meaning the Creative Fires of Mankind, carries works by local artists in a variety of mediums, as well as the Greg Rich/Gibson collection of art instruments—guitars and banjos, selling from $10,000 to $250,000, that are hand decorated with pearl, abalone, brass, copper and gold. **Exposures Gallery of the West** (520-204-1477) shows life-size and monumental bronze sculptures, as well as works in other mediums. The **Compass Rose Gallery** (520-282-7904) offers a fascinating collection of antique maps, hand-colored prints and historic photographs, many pertaining to the region. **The Clay Pigeon** (520-282-2862) specializes in hand-crafted Southwestern crafts such as the whimsical rabbit sculptures of Jeanne Stevens-Sollman and handmade musical instruments. ~ 671 Route 179, Sedona.

Shopping enthusiasts will also want to visit **Oak Creek Factory Outlet**, a mall located south of town. This is factory-direct outlet shopping with a difference. The factories represented include **Capezio** (520-284-1910), **Jones of New York** (520-284-1919),

Sedona's Sumptuous Spas

If Sedona's natural beauty or the energy of its vortexes isn't enough to heal what ails you, then a massage or spa visit might just be the thing. In Sedona, there's a staggering range of services to chose from, so first you'll have to decide if you want just a massage (and what kind of massage you want) or the full spa treatment (aerobics, sauna, aromatherapy, herbal body wrap, inhalation room and facial).

Here's a quick review of a few popular terms and techniques: **Aromatherapy** employs essential, aromatic oils from flowers, plants, fruits and other natural substances as sensory relaxants. **Shiatsu** is a 5000-year-old Japanese massage technique using focused pressure to balance the body's energy flow. Classic **Swedish massage** involves kneading and stroking aimed at increasing circulation. **Deep tissue massage** is a technique used to release built-up tension; **muscle sculpting** is a form of deep tissue massage characterized by firm but slow strokes. **Reflexology** is massage therapy of the hands and feet.

If you're staying at one of Sedona's resorts, you probably have access to at least a therapeutic massage that will incorporate a variety of techniques such as muscle sculpting and reflexology. Guests at **Poco Diablo Resort**, for example, can make an appointment for a half-hour (about $30) or one-hour (about $60) therapeutic massage conducted in the massage suite at the tennis clubhouse. ~1752 South Route 179; 520-282-7333 ext. 137.

For the works—massage, facials, steam and inhalation rooms, body wraps—you'll have to ante up a hefty fee for a stay at a resort like **Enchantment**, where room rates start at $295 a night. Everything else costs extra: massages range from around $80 for 50 minutes to over $100 for 80 minutes. Fees for body wraps start at around $90. ~ 525 Boynton Canyon Road; 520-282-2900.

The health spa at **Los Abrigados Resort** is open for day use for a fee of $20. The fee is waived, however, if you take a massage, body wrap or other spa treatment. Massages are about $40 for a half hour to about $110 for a 90-minute session. ~ 160 Portal Lane; 520-282-1777.

Set on the banks of Oak Creek, **Therapy on the Rocks** specializes in something called "myofascial release," which targets the body's connective tissue. Swedish and deep tissue massages are also offered, and you can opt to have the massage outside on the deck overlooking the creek. An hour-long massage costs about $75. ~ 676 North Route 89A; 520-282-3002.

Mikasa (520-284-9505), **Izod/Gant** (520-284-9844) and **Anne Klein** (520-284-0407)—designer goods at discount prices. ~ Route 179, Oak Creek.

NIGHTLIFE   Sedona has surprisingly little nightlife. One exception is the **Dahl and DiLuca**, where you can enjoy piano music on Friday, Saturday and Sunday evenings. This is a favorite gathering spot for locals who come here to relax, socialize and enjoy the tasty Italian specialties. ~ 2321 West Route 89A, Sedona; 520-282-5219.

Other than that, try the lounges in the major resort hotels (Poco Diablo has a small but popular sports bar, for example) or call the **Sedona Arts Center** for its current schedule of theatrical and concert performances. It features artwork by local and regional artists; in addition, plays and musical performances are also held here. ~ Route 89A at Art Barn Road, Sedona; 520-282-3809.

PARKS   **SLIDE ROCK STATE PARK** 🏃 🏊 Very popular with students from the Northern Arizona University, this swimming area midway between Flagstaff and Sedona in the heart of Oak Creek Canyon is almost always packed during warm-weather months. It is like a natural water park, with placid pools, fast-moving chutes and a wide, flat shoreline of red sandstone for sunbathing. The state park also includes the Pendley homestead, which is listed on the National Register of Historic Places, and acres of apple orchards. Visitors are not allowed to pick the apples, but cider made from them is sold at a stand on the trail to the swim area. When rangers are available they lead nature/historical walks on Saturdays. You'll find a picnic area, restrooms, a volleyball court, a nature trail and a snack bar. Day-use fee, $5. ~ Located seven miles north of Sedona via Route 89A in Oak Creek Canyon; 520-282-3034.

RED ROCK STATE PARK 🏃 🚴 ⛵ Beautiful Oak Creek runs through this 286-acre park situated in the heart of Red Rock Country. Naturalists offer guided walks daily along the six-mile trail system dotted with sycamore and cottonwood trees. One route leads to a 1948 house that resembles an Indian pueblo and, sitting atop a hill, affords great views of the area. The visitors center has natural history exhibits and videos. Fishing is allowed on Oak Creek, with catches including warm-water catfish and sunfish. There are picnic areas, restrooms and a visitors center. Day-use fee, $5. ~ Drive four miles southwest of Sedona on Route 89A, then turn south on Lower Red Rock Loop Road; the park appears in three miles; 520-282-6907.

DEAD HORSE RANCH STATE PARK 🏃 ⛵ This 325-acre park, located along the Verde River, has both desert and lush areas that can be enjoyed by walking the extensive hiking trails. Fishing is allowed in the Verde River and the four-acre lagoon, which is stocked with catfish and trout. There are picnic tables, restrooms and showers. Day-use fee, $4 per vehicle. ~ From Cottonwood, take Main Street to 10th Street, then go north for about a mile; 520-634-5283.

▲ There are 45 sites plus an overflow area for self-contained RVs; $10 per night for no hookups, $15 per night with hookups.

▼▼▼▼▼▼▼▼▼▼
Jerome

Jerome, located southwest of Sedona on Route 89A, is one of Arizona's most intriguing ghost towns. In the first decades of the 20th century it was a rich silver mining district and, with a population of 15,000, was the fifth-largest city in Arizona. After having been completely abandoned in the 1950s, it was resettled by hippies in the late 1960s and now is a thriving artists' colony with a population of about 500 people.

SIGHTS

The history of Jerome's mining era is brought to life in three museums. The old Douglas Mansion in **Jerome State Historic Park** at the lower end of town offers an informative 25-minute video called "Ghost Town of Jerome," a three-dimensional model of Jerome showing the underground shafts and tunnels and a mineral exhibit. Admission. ~ Douglas Road; 520-634-5381.

For a look at mining tools, old photos, and other exhibits about old-time copper mining enter the **Jerome Historical Society Mine Museum**. Admission. ~ Main Street; 520-634-5477.

The **Gold King Mine Museum** has a re-created assay office, a replica mine shaft and a petting zoo. Admission. ~ Perkinsville Road; 520-634-0053.

The real pleasure of Jerome lies in strolling the streets that switchback up Cleopatra Hill, browsing in the shops along the way and admiring the carefully preserved turn-of-the-century architecture. Many of the town's buildings were constructed of massive blocks of quarried stone to withstand the blasts that frequently shook the ground from the nearby mine. The entire town has been declared a National Historic Landmark.

A historic railroad that carries sightseers through some of Arizona's most spectacular country is the **Verde River Canyon Excursion Train**. Revived in November 1990, this train achieved instant popularity as a major tourist attraction. It takes passengers on a 40-mile round trip from Clarkdale, just below Jerome. The diesel-powered train winds along sheer cliffs of red limestone in curve after curve high above the Verde River, through a long, dark tunnel, over bridges, past gold mines and Indian Ruins, to the ghost town of Perkinsville and back. Admission. ~ 300 North Broadway Street, Clarkdale; 520-639-0010.

LODGING   One of the chief delights of visiting Jerome is the chance to stay in a historic landmark, a growing number of which are being converted to bed-and-breakfast inns. Some even claim to be haunted by their colorful past residents.

Built for the mining company's chief surgeon in 1917, the **Surgeon's House** is a stately blonde stucco, tile-roofed home with colorful terraced gardens facing the Verde Valley. Along with three spacious rooms and suites in the main house, there is a guest cottage decorated with vibrant Guatemalan textiles, stained-glass window hangings, terra-cotta tiles, an old-fashioned upright bathtub painted Chinese red and a secluded patio. Guests have access to the gardens. Complimentary beverages, snacks and a hearty breakfast are included. ~ P.O. Box 998, Jerome, AZ 86331; 520-639-1452, 800-639-1452; www.virtualcities.com. MODERATE TO DELUXE.

Hillside House is a charming and historic old home nestled on the slopes of Cleopatra Hill and surrounded by fruit orchards. The inn is a private home with just one accommodation: a two-room suite located downstairs with its own private entrance and access to a garden patio. In addition to the bedroom, the suite has a sitting area with a bunk bed, refrigerator and microwave. ~ P.O. Box 305, Jerome, AZ 86331; 520-634-5667. MODERATE.

An 1898 Victorian bed and breakfast, the **Ghost City Inn** features four rooms with shared baths and one room with a private bath. Visit the Old West in the "Satin and Spurs" room or float away in the "Champagne and Propane" room. There's also a jacuzzi to relax in. ~ 541 North Main Street; 520-634-4678, 888-634-4678. MODERATE.

DINING   In Jerome, the elegant place to dine is the **House of Joy**, a former house of ill repute whose past is recalled in the decor—red lights, red candles, red flowers, red placemats, red everything. The menu features veal, lamb and poultry. Seating is by reservation only—call at least a month in advance. Open for dinner on weekends only; for reservations call after 9 a.m. Saturday or Sunday. ~ 416 Hull Avenue; 520-634-5339. DELUXE TO ULTRA-DELUXE.

The walls at the **Jerome Grill** are decorated with picks, axes and scores of photographs outlining the town's mining heyday. Breakfast goodies include omelets, French toast and huevos rancheros. For lunch, fill up on burgers, sandwiches, meatloaf or chicken-fried steak. No dinner. ~ 309 Main Street; 520-634-5094. BUDGET.

For breakfast or lunch, try the **Flatiron Cafe**, serving pastries, vegetarian dishes and panini sandwiches along with gourmet coffees and teas in historic surroundings. ~ 416 Main Street; 520-634-2733. BUDGET.

Jerome Palace Haunted Burger is a meateater's delight, specializing in grilled steaks, chicken and ribs served in a cozy dining room with a fireplace and 90-mile views of the Verde Valley. Both indoor and outdoor seating are available. ~ 401 Clark Street; 520-634-0554. BUDGET TO MODERATE.

Many of Jerome's residents are arts-and-crafts people, and a stroll **SHOPPING** up and down the town's switchback main street will take you past quite a few intriguing shops that offer pottery, jewelry, handmade clothing, stained glass and other such wares.

Rattan couches with fluffy pillows beckon people inside the two-story **Designs on You** shop that sells natural fiber clothing, shoes and lingerie. ~ 233 Main Street; 520-634-7879.

You can watch jewelers create contemporary designs at **Aurum Jewelry**. About 40 local artists show their work here, which ranges from a sculptured iron spoon and fork to belt buckles, bolo ties, custom knives and jewelry. ~ 369 Main Street; 520-634-3330.

In the last few years, the heart of the working art movement in town has been centered at the **Old Mingus Art Center**, which is now filled with studios and galleries carrying everything from paintings to blown glass. The biggest is the **Anderson/Mandette Art Studios** One of the largest private art studios in the country, it feels more like a museum as you walk through it. One level contains working studios and an 11' x 17' canvas titled *Grand Canyon*. Upstairs, paintings hang by Robin Anderson and Margo Mandette. ~ Route 89A; 520-634-3438.

The Old West saloon tradition lives on in Jerome, where the **NIGHTLIFE** town's most popular club is the **Spirit Room** in the old Conner Hotel. There is live music on weekend afternoons and evenings and the atmosphere is as authentic as can be. Cover. ~ 166 Main Street at Jerome Avenue; 520-634-8809.

Continuing southwest on Route 89A, in the next valley, **Prescott** sits the city of Prescott, the original territorial capital of Arizona from 1864 to 1867. President Abraham Lincoln decided to declare it the capital because the only other community of any size in the Arizona Territory, Tucson, was full of Confederate sympathizers. Today, Prescott is a low-key, all-American city with a certain quiet charm and few concessions to tourism. Incidentally, Prescott is located at the exact geographic center of the state of Arizona.

Built in 1916, the **Yavapai County Courthouse** sits at the heart **SIGHTS** of Prescott, surrounded by a green plaza where locals pass the time playing cards and chatting, and tourists rest awhile on park benches. Surrounding the plaza are many of the town's shops, in addition to historic Whiskey Row, where at one time some 20 saloons were open day and night.

The major sightseeing highlight in Prescott is the **Sharlot Hall Museum**, which contains a large collection of antiques from Arizona's territorial period, including several fully furnished houses and an excellent collection of stagecoaches and carriages, as well as the history of the Prescott area in photographs. Sharlot Mabridth Hall was a well-known essayist, poet and traveler who explored the wild areas of the Arizona Territory around the turn of the century. Seeing that Arizona's historic and prehistoric artifacts were rapidly being taken from the state, Ms. Hall began a personal collection that grew quite large over the next three decades and became the nucleus of this large historical museum. The museum's collections are housed in several Territorial-era buildings brought from around the county, including a home that was built of ponderosa pine logs in 1864 and used as a governor's mansion until 1867. The complex occupies a large park in downtown Prescott. ~ 415 West Gurley Street; 520-445-3122.

Probably the most unusual of Prescott's museums is the **Bead Museum**, displaying a phenomenal collection of beads, jewelry and other adornments from around the world with explanations of their uses as trade goods, currency, religious items and status symbols. Visitors to this one-of-a-kind nonprofit museum discover that there's more to beads than they ever suspected. Closed Sunday. ~ 140 South Montezuma Street; 520-445-2431.

The **Smoki Museum** (pronounced Smoke-eye) houses a large collection of American Indian artifacts from throughout the Southwest. (The Smoki were a group of white people who formed an organization in 1921 to perform American Indian dances at pa-

SHARLOT HALL

One of the most admired women in Arizona history was Sharlot Mabridth Hall, who arrived in Prescott in 1882. She helped manage the family ranch east of Prescott, passing time writing poetry and panning for gold. But in 1909 she became the territorial historian and the first woman in Arizona to hold a political office. In 1924, Hall was asked to go east and represent Arizona in the electoral college. Originally she turned down the offer, not having enough money for suitable clothes. But officials at the United Verde Mine saved the day, buying her a blue silk dress with a fine copper mesh coat. This "copper dress" was a hit back east and gave a free shot of publicity to the Arizona copper industry. Today, you can learn all about her in the Sharlot Hall Museum.

rades and festivals. The group eventually disbanded.) The museum also houses a library and the largest collection of the work of Kate Cory, a painter and photographer of Hopi life during the early 20th century. Closed November through April. Admission. ~ 147 North Arizona Street; 520-445-1230.

Prescott also has some other noteworthy museums. The **Phippen Museum of Western Art**, six miles north of town, honors cowboy artist George Phippen and presents changing exhibits of art of the American West. It is generally considered one of the best western art museums in the country. Closed Tuesday. Admission. ~ 4701 Route 89 North; 520-778-1385.

Thirty-four miles east of Prescott you'll find **Arcosanti**, a planned city that will eventually be home to 6000 people. Arcosanti was designed by famed Italian designer Paolo Soleri as a synthesis of architecture and ecology. The complex, which presently houses a gallery, a bakery, a café, a music center, a bronze foundry and a ceramics studio, is pedestrian-oriented, and its unusual buildings with domes, arches, portholes and protruding cubes make maximum use of passive solar heat. Tours are offered daily. Continuing construction is financed in part by the sale of handmade souvenir items such as Cosanti wind bells. Admission. ~ Route 17, Exit 262 at Cordes Junction; 520-632-7135.

LODGING

Prescott has several historic downtown hotels. The most elegant of them is the **Hassayampa Inn**, a 1927 hotel listed on the National Register. The lobby and other common areas have been restored to their earlier glory and furnished with antiques. The rooms have been beautifully renovated and all have private baths. Room rate includes a complimentary cocktail and breakfast in the Peacock Dining Room. ~ 122 East Gurley Street; 520-778-9434, 800-322-1927, fax 520-445-8590. DELUXE TO ULTRA-DELUXE.

With 160 rooms and suites, **Prescott Resort and Conference Center** is the largest lodging facility in the area. It sits on a hill just outside town with a commanding view of the surrounding countryside. Although rooms are large and come with cable TV and coffeemakers, the resort's biggest draw is probably the adjacent 24-hour casino, Bucky's, which has slots and poker machines. ~ 1500 Route 69; 520-776-1666, 800-967-4637, fax 520-776-8544; www.prescottresort.com. DELUXE.

A smaller hotel on a quiet side street is the **Hotel Vendome**. Rooms in this historic 20-room 1917 hotel have been nicely restored and decorated in the style of the era. There are also four two-room suites. Some have modern bathrooms, while others have restored clawfoot tub/showers. ~ 230 South Cortez Street; 520-776-0900, 888-468-3583, fax 520-771-0395; www.vendome hotel.com. MODERATE TO DELUXE.

Sitting atop Nob Hill with a view of Courthouse Square is **The Marks House**, a yellow Queen Anne Victorian bed and breakfast. Built in 1894, the house and its four guest rooms are decorated with antiques; all have feather beds and private baths. Mornings begin with a full family-style breakfast. ~ 203 East Union Street; 520-778-4632, 800-843-6275. MODERATE TO DELUXE.

A posh bed and breakfast in a 1902 main house with four guest houses is the **Prescott Pines Inn**. It has 13 Victorian-style guest rooms beautifully decorated in subdued color schemes. Some have fireplaces and others have kitchens. Sumptuous full breakfasts are served on rose-patterned china. Reservations are recommended. ~ 901 White Spar Road; 520-445-7270, 800-541-5374, fax 520-778-3665; www.prescottpinesinn.com. BUDGET TO MODERATE.

More modest rooms, all with private baths, are available at the **Hotel St. Michael**. The location couldn't be better for those who wish to enjoy the Wild West nightlife of Whiskey Row, on the same block. ~ 205 West Gurley Street; 520-776-1999, 800-678-3757, fax 520-776-7318. BUDGET TO MODERATE.

Prescott also has more than its share of low-priced, basic lodging from which to explore the wild canyons and forests surrounding the city. The Mediterranean-style **American Motel** boasts rooms decorated in adobe and terra-cotta hues, with some wonderful old murals on the walls. ~ 1211 East Gurley Street; 520-778-4322, fax 520-778-1324. MODERATE.

DINING

Prescott's finer restaurants include the **Peacock Dining Room** in the Hassayampa Inn. Here you'll find full lunch and dinner menus of Continental and American specialties in an elegant old-time atmosphere. An etched-glass peacock adorns the front door of this art deco dining room. Choose between seating at tables or semi-circular booths. Tiffany-style lamps add to the quaint atmosphere of this high-ceilinged establishment. Breakfast, lunch and dinner served Monday through Saturday, breakfast and dinner only on Sunday. ~ 122 East Gurley Street; 520-778-9434. MODERATE TO DELUXE.

A century-old general merchandise store that has been transformed into a popular restaurant, **Murphy's** is a walk through history. A leaded-glass divider separates the bar and restaurant sections decorated with photos of Prescott's mining heyday. Mahogany bar booths and a burgundy carpet add to the charm of this establishment. You can also enjoy a drink in the lounge offering views of Thumb Butte. Specialties include mesquite-broiled seafood and prime rib of beef along with fresh homebaked bread. ~ 201 North Cortez Street; 520-445-4044. MODERATE TO DELUXE.

With many plants and a creekside view, the **Porterhouse Restaurant** is a large, rustic-style establishment. It serves a number of steak and seafood dishes. Dinner only Monday through Saturday; brunch and dinner on Sunday. ~ 155 Plaza Drive; 520-445-1991. MODERATE TO ULTRA-DELUXE.

For home-style cooking in Prescott head to the **Dinner Bell Café**. It may not look like much from the outside, but give it a try and you'll find out why this is one of the most popular restaurants in central Arizona. For breakfast try the hubcap-size pancakes or three-egg omelettes. Lunch specials include pork chops, chicken-fried steak, ground round steak and hot roast beef. Be sure to sample the homemade salsa. ~ 321 West Gurley Street; 520-445-9888. BUDGET.

◀ HIDDEN

If sampling locally brewed handcrafted beer appeals to you, stop by **Prescott Brewing Company**, across the street from the courthouse, for lunch or dinner. A glass wall at the back of the bar lets you peek in on the brewing process. You can taste the results in the bar or in one of two dining rooms in this two-level publike eatery. The menu is varied enough—fish and chips, burgers, salads, fajitas, pasta and pizza—to appeal to most everyone in the family. ~ 130 West Gurley Street; 520-771-2795. BUDGET TO MODERATE.

For breakfast or lunch in Prescott, a very popular place in the downtown area is the **Plaza Café**, which serves an assortment of pancakes, omelettes and homemade soups. ~ 106 West Gurley Street; 520-445-3234. BUDGET.

◀ HIDDEN

Also good is the **Prescott Pantry** in the Iron Springs Plaza shopping center. This bakery-deli-wine shop has restaurant seating and offers ever-changing daily specials, hearty sandwiches, espresso and cappuccino and fresh-baked pastries. Closed Sunday. ~ 1201 Iron Springs Road; 520-778-4280. BUDGET.

Elmer Young started farming 80 acres in 1947, and now visits to his dream, **Young's Farm**, are an Arizona tradition. People gather here year-round, but crowds are especially thick during seasonal festivals. Treats include pumpkins, turkeys, sweet corn, vegetables and meat, as well as more unusual pumpkin butter, Hopi Corn jelly and fruit cakes. The place has a real down-home country feel. Open for breakfast and lunch. ~ East of Prescott at the intersection of Routes 69 and 169, Dewey; 520-632-7272. BUDGET.

Because it is old as Arizona towns go, and perhaps because of Sharlot Hall's recognition that it was important to preserve the everyday objects of 19th-century Arizona, Prescott is a good place for antique shopping. As in most antique hunting areas, some items offered for sale do not come from the Prescott area but have been imported from other, less visited parts of the country. Most, however, are the real thing, and antique buffs will find lots of great shops within walking distance of one another in the downtown

SHOPPING

area, especially along the two-block strip of Cortez Street between Gurley and Sheldon streets.

Some of the best places to browse are the indoor mini-malls where select groups of dealers and collectors display, such as the **Merchandise Mart Antique Mall**. ~ 205 North Cortez Street; 520-776-1728. **Prescott Antique & Craft Market** is another such mall. ~ 115 North Cortez Street; 520-445-7156. Nearby is the **Deja Vu Antique Mall**, which also features an old-fashioned soda fountain. ~ 134 North Cortez Street; 520-445-6732.

The bars that line Prescott's Whiskey Row have been in operation since the late 19th century, when this was one of the most notorious sin strips in the West.

Beside the historic Hotel St. Michael are a group of shops called **St. Michael's Alley**. The dozen or so shops include **Puttin' on the Hats** (520-776-1150), which has everything from Greek fisherman's hats to cowboy hats. **Lida** (520-771-0274) is a designer boutique that sells Southwestern-style clothing and jewelry made in their local factory. ~ 110 Montezuma Street.

An excellent gallery in town is **Sun West**. Arizona and local artists sell sculpture, pottery, furniture, paintings and jewelry, and there are also rugs woven by the Zapotec people. ~ 152 South Montezuma Street; 520-778-1204.

Other noteworthy galleries that exhibit and sell the works of local artists include the **Prescott Fine Arts Gallery**. ~ 208 North Marina Street; 520-445-3286. Visit **Mountain Artists Guild**. ~ 701 Ruth Street; 520-445-2510. There's also the **Yavapai College Gallery**. ~ In the performance hall on campus, 1100 East Sheldon Street; 520-445-7300.

Stuffed deer greet patrons at **The Cattleman's Shop**, where you will find Western wear ranging from frilly toddler cowgirl dresses to spurs. ~ 124 Whiskey Row; 520-445-8222.

NIGHTLIFE   Rock-and-roll, blues and country acts entertain on Friday and Sunday nights at **Piñon Pines Nite Club**. See what musicians come up with on Wednesday's live jam night. ~ 2701 East Route 89A; 520-445-9935.

Moctezuma's has live bands on Fridays and deejay tunes on Thursday and Saturday. Cover on weekends. ~ 144 South Montezuma Street; 520-445-1244.

Quieter is the **Eagle's Nest Lounge**, which offers dancing and live entertainment Tuesday through Saturday at the Prescott Resort and Conference Center. **Bucky's Casino** is adjacent to the hotel lobby and is open 24 hours. ~ 1500 Route 69; 520-776-1666.

Prescott has its own repertory theater company performing year-round at the **Prescott Fine Arts Theater**. It offers both a main stage and a Family Theater for child-oriented productions. ~ 208 North Marina Street; 520-445-3286.

WATSON LAKE PARK 🏃 🚤 🛶 A labyrinth of granite rock formations along Route 89 just outside of Prescott surrounds pretty little Watson Lake, a manmade reservoir that is locally popular for boating and catfish fishing. The area used to be a stronghold for Apache Indians. More recently, from the 1920s to the 1950s, there was a major resort at Granite Dells and some artifacts survive from that era. Hiking and rock climbing are popular pursuits here. There are restrooms, showers and a picnic area. ~ Located four miles northeast of Prescott on Route 89; 520-771-5841.

▲ There are 50 sites (no hookups); $12 per night.

PARKS

North Central Arizona is a popular region for both downhill and cross-country skiing.

▼▼▼▼▼▼▼▼▼▼▼▼
Outdoor Adventures

FLAGSTAFF AREA   Arizona's premier downhill ski area is the **Arizona Snowbowl**, located 14 miles north of Flagstaff on the slopes on Agassiz Peak, a 12,000-foot volcano in the San Francisco Peaks. Snowboarders can use the designated park or share the slopes with skiers. Snowbowl can get up to 250 inches of snow a year. The area has 30 runs, 4 chairlifts and a vertical drop of 2300 feet. The season runs from mid-December to mid-April. ~ Seven miles off Route 180, Snowbowl Road; 520-779-1951; snow report, 520-779-4577.

SKIING

For cross-country skiers, the **Flagstaff Nordic Center**, 16 miles north of Flagstaff in Coconino National Forest, maintains an extensive system of trails from mid-November through mid-March. The center offers equipment rentals, guided tours and a ski school. ~ Route 180; 520-779-1951.

For the most spectacular guided tour in town, sightsee from a hot-air balloon.

BALLOON RIDES

SEDONA AREA   See the Red Rock Country from the sky with **Red Rock Balloon Adventure**. All rides begin at sunrise and include a Continental-style meal. ~ 295 Lee Mountain Road, Sedona; 520-284-0040. Also hovering above is **Northern Light Balloon Expeditions**. Balloon rides last an hour and go over Sedona or along the Mogollon Rim depending on the winds. Each operator launches one trip a day at sunrise and follows it up with a picnic breakfast. ~ P.O. Box 1695, Sedona, AZ 86339; 520-282-2274.

Sedona has an extraordinary number of jeep tour services, offering everything from general sightseeing trips to spiritual inner journeys. Tours range from one hour to all day, and are fully guided.

JEEP TOURS

Pink Jeep Tours runs sightseeing trips in—what else—those flashy pink jobs you see darting around town. They provide off-road, backcountry tours of the Sedona red rock area, as well as trips to Indian ruins and petro-glyphs, which require a little hiking as well as jeep-ing. The tours, which range from one-and-a-half to four hours, focus on American Indian folklore, geology and wildlife appreciation. ~ 204 North Route 89A; 520-282-5000, 800-873-3662.

> The elevation drop from Flagstaff to Sedona is 2500 feet, and the temperature is often 20° higher in Sedona than in Flagstaff.

Ooh and ahh at the vista from 2000 feet up Schnebley Hill Road, or explore ruins in the Diamondback Gulch and Boynton Canyon backcountry with **Sedona Adventures Jeep Tours**. ~ 276 North Route 89A; 520-282-3500.

Whether you're looking for a Wild West sightseeing tour that traverses private ranchlands, or a New Age "Vortex Tour" where you can absorb the electromagnetic energy that is said to swirl among select stones in Boynton Canyon, the cowboy-garbed guides at **Sedona Red Rock Jeep Tours** can provide it; the emphasis on these one-and-a-half to two-hour trips is education and photography, so whichever tour you take, you'll doubtless learn as much as you ever wanted to know about the area. ~ 270 North Route 89A; 520-282-6826.

The Vortex Tour is the most popular of the eight different tours offered by **Earth Wisdom Tours**, all of which are intended to blend travel with spiritual wisdom and consciousness. Even the slightly skeptical visitor will find the lively, even intense, discussions that take place among the guide and passengers highly interesting metaphysical mini-lessons covering science and myth, personal growth and the secrets of the medicine wheel. ~ 293 North Route 89A, at Rollie's Camera Courtyard; 520-282-4714.

GOLF

While you might not be able to golf year-round here, most of the year offers excellent weather for hitting the greens.

FLAGSTAFF AREA   Tee off at the 18-hole public **Elden Hills Golf Resort**. There are clubs and golf carts for rent. Closed in winter. ~ 2380 North Oakmont Drive, Flagstaff; 520-526-5125.

SEDONA AREA   Sedona Golf Resort's 18-hole course designed by Gary Panks is ranked third in the state among public courses. Clubs are available for rent, and the use of a cart is included in the green fee. ~ 35 Ridge Trail Drive; 520-284-9355. Drive a wedge at the semiprivate, 18-hole, Robert Trent Jones–designed **Village of Oak Creek Country Club**. Carts and clubs can be rented. ~ 690 Bell Rock Boulevard, Sedona; 520-284-1660. Play the greens at the semipublic **Canyon Mesa Country Club**, a nine-hole executive course with red-rock views. Clubs and carts available for rent. ~ 500 Jacks Canyon Road, Sedona; 520-284-0036.

The nine-hole, par-three course at **Poco Diablo Resort** wends its way among challenging water hazards and sand traps as well as beautiful stands of willow trees. There are clubs for rent, but no carts; it is a walking course, and metal cleats are prohibited. ~ 1752 South Route 179, Sedona; 520-282-7333. Go for a hole in one on either (or both) of the two 18-hole courses at the public **Antelope Hills Golf Course**. There are clubs and carts for rent. ~ 1 Perkins Drive, Prescott; 520-445-0583.

There is not a lot of tennis in this area, but you should be able to find a few open courts. **TENNIS**

FLAGSTAFF AREA **Thorpe Park** has four lighted public courts. ~ Thorpe Park Road. The public **Bushmaster Park** has two lighted courts. ~ Alta Vista Street. You can call **Tennis Flagstaff** for more information. ~ 520-779-7690.

SEDONA AREA Sedona has no public tennis courts. For a fee, courts are available to the public at **Poco Diablo Resort**, with four courts, two of which are lighted. Hitting assistants and a ball machine are available, and there is a tennis pro on call. ~ 1752 South Route 179; 520-282-7333.

PRESCOTT In Prescott, six tennis courts are open to the public during the summer months at **Yavapai College**. Daylight hours only; no fee. ~ 1100 East Sheldon Street; 520-445-7300. Public summer courts are also found at **Prescott High School**, which has six courts. ~ 1050 North Ruth Street; 520-445-2322. **Ken Lindley Field** has four "sand" courts open for summer use. ~ East Gurley and Arizona streets; 520-445-5291.

The equestrian will find many riding opportunities in this region. **RIDING STABLES**

FLAGSTAFF AREA In Flagstaff, **Hitchin' Post Stables** offers a full range of guided horse and mule trips, from one-hour rides along the rim of Walnut Canyon to three-day pack trips, as well as sunset rides complete with a steak or chicken dinner. ~ 4848 Lake Mary Road; 520-774-1719. Year-round trips in Coconino National Forest are offered by **Flying Heart Barn**. ~ 8400 North Route 89, Flagstaff; 520-526-2788. Also in Flagstaff is **Ski Lift Lodge and Stables**, which has one-hour and longer guided tours and hayrides on the weekend. Closed in winter. ~ Route 180 at Snow Bowl Road; 520-774-0729.

SEDONA AREA **Legends Ranch** offers one- to two-and-a-half-hour-long tours of red-rock country. ~ 270 North Route 89A; 520-282-6826, 800-848-7728. For one-hour, two-hour, half-day or overnight rides through Coconino National Forest, contact **Trail Horse Adventures**. ~ 85 Five J Lane; 602-502-9536, 800-723-3538.

PRESCOTT **Granite Mountain Stables** provides guided horse rides in the Granite Mountain Wilderness. ~ 2400 West Shane Drive off Williamson Valley Road; 520-771-9551.

BIKING

As in the rest of the state, this region is fast becoming a mecca for biking.

FLAGSTAFF AREA   Flagstaff has about eight miles of paved trails in its **Urban Trail System and Bikeways System**, linking the Northern Arizona University campus, the downtown area and Lowell Observatory. Maps and information on the trail system are available upon request from the **Parks and Recreation Department**. ~ 211 West Aspen Avenue; 520-779-7690.

Outside the city, a popular route for all-day bike touring is the 36-mile paved loop road through Sunset Crater and Wupatki national monuments, starting at the turnoff from Route 89 about 20 miles northeast of town.

For mountain bikers, several unpaved primitive roads lead deeper into the San Francisco Volcano Field in **Coconino National Forest**. Check out the forest road that leads to the base of Colton Crater and SP Crater. For complete information, contact the **Peaks Ranger Station**. ~ 5075 North Route 89; 520-526-0866.

SEDONA AREA   The same network of unpaved back roads that makes the **Red Rock Country** around Sedona such a popular area for four-wheel-drive touring is also ideal for mountain biking. Get a map from one of the local bike shops and try the dirt roads leading from Soldier Pass Road to the Seven Sacred Pools or the Devil's Kitchen. Or follow the Broken Arrow Jeep Trail east from Route 179 to Submarine Rock. The Schnebly Hill Road climbs all the way north to Flagstaff, paralleling the Oak Creek Canyon Highway. The upper part of the road is steep, winding and very rough, but the lower part, through Bear Wallow Canyon, makes for a beautiful mountain biking excursion.

Bike Rentals   In Flagstaff, you can rent mountain bikes and obtain trail information at **Absolute Bikes**. They also offer repair service. ~ 18 North San Francisco Street; 520-779-5969. **Mountain Sports** is another full-service Flagstaff store with bikes and information. ~ 1800 South Milton Road; 520-779-5156. In Sedona, you'll find trail information, bike rentals and repairs at **Mountain Bike Heaven**. ~ 1695 West Route 89A; 520-282-1312. **Sedona Sports** also rents and repairs bikes. ~ Artesania Creekside Plaza, 251 Route 179; 520-282-1317.

HIKING

Lovers of the outdoors will delight in the number and variety of hiking trails this area provides. All distances for hiking trails are one way unless otherwise noted.

FLAGSTAFF AREA   Just north of Flagstaff rise the San Francisco Peaks, the highest in Arizona. Numerous trails start from Mount

Elden and Schultz Pass roads, which branch off Route 180 to the right a short distance past the Museum of Northern Arizona. Other trailheads are located in Flagstaff at Buffalo Park on Cedar Avenue and near the Peaks Ranger Station on Route 89. Most trails in the Flagstaff area close in winter.

North of the ranger station, off Route 180, the **Elden Lookout Trail** (3 miles) climbs by switchbacks up the east face of 9299-foot Mount Elden, with an elevation gain of 2400 feet and, waiting to reward you at the top, a spectacular view of the city and the volcano fields around Sunset Crater.

The **Fatman's Loop Trail** (2 miles), branching off of Elden Lookout Trail for a shorter hike with a 600-foot elevation gain, also offers a good view of Flagstaff.

From the Buffalo Park trailhead, the **Oldham Trail** (5.5 miles) ascends the west face to the top of Mount Elden. The longest trail on the mountain, this is a gentler climb. The Oldham Trail intersects Mount Elden Road three times, making it possible to take a shorter hike on only the higher part of the trail. **Pipeline Trail** (2.8 miles) links the lower parts of the Oldham and Elden Lookout trails along the northern city limit of Flagstaff, allowing either a short hike on the edge of town or a long, all-day loop trip up one side of the mountain and down the other.

Perhaps the most unusual of many hiking options in the strange volcanic landscape around the base of the San Francisco Peaks is on **Red Mountain**, 33 miles north of Flagstaff off Route 180. A gap in the base of this 1000-foot-high volcanic cone lets you follow the **Red Mountain Trail** (1 mile) from the end of the national forest access road straight into the crater without climbing. Not often visited by tourists, this is a great place to explore with older children.

◄ HIDDEN

For maps and detailed hiking information on these and many other trails in Coconino National Forest, contact the **Peaks Ranger Station**. ~ 5075 North Route 89; 520-526-0866; www.fs.fed.us/r3/coconino.

✔ **CHECK THESE OUT—UNIQUE OUTDOOR ADVENTURES**

• Arrive in the winter and you won't be disappointed with the ski runs at Arizona Snowbowl, located on the San Francisco Peaks. *page 147*

• Soar above Red Rock Country in one of the many colorful hot-air balloons. *page 147*

• Set aside a day to explore the unpaved primitive roads through the Coconino National Forest by bicycle. *page 150*

• Hike Devil's Bridge Trail in Boynton Canyon and you will be rewarded with vistas of canyonlands from atop a sandstone arch. *page 152*

SEDONA AREA   While every visitor to Flagstaff or Sedona drives through often-crowded Oak Creek Canyon, one of central Arizona's "must-see" spots, few stop to explore the canyon's west fork, a narrow canyon with sheer walls hundreds feet high in places, which is only accessible on foot. For more information on trails in this area, call the Sedona Ranger Station, 520-282-4119.

The trailhead for the **West Fork Trail** (14 miles) is in the parking lot (there is a parking fee) of the Call of the Canyon on the west side of Route 89A, ten miles north of Sedona. The first three miles of the fairly level trail, which pass through a protected "research natural area," are heavily used and easy to hike. Farther up, the trail becomes less distinct, requires repeatedly swimming through pools of water while floating your gear and leads into the Red Rock Secret Mountain Wilderness.

A very popular hiking spot in the Red Rock Country is Boynton Canyon, one of Sedona's four "Vortex" areas. According to Sedona's New Age community, Boynton Canyon is the most powerful of the Vortexes, emanating an electromagnetic yin/yang psychic energy that can be felt for miles around. Whether you believe in such things or not, it is undeniably beautiful. From the trailhead on Boynton Pass Road—a continuation of Dry Creek Road, which leaves Route 89A in West Sedona—the nearly level **Boynton Canyon Trail** (2.5 miles) goes up the canyon through woods and among redrock formations. There are several small, ancient Sinagua Indian cliff dwellings in the canyon. If you visit the ruins be aware that the dwellings are very fragile and are disappearing due to impact.

A right turn from Dry Creek Road on the way to Boynton Pass will put you on unpaved Forest Road 152, which is rough enough in spots that drivers of low-clearance vehicles may want to think twice before proceeding. One and a half miles up this road, the **Devil's Bridge Trail** (1 mile) climbs gradually through piñon and juniper country to a long red sandstone arch with a magnificent view of the surrounding canyonlands. You can walk to the top of the arch. Located three miles further, at the end of Dry Creek Road, is the trailhead for the **Vultee Arch Trail** (1.7 miles), which follows Sterling Canyon to another natural bridge.

PRESCOTT   There are many hiking trails in the national forest around Prescott. One of the most popular is the **Thumb Butte Trail** (1.4 miles), which goes up a saddle west of town, through oak and piñon woods, offering good views of Prescott and Granite Dells. The trail starts from Thumb Butte Park. To get there, go west on Thumb Butte Road, an extension of Gurley Street.

More ambitious hikers may wish to explore the **Granite Mountain Wilderness**. Of its several trails, the one that goes to the summit of the 7125-foot mountain is **Little Granite Mountain Trail** (3.3 miles), a beautiful all-day hike with an elevation gain of 1500 feet. For information on this and other trails in the area, contact the Prescott National Forest—Bradshaw District ranger station. ~ 2230 East Route 69, just east of Prescott; 520-445-7253.

▼▼▼▼▼▼▼▼▼▼▼

Transportation

One hundred and thirty eight miles north of Phoenix via **Route 17**, Flagstaff is located on **Route 40**, the main east–west route across northern Arizona. Grand Canyon-bound travelers leaving the interstate at Flagstaff have a choice between the more direct way to Grand Canyon Village, 79 miles via **Route 180**, or the longer way, 105 miles via **Route 89** and **Route 64**, which parallels the canyon rim for 25 miles. These routes combine perfectly into a spectacular loop trip from Flagstaff.

CAR

Another scenic loop trip from Flagstaff goes south on **Route 89A**, descending through Oak Creek Canyon to the town of Sedona in the Red Rock Country, a distance of 26 slow miles. From Sedona, Route 89A continues for 58 more miles through the historic mining town of Jerome, with a steep climb over Cleopatra Hill, to Prescott, the old territorial capital. From there, a 51-mile drive on Route 89 returns travelers to interstate Route 40 at Ash Fork, about 55 miles west of Flagstaff.

America West Express flies into the **Flagstaff Pulliam Airport** (520-556-1234) and **Prescott Municipal Airport** (520-445-7860).

AIR

Westwind Aviation (888-282-2037) and **Sedona Sky Treks** (520-284-2998) provide on-demand charter service for travelers from the **Sedona Airport** (520-282-4487).

Grayline Nava-Hopi Tours provides bus service to the Grand Canyon South Rim, as well as Flagstaff. ~ 114 West Santa Fe Avenue, Flagstaff; 520-774-5003, 800-892-8687.

BUS

Greyhound Bus Lines (800-231-2222) stops at the bus terminals in Flagstaff and Prescott. In Flagstaff, it's at 399 South Malpais Lane; 520-774-4573. In Prescott, it's at 820 East Sheldon Street; 520-445-5470.

Amtrak serves Flagstaff daily on its "Southwest Chief" route between Chicago and Los Angeles. The westbound passenger train stops in Flagstaff late in the evening, so arriving passengers will want to make hotel reservations in advance, with a deposit to hold the room late. Amtrak offers a shuttle bus service to the Grand Canyon for its Flagstaff passengers. ~ 1 East Santa Fe Avenue, Flagstaff; 800-872-7245.

TRAIN

Flagstaff has about a dozen car-rental agencies, most of them at the airport. Among the airport concessions are **Avis Rent A Car** (800-831-2847), **Budget Rent A Car** (800-527-0700) and **Hertz Rent A Car** (800-654-3131).

CAR RENTALS

Located downtown, and more convenient for those arriving by train or bus, is **Budget Rent A Car**. ~ Corner of Humphreys (Route 180 North) and Aspen streets; 800-527-0700. **Triple A Car Rental** will accept a cash deposit in lieu of a credit card. ~ In the lobby of the Crystal Inn; 520-774-7394. Also in Flagstaff is an office of **Cruise America**, a nationwide motorhome rental agency. ~ 824 West Route 66; 520-774-4707, 800-327-7799.

At the Sedona Airport, rentals are available from **Arizona Jeep and Car Rentals** (800-879-5337).

For rentals in Prescott try **Hertz Rent A Car** (Prescott Municipal Airport; 520-776-1399, 800-654-3131) or **Budget Rent A Car** (1031 Commerce Drive; 520-778-3806).

TAXIS

Flagstaff has more than its share of taxi companies because many public transportation travelers stop there en route to the Grand Canyon. These cabs will take you anywhere in central Arizona at any time of day or night. Sedona? Phoenix? No problem. Call **A Friendly Cab** (520-774-4444) or **Harper's Taxi** (520-779-1234). Shop and compare—rates vary.

Sedona's local taxi company is **Bob's Sedona Taxi** (520-282-1234). Another one is **Bell Rock Taxi** (520-282-4222).

Prescott's **Ace City Cab** (520-445-1616) offers discounted rates for senior citizens and physically challenged persons.

SEVEN

Western Arizona

Heading west, the mighty Colorado River pours out of the Grand Canyon, spreads itself into Lake Mead, proceeds through a succession of scenic lakes, resorts and riverfront coves, then rolls south until it reaches the Gulf of California. In its wake, visitors to the region will discover a number of unusual points of interest and unparalleled recreational opportunities—each one surrounded by a distinctive landscape, each one quite different from the others. Here, you'll find broad expanses of sparkling water, summer breezes whipping up whitecaps, waterskiers cutting crystal wakes, colorful sails curled above catamarans, and miles of sandy beaches—all along the Colorado River on Arizona's "West Coast."

Kingman is a good starting point for exploring Arizona's western edge. Set at the crossroads of Routes 93 and 40, the town is strategically placed for excursions to Lake Mead and Hoover Dam, Bullhead City/Laughlin and Lake Mohave, Lake Havasu and its London Bridge, and the Parker Strip and Quartzsite. Along the way, you can explore gold and silver mining ghost towns such as Oatman and Chloride, which cling to a tenuous existence amid scenic surroundings. From Kingman, there's also a steep road that leads to the alpine greenery of Hualapai Mountain Park, where you can picnic and camp.

About 80 miles north of Kingman, on Route 93, is manmade Lake Mead, which is shared by Arizona and Nevada. Created in the 1930s when the Colorado River was backed up by Hoover Dam, Lake Mead is a popular recreation area.

In the forbidding, rocky hills of western Arizona's Mojave Desert, real estate promoters used to sell lots in planned communities sight unseen to gullible people in the East. Most of these would-be towns never even came close to reality, but two "cities" set in the middle of nowhere along desolate stretches of the Colorado River have become the twin hubs of a genuine phenomenon.

Bullhead City, the fastest-growing city in Arizona, is an isolated resort and retirement community of about 28,000 people. Founded as the construction camp for Davis Dam, Bullhead City has no visible reason for its existence except daily sunshine, warm weather year-round, boating and fishing access to the Colorado River—and a booming casino strip across the river in Laughlin, at the extreme southern tip of Nevada.

Even more improbable than Bullhead City is Lake Havasu City, which the *Los Angeles Times* has called "the most successful freestanding new town in the United States." Though it enjoys a great wintertime climate and a fine location on the shore of a 45-mile-long desert lake, there is really no logical explanation for Lake Havasu City—except that, in the 1960s, chain saw tycoon Bob McCulloch and partner C. V. Wood Jr., planner and first general manager of Disneyland, decided to build it. Since their planned community had no economic base, they concluded that what it needed was a tourist attraction. They came up with a doozie—the London Bridge. Yes, the *real* London Bridge, bought at auction and moved block by massive granite block across the Atlantic, where it was reassembled over a channel to connect to an island in Lake Havasu. The unprecedented, seemingly absurd plan actually worked, and you can see the result for yourself today.

In addition to London Bridge, Lake Havasu City has an "English Village" to complement it. Nearby, the two sections of Lake Havasu State Park are well-developed recreational areas that take advantage of the lake's 45 miles of shore-line. The Windsor Beach Unit on the upper level of the lake has boat ramps, shaded picnic areas, campsites and more primitive camping areas accessible by boat. The Cattail Cove Unit has similar facilities, plus a marina, restaurant, store and boat rentals.

Near Parker Dam, which impounds Lake Havasu, Buckskin Mountain State Park attracts tube floaters, boaters and waterskiers. Hiking trails into the Buckskin Mountains lead to panoramic vista points, and, for some lucky hikers, sightings of desert bighorn sheep.

About halfway down the "coast," the Bill Williams River empties into the Colorado River just above Parker Dam. Upstream is Alamo Lake, a large manmade reservoir created for recreation and flood control. The lake has bass fishing, swimming, boating, canoeing and views of native wildlife, including the bald and golden eagle.

En route to these unusual Arizona communities, you'll have a chance to visit Havasu National Wildlife Refuge. Keep a sharp eye and you may glimpse a bald eagle, peregrine falcon or desert bighorn sheep, along with a wide variety of other fauna.

Downriver from Parker Dam, the town of Parker and the Colorado River Indian Reservation serve as trade centers and jumping-off points for more recreation. Farther south, the town of Quartzsite, which is more a sprawling RV park than a city, attracts several hundred thousand people late January and early February for its annual rock and mineral shows.

▼▼▼▼▼▼▼▼▼▼
Kingman Area

At the crossroads of Routes 40 and 93, Kingman has earned a reputation as a comfortable stopover for travelers hurrying between Phoenix and Las Vegas or Los Angeles and Albuquerque. It is also a natural hub for leisurely trips to nearby ghost towns, Hoover Dam, Lake Mead and other recreational resorts along the Colorado River.

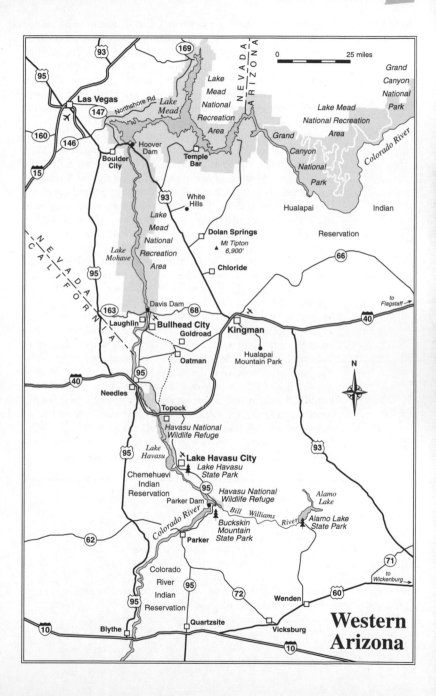

Western Arizona

SIGHTS   **Kingman** was named for surveyor Lewis Kingman, who passed through the area in 1892 while charting a railroad route between Needles, California, and Albuquerque, New Mexico. The railroad camp subsequently built here took his name, but the town didn't flourish until the early 1900s, when silver and copper deposits were discovered in the surrounding hills. The mines were depleted by the 1940s, but the town survived as an important pit stop for travelers on the Santa Fe railway and old Route 66.

With more than 30 motels and 50 restaurants, modern-day Kingman continues its tradition as a key provisioning center. Most of the commercial activity has shifted to Motel Row—East Andy Devine Avenue—and suburban shopping centers, but there are a few historical gems around town worth seeing. To find out about them, stop at the **Powerhouse Visitor Center**, which dispenses maps, brochures and a listing of the area's annual events and festivals. Be sure to ask for a map of downtown's historic district tour. ~ 120 West Andy Devine Avenue, Kingman; 520-753-6106.

An interesting stop is the **Mohave Museum of History and Arts**, which gives visitors a glimpse of many of the unusual aspects of western Arizona. A mural and dioramas in the lobby depict the settlement of the region and show how camels used to be used as beasts of burden in these parts. Kingman is the source of much of the turquoise mined in the United States, and the museum has a fine collection of carved turquoise objects. American Indian exhibits include portrayals of the traditional ways of the Hualapai and Mohave tribes. Other rooms contain a collection of paintings of U.S. presidents and their first ladies by artist Lawrence Williams, as well as memorabilia of the town's most famous native son, the late actor Andy Devine. Closed weekend mornings. Admission. ~ 400 West Beale Street, Kingman; 520-753-3195.

A drive through the older section of Kingman, away from the chain-store motels and generic coffee shops, reveals a turn-of-the-

✔ CHECK THESE OUT—UNIQUE SIGHTS

- Plummet 21 stories to the floor of the limestone **Grand Canyon Caverns** and view three-million-year-old crystals and fossils. *page 159*
- Descend into the bowels of the **Hoover Dam,** an engineering feat that supplies electricity to Arizona, Nevada and southern California. *page 163*
- Travel the Colorado River and learn the history of the area aboard the paddlewheel steamer named **Colorado Belle.** *page 166*
- Walk across the **London Bridge**—yes, the original bridge from England that was moved to Lake Havasu City in 1968. *page 174*

century downtown area that is gradually being revitalized. For the time being, you can still admire the architectural splendor the proud buildings once enjoyed, from Victorian mansions to simple adobe shacks. Some of the sights on the chamber's historic district tour include the Spanish-Colonial **Santa Fe Railroad Depot** at Andy Devine Avenue and 4th Street; the mission revival-style IOOF building at 5th and Beale streets; the classic Greek-style tufa-stone, glass-domed **Mohave County Courthouse** at Spring and 4th streets; and, just east of the museum, **Locomotive Park**, a collection of early train locomotives, with a 1927 Baldwin steam engine and bright red caboose as the centerpiece.

To step even further into the area's past, drive to the old gold-mining town of **Oatman**, about 25 miles southwest of Kingman via Route 66. Founded in 1906 and mostly abandoned in 1942, Oatman is a funky collection of rickety, Old West buildings—some look ready to collapse, while others are occupied by souvenir stores and yogurt shops. This is one of the better preserved of Arizona's ghost towns, thanks largely to the fact that it has been used several times as a movie set. In addition, a healthy tourist trade keeps the town going. Tourism also keeps dozens of wild burros, descendants of the work animals who once hauled gold ore out of the local mines, loitering in the streets of Oatman. They've learned that panhandling snacks from sightseers beats scrounging around for food in the Mojave Desert any day. Weekends are lively with country music and staged shootouts in the streets.

◄ *HIDDEN*

Besides the usual assortment of antique and curio shops, the **Oatman Hotel** features a downstairs museum of old movie posters, rusty mining equipment and period antiques. In 1939, Carole Lombard and Clark Gable spent their wedding night here after getting married in Kingman. One of her dresses is displayed in the honeymoon suite. ~ Route 66, Oatman; 520-768-4408.

A more pristine example of an Arizona ghost town is **Chloride**, located about 23 miles northwest of Kingman via Route 93. Named for the salt deposits in the surrounding hills, Chloride is a weathered gathering of wood-planked buildings, miner's shacks and processing mills. Although not as rehearsed as Oatman's, the townsfolk put on amateurish skits and shootouts on the weekend. Although the high melodrama would be better accompanied by a player piano, everyone seems to have a good time. The sights here include several galleries and antique shops, and a bed and breakfast next door to Shelp's General Store.

About an hour's drive east of Kingman are the **Grand Canyon Caverns**, limestone caves with selenite crystals and marine fossils dating back three million years. Guided tours begin with a 21-story elevator ride below ground to the cavern floors for a 45-minute walk along lighted trails equipped with handrails. Above ground are a historical museum, gift shop and restaurant. Admission. ~ Route 66, 12 miles east of Peach Springs; 520-422-3223.

LODGING   It seems nearly every motel chain is represented in Kingman. Most are located along East Andy Devine Avenue and West Beale Street, and provide dependable lodging. Among the nicer ones, the **Quality Inn** features modern guest rooms, some equipped with kitchenettes and refrigerators. Fitness buffs will like its pool, sauna and workout room. ~ 1400 East Andy Devine Avenue, Kingman; 520-753-4747, 800-869-3252. BUDGET.

In the downtown area, the **Arizona Inn** is within walking distance from the historic downtown sights. Comfortable rooms are decorated with dark-wood furniture and cool pastels. ~ 411 West Beale Street, Kingman; 520-753-5521, fax 520-753-6579. BUDGET.

HIDDEN ▶   In the ghost town of Oatman, the old **Oatman Hotel** has reopened as lodging for overnight guests. The authentic two-story adobe with arched facade and corrugated iron walls and ceilings may induce you to take a room, as it did Clark Gable and Carole Lombard on their wedding night after a surprise ceremony in Kingman. Oatman was on the main highway—Route 66—to Hollywood back then, and has ten restored rooms. ~ Route 66, Oatman; 520-768-4408. BUDGET.

DINING   Dozens of chain restaurants and coffee shops line East Andy Devine Avenue in Kingman, but for some local flavor try **The Kingman Deli**, where the chili is thick and spicy, and there are over three dozen types of sandwiches. Sample the popular "Sneaky Snake" with ham, turkey, roast beef and swiss cheese or the "Tumbleweed" with cucumber, avocado, sprouts, tomatoes and swiss cheese. No dinner. Closed Sunday. ~ 419 East Beale Street, Kingman; 520-753-4151. BUDGET.

Or you can stop in for a pastry and an espresso at the **Oldtown Coffeehouse** located in the historic Kayser House, a quaint 1920s bungalow that's part of the downtown tour. At lunch, this friendly café caters to local businesspeople who come for the homemade chili, quiche and sandwiches. No dinner. Closed Sunday. ~ 616 East Beale Street, Kingman; 520-753-2244. BUDGET.

SHOPPING   Most of Kingman's commercial activity takes place along Beale Street and Andy Devine Avenue, parallel one-way streets that form a loop through the downtown area. The two merge at the eastern end, where there are a pair of regional shopping centers. There's not much in between, except the **Oldtown Coffeehouse**, a store and café where you can purchase gift baskets, candles and gourmet coffees, teas and foods. ~ 616 East Beale Street, Kingman; 520-753-2244.

You won't find Kitty or Festus at the **Long Branch Saloon,** but **NIGHTLIFE** you can make a spectacle of yourself on karaoke nights—Monday and Tuesday—or kick up your heels to live country-and-western music Wednesday through Saturday. ~ 2255 Airway Avenue, Kingman; 520-757-8756.

Bluegrass and acoustical artists play to a packed house Friday evenings at the **Oldtown Coffeehouse.** On the second Friday of every month there are poetry readings by local poets. ~ 616 East Beale Street, Kingman; 520-753-2244.

Or you can catch a flick at **The Movies.** ~ 4055 Stockton Hill Road, Kingman; 520-757-7985.

HUALAPAI MOUNTAIN PARK 🏃 This island of forested slopes **PARKS** in the middle of the Mojave Desert is a locally popular picnicking, camping and hiking area. These mountains were once the ancestral home of the Hualapai Indians, until they were forced to relocate by the U.S. military in the 1870s. The Hualapai, whose name translates to "Pine-tree folk," now live farther north on a reservation as the west end of the Grand Canyon. Managed by the Mohave County Parks Department, the park offers cool, protected habitat for wildlife including deer, elk, coyotes and occasional mountain lions. There are picnic areas, restrooms, cabins, softball diamond, hiking trails, winter snow play area. ~ Located 14 miles southeast of Kingman on the paved Hualapai Mountain Park Road; 520-757-0915.

▲ There are 70 tent sites, as well as 11 RV hookups available May to September; $8 per night for tent sites, $15 for hookups. Besides tent and RV campgrounds, there are 14 cabins built in the 1930s as part of a Civilian Conservation Corps camp that can be rented for the night ($25 to $55 per night). Reservations are required for the cabins. ~ 520-757-0915.

Downriver from the Grand Canyon, the Colorado ▼▼▼▼▼▼▼▼▼▼▼ River becomes a series of manmade desert lakes formed **Lake Mead Area** by the dams of the Colorado River Project, which provides: electricity for Southern California, a steady supply of irrigation water for Imperial Valley agriculture, and flood control for all the communities along the once-raging river. With Nevada and California on the other side, the river and lakes form the Arizona state line.

The largest of the reservoirs is 110-mile-long **Lake Mead,** about **SIGHTS** 80 miles north of Kingman on Route 93, not far from Las Vegas. The lake was created when the Colorado River was backed up by Hoover Dam from 1935 to 1938. Attracting more than ten million visitors annually, Lake Mead is a popular destination for boating, fishing, windsurfing, waterskiing, lying on the beach or exploring hidden coves and inlets by houseboat. The sheer size of the lake—822 miles of shoreline and nine trillion gallons of water —and the surrounding jagged canyons and desert sand dunes are reason enough to visit the largest manmade lake in the United States.

The lake is especially popular with anglers, who take a run at largemouth bass, rainbow, brown and cutthroat trout, catfish and black crappie. Striped bass, which can reach 50 pounds, are the most popular game fish in recent years.

A good way to learn about the lake is to stop at the **Lake Mead Visitors Center**. Located midway between Boulder City and Hoover Dam, the center's botanical garden, exhibits and short movie shown periodically throughout the day describe the area's history and attractions. There are also books for sale that can provide more in-depth information on the area's history, flora and fauna. ~ Route 93 and Lakeshore Road, Boulder City, NV; 702-293-8906, 702-293-8990; www.nps.gov/lame.

The easiest way to access Lake Mead from the isolated Arizona shore is at **Temple Bar Marina**. There's lodging, a café, gas and provisions here. This is the last outpost for supplies if you plan to boat north of Temple Bar. ~ Reached by a well-marked, paved 28-mile road that turns off Route 93 about 55 miles north of Kingman; 520-767-3211, 800-752-9669.

Although more remote, **South Cove/Pearce Ferry** is recommended for its scenic vistas of the lake and craggy peaks of Iceberg Canyon, about 46 miles east of Hoover Dam. Take Route 93 north from Kingman about 40 miles to the Dolan Springs turnoff and drive east. After passing Dolan Springs, you'll enter a massive forest of Joshua trees and the retirement resort of Meadview. Soon, you'll begin to catch glimpses of Lake Mead, from atop Grapevine Mesa. South Cove has only a boat ramp, a picnic area and toilets, but it offers a serene respite, accented by the deep blue waters of Lake Mead and rough-hewn mountains that frame it. The final four-mile stretch of dirt road to Pearce Ferry drops down through steep canyon walls and granite buttes. At the shoreline are primitive camp sites, a picnic area, an unpaved boat ramp and plenty of peace and quiet. If the rocky granite corridors remind you of the Grand Canyon, it's because the park's western boundary is just a mile east of here.

There's also a scenic drive that runs along the Nevada side of the lake, where there are more marinas, a campground, a popular public beach and a few resorts. Take Route 166 from Boulder City through the washes and canyons above the lake until you reach **Northshore Road** (Routes 147 and 167). You can stay on the highway that follows the shoreline all the way to the Valley of Fire State Park, or drop down to the lake at Las Vegas Bay, Callville Bay, Echo Bay or Overton Beach. You'll find food and facilities at all four resorts.

Lake Mead Cruises offers a **Hoover Dam cruise** aboard a three-deck paddleboat, the *Desert Princess*. The 100-foot-long sternwheeler is the largest vessel to ply the waters of the lake, and features a snack bar, two glass-enclosed decks, an open promenade deck, an 80-seat dining room, cocktail lounge and dancefloor. The late afternoon cruise features a sunset dinner and stunning views of illuminated Hoover Dam. Cruises leave several times a day from the Lake Mead Cruises landing, a half mile beyond the Lake Mead Marina. ~ Lake Mead Marina: 322 Lakeshore Road, Boulder City, NV; 702-293-3484; Lake Mead Cruises: 702-293-6180.

Hoover Dam, which impounds Lake Mead, was a tourist attraction in the area even before the first casino was built on the Las Vegas Strip. This gigantic dam rises 726 feet above the river and generates four billion kilowatt-hours of electricity in a year. Containing over three million cubic yards of concrete, it was completed in 1935. Its Depression-era origins are evident in the art deco motifs that decorate the top of the dam. Notice the 30-foot-tall art nouveau figures outside—the Winged Figures of the Republic, cast in bronze by sculptor Oskar Hansen, and a terrazzo floor patterned with mystical cosmic symbols.

One of the guided tours, which takes about 35 minutes, begins with an elevator ride to the base of the dam. You'll feel the temperature drop as you descend—the dam's interior averages between 55 and 60 degrees year-round. At the base you'll

HOOVER DAM

Long before gambling became king, Hoover Dam was the number-one tourist attraction in Nevada. Completed in 1935, the dam was touted as the Eighth Wonder of the World. And for good reason. The dam is one of the world's engineering marvels. The horseshoe-shaped plug that holds back two-years' flow of the mighty Colorado River is as tall as a 54-story building. The base is 600 feet thick and contains enough concrete to build a two-lane highway from San Francisco to New York. Inside, there's as much reinforced steel as in the Empire State Building. The dam took five years to build, at a cost of $175 million. At the peak of construction, 5000 workers labored night and day. An average of 50 injuries a day and 94 deaths were recorded before the flood gates were closed and Lake Mead began to fill.

enter a monumental room housing the seven-story-high turbines that took three years to build and assemble, and which generate four billion kilowatt-hours of electricity.

The base of the dam is honey-combed with tunnels. One leads to a 30-foot diversion pipe; another to an outdoor observation deck where you can enjoy a fish-eye perspective of the dam and the rugged canyon it bridges. Returning to the top, you'll find a snack bar and souvenir shop. A more in-depth tour is offered at the dam and power plant. The "hard hat tour" takes about an hour, and leads you through the shaft gallery, the needle valve house, and the seepage gallery. You even get to keep the hat when it's over. Keep in mind that Nevada time is one hour earlier than Arizona's. Guided tours begin at the **Hoover Dam Visitors Center** and take visitors down into the interior of the dam on an elevator. Admission. ~ 702-294-3524; www.hooverdam.com.

LODGING & DINING   The only lodging on the Arizona shore of Lake Mead is at **Temple Bar Marina**, where you can rent a room at the modern motel, or one of the older cabins with kitchenettes. There is also a restaurant, cocktail lounge, campground, RV park, boat-launching ramp, fuel dock and store. This is the last outpost for supplies if you plan to boat north of Temple Bar. Limited menu in January and February. ~ 520-767-3211, 800-752-9669, fax 520-767-4514. BUDGET TO MODERATE.

There's a motel on the Nevada shore of the lake at **Echo Bay Resort and Marina**. Along with a restaurant and lounge, the motel offers modern rooms, an RV village and an airstrip for light aircraft (day-use only). ~ Overton, NV; 702-394-4000, 800-752-9669; www.sevencrown.com. BUDGET TO MODERATE.

About a half mile north of the Boulder Beach, **Lake Mead Resort and Marina** has hundreds of boat slips and a popular floating restaurant, coffee shop and cocktail lounge. The marina operates a **lodge** (702-293-2074), located just down the road, with 42 budget-priced rooms. Limited menu off-season. ~ 322 Lakeshore Road; 702-293-3484.

Farther north, the **Las Vegas Boat Harbor** has more boat slips, a restaurant, a picnic area and a campground ($10) with water but no electric hookups. ~ P.O. Box 91150, Henderson, NV 89009; 702-565-9111.

You can also camp or park your RV at **Callville Bay Resort Marina**, which has a boat launch, store, snack bar and cocktail lounge. The marina rents anything from jet skis to 65-foot houseboats. ~ HCR-30, Box 100, Las Vegas, NV 89124; 702-565-8958.

PARKS   **BOULDER BEACH** Most of Lake Mead's shoreline consists of rocks and gravel, but you can spread a beach towel at Boulder Beach. The two miles of beach and the clear water of Lake Mead attract year-round sunbathers. The clear water and warm temperatures attract divers, who can explore the sunken yachts *Tortuga* (near the Boulder Islands) and the *Cold Duck* (submerged in 35 feet of water), as well as the remains of Hoover Dam's asphalt factory. There are picnic areas, restrooms, a ranger station, a restaurant and convenience store nearby. ~ Located two miles north of the Lake Mead Visitors Center; 702-293-8990.

▲ There are 150 sites; $10 per night for tents and RVs (no hookups).

Bullhead City/Laughlin Area

Bullhead City, 35 miles west of Kingman via Route 68, may be Arizona's fastest-growing city, but it owes its prosperity to Laughlin, Nevada, on the far side of the river. The city of Laughlin is a shimmering riverfront resort that has blossomed into Nevada's third-largest gambling center. Because it has few residential and commercial areas of its own, most of the thousands of people who work there live, shop and send their kids to school in its Arizona sister, Bullhead City. The closest gambling zone to the greater Phoenix area, Laughlin is packed to overflowing every weekend. The rest of the week, the casinos, buffets, lounges and showrooms play host to motorhome nomads who appreciate the opportunity to avoid Las Vegas traffic and avail themselves of Laughlin's vast, free RV parking lots.

> In Nevada, near Echo Bay, is Rogers Spring, a warm-water oasis where prehistoric Indians once camped.

But gambling isn't the only attraction in the Bullhead City/ Laughlin area. The Colorado River and nearby Lake Mohave are major draws, offering year-round water sports such as swimming, boating, fishing and waterskiing. Also within short driving distance are ghost towns, historic mines, and intriguing lost canyons waiting to be explored.

SIGHTS

Commercial boat cruises are also a popular pastime. Before the bridge across the Colorado River was built in the mid 1980s, visitors used to park on the Arizona side of the river and ride passenger ferries across to the casinos on the Nevada shore. Now, on busy weekends when parking lots in Laughlin are full, the ferries still carry people across the river, making for a brief, fun, and, best of all, free cruise. Several companies also offer longer riverboat sightseeing tours down the river from casino docks. One is **Laughlin River Tours**, which runs the *Edgewater Belle* and the *Celebration* paddlewheel steamers from the Edgewater Casino dock or the Flamingo Hilton dock. ~ P.O. Box 29279, Laughlin, NV 89028; 702-298-1047, 800-228-9825. **Desert Recreation, Inc.** operates a blue-water yacht that departs from Harrah's for a journey up to Davis Dam. ~ 2900 South Casino Drive, Laughlin; 702-298-6828, 800-742-3224.

Bullhead City was incorporated in 1984, but it was founded in 1945 when it was the construction camp for Davis Dam, three miles upstream. The town, named for a rock formation now submerged by Lake Mohave, is a collection of lowrise housing tracts, shopping centers and mobile home parks. New housing developments and retirement communities along the Colorado River—Riviera, Fort Mohave and Golden Shores—have extended Bullhead City's outskirts as far south as Topock, at the junction of Route 40.

The best time to visit Bullhead City/Laughlin is in the winter and spring months, when the daytime temperatures range from 65 to 80°. Temperatures in July and August can reach an astounding 120° or more, making this area the hottest spot in the nation.

There's not much to see or do in Bullhead City, unless pre-fab homes and tilt-up shopping centers are your idea of excitement. So it's no surprise that the most-visited attraction in the area is the strip of ten casinos across the water on the river's western shore. Unlike their larger cousins on the famed Las Vegas Strip, the Laughlin hotel/casinos are close together and are easily accessible by a concrete strand that follows the river. The best is the **Colorado Belle**, a 600-foot replica of a Mississippi steamboat, complete with three decks and four black smokestacks. In the evening, the paddlewheel "turns" by strobe light. Inside, the decor is turn-of-the-century New Orleans, with lots of plush red carpeting, glass-globe lamps, brass railings and wrought-iron fixtures. The cluster of shops on the mezzanine level has several restaurants and an old-fashioned candy store. ~ 2100 South Casino Drive, Laughlin; 702-298-4000, 800-477-4837.

For a bit of Dodge City by the river try the **Pioneer Hotel and Gambling Hall** next door. The two-story hotel looks like a U-shaped fort, finished with weathered wood panels. The facade of the casino entrance suggests a Wild West boarding house. Swinging doors and a wooden porch lead into a hectic casino, decorated with dark-wood floors and distressed paneling. On the river side of the hotel is a waving neon cowboy—River Rick. He's Laughlin's version of Vegas Vic. The grounds facing the river include a lush flower garden, green grass and shade trees. ~ 2200 South Casino Drive, Laughlin; 702-298-2442, 800-634-3469.

Also worth visiting is the **Don Laughlin's Riverside Resort**. Be sure to stop in at the antiques shop just off the casino. The small but interesting collection consists of slot machines, jukeboxes, vintage radios, antique cars and a variety of old neon signs. On display, but not for sale, are antique slots from Don Laughlin's personal collection, including a 1938 vest pocket slot machine and

Don't Be Spooked

Arizona has two types of ghost towns—those that have been completely and irrevocably abandoned to the ravages of time and those that have risen into new life thanks to tourism. Good examples of both types can be found along the beat-up old segment of Route 66 that climbs and winds over the mountains between Kingman and Topock near the state's western boundary.

Goldroad, a once-prosperous town whose residents dug $7 million worth of gold ore out of the desert hillsides between 1901 and 1931, is just about gone now. All that remains are mine shafts, a few crumbling adobe walls and stone foundations.

Oatman, just two miles away, was another gold-mining town of about the same size, founded at about the same time as Goldroad and abandoned around the same time. The old buildings still stand. Some are boarded up, but many others have become curio shops and snack bars. People today come from all over the state on weekends to wander through town.

Why the difference? The landowners of Goldroad destroyed their buildings on purpose to reduce their property-tax assessments. In Oatman, though, a small group of "never say die" citizens survived the lean years by selling refreshments to passers-by on the old highway. Eventually, Hollywood discovered Oatman and used it as a set for several Western movies, including *How the West Was Won*. People around Oatman realized early on that one day old buildings might be worth more than the gold ore that some say still lies in the ground beneath both Goldroad and Oatman.

In recent years, Oatman has been declared a National Historic District, as have other famous Arizona ghost towns like the copper-mining towns of **Jerome** and **Bisbee** and the silver boom town of **Tombstone**. Historic status assures their continued survival and prosperity by offering special tax breaks to investors who restore the old buildings and by prohibiting anyone from tearing them down. Bed and breakfasts, cafés and yogurt shops are springing up behind the old storefronts, and parking is becoming a problem.

Without tourism as an economic base and incentive for preservation, there'd be no opportunity to wander the streets of a town from yesteryear. For those travelers with vivid imaginations, a good local history book and an urge to explore away from the well-trodden paths, the nearly vanished towns also have something special to offer. There's history unadorned in the dusty remains of places like **White Hills** and **Mineral Park** north of Kingman, **Walker** and **McCabe** in the national forest near Prescott and **Stanton** and **Weaverville** north of Wickenburg, as well as dozens of sites in the southeast part of the state. The **Arizona Office of Tourism** publishes a free brochure telling how to find these and other ghost towns. ~ 2702 North 3rd Street, Phoenix, AZ 85004; 602-230-7733, 800-842-8257.

a 1931 slot that paid off in golf balls. The resort also has a 34-lane bowling center. ~ 1650 South Casino Drive, Laughlin; 702-298-2535, 800-227-3849.

The **Davis Dam and Powerplant** was built in 1953 to produce hydroelectric power and regulate water delivery to Mexico. The powerplant, located downstream from the dam embankment on the Arizona side of the river, is no longer open to the public, but you can walk across the top of the dam for a scenic view of the Colorado River and the Bullhead City/Laughlin area downstream. ~ About three miles north of Bullhead City on Route 68; 520-754-3628.

Behind the dam lies **Lake Mohave** (part of the Lake Mead National Recreation Area), which extends 67 miles upstream to Hoover Dam. The long, narrow lake (four miles across at its widest point) provides a multitude of recreational opportunities, including fishing, boating, waterskiing and windsurfing.

Lake Mohave is accessible at only two points in Arizona: Willow Beach, off Route 93 about 60 miles north of Kingman, and Katherine Landing, six miles north of Bullhead City and Laughlin. **Lake Mohave Resort**, six miles north of Bullhead City, rents houseboats and other craft for use on Lake Mohave. ~ Katherine Landing; 520-754-3245, 800-752-9669. **Willow Beach Harbor** also provides rentals. ~ 520-767-4747.

On the Nevada shore of Lake Mohave is **Cottonwood Cove Resort**. Facilities include a marina, a motel, a restaurant, boat rentals, a campground and an RV park. ~ 702-565-8958.

LODGING   On Sunday through Thursday nights, rooms cost significantly less in the casino hotels of Laughlin, Nevada, than they do in Bullhead City on the Arizona side of the Colorado River. In fact, on weeknights, you can rent a spacious, modern room with a king-size bed, remote control television, art prints and designer wallpaper in Laughlin for about the same rate as a plain, somewhat threadbare room in an aging mom-and-pop motel by the interstate in Kingman.

For most visitors to the Bullhead City/Laughlin area, there is probably not much point to staying on the Arizona side of the river. Most of the motels in Bullhead City are clean and modern but unexceptional, and room rates tend to run higher than in the Laughlin casino hotels. They seem to thrive on weekend and peak-season overflows.

It's hard to believe that a number of people with aversions to the gambling scene would go out of their way to stay in Bullhead City when they could as easily proceed south to the more family-oriented Lake Havasu City. But if they did, they'd find good non-casino lodging in Bullhead City at the **Bullhead River Lodge**. It is an all-suite motel that rents by the week or month, ideal for fam-

ilies, with a boat and fishing dock available for use at no charge.
~ 455 Moser Avenue, Bullhead City; 520-754-2250. BUDGET.

Operated by the same folks who run Bullhead River Lodge,
Hilltop Hotel has 57 rooms and suites. Laundry facilities are available, as well as beach dock, fishing and boating privileges at Bullhead River Lodge. ~ 2037 Route 95, Bullhead City; 520-758-6620,
fax 520-758-6612. BUDGET.

Just a stone's throw from the Colorado River, **Gretchen's Inn**
is a small but modern hostelry, with a Southwest motif. The
rooms, some with river views, are exceptionally large and tastefully decorated. Suites and kitchenettes are available. ~ 1081
Route 95, Bullhead City; 520-754-2440, fax 520-754-2526.
BUDGET TO MODERATE.

Set on a prime lakefront location, the **Lake Mohave Resort**
features a private marine, beach area and landscaped grounds for
spotting quail, roadrunners and jackrabbits. Accommodations,
which are basic motel-style rooms decorated with blue fabrics and
desert artwork, all face the lake. ~ Katharine Landing just above
Davis Dam; 520-754-3245, 800-752-9669, fax 520-7541125;
www.sevencrown.com. BUDGET.

Although there are 10,000 hotel rooms in Laughlin, busy weekends often attract up to 50,000 visitors. You don't need a calculator to figure the result: Reservations are a must. Like their Vegas
cousins, the hotels in Laughlin offer the basic amenities—casinos,
bars, restaurants, inexpensive buffets and lounge entertainment
—and the guest rooms are comparable. Most hotel accommodations in Laughlin are in the budget range during the week and in
the moderate-to-deluxe range on the weekend, but they can be
in short supply. Laughlin's strip consists of ten casino hotels.

Top of the line and the closest to the bridge across the river
from Bullhead City, is **Don Laughlin's Riverside Resort Hotel and
Casino**. The resort's owner conceived the idea of promoting a
casino strip here, founded the town that is named after him, and

▼▲

✔ CHECK THESE OUT—UNIQUE LODGING

- *Budget:* Stay at the historic **Oatman Hotel** and ask to see the simple room where Clark Gable and Carole Lombard spent their honeymoon. *page 160*
- *Budget:* Cross the Nevada border and check into the **Colorado Belle**, a showy casino-hotel shaped like a Mississippi steamboat. *page 170*
- *Budget to moderate:* Motor up to the **Temple Bar Marina**, the only waterfront accommodations on Lake Mead. *page 164*
- *Moderate to deluxe:* Go sailing, boating and waterskiing until your heart's content when you're a guest at the **Nautical Inn**. *page 175*

Budget: under $70   Moderate: $70–$110   Deluxe: $110–$180   Ultra-deluxe: over $180

in 1966 converted the old Riverside Bait Shop on this site into Laughlin's first casino. Since then, it has added a 26-story hotel tower, a second swimming pool and a nonsmoking casino. ~ 1650 Casino Drive, Laughlin; 702-298-2535, 800-227-3849, fax 702-298-2614; www.riversideresort.com. BUDGET.

For gorgeous river views, check out the **Edgewater Hotel**, whose frosty-white, 26-story tower has the most rooms fronting the Colorado. All 1402 guest rooms and 26 suites are comfortable and tastefully decorated. At the dock, pay for a river cruise on the *Edgewater Belle* paddleboat. ~ 2020 South Casino Drive, Laughlin; 702-298-2453, 800-677-4837, fax 702-298-8165; www.edgewater-casino.com. BUDGET TO ULTRA-DELUXE.

For half the year, Bullhead City, AZ is one hour ahead of Laughlin, NV, which is in another time zone. The rest of the time Nevada switches to Daylight Savings and you won't need to adjust your watch each time you cross the Colorado River.

Some of the other hotels are famous-name spin-offs from well-known Las Vegas and Reno establishments, such as the **Flamingo Hilton**, where ribbons of pink neon wrap through the casino and restaurants. The 1914 rooms in the shiny pink twin towers are typically Hilton—spacious and modern, and decorated in festive colors. Hotel amenities include six restaurants, a production show and a beautifully landscaped garden overlooking the river. ~ 1900 South Casino Drive, Laughlin; 702298-5111, 800-352-6464, fax 702-298-5177; www.hilton.com. MODERATE.

Or try the **Golden Nugget** where you're serenaded by songbirds as you check in. (The cage housing the birds is just for show—they're mechanical!) The theme at the Nugget is jungle: a giant waterfall as you enter, plenty of green plants and 300 rooms done in tropical decor. The Tarzan lounge, four restaurants and a gift emporium are some of the hotel's amenities. ~ 2300 South Casino Drive, Laughlin; 702-298-7111, 800-950-7700, fax 702-298-7122. BUDGET.

The **Colorado Belle**, a showy casino hotel shaped like a giant riverboat midway down the strip, was created by the same company that owns Circus Circus and the Excalibur in Las Vegas. ~ 2100 South Casino Drive, Laughlin; 702-298-4000, 800-477-4837; www.coloradobelle.com. BUDGET.

The covered terrace and pool area at **River Palms Resort and Casino** with its palm trees, green lawns and river view is a great spot for lounging. Inside, the 1000 rooms are bright and airy with plush carpeting, smoked-glass tables and velour-upholstered chairs. Be sure to check out the casino with its high ceilings and tropical decor. ~ 2700 South Casino Drive, Laughlin; 702-298-2242, 800-835-7903, fax 702-298-2196; www.rvrpalm.com. BUDGET TO ULTRA-DELUXE.

Just around a bend in the river is **Harrah's Laughlin**, which sits in a private cove at the south end of casino row. The cove fronting the hotel offers the only sandy beach on casino row. With a south-of-the-border theme, fiesta colors are splashed throughout the casino, four restaurants, three bars and the 1600 guest rooms. ~ 2900 South Casino Drive, Laughlin; 702-298-4600, 800-427-7247, fax 702-298-6896; www.harrahs.com. BUDGET TO DELUXE.

It's not the Reading, but you can ride the rails on a mini-passenger train at the **Ramada Express**. The narrow-gauge railroad shuttles you on a 15-minute ride from the parking lot to the casino, decorated like a Victorian railroad station. Guest rooms in the 1500-room towers behind the casino feature either mint green or deep earth-tone colors, dark-wood furniture and brass lamps and fixtures. ~ 2121 South Casino Drive, Laughlin; 702-298-4200, 800-243-6846, fax 702-298-6403. BUDGET TO MODERATE.

DINING

Along with a nice view of Lake Mohave, Lake Mohave Resort's restaurant **Tail of the Whale** serves a tasty grilled catfish and other seafood dishes, plus steaks and chops. ~ Katherine Landing just above Davis Dam; 520-754-3245. MODERATE.

In Laughlin, hit the casinos for inexpensive feasts. Just about every hotel on Casino Row has an all-you-can-eat buffet featuring 40 or more items, in the budget range for dinner and almost absurdly affordable—no more than you'd spend at a franchise hamburger joint—for breakfast and lunch. To sweeten the deal even more, two-for-one buffet coupons are included in free "fun books" widely distributed in visitors centers and truck stops in Kingman and elsewhere along Route 40. The largest buffet in town is located at the **Edgewater Hotel**. ~ 2020 South Casino Drive, Laughlin; 702-298-2453. BUDGET.

Each casino also has a full-service 24-hour coffee shop, most of them featuring breakfast specials priced between 99 cents and $1.99. Notable among the 24-hour casual places is **Flamingo Diner**, a classic '50s-style diner and coffee shop. ~ Flamingo Hilton, 1900 South Casino Drive, Laughlin; 702-298-5111. BUDGET TO MODERATE.

Many, though not all, casinos also have slightly more upscale fine dining restaurants. **Harrah's Laughlin** offers an intimate atmosphere and a riverside view at William Fisk's Steakhouse (reservations required) or authentic Mexican fare at La Hacienda. ~ 2900 South Casino Drive, Laughlin; 702-298-4600. MODERATE TO DELUXE.

Another option is the **Prime Rib Room**, where you can supervise the carving at your table. ~ Riverside Resort, 1650 South Casino Drive, Laughlin; 702-298-2535. BUDGET. Yet another choice is the **Alta Villa** for Continental-style cuisine. ~ Flamingo Hilton,

1900 South Casino Drive, Laughlin; 702-298-5111. MODERATE TO DELUXE.

In the **Colorado Belle**, seafood is a specialty in the casually classy Orleans Room. Dinner only. ~ 2100 South Casino Drive, Laughlin; 702298-4000. MODERATE TO ULTRA-DELUXE.

River Palms serves fine American and Continental selections in Madeleine's Lodge, designed in a hunting lodge theme with wood-beamed ceiling and big stone fireplace, all so convincing that you may forget that you're in a casino. Dinner only. ~ 2700 Casino Drive, Laughlin; 702-298-2242. MODERATE TO ULTRA-DELUXE.

Country cooking is never out of reach at the **Boarding House Restaurant** at the Pioneer Hotel, where you can feast on a dinner of fried chicken, barbecued ribs, prime rib or baked ham. These entrées are also available during the Saturday buffet. Go easy on the cornbread and save room for homemade strawberry shortcake. ~ 2200 South Casino Drive, Laughlin; 702-298-2442. BUDGET TO MODERATE.

SHOPPING   Shoppers will delight in the bargains found at **Horizon Outlet Center**, which brings together more than 50 shops offering everything from clothing, shoes and jewelry to perfumes and luggage. Among them are **Bugle Boy, Reebok/Rockport, Maidenform, Samsonite, Levi's** and **Polo Ralph Lauren**. ~ 1955 South Casino Drive, Laughlin; 702-298-3003.

NIGHTLIFE   Nightlife on the river all happens in Laughlin where each of the casinos has at least one, often two, cocktail lounges that don't charge for watching musical acts that perform here while practicing for Las Vegas. Only one of the casinos has a showroom where name acts appear: **Don's Celebrity Theater** hosts such performers as Roy Clark, the Smothers Brothers, the Oakridge Boys, Debbie Reynolds and Willie Nelson. Cover. ~ Don Laughlin's Riverside Resort, 1650 Casino Drive, Laughlin; 702-298-2535.

Also at the Riverside, the **Western Dance Hall** features dancing to country music (live or videotaped), and the **Western Ballroom** hosts a Sunday afternoon big band dance.

The town's only production show is staged at the **Silver Bullet Showroom** in the Flamingo Hilton. Past acts have included top impersonators and a Broadway-style revue. **Flamingo Spring and Fall Concert Series** at the Flamingo's outdoor amphitheater usually features nostalgic acts the likes of Wayne Newton, the Doobie Brothers and Jerry Lee Lewis. Cover at both facilities. ~ 1900 South Casino Drive, Laughlin; 702-298-5111.

PARKS   The **Colorado River** and **Lake Mohave** provide a multitude of recreational activities, including boating, fishing, waterskiing, scuba diving and windsurfing. Landlubbing hikers will love the desert and canyons surrounding Bullhead City/Laughlin. Lake Mohave above **Davis Dam** actually resembles the river below the dam—the lake stretches for 67 miles through jagged canyons and rocky mountains. At its widest point, it is only four miles from shore to shore.

KATHERINE LANDING Located just 640 feet above sea level along Lake Mohave, Katherine Landing's flora and fauna is representative of the surrounding Mojave Desert. Short hikes into the area reveal desert shrubs, cacti and roadrunners, as well as views of the Black and Newberry Mountains in the distance. There's striped bass, bluegill and channel catfish for anglers, and there's good swimming at South Telephone Cove. There are a picnic area, restrooms, pay showers, laundry facilities, a full-service marina with boat rentals, fishing tackle and water-ski rentals, a motel, a restaurant and grocery store, and a visitors center. ~ Located just north of Bullhead City off of Route 68; 520-754-3272.

▲ There are 170 campground sites, each with a barbecue grill, picnic table and running water; $10 per night.

DAVIS CAMP COUNTY PARK Here at the only public beach on the Colorado River you'll find a stretch of sandy beach where you can swim, fish or launch a jet ski. You can angle here for striped bass, catfish and trout, and there's a marked off swimming area good for children. At the south end of the park is a marsh that's home to variety of birds and other small wildlife. There are restrooms, showers, laundry facilities, barbecue grills and ramadas with picnic tables. Day-use fee, $3. ~ Located about one mile north of Laughlin on the Arizona side of the river; 520-754-4606.

▲ There are 141 sites with full hookups ($15 per night), 30 sites with partial hookups ($11 per night) and an open area for tent camping ($8 per night).

WILLOW BEACH Nearby, you can tour the Willow Beach National Fish Hatchery that keeps Lake Mohave stocked, and its small exhibit room where you can learn about the Colorado River's history. Bait, tackle and fishing licenses are available at the dock; try for trout and striped bass. There are restrooms, picnic grounds, barbecue grills, boat rentals, fuel and a grocery store. ~ On Lake Mohave about 14 miles south of Hoover Dam off of Route 93; 520-767-4747.

Lake Havasu Area

About 20 miles upstream from Parker Dam, Lake Havasu may be the prettiest dammed lake along the Colorado River. Cool and bright blue in the heart of the desert, this 46-mile-long lake has become a very popular recreation area.

SIGHTS   Lake Havasu's main claim to fame is **London Bridge** in Lake Havasu City; except for the Grand Canyon, the bridge is the most visited tourist attraction in Arizona. The audacity and monumental pointlessness of the city fathers' moving the bridge here when the city of London decided to replace it draws curiosity seekers in droves. To believe it, you have to see it.

Originally built in 1825 to replace a still older London Bridge that had lasted 625 years, this bridge was sold at auction in 1968. Lake Havasu City's promoters bought it for $2,460,000. The 10,000 tons of granite facing were disassembled into blocks weighing from 1000 to 17,000 pounds each, shipped and trucked 10,000 miles to this site and reconstructed on the shore of Lake Havasu when the city was practically nonexistent. Then a canal was dug to let water flow under the bridge.

It is 49 feet wide and 928 feet long, and you can drive or walk across it. Every year, millions do. Is it worth seeing? Absolutely! It's a giant object lesson in the fine line between madness and genius—and one of the strangest things in Arizona.

To add more British atmosphere, the developers built an English-style village nearby. Here, you'll find a double-decker bus, a London cab, a bright-red wooden phone booth and a somewhat authentic Liverpool pub—the City of London Arms. In recent years, however, the "shoppes" in the English village have begun to look more like Coney Island than Piccadilly Circus, with a slew of T-shirt and ashtray souvenir stores, fast-food stands that dispense flavorless fish-and-chips, even a Wild West gift shop. For more information about the bridge and the surrounding area head for the **Lake Havasu Chamber of Commerce.** ~ 314 London Bridge Road; 520-855-4115, 520-453-3440.

Nevertheless, the stately London Bridge is an impressive sight with its sweeping arches of chiseled granite. A great time to see it is at night, when it glows against the cobalt sky.

In **Lake Havasu City**, a number of boats offer sightseeing tours from London Bridge, including the large Mississippi riverboat

RIVER OF THE DAMMED

Davis Dam is one of three dams operating to control flooding and produce hydroelectric power along the Colorado River. Along with the other two—**Hoover Dam** to the north and **Parker Dam**, about 80 miles downstream—they form the Lower Colorado River Dams project. They also divert river water to form three lakes: Lake Mead, Lake Mohave and Lake Havasu. Another six large dams in Colorado, Utah and New Mexico also control the waters of the mighty Colorado.

replica *Dixie Belle*. ~ 520-453-6776, 520-855-0888. **Bluewater Jet Boat Tours** runs daily boat excursions from London Bridge to Topock Gorge and the Havasu National Wildlife Refuge. ~ 520-855-7171.

In the little town of **Topock**, located midway between Bull-head City and Lake Havasu City at the junction of Route 40 and Route 95 South, Jerkwater Canoe and Kayak Co. rents canoes and kayaks to explore otherwise inaccessible areas of the **Havasu National Wildlife Refuge**. The company can also provide directions to the beautiful **Topock Gorge**, ancient petroglyph sites and the **Topock Maze**, where Mohave Indians used to go to cleanse their spirits after long journeys. ~ Jerkwater Canoe and Kayak Co.; 520-768-7753.

◄ *HIDDEN*

Across the bridge from the Olde English Village, on the island, the **Nautical Inn** has a golf course, as well as a private dock with waterskiing, sailing, boating and jet-skiing equipment for guests. All the guest rooms are on the waterfront. Each carpeted unit comes with two queen-sized beds, a patio and direct access to the lawn and beach. The suites include refrigerators and kitchenettes. ~ 1000 McCulloch Boulevard, Lake Havasu City; 520-855-2141, 800-892-2141, fax 520-453-5808. MODERATE TO DELUXE.

LODGING

Within a half-mile of the bridge, 64 standard motel rooms are available at the **Windsor Inn**, which has a pool and spa. ~ 451 London Bridge Road, Lake Havasu City; 520-855-4135, 800-245-4135, fax 520-855-3583. BUDGET. The **Days Inn** also has similar accommodations, with a pool. ~ 2190 McCulloch Boulevard, Lake Havasu City; 520-855-4157, 800-982-3622, fax 520-453-1514. MODERATE.

Spacious one- and two-bedroom suites are available at the **Sands Vacation Resort**. Pictures of the Southwest decorate the pastel walls of these courtyard units. Each carpeted suite includes a living room, dining area and kitchenette. A sauna, jacuzzi and fitness center are on the premises. ~ 2040 Mesquite Avenue, Lake Havasu City; 520-855-1388, 800-521-0360, fax 520-453-1802; www.interworldnet.net/sands. MODERATE.

Lake Havasu City, oddly, has virtually no high-priced haute cuisine, but it does have a good selection of pleasant, affordable restaurants. A good place for salads, steaks and seafood is **Shugrue's** in back of the Island Fashion Mall, which has an unbeatable view of London Bridge from the island side through tall wraparound windows. Fresh bakery goods are the specialty. ~ 1425 McCulloch Boulevard, Lake Havasu City; 520-453-1400. MODERATE TO ULTRA-DELUXE.

DINING

Next door to Shugrue's, **Barley Brothers** microbrewery cooks pizzas in a wood-burning oven and also serves salads, pasta, rotisserie chicken, ribs and sandwiches. ~ 1425 McCulloch Boulevard, Lake Havasu City; 520-505-7837. MODERATE.

Also on the island, the **Captain's Table**, in the Nautical Inn, serves seafood and traditional American menu selections with a lakeside view. ~ 1000 McCulloch Boulevard, Lake Havasu City; 520-855-2141. BUDGET TO DELUXE.

Away from the water, a local favorite is **Krystal's**, featuring specialties such as Alaskan king crab legs, lobster tails and mahi-mahi. ~ 460 El Camino Way, Lake Havasu City; 520-453-2999. MODERATE TO ULTRA-DELUXE.

Another long-time local favorite is **Nicolino's Italian Restaurant**, serving 30 varieties of pasta. ~ 86 South Smoketree Avenue, Lake Havasu City; 520-855-3484. BUDGET TO DELUXE.

In the English Village on the mainland side of the bridge, there's the usually busy **Mermaid Inn**, serving fish and chips, clam strips and hamburgers. ~ 401 English Village, London Bridge, Lake Havasu City; 520-855-3234. BUDGET.

SHOPPING   Arizona's "West Coast" holds a number of enticements for visitors, but shopping isn't one of them. The most interesting shopping district in the area is the **Olde English Village** on the mainland side of London Bridge in Lake Havasu, and the most remarkable thing about it, other than its vast expanse of bright-green lawn in the heart of one of America's most desolate deserts, is that the land on which it was built was owned by the city of London—making the bridge a symbolic link between London and Lake Havasu City. The cute Olde English buildings housing the shops and snack bars remind us that the city and the bridge were the brainchild of the retired general manager of Disneyland. The Olde English Village has about two dozen theme gift shops such as the London Arms Gift Shoppe, the Copper Shoppe, the Gallerie of Glasse and the Curiosity Shoppe, as well as the London Bridge Candle Factory, which claims to be the world's largest candle shop. ~ 520-855-0888.

At the other end of the bridge, the **Island Fashion Mall** houses a dozen shops selling men's and women's fashions, sportswear and fine jewelry. ~ 1425 McCulloch Boulevard, Lake Havasu City; 520-855-6274.

NIGHTLIFE   In addition to Lake Havasu City's hotels cocktail lounges, a nice spot for an intimate encounter is **London Arms Pub and Restaurant**, a British-style pub and microbrewery that looks transplanted from Walpole Street. It has a used-brick facade, a "Big Ben" clock tower, two outdoor patios (one a replica of Hyde Park), a wrought-iron fence, stately carriage lamps and private leather-lined booths. ~ 422 English Village, Lake Havasu City; 520-855-8782.

Grab a "desert martini" (a beer with an olive in it) or settle
for standard beer and wine at the **Desert Martini**. This pool hall
also features darts, shuffleboard and five TVs. ~ 2120 McCulloch
Boulevard, Lake Havasu City; 520-855-1818.

LAKE HAVASU STATE PARK 🚶 ⛵ 🏕 ⛺ 🚤 🛥 🛶 This shore-   **PARKS**
line park area in and around Lake Havasu City encompasses
most of the Arizona shore of this broad blue lake nestled among
stark, rocky desert hills. The park has a campground and a rocky
swimming beach at Windsor Beach, north of the center of town.
Fish for largemouth bass, striped bass and catfish. There are picnic areas, restrooms, showers, and nature trails. Day-use fee, $4
weekdays, $7 weekends. ~ The main automobile accessible area
is at Windsor Beach. Other areas of the park, which includes most
of the east shore of Lake Havasu, are only accessible by boat; 520-
855-2784.

▲ The 74 sites at Windsor Beach (520-855-2784) cost $12
per night. Also available are 125 primitive boat-in sites along
the shore in the Aubrey Hills Natural Area, south of Lake Havasu City, operated by the BLM (520-505-1200); some sites have
vault toilets, picnic tables and shade structures; $10 per night
per boat.

CATTAIL COVE STATE PARK 🚶 ⛵ 🏕 ⛺ 🚤 🛶 About 15
miles south of Lake Havasu City, Cattail Cove is a 2000-acre
lakeside park with ample recreational opportunities. Fishing yields
crappie, bluegill and striped and largemouth bass. Nearby, Sandpoint Marina and RV Park (520-855-0549) has a restaurant, groceries, laundry facilities and boat rentals. Facilities include picnic
areas, restrooms, showers and concessions. Day-use fee, $4 per
vehicle Monday through Thursday, $7 per vehicle Friday through
Sunday. ~ Located off Route 95, 15 miles south of Lake Havasu
City; 520-855-1223.

▲ There are 66 sites; $10 per night, $15 with hookups.

HAVASU NATIONAL WILDLIFE REFUGE 🚶 🛶 🚤 🛶 Nature
buffs will enjoy this wildlife refuge, which straddles the Colorado
River from Topock, 20 miles north of Lake Havasu City, to Mesquite Bay, just north of the city. Hikers through the marshy trails
are often rewarded with views of a bald eagle, peregrine falcon,
or a number of winter visitors: snow and Canada geese and other
waterfowl. There are restrooms at Catfish Paradise and Mesquite
Bay; showers and laundry facilities at 5-Mile Landing. ~ The
refuge headquarters is at 315 Mesquite Avenue, Needles, CA. To
get to the park from Lake Havasu, go north on Route 95 to Route
40, and drive nine miles west to the exit marked Havasu National
Wildlife Refuge (Mohave County 227); 760-326-3853.

▲ There are 40 sites at 5-Mile Landing on Topock Marsh; $7 per night ($14.50 per night with hookups); information, 520-768-2350.

Parker Dam Area

Downstream from Parker Dam, which impounds Lake Havasu, the Colorado River flows through the Colorado River Indian Reservation to Parker, a nondescript trade center about 35 miles south of Lake Havasu City. Just two miles north of Parker, Headgate Rock Dam impedes the Colorado to form Lake Moovalya, an 11-mile stretch of water recreation better known as "The Parker Strip."

SIGHTS

Parker was nothing more than a postal stop until the railroad came through in 1908. Most of the town's development, however, occurred after the river was dammed and tourists began flocking to the lakes upstream. Recreation remains Parker's main reason for existing, along with a moderate climate that attracts several thousand snowbirds, mostly retirees, each winter.

The town itself has little to offer; many of its 3000 citizens live in wall-to-wall RV parks scattered across the scrub-brush hillsides, dotted with an occasional red-tile-roof home. Despite Parker's lackluster appeal, the area is besieged by visitors who enjoy year-round boating, waterskiing and inner-tubing (there's even an annual seven-mile inner-tube race) along the scenic Parker Strip.

The city's main attraction is the **Colorado River Indian Tribes Museum**, a storehouse of prehistoric American Indian artifacts from the Anasazi, Hohokam and other tribes, as well as dioramas of pueblos and other dwellings, crafts and folk art of the more modern Mohave, Chemehuevi, Navajo and Hopi people. Most interesting is the photo gallery of early reservation life and archival library of old manuscripts, books and other documents. Visit the gift shop before leaving; it has a good assortment of American Indian publications, baskets, beadwork and other crafts. Closed weekend mornings. ~ 2nd Avenue and Mohave Road, Parker; 520-669-9211.

About 15 miles upstream sits **Parker Dam**, a virtual twin to Davis Dam. One significant difference is you that can see only one-third of Parker Dam; the bedrock foundation is 235 feet below the riverbed. Like its upstream cousin, Parker Dam is open for self-guided tours. Be sure to step into the turbine room and watch the massive generator shaft spinning. ~ 520-663-3712.

If you'd like a change of pace, drive 34 miles south on Route 95 to the town of **Quartzsite**, the site of one of the strangest reunions in Arizona, and possibly the world. Although the dusty scrub-brush town—if you can call it that—consists of just a few motels, restaurants, and RV parks, each winter its population swells from several hundred to several hundred thousand. The reason?

The **Quartzsite Gemborees**, six shows resembling Bedouin bazaars for rock-swappers and gem collectors. Held in late January and early February, the festivals attract droves of rock and gem aficionados for a metallurgical freakout. In addition to the hundreds of booths, where you can buy everything from healing crystals to 5000-pound slabs of quartz, the festivals feature flea markets, antique and collectibles shows, a rodeo, camel and ostrich races, country music, an auto show—all choreographed in the tradition of Hunter Thompson. Started in 1964 by a rag-tag group of rock hounds, the original event has grown to six annual shows, becoming Quartzsite's main reason for existence. For further details about the Quartzsite Gemborees, contact Howard Armstrong at P.O. Box 2801, Quartzsite, AZ 85346; 520-927-5213.

LODGING

You won't find a bellhop in this part of the country, but there are clean rooms at **El Rancho Motel**, along with a few kitchenettes, microwave ovens, refrigerators, a pool and in-room coffee. ~ 709 California Avenue, Parker; 520-669-2231, fax 520-669-8777. BUDGET.

Traveling families will like the **Stardust Motel** because of its oversized rooms and mini-suites, all with refrigerators and microwave ovens, all clean and well maintained. The motel also has a pool. ~ 700 California Avenue, Parker; 520-669-2278, fax 520-669-6658. BUDGET.

DINING

One of the best places to eat in Parker is **El Palacio Restaurant**, a bustling Mexican restaurant with hand-painted pottery and other folk art on the walls. The food is spicy, hot and delicious, especially the pork tamales, menudo and chile rellenos. ~ 1885 Route 95, Parker; 520-763-2494. BUDGET TO MODERATE.

For home-cooked American dishes, try the **Paradise Cafe**, a formica-topped, family-run eatery that caters to regular locals who feast on the barbecued chicken, pork ribs, fish and chips and homemade pies. ~ Route 95 at Riverside Drive, Parker; 520-667-2404. BUDGET TO MODERATE.

PARKS

LA PAZ COUNTY PARK You can spread a beach towel or picnic blanket at this grassy recreational area. Located along a one-mile stretch of the Colorado River, the park is perfect for a relaxed family outing. Common catches for anglers are bass, catfish, bluegill, striper, flathead and perch. Swimming is good at the sandy beach. There are covered ramadas, barbecue grills, picnic tables, restrooms, showers, tennis courts, a baseball field and a playground. Day-use fee, $2 per person. ~ About eight miles north of Parker via Route 95; 520-667-2069.

▲ About a third of the park is open to tent camping; $10 per night. There are also 30 ramada sites ($12 per night) and 114

RV sites with full hookups ($15 per night). All camping fees are for two people; there's a $2 charge for each additional person.

BUCKSKIN MOUNTAIN STATE PARK 🏃 🚶 ⛴ 🛥 🚤 ⛵ This state park located near Parker Dam caters to tube floaters, boaters and waterskiiers. But you can also hike the nature trails in the mountains that surround the eastern edge of the park. In addition to panoramic vistas of the Colorado River, hikers can sometimes catch a glimpse of desert bighorn sheep that roam the area. Fish for bass, bluegill and catfish. There is a picnic ground, restrooms, gas dock, inner-tube rentals and snack bar. Day-use fee, $4 weekdays per vehicle, $7 weekends. ~ Buckskin Mountain is on Route 95, about 11 miles north of Parker. The River Island Unit is another one and a half miles north of Buckskin Mountain; 520-667-3231.

▲ Buckskin Mountain has 89 sites (water and electric hookups, $15 per night; cabañas, $20 per night). River Island offers 37 sites (some with water hookups; $12 per night). Restrooms and showers are available at both campgrounds.

ALAMO LAKE STATE PARK ⛴ 🛥 🚤 ⛵ The main draw at this 5642-acre park is the fishing. The 3000-acre Alamo Lake offers up bass, bluegill, crappie and catfish; get your fishing license from the park concessions stand. Water activities such as waterskiing are another popular pastime. Facilities include a playground, picnic areas, a concession stand, restrooms and showers. Day-use fee, $4. ~ Located about 100 miles from Parker. Take Route 95 from Parker, continue on Route 72 to Route 60. It's about 40 miles from Wenden; 520-669-2088.

▲ There are 250 sites: $16 per night for hookups; $10 per weekend night for undeveloped sites; $8 per weeknight for undeveloped sites.

▼▼▼▼▼▼▼▼▼▼▼▼▼▼
Outdoor Adventures

This region offers some of Arizona's best fishing. It's open season on all fish year-round at Lake Mead and the abundant Colorado River.

FISHING

LAKE MEAD AREA   There's plenty of catfish, bluegill, crappie and striped bass, often tipping the scales at 30 pounds, at **Lake Mead**. Spring and fall are the best seasons. One of the best spots for bass is near the Las Vegas Boat Harbor because of the wastewater nutrients that dump from the Las Vegas Wash. The Overton arm of Lake Mead is one of the best areas for striped bass, whose threadfin shad schools often churn the water in their feeding frenzies. Also worth trying are Calico Basin, Hemenway Harbour the Meadows, Stewarts Point and Meat Hole. For tips on other spots, ask any park ranger or try any of the marinas, which also sell licenses, bait and tackle. For example, **Lake Mead Marina**

rents fishing boats with tackle included and sells bait and fishing gear at the marina store. ~ 322 Lakeshore Road; 702-293-3484. Also on the lake is the **Las Vegas Bay Marina**. ~ Lake Mead Drive; 702-565-9111. **Callville Bay Resort Marina** has licenses, bait and tackle. ~ HCR 30, Box 100, off Northshore Road; 702-565-8958. **Echo Bay Resort and Marina** is a good spot to fulfill your fishing and boating needs. ~ 702-394-4000. **Temple Bar Marina** also sells bait. ~ 520-767-3211. For fishing guide services, contact **Karen Jones**, who leads six-hour trips on a 24-foot triple pontoon boat. ~ 702-566-5775, cellular 702-497-5902.

BULLHEAD CITY/LAUGHLIN AREA Fishing is also excellent along the **Colorado River** near the Bullhead City/Laughlin area. Anglers can fill their creels with striped bass, rainbow trout, bass, catfish, bluegill and crappie. A good spot is the cold water below Davis Dam. There's also good fishing above the dam on **Lake Mohave**, noted for its rainbow trout and bass.

This is one of the wettest parts of the state and opportunities for water sports abound.

WATER SPORTS

LAKE MEAD AREA On Arizona's West Coast, you can skip across Lake Mead in a power or ski boat, or simply relax under sail or on the deck of a houseboat. For rentals in the Lake Mead area, try the **Callville Bay Resort Marina**. ~ HCR 30, Box 100, off Northshore Road; 702-565-8958. **Lake Mead Marina** also has rentals. ~ 322 Lakeshore Road; 702-293-3484. Another place to rent boats at the north end of Lake Mead is **Echo Bay Resort and Marina**. ~ 702-394-4000.

BULLHEAD CITY/LAUGHLIN AREA In the Bullhead City/Laughlin area, waterskiing is permitted along the Colorado River from Davis Dam to Needles. The sparsely populated area just below Bullhead City is the best choice. You can also waterski on Lake Mohave north of Davis Dam. For boat rentals and equipment, check out **Lake Mohave Resort**. ~ Katherine Landing; 520-754-3245.

LAKE HAVASU AREA The lower Colorado River and Lake Havasu are a mecca for watersport enthusiasts, and craft of all kinds are available for rent. In Lake Havasu City, pontoon boats are available at **Island Boat Rentals**. ~ 1580 Dover Avenue; 520-453-3260. **Havasu Springs Resort** rents fishing boats, houseboats, pontoons and runabouts. ~ Route 95, Parker; 520-667-3361. **Bluewater Boat Rentals** has pontoon boats and power boats for fishing and waterskiing. They also provide charter boat tours of Topock Gorge and trips to Laughlin, Nevada. ~ 501 English Village; 520-453-9613, 888-855-7171. Fifteen miles south of Lake Havasu City, **Sandpoint Marina** rents fishing boats, pontoon boats and houseboats. ~ 520-855-0549.

RIVER
RUNNING

The four-mile stretch of Colorado River from Hoover Dam to Willow Beach is open year-round to rafts, canoes and kayaks, but the best time is spring and fall. Expect to see birds and other desert wildlife in this steep-walled wilderness canyon. It's smooth water all the way, with no rapids, and there are well-marked hot springs along the river bank. River running requires a permit from the **Hoover Dam Canoe Launch**. Only 30 permits are issued a day; advance reservations required. ~ 702-293-8204. For canoe and kayak rentals, try **Boulder City Water Sports**. ~ 1108 Nevada Highway, Boulder City, NV; 702-293-7526. It's not exactly white-knuckle rafting, but you can float down the Colorado River from Hoover Dam to Willow Beach and see waterfalls, hot springs and geological formations. For organized raft trips, contact **Black Canyon, Inc.** ~ 1297 Nevada Highway, Boulder City, NV; 702-293-3776.

GOLF

KINGMAN AREA   Kingman visitors won't be disappointed with the semiprivate 18-hole golf course and driving range at **Valley Vista Country Club**, which boasts some of the best greens in Arizona. Clubs and cart rentals are available. ~ 9686 Concho Drive; 520-757-8744. The 18-hole **Kingman Municipal Golf Course** is a high desert course with challenging water hazards and sand traps. Soft spikes required. Cart and clubs can be rented. ~ 1001 East Gates Road; 520-753-6593.

LAKE MEAD AREA   Serving the Lake Mead and Hoover Dam area is the 18-hole **Boulder City Municipal Golf Course**, one of the prettier courses in the greater Las Vegas area, with shade trees and bright green greens. Green fees include a cart, and club rentals are available. ~ 1 Clubhouse Drive, Boulder City, NV; 702-293-9236.

BULLHEAD CITY/LAUGHLIN AREA   In Laughlin, tee off at the 18-hole **Emerald River Golf Course**, a target desert course with narrow fairways and small greens. The USGA rates it the most challenging course in Nevada. There are clubs for rent, and the green fee includes the use of a cart. ~ 1155 West Casino Drive, Laughlin; 702-298-0061. In Bullhead City play the greens at the nine-hole, par-three **Riverview Golf Course**, which features lots of water hazards. There are rental carts and clubs. ~ 2000 East Ramar Road; 520-763-1818. Also in Bullhead City is the nine-hole, semiprivate **Chaparral Country Club**. Club and cart rentals available. ~ 1260 East Mohave Drive; 520-758-3939. The 18-hole **Desert Lakes Golf Course** is about 12 miles south of the Laughlin/Bullhead City bridge. Club rentals are available and carts are included in the green fee. ~ 5835 Desert Lakes Drive, Fort Mohave, AZ; 520-768-1000.

LAKE HAVASU AREA   Golfers can choose from two excellent courses around Lake Havasu. The first is the **Queen's Bay Golf**

Course, a nine-hole, par-three executive course with cart and club rentals. ~ 1477 Queen's Bay Road; 520-855-4777. You'll hope your score is falling down, falling down at the semiprivate **London Bridge Golf Club**. It has two 18-hole desert courses lined with palm trees. There are carts and clubs for rent. ~ 2400 Clubhouse Drive; 520-855-9096. Tee off amid magnificent surroundings at the 18-hole, par-72 championship **Emerald Canyon Golf Course**. A putting green, driving range and pro shop are on the premises. Clubs, carts and lessons are available. ~ 72 Emerald Canyon Drive, Parker; 520-667-3366.

TENNIS

Courts are fairly easy to come by if you want to rally away the endlessly sunny days.

BULLHEAD CITY/LAUGHLIN AREA   In Laughlin guests can use the **Flamingo Hilton Hotel**'s three lighted courts. ~ 1900 South Casino Drive, Laughlin; 702-298-5111. The **Riverview RV Resort** has two lighted courts for the exclusive use of campers staying at the resort; no fee. A tennis pro is on call. ~ 2000 East Ramar Road, Bullhead City; 520-763-5800.

LAKE HAVASU AREA   Tennis courts are open to the public for a fee in Lake Havasu City at **London Bridge Racquet and Fitness Center**. There are six courts, of which four are lighted. The center has a tennis pro. ~ 1425 McCulloch Boulevard; 520-855-6274.

HIKING

Hikers will be happy with all the forest and canyons this area has to offer. All distances listed for hiking trails are one way unless otherwise noted.

KINGMAN AREA   **Hualapai Mountain Park**, 14 miles southeast of Kingman, has an extensive network of hiking trails through piñon, oak, aspen and ponderosa forest teeming with bird and animal life. Six interconnecting trails totaling six miles, starting from the **Aspen Springs Trail** (1 mile) allow you to custom-design your own hike. Aspen Springs Trail connects with the **Potato Patch**

▸▸▸◂

✔ CHECK THESE OUT—UNIQUE OUTDOOR ADVENTURES

- Set up camp at Hualapai Mountain Park, once the ancestral home of the Hualapai people. *page 161*
- Bring your rod and tackle to Lake Mead, where the catfish, bluegill, crappie and striped bass are abundant. *page 180*
- Run the spring rapids on the Colorado River in a raft, canoe or kayak. *page 182*
- Wind your way along the Mohave Sunset Walking Trail, and enjoy the commanding views of Lake Havasu. *page 184*

Loop (4-mile loop) and from that trail various spur trails take off—the short and easy **Stonestep Lookout Trail** (.04 mile), and the slightly more ambitious **Aspen Peak Trail** (.7 mile), **Hayden Peak South Trail** (.8 mile) and **Hayden Peak West Trail** (.6 mile).

BULLHEAD CITY/LAUGHLIN AREA   A wonderful, little-known wintertime hike is **Grapevine Canyon** (1 mile). There is no clearly defined trail, but you will have no trouble tracing the tracks of other hikers up the wash along the canyon floor. Some rock scrambling is involved. At the mouth of the canyon are many petroglyphs that nomadic American Indians scratched into the sandstone with their *atl-atls*, or throwing sticks, an estimated 1200 years ago. Farther up the canyon, a thin waterfall flows year-round. The presence of water attracts nocturnal wildlife, and you may see tracks of badgers, skunks, desert bighorn sheep and even mountain lions. The wild grapes that grow here give the canyon its name. Grapevine Canyon is in Nevada, 13 miles west of the Laughlin/Bullhead City bridge on Route 163 and one and a half miles in on the clearly marked, unpaved road to Christmas Tree Pass. There is a parking area near the mouth of the canyon.

HIDDEN ▶

LAKE HAVASU AREA   The **Mohave Sunset Walking Trail** in Lake Havasu State Park begins at Windsor Beach and winds for two miles through a variety of terrains from lowlands dense with salt cedar to ridgelines commanding beautiful views of the lake. Signs along the sometimes hilly trail identify common Mojave Desert plant life.

▼▼▼▼▼▼▼▼▼▼

Transportation

CAR

On Arizona's "West Coast" along the lower Colorado River, the Bullhead City/Laughlin area is reached by exiting **Route 40** at Kingman and driving 26 miles on **Route 68** through the most starkly stunning scenery in the Mojave Desert, or by exiting Route 40 at Topock, 12 miles east of Needles, California, and driving 35 miles north on **Route 95**. The other major Colorado River resort, Lake Havasu City, is 21 miles south of Route 40 on Route 95. A fascinating back-road route connecting Route 95 with Route 40 at Kingman goes through the historic town of Oatman on its steep climb over Sitgreaves Pass, a drive challenging enough to evoke amazement at the fact that this numberless road used to be part of Old Route 66, the main highway across the Southwest to Los Angeles in the days before the interstate was built.

AIR

The **Bullhead City–Laughlin Airport** (520-754-2134) is serviced by America West, Sun Country and Sun West; the **Kingman Airport** (520-757-2134) in Kingman and the **Lake Havasu City Airport** are serviced by America West.

Greyhound Bus Lines (800-231-2222) stops at two bus terminals in western Arizona. They are in Kingman at 3264 Andy Devine Parkway, 520-757-8400; and in Laughlin at the Riverside Resort, 1650 South Casino Drive, 702-298-2535.

BUS

Amtrak (800-872-7245) provides service to Kingman (4th and Andy Devine streets) and Needles, CA (900 Front Street), which is close to Lake Havasu.

TRAIN

Car-rental agencies at the Bullhead City–Laughlin Airport are **Avis Rent A Car** (800-331-1212) and **Hertz Rent A Car** (800-654-3131). Hertz also has rental cars at the Kingman Airport.

CAR RENTALS

EIGHT

South Central Arizona

 Rising up out of the very center of the rugged south central Arizona landscape is the biggest metropolis between southern Texas and California and the eighth largest in the country—you could say Phoenix is a city taking flight. The population of Phoenix proper is 1,210,420, which balloons to 2,721,750 when you include the 23 satellite towns that blend seamlessly along the valley of the Salt River. Some thousand families a month set up homes in the broad river valley as subdivisions and shopping centers mushroom.

Inadvertently, it was the American Indian's handiwork that led to the birth of Phoenix and lured more white men to the area. Upon discovering the Hohokam canals in 1867, a prospector named Jack Swilling realized that people could successfully farm the desert. He began dredging the prehistoric ditches, homesteading farmers arrived, and before long what is now the largest city in the state was flourishing.

Phoenix today is a far cry from the era of the Hohokam Indians. The Hohokam, meaning "those who vanished," built a network of irrigation ditches to obtain water from the Salt River, part of which is still in use today. Then, as now, irrigation was vital to Phoenix. So much water is piped in to soak fields, groves and little kids' toes that the desert air is actually humid—uncomfortably so through much of the summer. Lettuce, melons, alfalfa, cotton, vegetables, oranges, grapefruit, lemons and olives are grown in abundance in the irrigated fields and groves, lending a touch of green to the otherwise brown landscape. Boating, waterskiing, swimming and even surfing—in a gigantic, mechanically activated pool—are splendid byproducts.

Did we mention sports? Whatever your game may be, this is sports heaven. In professional competition, Phoenix has baseball (the Triple-A Firebirds), hockey (the Roadrunners), football (the Cardinals) and basketball (the Suns). Plus, the Arizona State University Sun Devils play football, basketball and baseball. Still other spectator sports include rodeos and horse racing. For the active set, there are 125 golf courses and hundreds of tennis courts, as well as bike, jogging and horse-riding trails, and opportunities for all kinds of other pursuits.

The action here isn't all on the field. The city has completed a $1.1 billion redevelopment of the downtown that began in 1988. Testimony to the effort are the glitzy Arizona Center, the Mexican-themed Mercado and the 18,000-seat America West Arena next to the Civic Center Plaza.

Metropolitan Phoenix, or the Valley of the Sun, originated in 1850 on the banks of the Salt River and became the capital of the Arizona Territory in 1889. At one time, nearly 25,000 Indians were the exclusive inhabitants of Arizona. The earliest were the Hohokam who thrived from 30 A.D. until about 1450 A.D. Signs of their settlements remain intact to this day. Two other major tribal groups followed: the Anasazi in the state's northern plateau highlands, and the Mogollon People, in the northeastern and eastern mountain belt.

In the mid-1500s, the conquistadors arrived, carrying the banner of Spain. They were looking for gold and seeking souls to save. The Spanish-Mexican influence is still strongly evident throughout the Southwest. And the gold prospector eventually became the very symbol of the Old West—an old man with a white beard, alone with his trusted burro, looking to strike it rich. You only have to go 30 miles east of Phoenix into the Superstition Mountains to find the lore and the legend and the lure of gold still very much alive today.

With the construction of the first railroad in 1887, fast-paced expansion took hold as Phoenix drew settlers from all over the United States. In 1889 it was named the capital of the Arizona Territory, and statehood was declared in 1912.

Once hailed as the agricultural center of Arizona, Phoenix by 1920 was already highly urbanized. Its horse-drawn carriages represented the state's first public transportation. Its population reached 29,053 and the surrounding communities of Tempe, Mesa, Glendale, Chandler and Scottsdale added 8636 to the count. As farmers and ranchers were slowly being squeezed out, these years of Phoenix's development saw a rugged frontier town trying to emulate as best it could famous cities back East. It had a Boston store, a New York store, three New England–style tea parlors and a number of gourmet shops selling everything from smoked herring to Delaware cream cheese. The region's dry desert air also began to attract scores of "health-seekers." The advent of scheduled airline service and the proliferation of dude ranches, resorts and other tourist attractions changed the character of the city still further.

Today, high-tech industry forms the economic core of Phoenix, while tourism remains the state's number-two job-producer. Not surprisingly, construction is the city's third major industry. But Phoenix retains a strong community flavor. Its downtown area isn't saturated with block after block of highrises and apartment houses. The city and all its suburbs form an orderly, 800-square-mile pattern of streets and avenues running north and south and east and west, with periphery access gained by soaring Los Angeles–style freeways. Beyond are the mountains and desert, which offer an escape from city living, with camping, hiking and other recreational facilities.

If the desert isn't your scene, neighboring Scottsdale just might be. Billing itself as "The West's Most Western Town," Scottsdale is about as "Western" as Beverly Hills.

Scottsdale's population of over 200,000 appears to be made up primarily of "snow birds" who came to stay: rich retirees from other parts of the United States who enjoy the sun, the golf courses, the swimming pools, the mountains, the bolo ties and the almost endless selection of handicraft shops, boutiques and over 100 art galleries. Actually, retired persons account for only 20 percent of this fast-growing city, whose median adult age is 39. There are far more yuppies than grandmas.

Scottsdale was only desert land in 1888 when U.S. Army Chaplain Winfield Scott bought a parcel of land located near the Arizona Canal at the base of Camelback Mountain. Before long, much of the cactus and greasewood trees here had been replaced by 80 acres of barley, a 20-acre vineyard and 50 orange trees. Scottsdale remained a small agricultural and ranching community until after World War II. Motorola opened a plant in Scottsdale in 1945, becoming the first of many electronics manufacturing firms to locate in the valley.

Less than a quarter-mile square in size when it was incorporated in 1951, Scottsdale now spreads over 150 square miles. Its unparalleled growth would appear never-ending except that the city is now braced up against the 50,000-acre Salt River Indian Reservation, established in 1879 and home of the Pima and Maricopa people who haven't let their juxtaposition with one of the nation's wealthiest communities go unrewarded. The reservation boasts one of the largest shopping areas in the Southwest, a junior college, thousands of acres of productive farmland and future hotel sites.

The network of satellite communities that surrounds the Phoenix-Scottsdale area, like random pieces of a jigsaw puzzle, is primarily made up of bedroom communities. Tempe to the south is home of Arizona State University. Burgeoning Glendale, to the northwest, was originally founded as a "temperance colony" where the sale of intoxicants was forever forbidden. Mesa, to the east, covering 100 square miles, is Arizona's third-largest city. Carefree and Cave Creek, to the north, are two communities sheltered by the Sonoran Desert foothills and surrounded by mountains. Carefree was planned for those who enjoy fun-in-the-sun activities like tennis, golf and horseback riding. Cave Creek, a booming ranching and mining center back in 1873, thrives on its strong Western flavor. A bit hokey, but fun. Like fallout from a starburst, these and other neighboring communities all revolve around the tempo, pace and heartbeat of the Phoenix-Scottsdale core.

Beyond the urban centers, you can pull up to a gas station that's the last one from anywhere, visit honky-tonk saloons, skinny-dip in a mountain lake, pan for gold, meet dreamers and drifters. The best way to see the West is to be part of it, to feel the currents of its rivers or the steepness of its hills underfoot. South central Arizona certainly offers ample opportunity.

Phoenix
▼▼▼▼▼▼▼▼▼

The history of south central Arizona unravels in smooth, easy chapters through Phoenix's museums and attractions, particularly highlighting its Indian heritage. But this is by no means all you'll find here. The city is also a bustling art mecca, evident from the moment visitors arrive at Sky Harbor Airport, with its array of contemporary and Western artworks on display. The airport's program of changing art exhibits, in conjunction with the Phoenix Art Commission, is a model for similar programs at airports throughout the country. You'll also find art everywhere in the city. Along Squaw Peak Freeway, a ten-mile stretch that connects downtown Phoenix with the city's northern suburbs, you may think you're seeing things, and you are. The freeway is lined with 35 giant three- and four-foot sculptures—vases, cups, Indian-style pots and other utensils, all part of the city's public arts project "to make people feel more at home with the freeway." Not everyone in Phoenix loves the idea. Detractors have dubbed the freeway art project "Chamber Pots of the Gods."

Surely the last of the rugged Marlboro men can still be seen astride handsome, well-groomed horses in Phoenix, but they're not riding off into the sunset, never to be seen again. Chances are they're heading into the vast expanse of desert land that still surrounds the city proper to recharge their motors. Long considered a scourge of man, arid and untamable, the desert with its raw awesome beauty is now considered by many as the last vestige of America's wilderness. Numerous tour operators offer guided jeep and horseback tours into the desert, but as any Arizonian will tell

South Central Arizona

you, the desert is best appreciated alone. Southwestern Indians have long known the secrets of the desert. Now the settler man comes to turn his face skyward into the pale desert sun.

But whether the city proper or its environs are your scene, trying to take in all the sights and sounds in one trip is a bit like counting the grains of sand in a desert. We suppose it can be done, but who on earth has the time? To help you on your quest, here are some of this city's highlights.

SIGHTS   Phoenix's once lackluster downtown is starting to reap the benefits of some $1.1 billion worth of cultural and architectural enhancements in progress since the late 1980s. A focal point of the new **Phoenix Municipal Government Center**, which includes a new city hall, is one of the city's oldest landmarks—the **Orpheum Theater**, a magnificent 1929 Spanish baroque revival building that was once considered the most luxurious playhouse west of the Mississippi River. Recently restored, the theater gives free public tours of the exterior and is a showcase for performing arts, community and civic events, ballet, children's theater, film festivals and other special events. ~ 203 West Adams Street; 602-252-9678.

Other improvements are making downtown more pedestrian-friendly, such as the **Margaret T. Hance Deck Park**, a 29-acre greenbelt stretching from 3rd Street to 3rd Avenue, with wooded areas, fountains and a Japanese garden symbolizing Phoenix's ties to sister city Hemeji, Japan.

Southwestern anthropology and primitive arts are showcased at **The Heard Museum**. The ten exhibition galleries on three levels include a Hopi kachina collection, Cochi storyteller figures, pottery by Maria Martinez, silver and turquoise jewelry, basketry, blankets and other American Indian crafts. The recently expanded museum also includes an education pavilion, a working artist studio and a giftshop and bookstore. Admission. ~ 22 East Monte Vista Road; 602-252-8840.

● ●

✔ CHECK THESE OUT—UNIQUE SIGHTS

- Bring the kids to the world's largest firefighting museum, aptly named the **Hall of Flame Museum**, where old-time firefighting equipment and hundreds of artifacts are on display. *page 194*
- Stride through **Rawhide Arizona's 1880 Western Town** and dodge real sheep and shootouts while exploring rickety Main Street. *page 207*
- Venture into Tonto National Forest and gaze at **Tonto Natural Bridge**, the largest natural travertine bridge in the world. *page 228*
- Delve into the past at **Casa Grande Ruins National Monument**, where you'll see Indian dwellings built in the 1300s. *page 229*

The **Phoenix Art Museum**, which features exhibits on Western, Asian, Latin American, contemporary and decorative arts, has an outstanding costume collection that includes accessories and textiles. The renovated museum also presents temporary exhibitions on tour from other major museums. In addition, children can engage in hands-on fun at Artworks, an interactive gallery. Call for specific exhibition information. Closed Monday. Admission. ~ 1625 North Central Avenue; 602-257-1880.

The **Arizona State Capitol Museum** was built in 1900 to serve as the Territorial Capitol. The building has been restored to the 1912 era when Arizona won statehood. Guided tours feature permanent exhibits in the Senate and House Chambers, the Governor's Suite and the Rotunda. A wax figure of the state's first governor, George Hunt, is seated at his partnership desk surrounded by period furnishings. Major artifacts include the original silver service taken from the USS *Arizona* before the battleship was sunk at Pearl Harbor and the roughrider flag carried up Cuba's San Juan Hill during the Spanish-American War. Closed weekends. ~ 1700 West Washington Avenue; 602-542-4675.

Mineral and ores from Arizona and the rest of the world are displayed at the **Arizona Mining and Mineral Museum**, one of the finest of its kind in the Southwest. Closed Sunday. ~ 1502 West Washington Avenue; 602-255-3791.

Over at the **Hall of Fame Museum** you will find rotating exhibits dedicated to the people who made Arizona what it is today. Crammed with artifacts, each section offers insight on the colorful lives of pioneers who built this state. Closed weekends. ~ 1101 West Washington Avenue; 602-255-2110.

The **Mercado** is composed of half a dozen commercial buildings patterned on a traditional Mexican village. This two-block-long complex includes shops offering handicrafts from Mexico, American Indian jewelry and crafts, and is in the process of adding dining and entertainment venues. Beautiful courtyards add to the charm of this eclectic complex. ~ Van Buren Street between 5th and 7th streets; 602-256-6322.

Museo Chicano features changing exhibits ranging from local to international focus. Latino culture, arts and history are exhibited, as well as the work of well-known and emerging artists. In addition, the museum offers a popular series of cultural programs and performing arts events, such as the Mexican Ballet Folklorico with live mariachi bands. The museum store features Latino fine and folk art, bilingual books and hundreds of posters; it also hosts author readings and book signings. Closed Sunday and Monday. Admission. ~ 25 East Adams Street; 602-257-5536.

Heritage Square is a Southwestern time warp featuring four turn-of-the-century homes: the **Arizona Doll and Toy Museum**; the **Rosson House**, an 1895 Eastlake Victorian that contains a beautiful collection of period furniture; the **Silva House**, a Victorian-style bungalow that has exhibits ranging from turn-of-the-century swimsuits to origami; and the **Stevens-Haustgen House**. There is an admission charge at the Rosson House and the Arizona Doll and Toy Museum. ~ Heritage Square, 115 North 6th Street; 602-262-5071.

The **Phoenix Museum of History**, located in the Heritage and Science Park next to Heritage Square, focuses on the territorial history of Phoenix from prehistoric times to the 1930s. Many displays are interactive and involve personal stories and historical figures; others include an impressive printing press exhibit and one of the state's oldest mining locomotives. There is a library for research and browsing, as well as a gift shop. Admission. ~ 105 North 5th Street; 602-253-2734.

For a glimpse into the Hohokam tribe's past, visit the **Pueblo Grande Museum**. The exhibits include a prehistoric Hohokam ruin, a permanent display on this legendary tribe and a changing gallery featuring Southwestern Indian arts, crafts and archaeology. Of special interest is an outdoor trail that leads visitors to the top of a Hohokam platform mound. There is also an interactive exhibit for children. Admission. ~ 4619 East Washington Street; 602-495-0901.

Also next to Heritage Square is the **Arizona Science Center**, which is outfitted with a planetarium, a giant-screen theater, and 350 hands-on exhibits. Admission. ~ 600 East Washington Street; 602-716-2000.

Located not far from the central Phoenix museums is the **Desert Botanical Garden** where more than 20,000 plants from desert lands of Africa, Australia, North and South America are displayed. You can see this beautiful garden via a self-guided nature walk or a group tour. Featured is a 35-acre showcase of native Sonoran desert plants, a saguaro forest, a mesquite thicket, a desert stream and an upland chaparral habitat, complete with historic American Indian dwellings. The botanical garden reopened in 1997 after a $2 million improvement project, adding new trail exhibits and interactive displays as well as "islands" of shade that offer relief from the often brutal afternoon sun. Admission. ~ 1201 North Galvin Parkway; 602-941-1225.

Nearby is the **Phoenix Zoo** which uses natural settings, including a four-acre African Savanna, to showcase over 1300 mammals, birds and reptiles. Phoenix newcomers are frequently startled to find themselves driving along busy Van Buren alongside a family of trumpeting elephants. For a convenient zoo overview take the Safari Train. Popular highlights are the World Herd of Arabian Oryx, a rare Sumatran tiger exhibit and the Baboon Kingdom. Children will especially enjoy the hands-on participatory ex-

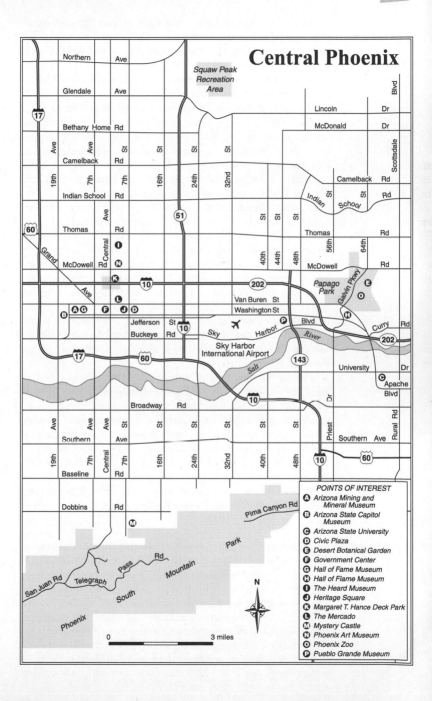

Central Phoenix

Northern Ave

Squaw Peak Recreation Area

Glendale Ave

Blvd

Lincoln Dr

McDonald Dr

Bethany Home Rd

Scottsdale

Ave
Ave
St
St
St
St

Camelback Rd

19th
7th
7th
16th
24th
32nd

Camelback Rd

Indian School Rd

Indian School

Ave

Thomas Rd

St
St
St

Thomas Rd

Grand

Central Rd

I
N

40th
44th
48th

56th
64th

McDowell Rd

K

McDowell Rd

Papago Park

Galvin Pkwy

E
O

Ave

10

202

L

Van Buren St

H

A **G**
F
J **D**

Washington St

B

Curry Rd

Jefferson St

10

Sky Harbor Blvd

P

202

Buckeye Rd

River

Sky Harbor International Airport

17
60

Salt

143

University Dr

C

Apache Blvd

10

Priest Dr

Broadway Rd

Ave
Ave
Ave
St
St
St
St
St
St

Rural Rd

Southern Ave

Southern Ave

19th
7th
Central
7th
16th
24th
32nd
40th
48th

10

60

Baseline Rd

Dobbins Rd

M

Pima Canyon Rd

Park

San Juan Rd
Telegraph Pass Rd

Mountain

South

Phoenix

N

0   3 miles

POINTS OF INTEREST
A Arizona Mining and Mineral Museum
B Arizona State Capitol Museum
C Arizona State University
D Civic Plaza
E Desert Botanical Garden
F Government Center
G Hall of Fame Museum
H Hall of Flame Museum
I The Heard Museum
J Heritage Square
K Margaret T. Hance Deck Park
L The Mercado
M Mystery Castle
N Phoenix Art Museum
O Phoenix Zoo
P Pueblo Grande Museum

hibit called the Animal Encounters show. Be sure to visit the one-acre tropical rainforest, the home of 15 bird and animal species adopted from around the world. Admission. ~ 455 North Galvin Parkway; 602-273-1341.

The largest firefighting museum in the world is the **Hall of Flame Museum**. On display are more than 90 restored hand-drawn, horse-drawn and motorized fire engines and hundreds of artifacts. Special games, exhibits and programs, all stressing fire safety, are offered for children. You'll also find a firefighting library and a theater where videos are shown. Admission. ~ 6101 East Van Buren Street; 602-275-3473.

Tucked away in the foothills of South Mountain Park, the **Mystery Castle** is an 18-room extravaganza fashioned from native stone, sand, cement, water, goat's milk and Stutz Bearcat wire-rim wheels. Warmed by 13 fireplaces, the parapeted castle has a cantilevered stairway, chapel and dozens of nooks and crannies and is furnished with Southwestern antiques. It's known as the "mystery" castle because the builder, Boyce Luther Gulley, thinking he was about to die from tuberculosis, ran away from his Seattle home in a Stutz Bearcat and devoted 15 years to the construction project. It was only after his death in 1945 that the missing builder's family learned of his whereabouts and inherited the castle. Closed Monday through Wednesday from October through June; closed July through September. Admission. ~ End of Mineral Road; 602-268-1581.

Pioneer Arizona Living History Museum re-creates an Old West town using mostly original buildings—a church, schoolhouse, printing shop and blacksmith shop—and featuring costumed interpreters. Living history exhibitions include cooking, gardening and sewing. At the opera house you'll see melodramas and historic performances all themed to the territorial period, 1858 to 1912. Of special interest is one of our nation's last remaining herds of colonial Spanish horses. You can also enjoy the picnic area and a restaurant. Closed June through September. Admission. ~ 3901 West Pioneer Road (Pioneer Road exit off of Route 17); 602-465-1052.

LODGING As a major resort and convention center, the Valley of the Sun features some of the most spectacular hotel resorts in the country. It has had the rare distinction of having more *Mobil Travel Guide* Five Star resorts (three of the twelve top-rated resorts nationwide) than any other city in the United States (see "Spoil Yourself" in this chapter). Yet it's not without its share of budget- and moderate-priced hotels and motels, and proliferating bed and breakfasts.

An elegant scene of the past is mirrored in the glossy facade of the present with the rebirth of the **San Carlos Hotel** in the heart of downtown. Built in 1927, the seven-story San Carlos is undergoing a multimillion-dollar restoration while keeping its charm intact—a crystal chandelier and period furnishing in the lobby, original bathtubs, basins and furniture in the 130 guest rooms and nine suites. Deep carpets line the hallways. The San Carlos is one of the largest hotels listed in the National Register of Historic Places. ~ 202 North Central Avenue; 602-253-4121, 800-528-5446, fax 602-253-6668. DELUXE.

The 24-story **Hyatt Regency Phoenix** is across from Civic Plaza downtown. With 712 rooms, it's the city's largest hotel. It has a heated swimming pool, exercise equipment, a café, lounges and a revolving roof-top dining room. Rooms are smallish but tastefully furnished in a light, Southwest style. ~ Located on 2nd and Adams streets; 602-252-1234, 800-233-1234, fax 602-254-9472. ULTRA-DELUXE.

For luxurious accommodations located in the heart of the upscale Biltmore area, check out **Embassy Suites**. Walk through the doors and your first sight is a huge atrium complete with palm trees, tropical plants and waterways shimmering with goldfish. With the price tag comes a complimentary cooked-to-order breakfast. The 233 modern two-room suites each offer a microwave oven, wet bar, refrigerator and dining area. ~ 2630 East Camelback Road; 602-955-3992, 800-362-2779, fax 602-955-6479. ULTRA-DELUXE.

The **Pointe Hilton Resort at Squaw Peak** is an all-suite resort on 180 acres near the Phoenix Mountain Preserve. The architecture and ambience here are a cross between Southwestern and Mediterranean. The 576 suites have French doors in the bedrooms that open to private balconies, as well as desks, marble bathroom countertops and fully stocked mini-bars. There are also 78 one- and two-bedroom villas. Amenities include the use of a nearby 18-hole golf course, tennis courts, a fitness center, swimming pools, miniature golf and the Coyote Camp to keep the kids oc-

▸▸◂◂◂◂

✔ CHECK THESE OUT—UNIQUE LODGING

- *Budget:* Make your pocketbook happy as you bed down at **Pyramid Inn**, an attractive two-story brick inn in Phoenix. *page 196*
- *Moderate:* Laze around the pool at **Scottsdale's Fifth Avenue Inn** after a shopping spree in Scottsdale's premier shopping district. *page 209*
- *Deluxe:* Saddle up at the historic **Kay El Bar Ranch**, a dude ranch with hacienda-style accommodations. *page 226*
- *Ultra-deluxe:* Lose yourself at **The Boulders**, where 12-million-year-old granite boulders are the backdrop at this luxury resort. *page 225*

Budget: under $70   Moderate: $70–$110   Deluxe: $110–$180   Ultra-deluxe: over $180

cupied. ~ 7677 North 16th Street; 602-997-2626, 800-876-4683, fax 602-870-2797. ULTRA-DELUXE.

A find, price-wise, is the **Pyramid Inn**, an attractive two-story brick inn with 30 large rooms—peach and rust color themes predominating—and a swimming pool and free airport shuttle service. ~ 3307 East Van Buren Street; 602-275-3691, fax 602-267-0448. BUDGET.

For those interested in meeting fellow budget-travelers try the **Hostel Metcalf House**. Here's what you get: two dormitory-style rooms (men's and women's) with bunk beds for ten in each. Guests may use the kitchen and community room. ~ 1026 North 9th Street; 602-254-9803. BUDGET.

The **YMCA** has 139 rooms in an seven-story downtown building. It's good old Y-style, nothing fancy, but it's clean. For $2 extra, full use of the gym facilities and swimming pool is included. ~ 350 North 1st Avenue; 602-253-6181. BUDGET.

If you want to stay in shape while you're away, try the **Lexington Hotel and City Square Sports Club**, a hotel with 176 rooms, a restaurant and a lounge along with a full-scale athletic club facility including basketball and racquetball courts, sauna, steamroom and pool. Rooms are contemporary decor, but the workout's great. ~ 100 West Clarendon Avenue; 602-279-9811, 800-927-8483, fax 602-285-2932. MODERATE TO DELUXE.

Desert Sun Hotel offers 107 guest rooms with modern furnishings and various color themes. It has a restaurant, a lounge, a swimming pool, and the right price. ~ 1325 Grand Avenue; 602-258-8971, 800-227-0301, fax 602-256-9196. BUDGET TO MODERATE.

HIDDEN ►   The **Maricopa Manor** is a Spanish-style bed and breakfast situated in a garden-like setting of palm trees and flowers in the heart of north central Phoenix. Built in 1928, the inn has five individually decorated suites, all with private baths. Typical is the Library Suite with its canopied king-size bed, private deck entrance, handsome collection of leather-bound books and an antique work desk. The Manor Suite has a whirlpool tub and a fireplace. Guests may also use the inn's spacious Gathering Room as well as the formal living, dining, music rooms, patio, pool and gazebo spa. Continental breakfast is included in the room rate. ~ 15 West Pasadena Avenue; 602-274-6302, 800-292-6403, fax 602-266-3904; www. maricopamanor.com. DELUXE TO ULTRA-DELUXE.

DINING   Looking for a quick snack? Go to the **Arizona Center**, take the elevator or stairs to the second floor and, voilà! Here you'll find a whole array of attractive fast-food restaurants all sharing a mutual sit-down dining—**Sun Valley Smoothies, Gyros and Grill, Diego's Mexican Grill, Scotto Pizza, Teriyaki Temple, Chinese**

Cafe, and more. ~ Van Buren between 3rd and 5th streets; 602-271-4000. BUDGET.

At **Sam's Cafe** in the Arizona Center, a large patio set amidst fountains is one draw; good Southwestern cuisine is another. Start with *poblano* chicken chowder, then have chile-rubbed shrimp topped with lemon butter and *pico de gallo*, or Hannah's roasted chicken with jalapeño-garlic marinade, or the blackened salmon Caesar salad. If the weather is inclement (which it rarely is), indoor dining is also nice, with more fountains and terra-cotta colored walls. ~ 455 North 3rd Street; 602-252-3545. MODERATE TO DELUXE.

With a dozen aquariums scattered around the lobby and dining room, the **Golden Phoenix** appears to have the largest tropical fish population of any Arizona restaurant. While the decor of this stucco-style establishment offers few Asian touches, the kitchen does wonders with Mandarin dishes like *kung pao* shrimp and hot sizzling beef. ~ 1534 West Camelback Road; 602-279-4447. BUDGET TO MODERATE.

The chef at **Eddie's Grill** has elevated cooking to an art form by blending culinary traits from America's diverse ethnic groups into a "New American" cuisine. Try the toasted seafood wontons with raspberry-jalapeño sauce or grilled chicken breast with ginger cream sauce. As multicultural as this restaurant may sound, it's truly American at heart, from the U.S.-produced meats and vegetables to the wines and bottled water. Don't ask for Evian. Dinner only weekends. ~ 4747 North 7th Street; 602-241-1188. MODERATE TO DELUXE.

Christo's specializes in Northern Italian cuisine, which means less pasta in favor of meatier fare—chicken *zingarella*, osso bucco veal, rack of lamb—and fish dishes such as halibut topped with goat cheese, olive oil, garlic and sliced tomatoes. Sparkling stemware, crisp peach-and-white tablecloths and table flowers add a festive note. Lunch daily, dinner only on Saturday. Closed Sunday. ~ 6327 North 7th Street; 602-264-1784. MODERATE TO DELUXE.

If you're looking for a large, festive, family-oriented Mexican restaurant, **Carlos O' Briens** fits the bill. Exposed ductwork, hanging plants and modern artwork supply the ambience for chowing down on fajitas, enchiladas and chimichangas. ~ 1133 East Northern Avenue; 602-274-5881. BUDGET TO MODERATE.

A popular neighborhood restaurant, **Texaz Grill** really looks ◄ HIDDEN
like it was transferred over from Dallas with its neon beer signs, glowing jukebox and antique wall memorabilia (old Texas license plates and the like). Steaks come in a variety of sizes, from an eight-ounce fillet to an 18-ounce Lone Star, but the biggest seller of all is the chicken-fried steak served with heaps of mashed potatoes and buttermilk biscuits, just like in Texas. No lunch on Sunday. ~ 6003 North 16th Street; 602-248-7827. MODERATE.

Comfort is not a problem at **Richardson's,** where lots of plump pillows adorn pink faux adobe booths. This New Mexico–style eatery is irreverent (political commentary often livens up the chalkboards), intimate and lively, with lots of music and talk competing at loud decibels. Favorites here include the cilantro fettuccine with shrimp and the Santa Fe chicken with jalapeño hollandaise. ~ 582 East Bethany Home Road; 602-265-5886. MODERATE TO ULTRA-DELUXE.

And you thought diners went the way of the dinosaur. Step into **Ed Debevic's** and you'll find yourself back in the 1950s, complete with tabletop jukeboxes, photos of Marilyn, blue-plate specials, burgers, shakes and fries. The servers perform nostalgic dances of the '50s and '60s, and the low prices are right out of the past, too. ~ 2102 East Highland Avenue; 602-956-2760. BUDGET.

Greek Fest brings a bit of Mykonos to the desert with a taverna-like atmosphere of white walls, archways, beamed ceilings, handcrafted wallhangings and marble floors. A tasty meal can easily be made of the *mezethes*, or appetizers, which include panfried calamari, grilled octopus, hummus, house-made lamb sausage, phyllo-wrapped meat, cheese and spinach pastries and salads. Closed Sunday. ~ 1940 East Camelback Road; 602-265-2990. MODERATE TO DELUXE.

A colorful coffee house with a touch of bohemia is **Dos Barista's Coffeehouse** in the Town & Country Shopping Center. A red neon espresso sign in the window greets people; inside, red, yellow and turquoise colors add to the decor. Don't expect meals here—just good pastry and coffee. A bin of newspapers will keep you entertained, as will people-watching or the live folk music three nights a week and live storytelling every third Thursday. Some just stare at the unique wall of burlap bags. There are also a handful of outdoor tables. ~ 4743 North 20th Street; 602-957-2236. BUDGET.

What it lacks in decor, **Ham's** makes up for in great cooking. Specials change daily and include beef tips and noodles, fried chicken, barbecued beef and meatloaf, all served with heaps of mashed potatoes, veggies and biscuits. Closed Sunday. ~ 3302 North 24th Street; 602-954-8775. BUDGET TO MODERATE.

RoxSand, located in the Biltmore Fashion Park offers "transcontinental food"—in other words, a little bit of everything, from Thai to European. Dine amidst a cool black-and-white interior dotted with modern art and suffused with jazz music; the menu features chicken wrapped in phyllo with eggplant and hummus, duck with plum sauce, and jerked rabbit. ~ 2594 East Camelback Road; 602-381-0444. DELUXE TO ULTRA-DELUXE.

Christopher's Fermier Brasserie ("Farmers' Tavern") features chef-owner Christopher Gross' gourmet fare prepared with fresh local produce. The French-inspired cuisine includes specialties such as truffle-infused smoked sirloin, house-smoked salmon, and artichoke and tomato tart. The menu matches a wine with each entrée and provides a rotating selection of 100 vintages available by the glass. House-brewed beer is also an option, and the adjacent wine bar is open for morning coffee and pastries as well as cheese and seafood platters and after-meal (or late-night) cigars. Reservations recommended. ~ In Biltmore Fashion Park, 2584 East Camelback Road; 602-522-2344. MODERATE TO ULTRA-DELUXE.

At **Ayako of Tokyo**, teppanyaki chefs grill chicken, scallops, shrimp, filet mignon and lobster at your table. Each entrée comes with soup, salad, rice and vegetables. Rice paper screens add a Japanese touch to the decor of this restaurant graced with Oriental paintings and panels. There are also sushi and tempura bars, as well as a lounge. Dinner only on weekends. ~ 2564 East Camelback Road, Biltmore Fashion Park; 602-955-7007. MODERATE TO ULTRA-DELUXE.

Wright's is an open, airy dining room at the Arizona Biltmore with a menu featuring New American cuisine. There is raisin and pistachio french toast with warm fruit compote as well as snazzy egg dishes. The lunch and dinner menus are filled with pasta, seafood and meat dishes served with intriguing sauces. For dinner start with an appetizer such as salmon tartar with candied apples and foie gras vinaigrette; and then try an entrée such as Maine lobster raviolis with pan-seared scallops and reggiano cream, or braised veal osso bucco with porcini risotto and madeira glaze. Save room for one of their fabulous desserts. ~ 24th Street and Missouri Avenue; 602-954-2507. ULTRA-DELUXE.

Ever try duck tamales? Mix Southwest and French cuisine, as they do at **Vincent Guerithault**, and that's the result. You'll find a country French atmosphere, complete with floral seat cushions and dried floral table centerpieces, while diners enjoy chimichanga of lobster or grilled ahi tuna with papaya cilantro salsa. Top it off with crème brulée in, what else, a sweet "taco" shell. Valet parking is available in this establishment. ~ 40th Street and East Camelback Road; 602-224-0225. MODERATE TO ULTRA-DELUXE.

Havana Cafe offers the not-too-spicy cuisine of Cuba, Spain and South America in an atmosphere that's more a small, cozy café than in the style of Hemingway's Havana. *Chicharitas*, an appetizer of fried green plantain chips, will get the juices flowing. There's Cuban chicken marinated in orange juice, lime juice and garlic, and paella (for two), the house specialty; sausage; *sopa de ajo* (garlic soup); *escabeche*; *picadillo* and more. ~ 4225 East Camelback Road; 602-952-1991. MODERATE TO ULTRA-DELUXE.

HIDDEN ► A spot popular with the downtown office workers eager for a touch of home cooking, **Mrs. White's Golden Rule Cafe** offers pork chops, chicken, cornbread and cobbler. Get there early for a table. Open until 2 a.m. Friday and Saturday. Closed Sunday. ~ 808 East Jefferson Street; 602-262-9256. BUDGET TO MODERATE.

To the west of Phoenix, check out **The Spicery** located in the Catlin Court Shops District, a downtown area where historic homes have been preserved. This eatery is in a charming, 1895 Victorian house. It makes food the way mother used to—homemade soups, salads, chubby sandwiches, fresh-baked bread and pies. The Spicery offers high tea Tuesday through Saturday (by reservation only) and brunch on Saturday morning. Closed Sunday and Monday in summer. ~ 7141 North 59th Avenue, Glendale; 602-937-6534. BUDGET TO MODERATE.

SHOPPING Western wear would seem a natural when hitting the shopping scene—and you're right. There's a herd of places selling boots, shirts, buckles and whatever else you might want. If you're in the market for Western clothes, just to look the part or to get ready for your next rodeo appearance you might start with **Aztex Hats** offering the largest selection of Western hats in Arizona. ~ 15044 North Cave Creek; 602-971-9090. **Saba's Western Store**, in business since 1927, includes Barry Goldwater among its clientele. ~ 2901 West Bell Road; 602-993-5948. **Sheplers** is part of the world's largest Western-wear chain. ~ 9201 North 29th Avenue; 602-870-8085.

If you like malls and shopping complexes, get ready. Phoenix has them in great abundance. One entertainment complex that has helped revitalize the downtown Phoenix area is **Arizona Center**, with about 500 restaurants, bars and shops on two levels. It attracts people for dining, meandering through the three-acre garden area, browsing amidst the shops, or listening to live entertainment in the evenings. Shops here include **Arizona Highways Gift and Information Center** (602-257-0381), which offers travel books and information about the Grand Canyon State, while **Yippie-Ei-O** (602-495-1048) highlights Western home accessories, clothing and gift items. At **Phases of the Moon** (602-254-7533), you'll find ethnic, exotic and mystical women's jewelry, accessories and apparel. ~ 455 North 3rd Street; 602-271-4000.

Town & Country Shopping Center showcases more than 70 shops, restaurants and services. Red brick sidewalks, fountains and soft music set the tone at this outdoor shopping center. Highlights include **Jutenhoops** (602-957-8006) with a whimsical, funky blend of gifts, cards and jewelry. **Bookstar** (602-957-2001) offers a huge selection of new books. ~ 2021 East Camelback Road; 602-955-6850.

Located just blocks from the Town & Country Shopping Center, but infinitely more exclusive, is **Biltmore Fashion Park**. Stroll along brick-paved walkways lined with green trees and shrubs, and peek into the expensive galleries, restaurants, jewelry stores and clothing stores. For women's clothing, names include **Ann Taylor** (602-468-3339) and **Lillie Rubin** (602-954-8009). Larger stores featured here include **Saks Fifth Avenue** (602-955-8000) and **Macy's** (602-468-2100). ~ Camelback Road and 24th Street; 602-955-8400.

If you like malls and shopping complexes, get ready. Phoenix has them in abundance. One of the best is **Park Central Mall**, the city's oldest and best-known shopping center. The **Green Woodpecker** (602-266-7381), a large novelty gift shop, can be found here. ~ 3121 North 3rd Avenue; 602-264-5575. The **Metrocenter** is an enclosed double-deck mall that includes **Robinson's-May**, **Dillard's** and **Macy's**. ~ 9617 Metro Parkway West; 602-997-2641.

The Mercado, located downtown adjacent to the Phoenix Civic Plaza, is a festive mall and Mexican cultural center with colorful buildings, brick-lined streets and outdoor dining. Mexican shops and restaurants feature arts, crafts, fashions and good things to eat of the hot and spicy persuasion. ~ Van Buren Street between 5th and 7th streets; 602-256-6322.

For designer merchandise at legendary low prices, head for **Loehmann's**. ~ 3135 East Lincoln Drive; 602-957-8691.

Museum gift shops offer unique finds for selective shoppers. For instance, the **Phoenix Art Museum** carries books, posters, catalogs and art-replica gifts, and also has a special section for children. ~ 1625 North Central Avenue; 602-257-1880.

The **Desert Botanical Garden** has a gift shop offering foods, spices and jellies made from desert plants, as well as nature books and Southwestern souvenirs and crafts; plants are sold in an adjoining greenhouse. ~ 1201 North Galvin Parkway; 602-941-1225.

Don't drop just yet. Because after all those malls and other stores, we come to the farmers' markets! Every Thursday from 9 a.m. to 1 p.m., farmers from around the community sell their freshest produce at low prices in the courtyard at **Heritage Square**. ~ Monroe and 7th streets; 602-262-5071.

For a kicker, **American Park 'N Swap** is the largest open-air flea market in the Southwest, with over 2000 dealers selling or swapping everything from used office furniture and rare antiques to Indian jewelry and rare one-of-a-kind photos of Marilyn Monroe. Open Wednesday, Friday and weekends. ~ 3801 East Washington Street; 602-273-1258.

A small town south of Phoenix is the setting for the **Guadalupe Farmer's Market**. You will find fresh vegetables, exotic fruits

◄ HIDDEN

and dried chile peppers. ~ 9210 South Avenida del Yaqui, Guadalupe; 602-730-1945. A few blocks north is **Mercado Mexico** where Mexican pottery and ceramics are sold. ~ 8212 South Avenida del Yaqui, Guadalupe; 602-831-5925.

NIGHTLIFE   Nightlife in south central Arizona is as diverse and far-reaching as the area itself, from twanging guitars of country-and-western bands to symphony strings. There are Indian ceremonials and sophisticated jazz as well. To find out what's happening, check the entertainment pages of the *Arizona Republic* and the *Phoenix Gazette*.

If you feel adventurous, you might try **Midnight Rodeo**, where a deejay spins country-and-western and 1940s dance music. Closed Sunday through Wednesday. Cover. ~ 4029 North 33rd Avenue; 602-279-3800.

Phoenix Live in the Arizona Center is actually three nightclubs and a restaurant. **America's Original Sports Bar** has 70 jumbo screens and 62 regular TVs plus a boxing ring dance floor. **Decades** features a deejay spinning the music of the '70s, '80s and '90s, and **Little Ditty's** is a "dueling piano" bar, where you can sing along. Food is served, and of course plenty of drinks. With all that action you can work up a thirst. Weekend cover. ~ 455 North 3rd Street; 602-252-2502.

A major sports and entertainment center for downtown Phoenix is the 20,000-seat **America West Arena,** a venue for Phoenix Suns basketball games, concerts, ice shows and other special events. ~ 201 East Jefferson Street; 602-379-7800.

Sports Fever boasts a $250,000 sports memorabilia collection, 38 televisions, five giant video screens, pool tables, dart boards and a happy hour complimentary buffet on Friday. ~ 2031 West Peoria Avenue; 602-331-8033.

A valley institution for the two-step crowd, **Mr. Lucky's** has live country music upstairs and a deejay spins Top-40 rock-and-roll downstairs. Live bull-riding (!) Wednesday, Friday and Saturday. Closed Monday. Weekend cover. ~ 3660 West Grand Avenue; 602-246-0686.

"Home of the Nashville Stars," **Toolies Country** is a 600-seat frontier Western cabaret with dinner and dancing nightly to the music of big-name country entertainers. Closed Monday and Tuesday. Cover Thursday through Saturday. ~ 4231 West Thomas Road; 602-272-3100.

Timothy's is a cross between a restaurant and a nightclub. The ivy-covered cottage oozes romance with live jazz nightly in an intimate setting. Jazz festival posters cover the walls, and the paint-splattered beams add a bohemian twist. For that extra bit of class, valet parking is available. ~ 6335 North 16th Street; 602-234-2205.

The **Rhythm Room** is a sophisticated blues nightclub. Framed black-and-white photographs of blues greats hang on gray wood walls in this clean, uncluttered bar. Live bands play nightly, and a good-sized dancefloor in front of the stage invites audience participation. ~ 1019 East Indian School Road; 602-265-4842.

Char's Has the Blues has live rhythm-and-blues nightly. Inside this old house, intimate burgundy curtains cover the windows and people dance on worn wooden floors. Wall sconces and tiny Christmas lights provide the soft lighting. ~ 4631 North 7th Avenue; 602-230-0205.

Nightlife here isn't restricted to the bar and two-step scene. A more refined look at the arts flourishes here as well. **The Herberger Theater Center** is an ultramodern theater complex housing two separate theaters, **Center Stage** and **Stage West,** where professional theater performances take place. The Center features the **Ballet Arizona, Arizona Jewish Theater, Actor's Theater of Phoenix** and **Child's Play,** and is home to the **Arizona Theater Company,** which has performed in Phoenix for more than 25 years. ~ 222 East Monroe Street; 602-252-8497.

> It was the disappearance of the Hohokam Indians that led settlers to select the name "Phoenix" from the symbol of immortality of the ancient Egyptians.

The 2500-seat **Phoenix Civic Plaza and Symphony Hall** houses the Phoenix Symphony and stages entertainment ranging from opera and ballet to Broadway shows and top-name concert performers. ~ Located on 3rd Street between Monroe and Washington streets; 602-495-1999.

The nationally acclaimed **Arizona Opera Company** presents five operas per season in Symphony Hall, with classics such as Verdi's *Don Carlo* and Puccini's *La Boheme.* ~ The box office is located at 4600 North 12th Street; 602-266-7464.

SOUTH MOUNTAIN PARK 🚶 🚴 🐎   With 17,000 acres, this is the largest municipal park in the world, a vast rugged mountain range that was once American Indian hunting ground. A spectacular view of Phoenix can be seen from Dobbins Lookout, one of four scenic overlooks located 2300 feet above the desert floor. The park offers over 40 miles of well-marked hiking and riding trails. Its steep canyons reveal evidence of ancient American Indian artifacts and petroglyphs. Facilities include picnic areas, restrooms and a sunken concrete stage for park ranger lectures or impromptu sing-alongs. There is also an Environmental Education Center (602-534-6324) that has displays (some of them interactive) on the people, history, flora and fauna of the park. Park rangers are available for questions. ~ 10919 South Central Avenue; 602-495-0222.

PARKS

PAPAGO PARK 🚶 🚴 🐎 ⛵   A part of the Phoenix parks network since 1959, Papago is a neat blend of hilly desert terrain, quiet lagoons and glistening streams. The former American Indian townsite now offers golf, picnic sites, ballfields and fishing. Three lagoons are stocked with bass, catfish, bluegill and trout in winter. (It's free for kids 13 and under but an urban fishing license is required for all others.) Also within its boundaries are the Phoenix Zoo, the Desert Botanical Garden, and the Phoenix Municipal Stadium, where the Oakland A's hold their spring training. You'll also find firepits, restrooms, archery range, bike paths and running courses. ~ 625 North Galvin Parkway; 602-262-4599, 602-256-3220.

SQUAW PEAK RECREATION AREA 🏃 One of Phoenix's most familiar landmarks with its craggy, easily identifiable pinnacle, Squaw Peak is primarily known for its hiking trails. However, the rocky terrain has been moderately developed for other recreational pursuits as well, whether picnicking or curling up in the shade of a towering saguaro with an Edward Abbey tome on the evils of overdevelopment. The picnic ramadas have electricity. Other amenities include drinking water, firepits, tables, benches and restrooms. ~ 2701 East Squaw Peak Drive; 602-262-6696.

ESTRELLA MOUNTAIN REGIONAL PARK 🏃 🚲 🐎 With 19,840 acres, Estrella offers abundant vegetation and spectacular mountain views, with peaks within the Sierra Estrella Mountains reaching 3650 feet. The park offers excellent areas for hiking and riding, a rodeo arena and a golf course. Horse and hiking trails abound. There's an amphitheater for lectures and gatherings. Picnic areas and restrooms are located in the park. Day-use fee, $2 per vehicle. ~ Located 16 miles southwest of Phoenix on Route 10. Take Exit 126 onto Estrella Parkway and follow it five miles south to the park; 602-932-3811.

▲ There are a few sites available in the park's RV campground, which cost $8 without electricity or $15 with full hookups.

WHITE TANK MOUNTAIN REGIONAL PARK 🏃 🚲 🐎 Covering 26,337 acres of desert, canyons and mountains, White Tank is the largest park in the Maricopa County Park System. Elevations range from 1402 feet at the entrance to 4083 feet at the park's highest point. White Tank contains an excellent hiking, mountain bike and horse trail system, a seasonal flowing waterfall (reached by a mile-long self-guided hiker's trail) and American Indian petroglyphs scattered throughout. Two newly constructed wheelchair-accessible trails allow visitors with disabilities to view some of the park's petroglyphs. Facilities include picnic sites, restrooms and showers. Day-use fee, $2. ~ Located on Dunlap Avenue (which turns into Olive Avenue before reaching the park), 15 miles west of Glendale; 602-935-2505.

▲ There are 38 sites; $8 per night. Backpack camping is allowed (free); a backcountry overnight permit is required.

While gay activities are found throughout Phoenix, the highest concentration centers around the blocks between Camelback and Indian School roads and between 7th Avenue and 7th Street. This area is home to an array of gay lodging, cafés, bars, shops and nightclubs.

The Phoenix Gay Scene

LODGING

Larry's Bed & Breakfast is centrally located and features three antique-decorated guest rooms. Folks here may watch movies and play cards in the spacious living room, or lounge in the clothing-optional outdoor pool and jacuzzi. Women are welcome, but this is primarily a spot for gay men. A full breakfast is served. ~ 502 West Claremont Avenue; 602-249-2974. BUDGET.

You can stay for a week or a month at the gay-owned **Arizona Royal Villa Apartments**. Hotel rooms, junior suites and one-bedroom apartments are available here. All accommodations face the courtyard. The private grounds, located within a walled complex with keyed entry, include a clothing-optional swimming pool, jacuzzi and sunbathing area. Men only. ~ 1102 East Turney Avenue; phone/fax 602-266-6883, 888-266-6884; www.royalvilla. com. MODERATE.

The men-only **Arizona Sunburst Inn** is an L-shaped ranch house with seven large, comfortable rooms furnished in contemporary designs; some rooms have private baths while others share. Guests have access to a fully equipped kitchen. The outdoor heated pool and jacuzzi are clothing optional. Continental breakfast is served. ~ 6245 North 12th Place; 602-274-1474; members.aol. com/sunbrstinn. MODERATE.

DINING

Dine on all-American food in an art-deco atmosphere at the popular gay-owned **Pookie's Cafe**. This lively spot adorned with colorful stained-glass windows features a piano bar lounge plus more than 30 television screens playing music videos. Choose from a menu offering sandwiches, burgers, quesadillas, Buffalo wings and dinner specials such as steak and pasta. ~ 4540 North 7th Street; 602-277-2121. BUDGET.

Plaster parrots greet you as you enter **Arriba Mexican Grill** for a festive meal of New Mexican fare generously spiced with Hatch green chile. Dine on delectable shrimp fajitas, *carnitas* flavored with orange and lime, New Mexican enchiladas and fiery Taos tacos amid colorful handpainted murals, a fireplace and a fountain. Wash it down, if you're inclined, with some of the 22 brands of tequila. ~ 1812 East Camelback Road; 602-265-9112. BUDGET TO MODERATE.

SHOPPING

For a selection of 5000 gay, lesbian, bi and transgender titles, check out **Obelisk the Bookstore**. You'll find fiction and nonfiction as well as a variety of magazines. ~ 24 West Camelback Road; 602-266-2665.

Gay-owned **Pink Flamingos Antiques and Collectibles** is an entire house filled with antiques ranging from beautiful bedroom sets to collector's shot glasses and ashtrays. Closed Monday and Tuesday. ~ 2241 North 7th Street; 602-261-7730.

Unique on Central is a gay-owned shop offering a large selection of cards, gifts, music, videos, travel books and magazines. ~ 4700 North Central Avenue, Suite 105; 602-279-9691.

NIGHTLIFE   Perhaps the most popular gay bar in the city is **Charlie's**, where you can take clogging and square-dancing lessons three nights a week and dance to good ol' country-and-western music nightly. The scene is mostly men, from 21 to 81 years of age. ~ 727 West Camelback Road; 602-265-0224.

At **Harley's Club 155 West** you'll find a mixed crowd dancing to Top-40 and house music every night of the week. ~ 155 West Camelback Road; 602-274-8505.

Both men and women frequent **BS**, a video/dance bar that has an outdoor patio and features house music on most nights. Monday is retro/comedy video, Thursday is college night and Sunday features an afternoon barbecue and evening karaoke. ~ 7125 East 5th Avenue; 602-945-9028.

For nightly live entertainment from jazz to karaoke to drag shows, head to **Wink's Cabaret**, a neighborhood bar. ~ 5707 North 7th Avenue; 602-265-9002.

Join gay and lesbian sports enthusiasts at **Roscoe's on 7th**, a popular sports bar boasting 15 monitors and daily drink specials. ~ 4531 North 7th Avenue; 602-285-0833.

For a women's sports club that caters mostly to lesbians, head to **The Rose**. A large dancefloor and a lively game room are the attractions. Check out the free dance lessons on Friday night. ~ 4301 North 7th Avenue; 602-265-3233.

Wednesday and Saturday are leather nights at **Shooterz**. On other nights, cruising is the main event at this spacious bar. ~ 998 East Indian School Road; 602-266-5640.

Ain't Nobody's Bizness is a very pink women's bar (although gay men are welcome) with R&B and Top-40 dance music most evenings; there is live music (and a cover charge) on three Sundays each month. Stand-up comedy is featured on a regular basis and Monday is karaoke night. ~ 3031 East Indian School Road; 602-224-9977.

A sports bar with eight large video screens, plus pool tables, darts and shuffleboard, **Nasty Habits** attracts a primarily lesbian following, though gay men are welcome. ~ 3108 East McDowell Road; 602-231-9427.

The leather-and-Levis crowd works up a sweat on TRAX's large dancefloor Thursday through Sunday nights, when deejays spin high-energy tunes. Cover on Friday and Saturday. ~ 1724 East McDowell Road; 602-254-0231.

Over by the airport stands Phoenix's oldest gay bar, Nu–Towne Saloon. Sunday and Tuesday drink specials ensure a convivial bunch at this popular hangout. ~ 5002 East Van Buren Street; 602-267-9959.

Scottsdale

Like neighboring Phoenix, Scottsdale is proud of its frontier heritage, which can be traced at a number of locations in and near the town. In the Old Scottsdale section, where only 35 years ago Lulu Belle's and the Pink Pony were the only two watering holes for miles around, the buildings all have false fronts, handcrafted signs and hitching posts, and horses still have the right of way. Many restaurants feature waiters and waitresses in period dress. The women have teased hairdos, and the men are all called Slim, Ace, Tex, Shorty and Stretch.

But that's about as *Western* as it gets. Otherwise, Scottsdale is chic, elegant and expensive. Amid its ties to the past, Scottsdale is a showplace of innovative architecture. The Frank Lloyd Wright Foundation is located here (at Taliesin West), as is the Cosanti Foundation, design headquarters for the controversial prototype town of Arcosanti, some 30 miles from Prescott, where building and nature are being fused.

SIGHTS

Don't miss **Rawhide Arizona's 1880 Western Town** with its colorful variety of rides and attractions, shops, a steakhouse and a saloon—all mostly located along a rickety Main Street where visitors dodge real sheep and goats. Western shootouts, fiddlers, a gypsy fortuneteller, stunt shows, a carriage exhibit, a covered-wagon circle and an Old West museum are all part of the fun. ~ 23023 North Scottsdale Road; 602-502-1880.

Taliesin West/Frank Lloyd Wright Foundation, a National Historic Landmark owned by the Frank Lloyd Wright Foundation, was the architect's Arizona home and studio. Situated on 600 acres of rugged Sonoran Desert, this remarkable set of buildings still astounds architectural critics with its beauty and unusual forms. A variety of guided tours are offered. There's also a lecture series. Admission. ~ 12621 North Frank Lloyd Wright Boulevard; 602-860-2700.

WestWorld is a special events facility with a restaurant and large arena hosting the world's largest Arabian horse show, automobile auctions, polo matches, rodeos and musical entertainment. Admission. ~ 16601 North Pima Road; 602-483-8800.

Lots of green lawn, fountains and almost 20 sculptures lure families to the **Civic Center Mall**. ~ Bounded by Indian School Road, Brown Avenue, 2nd Street and Civic Center Boulevard. In addition, culture thrives here with the Center for the Arts and an outdoor amphitheater hosting live performances year-round. After the show, stop by one of the restaurants or shops lining the mall's periphery. For more information, contact the **Center for the Arts**. ~ 7380 East 2nd Street, Scottsdale; 602-994-2787.

The Buffalo Museum of America displays such items as Buffalo Bill's hunting rifle, buffalo props from motion pictures and photos of buffalos. Closed Saturday and Sunday. Admission. ~ 10261 North Scottsdale Road, Scottsdale; 602-951-1022.

Fleischer Museum has rotating shows and permanent exhibits devoted to "American Impressionism, California School," with artwork from that stylish period between the 1880s and the 1930s, including misty, dreamlike landscapes, and architectural and still-life paintings. The museum also has an expanded permanent collection of the works of Russian and Soviet Impressionism from the Cold War era. ~ 17207 North Perimeter Drive; 602-585-3108.

LODGING

Holiday Inn–Old Town is located in the heart of "Old Town," close to everything. Its 206 rooms have a Southwestern motif. There are a lounge with nightly entertainment, a restaurant, a swimming pool and tennis courts. ~ 7353 East Indian School Road; 602-994-9203, 800-695-6995, fax 602-946-8084; www.holidayinnscottsdale.com. DELUXE.

A courtyard—complete with a lagoon, two pools (one with a sand beach and a waterslide) and a jacuzzi—is the center of attention at **SunBurst Resort**. Decked out in contemporary Southwestern decor, the 210 rooms and 5 suites feature French doors and private balconies and are equipped with satellite TV, coffeemakers, minibars and double phone lines. With a restaurant/lounge and a fitness room on-site, you won't have to abandon this modern oasis. ~ 4925 North Scottsdale Road; 602-945-7666, 800-528-7867, fax 602-946-4056; www.sunburstresort.com. ULTRA-DELUXE.

The **Scottsdale Plaza Resort** is a true find. Set within 40 acres, with 404 rooms, 180 of them suites, the resort features Spanish Mediterranean–style villas throughout, accented with courtyard swimming pools. The rooms are large and styled with Southwestern furnishing and art. Fountains, palm trees, earth-tone tiles, mauve carpeting, acres of fresh-cut flowers and potted greens add cooling touches. There are swimming pools, outdoor spas, tennis courts, indoor racquetball courts, a pro shop, a gym and a putting green. ~ 7200 North Scottsdale Road; 602-948-5000, 800-832-2025, fax 602-998-5971; www.tspr.com. ULTRA-DELUXE.

If you're looking for a gem of a mini-resort, try the 56-room **Best Western Papago Inn & Resort**. Amenities include a heated pool, sauna, lounge and dining room. Guest rooms all overlook a treed and flowered interior courtyard and swimming pool. Environmental "green" rooms—nonsmoking rooms with air and water filter systems—are available for a charge. ~ 7017 East Mc-Dowell Road; 602-947-7335, 800-528-1234, fax 602-994-0692. DELUXE.

Why go to a water park when the **Hyatt Regency Scottsdale** is around? Lounge on the sand beach, take a dip in the jacuzzi beneath a Greek water temple, or swim in the ten pools connected by a network of fountains, waterfalls, and a three-story waterslide. The 493 rooms, suites and *casitas* are modern with Sonoran desert tones. Amenities here include a health spa, three restaurants, golfing, tennis and horseback riding. ~ 7500 East Doubletree Ranch Road; 602-991-3388, 800-554-9288, fax 602-483-5540; www. hyatt.com. ULTRA-DELUXE.

Holiday Inn–Sunspree Resort, located on 16 lushly landscaped acres in the heart of Scottsdale, has 200 guest rooms (including 17 one- and two-bedroom suites). All are decorated in contemporary, upscale style. Recreational facilities include tennis courts, a pool, nearby golf, jogging trails and horseback riding. ~ 7601 East Indian Bend Road; 602-991-2400, 800-852-5265, fax 602-998-2261; www.arizonaguide.com/sunspree. DELUXE.

Scottsdale's Fifth Avenue Inn, a secluded retreat right in the heart of Scottsdale's premier shopping district, sprawls out around a central courtyard with a large heated swimming pool. Its 92 guest rooms feature desert colors, king and double queen beds, and separate dressing areas. Rates includes breakfast. ~ 6935 5th Avenue; 602-994-9461, 800-528-7396, fax 602-947-1695. MODERATE.

Holiday Inn Hotel and Suites is a four-story, all-suite, hotel designed in a courtyard setting with a heated pool and spa and a restaurant on the premises. Each of the hotel's two-room suites is styled in desert mauve and teals with light Southwestern contemporary furnishings. ~ 7515 East Butherus Drive; 602-951-4000, 800-334-1977, fax 602-483-9046. DELUXE.

Adjacent to the Tonto National Forest, **Desert Farren Hacienda** offers five hacienda-style guest rooms with private baths and European down comforters. You will find many opportunities to enjoy the beauty of the desert and saguaro cacti—from hiking the trails that meander the inn's 20 acres, to bicycling, swimming or playing golf or tennis at a nearby country club. If you overdo it in the day, soak in the hot tub at night. ~ P.O. Box 5550, Carefree, AZ 85377; 602-488-1110, 888-488-1110. ULTRA-DELUXE.

DINING

In the heart of the Scottsdale shopping district is **Jacqueline's Marketplace & Cafe**, an upscale, whimsical café/shop with lots of Southwestern gifts and bright coyote paintings and cards by artist Holly Haas. For dining, choices include table service or self-service, selecting from the wide variety of pastas, salads and sandwiches. The outdoor patio with its plants, brick walls and Southwestern tiles are a favorite in warm weather. Breakfast and lunch only. ~ 7303 East Indian School Road; 602-947-8777. BUDGET TO MODERATE.

Julio G's, established in 1934, somehow manages to combine a '30s art deco, Santa Fe and Mexican truck-stop decor—ceiling fans, black-tile walls and framed vintage-Mexican advertisements —into a trendy contemporary look. The food is much more clearly defined: *pollo magnifico*, beef tacos, bean tostadas, steaming bowls of rice and beans, chili con carne and tortillas. The staff is friendly and attentive. ~ 7633 East Indian School Road; 602-423-0058. BUDGET TO MODERATE.

For burgers, chicken and appetizers in a trendy eatery, stop by **AZ88**. The furnishings are made of glass, wood and steel and there are lots of climbing vines and floor-to-ceiling windows that overlook the green Civic Center Mall. Fresh flowers dot tabletops and contemporary urban music plays in the background for a lively meal. ~ 7353 Scottsdale Mall; 602-994-5576. BUDGET TO MODERATE.

Baby Kay's Cajun Kitchen is the place for crawfish étouffée, jambalaya, deep-fried catfish and Louisiana beers. Inside, the decorative motif is, naturally, Cajun, with crawfish nets on the walls and tablecloths printed with Mardi Gras masks, while a large patio offers seating around an outdoor fireplace. ~ 7216 East Shoeman Lane; 602-990-9080. MODERATE.

Any restaurant that combines American decor with traditional Greek flourishes has to be interesting. The food at **Blue Note Cool Cafe** runs from chicken and burgers to Greek omelettes and Gyro platters. There's also nightly live music. ~ 8040 East McDowell Road; 602-945-9573. BUDGET.

Malee's on Main Thai Gourmet is a charming little spot with a bar in one corner, tables inside and a patio, weather permitting, for dining outside. Attractive tableware is set against sandalwood- and eggplant-colored tablecloths. Popular with the art crowd (in Scottsdale that covers a wide swath), the restaurant has an extensive menu that comes in various degrees of spiciness. Dinner only on Sunday. ~ 7131 East Main Street; 602-947-6042. MODERATE TO DELUXE.

One of the oldest Mexican restaurants in Scottsdale (also considered the finest by many) is **Los Olivos Mexican Patio**. The restaurant was founded in 1945, but the adobe building in which it's located was built in 1928 and is officially listed as one of

Scottsdale's historic landmarks. Large and rambling, with viga ceilings, it has several individual dining rooms inside and patio dining outside. The Mexican cuisine served is primarily Sonoran —enchiladas, seasonal green corn tamales, chimichangas, *chile rellenos* and steak *picado*. The decor is festive (clay pots, flowers and piñatas) and there's live music and dancing on weekends. Aficionados rate its margaritas among the best in the state. ~ 7328 East 2nd Street; 602-946-2256. BUDGET TO MODERATE.

Located in the Phoenician resort, **Mary Elaine's** is classically elegant, decorated in soft shades of beige, gray and peach, with lavish touches such as 18th-century Italian oil paintings, German crystal stemware and romantic outdoor patios. The restaurant's menu draws on the flavors of Europe, North Africa and Asia, with such specialties as garlic and herb-crusted rack of lamb, grilled salmon with gazpacho vegetables and tomatillo chile coulis. ~ 6000 East Camelback Road; 602-423-2530. MODERATE TO ULTRA-DELUXE.

A traditional breakfast spot (it also serves lunch) is **The Original Pancake House,** in business over 40 years, serving up steaming stacks of golden flapjacks, topped with melted butter, honey, maple syrup, berries or whatever's your pleasure. The restaurant is small—eleven tables and ten booths. The decor is Southwestern with light green and tan colors dominating. Large picture windows in front keep it bright and cheerful. ~ 6840 East Camelback Road; 602-946-4902. BUDGET.

Dark hardwood tables and white limestone walls add to the Southwestern ambience at the bi-level **Z'Tejas Grill**. Try the voodoo tuna blackened with a spicy soy mustard and black pepper vinaigrette, followed by ancho chile fudge pie. The Southwestern cuisine is also laced with flavors from Louisiana. ~ 7014 East Camelback Road; 602-946-4171. MODERATE TO DELUXE.

▸▸

✔ CHECK THESE OUT—UNIQUE DINING

- *Budget:* Inhale the aroma of fresh coffee at the Caribbean-style **Coffee Plantation,** which roasts its own beans. *page 220*
- *Moderate:* Get a feel for the Lone Star State at the **Texaz Grill** and chow down on chicken-fried steak with all the fixin's. *page 197*
- *Deluxe*: Go French at **Voltaire**, where candlelight and crystal enhance sweetbreads sautéed in lemon butter and chicken à la Normande. *page 212*
- *Ultra-deluxe:* Indulge in Maine lobster ravioli with pan-seared scallops and other New American fare at **Wright's**. *page 199*

Budget: under $8   Moderate: $8–$16   Deluxe: $16–$24   Ultra-deluxe: over $24

Voltaire is a bastion of French gastronomy, all candlelight and crystal. Boned chicken à la Normande with apples, sautéed sand dabs, rack of lamb and sweetbreads sautéed in lemon butter and capers highlight the extensive menu. Closed Sunday. ~ 8340 East McDonald Drive; 602-948-1005. DELUXE.

Don't be surprised if your waiter breaks into song after you've ordered at **Ristorante Sandolo**, an Italian café known for their singing servers. The restaurant dishes out Venetian-style entrées and gourmet pizzas, followed by complimentary *sandolo* (similar to gondola) rides on the waterway winding through the Hyatt Regency Scottsdale. ~ 7500 East Doubletree Ranch Road; 602-991-3388. MODERATE TO DELUXE.

People flock to **Coco Pazzo** to eat Italian cuisine amidst faux Roman ruins, giant pillars and halogen lights. Jazz sets the mood, and dining on the authentic Tuscan-style meat and seafood entrées and homemade pastas can be done indoors or out on the sun-warmed patio. ~ 4720 North Scottsdale Road; 602-946-9777. MODERATE TO ULTRA-DELUXE.

With the success of her popular Tucson restaurant of the same name, chef Donna Nordin has branched out with another **Café Terra Cotta**, this one in Scottsdale's Borgata shopping center. Colorful and casual, with green chairs and little pots of cacti on the tables, stand-out dishes include a chile relleno stuffed with grilled shrimp in a red chile chipotle sauce, sea bass enchiladas and pork tenderloin *adobada* with apricot chutney. ~ 6166 North Scottsdale Road; 602-948-8100. MODERATE TO DELUXE.

House of Yang is small, only a few tables and chairs, and it appears to do a large takeout business. But whether you eat in or take out, the House of Yang is a course in Chinese cuisine, serving Szechwan, Hunan, Mandarin and Cantonese. Shrimp with lobster sauce—shrimp, onions and peppers, stir-fried and topped with a black bean sauce—comes with rice, won tons and an egg roll. Mongolian beef is thinly sliced beef served with egg roll, fried rice and won tons. ~ 13802 North Scottsdale Road; 602-443-0188. BUDGET TO MODERATE.

Rawhide Steakhouse and Saloon is the place to belly up to the bar in Scottsdale's popular Old West frontier town. There's good things to eat, too—mesquite-broiled steaks, prime rib, barbecued chicken, baby back ribs and even fried rattlesnake. The saloon section has an antique bar, gambling tables (but no gambling), "crooked" card dealers and live country music. ~ 23023 North Scottsdale Road; 602-563-5600. MODERATE TO ULTRA-DELUXE.

Greasewood Flats is a hot dog, chili and beer kind of place housed in an old graffiti-covered wooden shack in what appears to be a Western junkyard, with discarded school desks, wooden wagons, saddle frames, wagon wheels, milk cans and egg crates all around it. But folks line up to get in. Live music Thursday through Sunday. ~ 27000 North Alma School Road; 602-585-9430. BUDGET.

The **Marquesa** is one of the top restaurants in the valley. Even people who normally avoid hotel dining rooms flock to this one in the Scottsdale Princess Resort to soak up all of its Old World Spanish ambience and nibble on *tapas* before settling down to more serious pursuits. Roast loin of lamb wrapped in cabbage with chorizo sausage, artichokes and stoneground mustard–rosemary sauce, for instance, or steaming Mediterranean-style paella for two. The Marquesa is also known for its excellent wine list. Dinner only, plus Sunday brunch. ~ 7575 East Princess Drive; 602-585-4848. ULTRA-DELUXE.

Get out of town one evening and treat yourself to a breathtaking view of pristine desert landscape and the city lights beyond from **The Peaks** at Pinnacle Peak. Specialties here are baby-back ribs, prime rib and seafood, all with an Asian/Southwestern flair. The restaurant also has an extensive wine list. ~ 8711 East Pinnacle Peak Road; 602-998-2222. MODERATE TO DELUXE.

Don't wear a necktie if you're going to the **Pinnacle Peak Patio** because they'll snip it off and hang it from the rafters. That's part of the appeal of this highly informal Western-style steak house where 16-ounce mesquite-broiled steaks, with all the beans and fixin's, top the menu and the walls reverberate with the sounds of live country bands nightly. ~ 10426 East Jomax Road; 602-967-8082. BUDGET TO DELUXE.

Shells Oyster Bar & Seafood is the best known of the four restaurants located at Marriott's Mountain Shadows Resort. Live miniature fish swim in an illuminated aquarium. The decor is elegant, bright and airy, with polished brass, etched mirrors and natural wood finishes. Seafood entrées come in a variety of preparations—flame broiled, steamed, sautéed, pan-fried or blackened Cajun style, accompanied by a selection of special butters and sauces. Dinner only. ~ 5641 East Lincoln Drive; 602-948-7111. DELUXE TO ULTRA-DELUXE.

SHOPPING

The **Borgata of Scottsdale** may just be a harbinger of a striking new trend in shopping centers—mini-theme-park shopping malls —this one, a 14th-century-style village with medieval courtyards. International fashions, fine jewelry, unusual gifts, a book and music store and a spate of art galleries await. ~ 6166 North Scottsdale Road; 602-998-1822.

Despite the trendy intrusions, **Scottsdale Fashion Square** remains the city's most fashionable shopping complex. It features top-quality stores like **Neiman Marcus** (602-990-2100), **Dillard's** (602-949-5869) and **Robinson's-May** (602-941-0066). There's

Text continued on page 216.

Spoil Yourself

The American West is big and grand—how inconsistent it would be if its great resort hotels were not just a reach beyond all expectation. And Central Arizona is home to some of the biggest and grandest around.

Inspired by Frank Lloyd Wright and designed by Albert Chase McArthur, the refurbished **Arizona Biltmore** has maintained an aura of ease and luxury since its opening in 1929. From its palm-lined drive, elaborate high portico and immense lobby to its bright, handsomely furnished guest rooms, the 750-room Biltmore is as dramatic and visually exciting as it is comfortable. The "Jewel of the Desert" provides a full range of activities: golf courses, tennis courts, pools, a waterslide and a spa, salon and fitness center. ~ 24th Street and Missouri Avenue, Phoenix; 602-955-6600, 800-950-0086, fax 602-954-2548; www.arizonabiltmore.com. ULTRA-DELUXE.

Another ultra-deluxe establishment in Phoenix, to say the least, is **The Phoenician**, the most prestigious and talked-about resort in the Valley of the Sun. Sprawled over 250 acres along the sun-dappled flanks of Camelback Mountain, it's set within a tiered oasis of waterfalls and pools, the largest of which is tiled entirely with mother-of-pearl. Its 581 guest rooms are large and lavish with most situated in the main hotel, others in surrounding *casitas*. There are also 107 *casita* units with parlor suites that have hand-carved travertine fireplaces. If you really want to make a night of it, there are 4 presidential and 69 luxury suites. Recreational facilities run the gamut—a 27-hole golf course, lighted tennis courts, tournament croquet and a health and fitness spa. ~ 6000 East Camelback Road, Scottsdale; 602-941-8200, 800-888-8234, fax 602-947-4311; www.thephoenician.com. ULTRA-DELUXE.

The Scottsdale Princess, an ultra-luxury resort set against the dramatic backdrop of the McDowell Mountains, has 650 rooms. It's one of the Valley's largest hotels. Set on 450 elaborately landscaped acres with a central courtyard, waterfall, three swimming pools and 18th-century Spanish Colonial architecture, the Princess is one of the most visually arresting of its kind. The rooms are large, decorated in Southwestern furnishing, with a hint of Santa Fe. The grounds include seven tennis courts, a fitness center and two championship golf courses. ~ 7575 East Princess Drive, Scottsdale; 602-585-4848, 800-344-4758, fax 602-585-9895; www.cphotels.ca. ULTRA-DELUXE.

With 448 rooms, **Marriott's Camelback Inn** outside Scottsdale is yet another glorious world-class retreat dramatically nestled in the foothills between the Camelback and Mummy mountains, where landscaped paths wind through gardens of cactus and desert palms. Its Southwestern pueblo architecture and adobe-style *casitas* blend harmoniously into the stunning desert background. For the sportsminded there are championship golf and tennis, swimming, trail rides, weekly cookouts and fitness facilities. ~ 5402 East Lincoln Drive, Paradise Valley; 602-948-1700, 800-242-2635, fax 602-951-5452; www.camelbackinn.com. ULTRA-DELUXE.

Marriott's Mountain Shadows Resort and Golf Club offers palm trees, sparkling streams and lakes, and that's just the golf course. At the foot of Camelback Mountain, with over a hundred acres of land, Mountain Shadows seems designed for the sports devotee. Along with its 18 hole, executive par-3 golf course (#4 in the nation), it has lighted tennis courts, putting greens and swimming pools. The hotel's 337 guest rooms are designed in muted Southwestern colors, each with a private terrace. The resort has four restaurants. ~ 5641 East Lincoln Drive, Scottsdale; 602-948-7111, 800-782-2123, fax 602-951-5430; www.mountainshadows.com. ULTRA-DELUXE.

Who says the West is wild? The **Wigwam** west of Phoenix is an upper-upper-scale resort on 75 acres of what was originally virgin desert. The design is pueblo-style, with 331 desert-brown adobe *casitas* set in a lavish golf and country-club setting—towering palms, green lawns, cascading flowers and fragrant orange trees. Through the use of building materials native to the Southwest, architecture blends with nature. Slate, stone and wood surfaces are accented with Indian themes and desert colors. Championship golf courses, riding, tennis, swimming and other activities keep the body occupied while the mind relaxes. ~ 300 Wigwam Boulevard, Litchfield Park; 602-935-3811, 800-327-0396, fax 602-935-3737; www.wigwam resort.com. ULTRA-DELUXE.

even a shop for the kiddies—**The Disney Store** (602-994-9616).
~ 7000 East Camelback Road; 602-990-7800.

Fifth Avenue Shops comprise the landmark shopping area in
the heart of downtown Scottsdale, a sprawl of specialty shops,
boutiques, bookstores, galleries, jewelry stores, American Indian
crafts shops and restaurants, over 200 in all by latest count. ~
7121 East 5th Avenue; 602-946-7566. Among
them, **Sewell's Indian Arts** carries American Indian
jewelry, kachinas, Pueblo pottery and Navajo sandpaintings. ~ 7087 5th Avenue; 602-945-0962. **Kac-
tus Jock** has casual apparel and active wear, as well as
Southwestern gifts. ~ 7121 5th Avenue, #7; 602-946-
7566.

> After New York City
> and Santa Fe, Scottsdale
> is the busiest art center
> in the country, with
> more than 200
> galleries.

Arizona Sun Products has fun gift items, but specializes in
a wonderful moisturizer containing native plants such as
aloe vera, jojoba, wild roses and cacti. A colorful desert scene on
the front makes it a good souvenir, too. ~ 7136 East 5th Avenue;
602-941-9067.

Elsewhere, mystery lovers should seek out **The Poisoned Pen**,
a mystery bookstore specializing in crime, detective and suspense
books from American and British publishers. ~ 7100-D East Main
Street; 602-947-2974.

For you cowpokes, **Porters** is one of the oldest names in Scottsdale cowboy gear and features top-of-the-line name brands. ~
3944 North Brown Avenue; 602-945-0868.

Scottsdale's many art galleries offer contemporary works, Indian art, Western and Old Masters. If you're interested in the local
art scene, the **Scottsdale Gallery Association** conducts Art Walks
every Thursday, from 7 to 9 p.m., visiting many of the leading
galleries. ~ 602-990-3939.

At other times of the year, the Art Walks are conducted on
the third Thursday of each month. Walks begin at the **Scottsdale
Center for the Arts**. ~ 7380 East 2nd Street; 602-994-2787.

If you want to check out the art scene on your own, consider
Arizona West Galleries, which specializes in Western and Civil
War relics and American 19th- and 20th-century Western art, including works by Frederic Remington, Charlie Russell and May-
nard Dixon. Closed Sunday. ~ 7149 Main Street; 602-994-3752.

The **Biltmore Galleries** also has 19th- and 20th-century art,
including works by early New Mexico master Nicolai Fechin,
Joseph Sharp and Ernest Blumenschein. ~ 7113 Main Street; 602-
947-5975.

Packaged gift items featuring one of Arizona's most flavorful
products are available at the **Sphinx Date Ranch**. ~ 3039 North
Scottsdale Road; 602-941-2261.

Buck Saunders Gallery, the oldest gallery in Scottsdale, represents Arizona's best-known, best-loved artist, Ted De Grazia,

along with other American Indian and Southwestern artists. ~ 2724 North Scottsdale Road; 602-945-9376.

A unique assortment of boutiques and gift shops can be found at **El Pedregal Festival Marketplace**. Beautiful hand-painted silk, cotton gauze and velour fashions for women in desert sunset colors and jewel tones can be found at **Carole Dolighan** (602-488-4505). **Gallery 10** (602-994-0405) features contemporary American Indian and Western ceramic art, jewelry, kachinas and paintings. ~ 34505 North Scottsdale Road.

Glenn Green Galleries uses the elegant grounds of the posh Phoenician Resort (the gallery is in the hotel's retail corridor) to display the mammoth bronze and stone sculptures of famed Indian artist Alan Houser, as well as sculptors Paul Moore and Eduardo Oropeza. ~ 6000 East Camelback Road; 602-990-9110.

J. R. Fine Arts handles serigraphs, lithographs, oils and sculpture, including those by top contemporary painters Leroy Neiman and Earl Biss. ~ 4151 North Marshall Way; 602-945-7856.

All-American crafts in a variety of mediums—ceramics, wood, fabric, paper and glass—are showcased at **Mind's Eye Gallery**. ~ 4200 North Marshall Way; 602-941-2494.

Contemporary American Indian art is the focus of **Lovena Ohl Gallery** where there are sculptures by Larry Yazzie, paintings by David Johns and Tony Da, and pottery, jewelry and Kachina dolls by a variety of artists. ~ 4251 North Marshall Way; 602-945-8212.

To get your practical shopping done in one convenient stop, drive to **Scottsdale Pavilions**, a 1.2 million-square-foot complex that includes a pharmacy, clothing stores, fast-food stops, a bookstore and a home improvement store. ~ Corner of Pima and Indian Bend roads; 602-866-0900.

NIGHTLIFE

For starters, try the big-band sounds at the Royal Palm Inn's **El Mirage Lounge**. ~ 5200 East Camelback Road; 602-840-3610. At the spirited **Rawhide Arizona's 1880 Western Town**, live country-and-western bands perform nightly at both the steakhouse and saloon. ~ 23023 North Scottsdale Road; 602-502-5600. A live guitarist plays flamenco music Wednesday through Saturday, while Caribbean steel drums entertain Sunday through Tuesday at the Hyatt Regency Scottsdale's **Lobby Bar**. ~ 7500 East Doubletree Ranch Road; 602-991-3388. For some action at a sports bar, try **JD's Lounge** at the Scottsdale Plaza Resort. ~ 7200 North Scottsdale Road; 602-948-5000.

There's a lot of rockin' going on at the **Blue Note Cool Cafe**, a '50s-style diner with two performance spaces. The Blue Note hosts R&B bands nightly, while classic rock musicians groove in the Cool Cafe Thursday through Saturday. The weekend cover charge admits you into both rooms. ~ 8040 East McDowell Road; 602-945-9573.

J. Chew & Company has live jazz nightly in an intimate, European-style pub with french doors leading to two outdoor patios with fireplaces. ~ 7320 Scottsdale Mall; 602-946-2733.

Scottsdale Center for the Arts, located in the beautifully sculptured Scottsdale Mall, hosts a variety of events, including the Scottsdale Symphony, guest performing artists, concerts, lectures, classic cinema and art exhibitions. During the summer, music lovers flock to the concerts held outside on the grassy lawn at the mall's east end. For a schedule, call 602-994-2787.

▼▼▼▼▼▼▼▼▼▼▼▼
Tempe/Mesa Area

Immediately east of Phoenix are the communities of Tempe and Mesa. Continuing out over the desert that stretches on to New Mexico are Apache Junction and Globe. It's as though, heading east, all the big-city sheen dissolves in degrees into the West of the Old West, the pace slows down and you can almost reach up and feel the sky in your hands.

SIGHTS

Bordered by Scottsdale, Mesa, Phoenix and Chandler, **Tempe** was founded in 1872 by Charles Turnbell Hayden who established the Hayden Flour Mill that year, now the oldest continuously operating business in Arizona. **Old Town Tempe** is where Tempe was originally founded, set up around the old Hayden Flour Mill. Today many of the early homes and buildings have been renovated and serve as restaurants, shops, offices and galleries. ~ North of University Street along Mill Avenue. Stop by the **Tempe Convention and Visitors Bureau** for maps and information. ~ 51 West 3rd Street, Suite 105; 602-894-8158.

Forming the character of Tempe is **Arizona State University** (602-965-9011), located in the heart of the city. Home of the Fiesta Bowl, it has the largest enrollment of any school in the Southwest. With its 700-acre main campus, where strikingly modern buildings rise from a setting of palm trees and subtropical plants, Arizona State provides the chiefly residential city with its main industry. A number of outstanding museums dot the campus and are open to the public. **Arizona State University Art Museum** has an extensive collection of American paintings, prints and crafts as well as artworks from Africa, Latin America and the South Seas. Closed Monday. ~ 602-965-2787. The **Museum**

FROM PAST TO PRESENT

For a trip back in time, visit the outstanding **Tempe Historical Museum**, which covers the history of Tempe from early Indian days to the present. Two changing galleries offer historic exhibits on the area. There are also hands-on displays for children. Closed Friday. Admission. ~ 809 East Southern Avenue; 602-350-5100.

of **Anthropology** includes archaeological, physical and sociocultural anthropology exhibits. Closed on weekends. ~ 602-965-6224. Highlight exhibits at the **Museum of Geology** focus on rare geologic specimens, seismographs and earthquake displays. Closed on weekends. ~ 602965-7065. Museum hours vary, so call ahead.

Just east of Tempe, you'll come to the town of **Mesa**. Situated on a plateau, Mesa in Spanish means "table." The town was founded by Mormons in 1883 and was long a farming community. Irrigation canals built by the Hohokam Indians were still used in Mesa until fairly recent times. For information on sights and services in Mesa, stop by the **Mesa Convention and Visitors Bureau**. ~ 120 North Center Street, Mesa; 602-827-4700.

Mesa Southwest Museum covers the history of the Southwest from the time of the dinosaurs to the settlement of the West, with hands-on exhibits inside. Closed Monday. Admission. ~ 53 North MacDonald Street, Mesa; 602-644-2230.

A find for aviation aficionados, the **Champlin Fighter Museum** has a collection of 30 restored fighters from World War I, World War II and the Korean and Vietnam wars. Historic weaponry is also displayed. An art gallery, video theater and pilot-memorabilia gift shop round out the bill. Admission. ~ 4636 Fighter Aces Drive, Mesa; 602-830-4540.

Twenty minutes north of Mesa is the **Out of Africa Wildlife Park** where lions, tigers, bears, wolves and reptiles do their things. There are shows, natural habitat viewing, cub-petting and a playground for the kids. There's also a gift shop and restaurant. Closed Monday. Admission. ~ 2 South Fort McDowell Road, Fountain Hills; 602-837-7779.

LODGING

Located in the heart of downtown Tempe is the **Tempe Mission Palms Hotel**, with 303 Southwestern-style rooms and a lobby that has a wonderful wooden registration desk with a granite top and intricate millwork. Nice touches in the rooms include paintings of pottery on the walls, pastel bedspreads, bathrooms with marbleized sinks and a small makeup bureau. Most rooms overlook the lush, palm tree–dotted courtyard with fountains and a swimming pool. Other amenities include a restaurant, a sauna, whirlpool, exercise room and tennis courts. ~ 60 East 5th Street, Tempe; 602-894-1400, 800-547-8705, fax 602-968-7677; www.mission palms.com. ULTRA-DELUXE.

Sprawling across 33 acres, the **Fiesta Inn** offers 270 Southwestern-style guest rooms. All have refrigerators and several are mini-suites. The fitness-minded will find a swimming pool, jacuzzi, a golf practice facility with a lighted driving range and putting greens, tennis courts and an exercise room. There's also a restaurant on the premises. ~ 2100 South Priest Drive, Tempe; 602-967-1441, 800-528-6481, fax 602-967-0224. DELUXE.

Wyndham Buttes Resort is a dramatic 353-room, four-story resort built into the mountainsides, with Southwestern styling and art throughout. All guest rooms feature a Southwestern decor or rose and earth tones, cactus and wood furnishings. It has two restaurants, a nightclub, pools, tennis courts and all of the modern trim and trappings associated with luxury resort living in the valley, including cascading waterfalls and four romantic mountainside whirlpools. ~ 2000 Westcourt Way, Tempe; 602-225-9000, 800-996-3426, fax 602-431-2422; www.buttes.com. ULTRA-DELUXE.

Cornerstone of downtown Mesa, the **Sheraton Mesa Hotel** has 273 rooms, contemporary furnishings, lounge, restaurant and swimming pool and an elegant lobby. ~ 200 North Centennial Way, Mesa; 602-898-8300, 800-456-6372, fax 602-964-9279; www.sheraton.com. ULTRA-DELUXE.

Buckhorn Mineral Wells is a motel and natural hot water mineral springs bath house where massages and therapeutic hot soaks are offered. The motel has 14 rooms in contemporary Southwest decor. ~ 5900 East Main Street, Mesa; 602-832-1111. BUDGET.

DINING

Housed in the Old Tempe train station, **Macayo's Depot Cantina** is charmingly decorated with historic photographs and train memorabilia. The menu is Southwest/Mexican, particularly good for mesquite broiled meats and seafood. ~ 300 South Ash Avenue, Tempe; 602-966-6677. BUDGET TO MODERATE.

Mill Landing is a handsome restaurant housed in a historic building in the downtown Old Town section of Tempe offering a variety of light meals, salads, soups, sandwiches and seafood specialties. There's dining in the patio, weather permitting. ~ 398 South Mill Avenue, Tempe; 602-966-1700. MODERATE TO ULTRA-DELUXE.

In a similar mold and building (the Andre, built in 1888), **Paradise Bar and Grill** specializes in mesquite-grilled entrées. ~ 401 South Mill Avenue, Tempe; 602-829-0606. MODERATE.

Casa Reynoso is one of the better Mexican restaurants in town, despite its modest appearance—vinyl booths and wrought iron. Try the *gollo burro* or *chile rellenos*. Closed Monday. ~ 3138 South Mill Avenue, Tempe; 602-966-0776. MODERATE.

The Coffee Plantation is a Caribbean-style coffeehouse and retail store in a plantation house. Beans are roasted daily in a rustic roasting shack. There's indoor and outdoor seating where espresso, cappuccino and specialty coffees are served, along with pastries and desserts, light lunch and dinner. ~ 680 South Mill Avenue, Suite 101, Tempe; 602-829-7878. BUDGET.

For Italian Continental cuisine, try **John Henry's**. Duck, lamb, steak, seafood and pasta are some of the favorites you can enjoy in this elegant, plant-filled dining room. Live music Tuesday through Saturday. Closed Sunday in summer. ~ 909 East Elliot Road, Tempe; 602-730-9009. MODERATE TO DELUXE.

Though the decor is plain and simple, the food is anything but at **Char's Thai Restaurant** where an exotic touch of the East comes to Tempe with such offerings as chicken soup with coconut milk, smoked beef salad, curried duck and seafood combinations in peanut sauce. There's also a good selection of Asian beers. ~ 927 East University Drive, Tempe; 602-967-6013. BUDGET TO MODERATE.

For a good solid breakfast or lunch, they don't come much better than the **Ripe Tomato Cafe** where it's always wall-to-wall people. It's a great find for breakfast, and the steak, sandwiches and Mexican specialty lunches aren't bad either. Breakfast and lunch only. ~ 745 West Baseline Road, Mesa; 602-892-4340. BUDGET.

Historic **Old Town Tempe** exudes ambience with its old-fashioned red-brick sidewalks and planters, tree-lined streets and quaint street lamps. Walk the area and you'll find dozens of shops and restaurants. With light music floating in the background, you can scan the shelves at the **Changing Hands Bookstore**, which has more than 50,000 new and used books on three floors. Specialties at the bookstore are spirituality, psychology, literature, women's issues and travel. ~ 414 South Mill Avenue, Tempe; 602-966-0203. For clothing, gifts and accessories from around the world, try **Mazar Bazaar** ~ 514 South Mill Avenue, Tempe; 602-966-9090.

SHOPPING

Those Were the Days! has one of the largest selections of books on antiques and collecting in the Southwest with more than 5000 new titles, as well as used, out-of-print and rare titles on antiques. As an added bonus, you can buy antiques and kitsch here as folk music constantly plays in the background. ~ 516 South Mill Avenue, Tempe; 602-967-4729.

Superstition Springs Center is the newest mega-mall in the Phoenix area. In addition to the usual mall lineup of anchor stores and chain specialty shops, this center has a full-size carousel for the kids, a desert botanical garden with more than 100 plants, a playground with a 15-foot-tall Gila Monster slide, several short hiking trails and a stage for free concerts. ~ Intersection of Power Road and the Superstition Freeway, Mesa; 602-832-0212.

East Side Art in Mesa offers modern paintings, posters and prints, as well as art supplies, classes and framing services. ~ 9919 East Apache Trail, Mesa; 602-986-5450. **Galeria Mesa** features contemporary art from around the country. ~ 155 North Center Street, Mesa; 602-644-2056.

The **Lenox Factory Outlet** offers selected seconds on the company's famous china and crystal products, as well as candles, silver and other tabletop accessories. ~ 2121 South Power Road, Mesa; 602-986-9986.

NIGHTLIFE   **Grady Gammage Memorial Auditorium**, at the Arizona State University campus in Tempe, is a 3000-seat auditorium designed by Frank Lloyd Wright. Its entertainment features range from Broadway productions to symphony orchestra concerts and ballet. Guided tours of the center are offered Monday through Friday. ~ Tour information: 602-965-4050. Gammage Auditorium: corner of Mill Avenue and Apache Street; 602-965-3434.

Serving dinner, drinks and laughs, the **Tempe Improv**, is a restaurant/comedy club which features a changing lineup of stand-up comics. Cover. ~ 930 East University Drive, Tempe; 602-921-9877.

The Butte's swinging **Top of the Rock Bar** with its 24-foot video screen and live entertainment on weekends is one of the hottest spots in town. ~ 2000 West Westcourt Way, Tempe; 602-225-9000.

A dance club with a 1950s motif, **Studebaker's** has DJs, vintage rock and a happy-hour dinner buffet. ~ 1290 North Scottsdale Road, Tempe; 602-829-8617.

Satisfy your urge to jump, jive and wail at **The Bash**, where swing bands take the stage on Thursday and Saturday. Don't know any steps? Lessons are offered Tuesday, Thursday and Saturday. On Friday night, deejays spin high-energy dance music. Cover. ~ 230 West 5th Street, Tempe; 602-966-8200.

Bandersnatch is big with the ASU college crowd, which means lots of beer including seven homemade brews. Live jazz and traditional Irish music twice a week. ~ 125 East 5th Street, Tempe; 602-966-4438. **Balboa Café** draws large crowds with live jazz and rock nightly. Occasional cover. ~ 404 South Mill Avenue, Suite 101, Tempe; 602-966-1300.

Chandler Center for the Arts has three stages hosting musical, dance and theater performances by local and national performers. In addition, artwork is displayed in the foyer and exhibit hall. Admission. ~ 250 North Arizona Avenue, Chandler; 602-786-2680, 602-898-5665, ext. 1910.

PARKS   **MCDOWELL MOUNTAIN REGIONAL PARK** 🚶🚲🐎 This 21,099-acre wilderness expanse 15 miles northeast of Scottsdale is one of the region's most scenic parks with an abundance of vegetation and majestic mountain views. Elevation ranges from 1600 feet at the southeast corner to 2000 feet along the western boundary. The area is ideal for camping, picnicking, horseback riding, hiking and mountain bike riding. Facilities include picnic areas, restrooms and showers. Day-use fee, $2 per vehicle. ~ Located via McDowell Mountain Road, four miles northeast of Fountain Hills; 602-471-0173.

▲ There are 76 sites (all with RV hookups); $15 per night.

From cactus flowers to remote mountain lakes, here is a region rich in scenic wonders. Best known for its dude-ranch resorts, mining towns, cool forests and desert playgrounds, this recreational paradise includes the Wild West town of Wickenberg—the Dude Ranch Capital of the World—the three-million-acre Tonto National Forest and some of the Southwest's better ghost towns.

North of Phoenix

Established in 1950, **Carefree** is a planned community set in the scenic foothills of the Arizona desert. To the north and east stretches the immense Tonto National Forest. Next door is the old-time town of **Cave Creek**. Once a booming mining camp in the 1880s (gold and silver), Cave Creek wasn't incorporated until a hundred years later. Sheep and cattle were raised here as well. Today Cave Creek leans heavily on its past, with its Frontier Town re-creation and annual spring rodeo. For more information contact **Carefree/Cave Creek Chamber of Commerce**. ~ 748 Easy Street, Carefree; 602-488-3381.

SIGHTS

Cave Creek Museum offers a living-history exhibit of the desert foothills region, with a restored 1920s tuberculous cabin and a 1940s church, as well as displays of pioneer living, ranching, mining, guns and American Indian artifacts. Open October through May, Wednesday through Sunday. ~ 6140 East Skyline Drive, Cave Creek; 602-488-2764.

At the peak of the gold rush, Wickenburg had more than 80 mines, with the town growing into what was Arizona's third-largest city at the time.

To the northwest, on Route 89, you will come to the site of the richest gold strike in Arizona. Named after the Austrian settler Henry Wickenburg, who discovered it, **Wickenburg** is primarily known today as a winter resort.

Frontier Street preserves Wickenburg's turn-of-the-century character with its old-time train depot now housing the **Wickenburg Chamber of Commerce** and some vintage wood and brick buildings. One, the Hassayampa, was once the town's leading hotel. Maps for a self-guided historic walking tour are available at the chamber office. ~ 216 North Frontier Street, Wickenburg; 520-684-5479, 800-942-5242; www.wickenburgchamber.com.

Before the town jail was built, the nearby **Jail Tree** was used to chain criminals. Friends and relatives brought them picnic lunches. Today the tree is on the property of the Chaparral Ice Cream Parlor, and tykes eat their ice cream cones there now, probably none the wiser. ~ Tegner Street and Wickenburg Way, Wickenburg.

Venture over to the **Desert Caballeros Western Museum**, which covers the history of Wickenburg and surrounding area with major exhibits divided into various rooms. "Period" rooms include the Hall of History and a Street Scene representing Wickenburg at the turn of the century. Others focus on 19th- and early-20th-century lifestyles. Its art gallery features American Indian art and Western masters of the past and present. There is a special display of cowboy gear. The Museum Park outside offers unique desert landscaping and plants. Admission. ~ 21 North Frontier Street, Wickenburg; 520-684-2272.

One of Arizona's newer attractions is **Robson's Mining World**, an old mining town that supposedly has the world's largest collection of antique mining equipment. Along with seeing the thousands of pieces of equipment, you can stroll through a mineral and gemstone museum, print shop, trading post and several other buildings. Admission. ~ Take Route 60, 24 miles west of Wickenburg to Route 71, then go four miles north to milepost 90; 520-685-2609.

To the northeast of Phoenix lies **Payson**, district headquarters for the Tonto National Forest. Payson provides a base camp for numerous scenic attractions within the forest primeval. Founded over a century ago as a tiny mining and ranching community, it now thrives on its recreation industry. **Payson Chamber of Commerce** offers information on the area. ~ 100 West Main Street, Payson; 520-474-4515.

Ten miles north of Payson, **Tonto Natural Bridge** in the Tonto National Forest, is the world's largest natural travertine bridge.

Payson Zoo has between 40 and 50 injured or orphaned exotic animals, including bears, baboons, a serval (a small cat from Africa), lemurs, pot-bellied pigs, javelinas, deer and coyotes. The owner takes guests on a personal tour and explains the history of each animal. Closed Thursday. Admission. ~ Lion Spring Road at Route 260, Payson; 520-474-5435.

A state historic monument, **Strawberry Schoolhouse**, is the oldest standing schoolhouse in Arizona. Built in 1885, its last class was held in 1916. The small mountain village at 6000 feet was named for the many wild strawberries that covered the area when pioneers first arrived. Open weekends only. Closed October through March. ~ Village of Strawberry; 520-476-3095.

WEATHER OR NOT? WHILE SOME LIKE IT HOT . . .

All of south central Arizona gets hot, despite the seemingly innocuous average annual temperature of 72°F. Winter is cool and clear, in the 60s; spring is breezy and warm, in the 90s; summer is torrid, often topping 100°, and that's when the monsoons come, the swift summer rainstorms that usually arrive late in the day with spectacular flashes of lightning and deep, rolling rumbles of thunder; autumn is marvelously dry and clear, in the 80s. Depending on your weather preference, choose your time to visit accordingly.

Located just northeast of Scottsdale, **The Boulders** is built directly   **LODGING**
against a stunning backdrop of 12-million-year-old granite boul-
der formations that soar hundreds of feet against the desert sky.
Situated on 1300 acres, the resort consists of a main lodge and 160
adobe-style *casitas*, each individually designed to fit the sculptured
contours of the desert and the rocks. The hotel is designed in
broad architectural sweeps and makes dramatic use of American
Indian and regional art and artifacts—Navajo blankets, weavings,
pottery, ceramics, paintings, stone sculptures and basketry. Guest
rooms feature earth-tone furnishings, hand-hewn, viga ceilings,
fireplaces, wet bars, ceiling fans and oversized windows for broad
desert vistas. ~ 34631 North Tom Darlington Drive, Carefree;
602-488-9009, 800-553-1717, fax 602-488-4118; www.slh.com.
ULTRA-DELUXE.

Tumbleweed Hotel is a small downtown Cave Creek hotel
made of white slumpstone brick, with 16 rooms in the main building and eight *casita*-style guest houses, all with modern Western-
style furnishings and decor. The hotel has a swimming pool. ~
6333 East Cave Creek Road, Cave Creek; 602-488-3668, fax 602-
488-2936. MODERATE.

Spread across 20,000 acres, the **Rancho de los Caballeros**
resort/guest ranch has a homey feel, having been owned by the
same family since it opened in 1947. Out here, boredom is impossible. There's golfing on a championship 18-hole course, horseback riding, a skeet and trap range, tennis courts, a swimming
pool and programs for the kids. The 79 rooms and suites are
Southwestern in style, with private patios and indoor sitting areas.
The ranch is on the full American plan. Closed from the end of
May to early October. ~ 1551 South Vulture Mine Road, Wickenburg; 520-684-5484, 800-684-5030, fax 520-684-2267; www.
sunc.com. ULTRA-DELUXE.

There's not a lack of activities at Merv Griffin's **Wickenburg
Inn**, a dude ranch that waits at the end of a dusty road. Choices
include playing on one of three tennis courts, viewing displays at
the Desert Nature Center, followed by hiking, swimming in one of
three pools, horseback riding, painting or jewelry making at the
arts-and-crafts center, or spending money in the gift shop. Many
of the 54 *casitas* have kitchenettes and cozy fireplaces beneath
beamed ceilings; nine lodge rooms provide additional accommodations. The room price includes all meals, daily horseback rides
and use of recreational facilities. ~ Route 89, eight miles north of
Wickenburg; 520-684-7811, 800-942-5362, fax 520-684-2981;
www.merv.com. ULTRA-DELUXE.

Flying E Ranch is a working cattle ranch—and guest ranch—   ◄ *HIDDEN*
complete with trail rides, hay rides and chuckwagon dinners on
its 20,000-acre spread. There are 17 rooms, plus a heated pool,
sauna and whirlpool, along with tennis and shuffleboard. Rates

are on the American Plan—all meals included. Closed May through October. ~ 2801 West Wickenburg Way, Wickenburg; 520-684-2690, 888-684-2650, fax 520-684-5304; www.flyinge ranch.com. ULTRA-DELUXE.

Another top-notch dude ranch in Wickenburg (this one's listed in the National Historic Register), the **Kay El Bar Ranch** has room for 24 guests in hacienda-style adobe buildings beneath huge salt cedar trees. The lobby has a stone fireplace, and outside there's a heated pool for soaking after those long hours in the saddle. All meals and horseback riding are included. Closed May through mid-October. ~ Off Rincon Road, Wickenburg; 520-684-7593, 800-684-7583, fax 520-684-4497; www.kayelbar.com. ULTRA-DELUXE.

The 80-room **Best Western Rancho Grande Motel** offers guests a pool, whirlpool and playground. Rooms are furnished in a Southwest-contemporary motif. ~ 293 East Wickenburg Way, Wickenburg; 520-684-5445, 800-854-7235, fax 520-684-7380. MODERATE.

Inn at Payson/Swiss Village Lodge is a handsome, two-story hotel with lots of Alpine flavor in the midst of a European-style village of shops and restaurants. Its 99 rooms have recently been renovated in "mountain Southwest" style. Some have fireplaces. A spa, swimming pool and conference center are on the premises. Rates include continental breakfast. ~ Route 87, Payson; 520-474-3241, 800-247-9477, fax 520-472-6564. MODERATE.

A landmark around these parts for years, **Kohl's Ranch Lodge** sits on the banks of Tonto Creek 17 miles east of Payson. Recently remodeled, many of the 49 rooms and cabins overlook the creek and are equipped with outdoor grills and patios. Cabins have stone fireplaces, vaulted ceilings and kitchenettes, and rustic furnishings. Amenities here include a restaurant, lounges, a gift shop, a pool and horseback riding. ~ Route 260 East, Payson; 520-478-4211, 800-331-5645, fax 520-478-0353; www.ilxresorts.com. MODERATE.

DINING

Crazy Ed's Satisfied Frog and Goat Sucker Saloon captures a bit of the Old West with wood tables, sawdust on the floor and weird things on the walls—animal heads, posters, old farm tools. House specialties include barbecued beef, pork, chicken and smoked meats. The Frog has its own microbrewery and produces four house brands. ~ 6245 East Cave Creek Road, Cave Creek; 602-488-3317. MODERATE TO DELUXE.

Another amphibian-named eatery, **The Horny Toad** is a rustic, informal restaurant with wooden tables and booths, seating about 150 for lunch and dinner. Specialties include fried chicken and barbecued ribs. ~ 6738 Cave Creek Road, Cave Creek; 602-997-9622. MODERATE TO DELUXE.

Don't be fooled by the delicate peach tablecloths and soft country and easy listening music. At **Charley's Steak House,** bring your appetite to chow down on thick steaks served with salad, baked potato, cowboy beans and dessert. ~ 1187 West Wickenburg Way, Wickenburg; 520-684-2413. BUDGET TO ULTRA-DELUXE.

La Casa Pequeña features chimichangas, burritos and chicken Acapulco in a pleasant, south-of-the-border atmosphere. There's music on weekends. ~ 911 South Beeline Highway, Payson; 520-474-6329. MODERATE.

A Western theme dominates in the Kohl Ranch Lodge's **Zane Grey Restaurant,** where painted cowboys cook over a campfire on one wall and a replica of an 1884 hotel, complete with stained-glass windows, covers another wall. Beneath the glow of a wagon-wheel chandelier, diners can enjoy barbecued ribs, chicken, steaks and seafood. ~ Route 260 East, Payson; 520-478-4211. MODERATE.

Sit out on the screened porch and enjoy the scenery at the **Heritage House Garden Tea Room.** The fare is light, with items such as a tarragon chicken sandwich followed by a slice of homemade pie. There are also soups and salads. Lunch only. Closed Sunday. ~ 202 West Main Street, Payson; 520-474-5501. BUDGET.

During the warm months there is an outdoor patio at **The Oaks,** where you can order fresh steaks and seafood. There's also plenty of indoor seating and two fireplaces at this 50-odd-year-old renovated ranch house. ~ 302 West Main Street, Payson; 520-474-1929. MODERATE.

Wickenburg has several Southwestern gift shops and art galleries. **SHOPPING** **Grit** specializes in gifts, apparel and Southwestern gourmet food such as cactus salsa, chile vinegar and chocolate fettuccine. ~ 70 East Apache Street, Wickenburg; 520-684-2132.

It's hard to miss **Ben's Saddlery & Shoe Repair,** with a life-sized horse on top of the building. The owner is a roper, and even if you're not in the market for authentic Western gear, it's fun to breathe in the heady smell of leather and saddle soap while walking down aisles stocked with spurs, saddles and boots. ~ 174 North Tegner Street, Wickenburg; 520-684-2683.

The **Gold Nugget Art Gallery** is housed in an adobe building built in 1863 that was once Old Fort Wickenburg, a U.S. Cavalry base. Inside these historic walls are original Southwestern woodcarvings, pottery, paintings, sculptures and designer jewelry. ~ 274 East Wickenburg Way, Wickenburg; 520-684-5849.

A fixture for two decades is the **Wickenburg Gallery,** which showcases national and regional fine art including sculpture, paintings and traditional Navajo weavings. ~ 10 West Apache Street, Wickenburg; 520-684-7047.

It's hard to decide just what's more satisfying at the **Heritage House**—shopping or porch-sitting. Some come to shop in this quaint 1925 house for furniture, handmade tablecloths, picture frames and afghans. Others just sit in the twig and wicker furniture on the porch, watching the world go by just beyond the picket fence. ~ 202 West Main Street, Payson; 520-474-5501.

Antique lovers have several options in Payson, with the majority of shops just off the Beeline Highway. Try **Payson Antiques**, housing dolls, furniture and primitives by a variety of dealers. ~ 1001 South Beeline Highway, Payson; 520-474-8988.

NIGHTLIFE   Cozy booths inside and a balcony with tables overlooking Tonto Creek outside draw people to **The Cowboy Bar** at Kohl's Ranch Lodge. The rustic log building has been around for years, as has the huge oak tree that grows through the ceiling. On weekends, bring your boots and dance to live country music. ~ Route 260 East, Payson; 520-478-4211.

PARKS   **TONTO NATIONAL FOREST**
Ranging from Sonoran Desert to sprawling forests of ponderosa pine, this national forest covers nearly 2.9 million acres. The Payson and Cave Creek districts are outdoor playgrounds for area residents who can enjoy tubing, rafting and fishing on the Verde River. Barlett and Horseshoe reservoirs serve as watersheds, wildlife habitats and recreational sites for camping, swimming, fishing and boating. **Tonto Natural Bridge**, the largest known travertine bridge in the world, is a popular attraction, as was Zane Grey's cabin until it burned down in 1990. (The Zane Grey Society has plans for its restoration.) The national forest has picnic areas, restrooms, showers, a marina, boat rentals, snack stands, a restaurant, and hiking and riding trails. ~ There is access to the forest via Route 87 north from Phoenix to the town of Payson, in the heart of Tonto National Forest. To reach Horseshoe and Bartlett reservoirs take the Cave Creek Road east from Carefree to the entrance of the forest. From here Forest Service Road 24 takes you north to Seven Springs Campground. Horseshoe Dam Road continues east seven and a half miles until it forks. Forest Service Road 19 (the right fork) takes you to Bartlett Reservoir and Forest Service Road 265 (the left fork) takes you to Horseshoe Reservoir. Cave Creek Ranger district: 602-488-3441. Payson Ranger district: 520-474-7900.

▲ There are 86 campgrounds; free to $17 per night. Group sites are available. Primitive camping is also allowed. Reservations are only needed for group sites in fee areas; call USFS Reservations, 800-280-2267. The brand-new Houston-Mesa Campground is conveniently located two miles from Payson. There are 75 tent/RV sites; $12 per night. Seven Springs Campground is on a remote spring and has good access to hiking trails. There are 25 tent/RV sites; no fee.

HASSAYAMPA RIVER PRESERVE 🦶 A green desert oasis, this riparian area along the Hassayampa River features a cottonwood-willow forest and other vital Sonoran Desert habitats that are being protected by the nonprofit Nature Conservancy. Sit by the banks of spring-fed Palm Lake, a four-acre pond and marsh habitat, and you might spot a great blue heron or snowy egret. Birdwatchers also gather here to see the more than 230 species of birds that pass through this migration corridor. Naturalists offer guided walks along paths ranging from desert areas with cacti to lush stretches along the river. Tours start at the visitors center; call ahead for schedule. There are restrooms and picnic areas. Closed Monday and Tuesday. ~ Located on Route 60, three miles southeast of Wickenburg near mile marker 114; 520-684-2772.

▼▼▼▼▼▼▼▼▼▼▼▼

South of Phoenix

Out beyond the metropolis, where the bright lights give way to American Indian archaeological sites, you'll find the homeland of the Pima and Maricopa Indians, the site of Arizona's only Civil War battlefield and cotton fields that stretch for miles. Also, mountain peaks, great fishing and, for the born-to-shop crowd, factory-outlet malls. It is an intriguing blend of old and new Arizona.

SIGHTS

Gila River Indian Center in the Gila River Indian Reservation has an Indian museum, gift shop and restaurant featuring authentic Indian fry bread and Southwestern food. Here, too, is **Heritage Park**, featuring about half a dozen mini Indian villages. The museum is free and you can also take an interpretive walking tour of Heritage Park conducted by an American Indian. Tours are available upon request; there is a fee. ~ Casa Blanca Road, off Route 10 via Route 387, Exit 175; 520-315-3411.

Farther south is **Casa Grande**, named for the ancient Indian dwellings northeast of town. Casa Grande is known primarily for cotton-growing, industry and the many name-brand factory-outlet stores that have mushroomed there in recent years. For additional information, contact **Greater Casa Grande Chamber of Commerce.** ~ 575 North Marshall Street, Casa Grande; 520-836-2125, 800-916-1515.

Casa Grande Ruins National Monument was originally built by the Hohokam Indians in the early 1300s; the village was abandoned by the end of that century. Four stories high, and covered by a large protective roof, the main structure is the only one of its size and kind in this area. (The monument grounds contain about 60 prehistoric sites.) The structure is easily viewed via a short path on a well-marked self-guided tour. There's a visitors center and museum where ranger talks are presented. Admission. ~ About 20 miles east of Casa Grande on State Route 87; 520-723-3172.

For cowboy fans, the **Tom Mix Monument**, honors the silent-movie cowboy star near the spot where he died in an auto wreck in 1940. "In memory of Tom Mix whose spirit left his body on this spot and whose characterizations and portrayals in life served to better fix memories of the Old West in the minds of living men," reads the inscription. ~ Pinal Pioneer Parkway 18 miles south of Florence; 520-868-9433.

LODGING

Francisco Grande Resort and Golf Club is where it's all at in Casa Grande. The tallest building in Pinal County (eight stories), the hotel's tower building contains most of its 112 rooms, while other motel-type rooms are located around the patio. Furnishings are Southwestern-style throughout including paintings of cowboys and Western landscapes on the walls. The hotel has a restaurant, lounge (with nightly entertainment), swimming pool and golf. ~ 26000 Gila Bend Highway, Casa Grande; 520-836-6444, 800-237-4238, fax 520-421-0544; www.franciscogrande.com. MODERATE TO DELUXE.

Holiday Inn at Casa Grande, a four-story, Spanish-style stucco building, has 175 rooms in contemporary style, an outdoor pool and spa, restaurant and lounge with live entertainment Friday and Saturday nights. ~ 777 North Pinal Avenue, Casa Grande; 520-426-3500, 800-858-4499, fax 520-836-4728. MODERATE.

Beautifully set in a 1930s adobe guest ranch surrounded by saguaro cacti, the **Inn at Rancho Sonora** offers six rooms with private baths and entrances plus three fully equipped cottages. Stroll through the enclosed brick courtyard, where a fountain spurts merrily, or take a dip in the outdoor pool and waterfall spa. Continental breakfast included. ~ 9198 North Route 79, Florence; phone/fax 520-868-8000, 800-205-6817; e-mail rancho@c2i2.com. MODERATE TO DELUXE.

DINING

Gila River Arts and Crafts Restaurant features Indian fry bread along with burritos, tacos, hamburgers, homemade pies and coffee. ~ Gila River Indian Reservation; 520-315-3411. BUDGET.

Mi Amigo Ricardo offers up hot and spicy Mexican specialties —chimichangas, enchiladas, frijoles, tamales, flautas and *posole* —with beer and wine to soothe the flames. The decor is Mexican, of course, and quite attractive. ~ 821 East Florence Boulevard, Casa Grande; 520-836-3858. BUDGET.

Bring a big appetite to the **Golden Corral**. It's a traditional Western steak house where owner Vicki Carlson cuts her steaks fresh daily and the salad bar has 150 items. ~ 1295 East Florence Boulevard, Casa Grande; 520-836-4630. BUDGET TO MODERATE.

Bedillon's is a restaurant and museum in two separate buildings. The museum features Indian artifacts and Western memorabilia. The menu offers a full range of American cuisine. Closed

Sunday and Monday. ~ 800 North Park Avenue, Casa Grande; 520-836-2045. BUDGET TO DELUXE.

A small, downtown Casa Grande bakery and café, **The Cook E Jar** serves up breakfast and lunch as well as take-out bakery goods (even wedding cakes) and sandwiches. Closed Sunday. ~ 100 West 2nd Street, Casa Grande; 520-836-9294. BUDGET.

Gila River Indian Center has a shop selling traditional American Indian crafts, silver and turquoise jewelry, sandpaintings, kachinas and baskets. ~ Gila River Indian Reservation; 520-315-3411.

SHOPPING

Casa Grande, the main town along Route 10 between Phoenix and Tucson, is the site of the largest number of factory-owned **outlet stores** in Arizona. More than 70 are located in two sprawling commercial malls off Route 10 (take Exit 194, Florence Boulevard). More than a million shoppers a year come to Casa Grande seeking bargains from such major firms as **Liz Claiborne, Samsonite, Bugle Boy, Royal Doulton** and **Reebok**. For information, call Factory Stores of America at 800-746-7872, or the Tanger Factory Outlet Center at 520-836-0897.

Arizona's climate is ideal for recreational pursuits—most of the time. But in the summer, dry heat can be deceiving and you may think it's cooler than it actually is. Keep summer exertion to a minimum and play indoors, where there's air-conditioning, if you can.

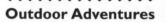

Outdoor Adventures

Three main rivers in south central Arizona, the Verde, the Salt and the Gila, all east of Phoenix, offer a wealth of recreational activities year-round. A number of companies provide rafting and tubing expeditions, with pick-ups, meals and guides included.

RIVER RUNNING

SCOTTSDALE **Cimarron River Co.** has guided two-hour scenic float trips for groups of ten or more on the lower Salt River. The gentle trips, which involve no whitewater, glide through Sonoran Desert landscapes with towering cliffs and stately saguaros. ~ 7902 East Pierce Street; 602-994-1199. **Desert Voyagers Guided Rafting Tours** offers a variety of half-day trips on the Verde and Salt rivers. ~ P.O. Box 9053, Scottsdale, AZ 85252; 602-998-7238.

TEMPE/MESA AREA In Mesa, **Salt River Recreation Inc.** rents large inner tubes and operates a shuttle to carry you up the Salt River so you can tube back down through easy whitewater. Closed October to mid-April. ~ North Bush Highway and Usery Pass Road, Mesa; 602-984-3305.

The Valley's extensive network of canals provides ideal, often shaded tracks.

JOGGING

PHOENIX If you want to jog during the hot summers stick to cooler early-morning hours. Phoenix's **Encanto Park**, three miles north of the Civic Plaza, is an excellent jogging trail.

SCOTTSDALE **Indian Bend Wash Greenbelt** is a dream trail for joggers. It runs north and south for the entire length of Scottsdale, including 13 winding miles of jogging and bike paths laid out within the Greenbelt's scenic system of parks, lakes and golf courses.

SWIMMING

There are so many swimming pools found in south central Arizona that gathering rain clouds, so it's said, are often colored green from all the chlorine.

PHOENIX Many public pools are available, over 30 in Phoenix alone. For starters, there's **Cactus Pool**. ~ 3801 West Cactus Road; 602-262-6680. You can also dive into **Grant Pool**. ~ 714 South 2nd Avenue; 602-261-8728. Make a splash at **Starlight Pool**. ~ 7810 West Osborn Road; 602-495-2412. **Washington Pool** will also cool you down. ~ 6655 North 23rd Avenue; 602-262-7198. For additional information and listings, call 602-258-7946. The pools are open only during the summer.

Arizona's broad central band stretches across the state in what visiting English author J. B. Priestley once described as "geology by day and astronomy by night."

Telephone Pioneer Pool is an option for people with disabilities, their families and friends. Closed Friday and Sunday and in December and January. ~ 1946 West Morningside Drive; 602-495-2404.

The Adobe Dam Recreation Area is home to **Water World** (602-581-8446), which features a wave pool, waterslides and an 1100-foot-long Zambezi River complete with little rapids. Closed Labor Day to Memorial Day. ~ Recreation area: Northwest of Adobe Dam, on Pinnacle Peak Road and North 43rd Avenue, Phoenix; 602-506-2930.

TEMPE/MESA AREA In Tempe, **Big Surf** includes a 300-foot surf slide and raft-riding in a gigantic, mechanically activated freshwater pool. Closed Labor Day to Memorial Day. Admission. ~ 1500 North McClintock Road; 602-947-7873. The **Kiwanis Park Wave Pool & Recreation Center** is open year-round with an indoor heated "wave pool" and water slide. ~ 611 All-American Way, Tempe; 602-350-5201.

BALLOON RIDES

For ballooning enthusiasts, the surrounding mountains provide the perfect setting to let it all hang out. Dozens of firms will be happy to take you up, up and away.

PHOENIX Float through the air with **Cloud Chasers Balloon Company**, which offers sunrise flights over the Sonoran desert, followed by a champagne breakfast. ~ 1716 West Butler Drive; 602-944-4080. You can soar in the skies over the north Phoenix area and Sonoran desert with **Adventures Aloft**. ~ 45 West Jefferson Street; 602-951-2650. **Hot Air Expeditions** has sunrise and candlelit sunset flights. ~ 2243 East Rose Garden Loop; 602-788-5555.

SCOTTSDALE   The **Unicorn Balloon Co.** will take you floating above the desert north of Scottsdale. Flights ascend to heights of 2000 feet and, at other times, glide just above the treetops to spot deer, javelinas, coyotes and other desert wildlife. The trip finishes with a champagne award ceremony in which passengers receive their "First Flight Certificate." ~ 15001 North 74th Street; 602-991-3666.

View desert wildlife and vegetation as you drift through the sky with **Adventures Out West**. Sunrise and sunset excursions conclude with champagne and treats. ~ P.O. Box 12009-266, Scottsdale, AZ 85267; 602-996-6100, 800-755-0935.

Try **Sky Masters School of Hang Gliding** for aero-tours and tandem instruction. They also provide equipment rentals, sales and service. ~ 1902 East Behrend Drive; 602-582-5904.

**HANG
GLIDING**

Dozens of stables, dude ranches and equestrian outfitters are available for saddling up and heading off into desert wilderness for a few hours or a few days under the supervision of a crusty trail boss. If ever there was a place for horsing around, this is it.

**RIDING
STABLES**

PHOENIX   Saddle up in Phoenix at **All Western Stables**. Guided horseback tours ranging in length from an hour to all day go through Phoenix's 18,000-acre Desert Park. ~ 10220 South Central Avenue; 602-276-5862.

SCOTTSDALE   For information on riding in Scottsdale, contact **Westworld Equestrian Center**. ~ 16601 North Pima Road; 602-483-8800. **Trail Horse Adventures** leads rides from the Westworld Equestrian Center and features barbecue and sunset excursions. ~ 16601 North Pima Road; 602-941-4756. **MacDonald's Ranch** takes riders through their 1300 acres of high-desert terrain. ~ 26540 North Scottsdale Road; 602-585-0239.

TEMPE/MESA AREA   **Papago Riding Stables** offers one- and two-hour wrangler-guided trips into the desert foothills of Papago Park, where knolls afford spectacular views of the greater Phoenix area. ~ 400 North Scottsdale Road, Tempe; 602-966-9793.

More than half of Arizona's 205 golf courses are located in south central Arizona, making Phoenix and environs the undisputed Golf Capital of the Southwest. Some of the country's finest courses can be found among its resorts, parks and country clubs.

GOLF

PHOENIX   One of the most spectacular is the **Wigwam Golf & Country Club** in Litchfield Park just west of Phoenix. This private club has three separate 18-hole courses with mature landscaping. Cart and club rentals available. ~ 451 North Litchfield Road; 602-935-9414. Among Phoenix's top public links is **Encanto Golf Course**, an 18-hole course with club rentals and a golf pro in residence. ~ 2705 North 15th Avenue; 602-253-3963. The 18-hole public **Papago Golf Course** has shade trees and challenging water hazards. There are cart and club rentals and a pro shop. ~ 5595 East Moreland Street; 602-275-8428. Nine-hole **Palo Verde Golf Course** is a third public course in Phoenix. Cart and club rentals available. ~ 6215 North 15th Avenue; 602-249-9930.

SCOTTSDALE   Top public courses include the 18-hole **Continental Golf Course**. Cart and club rentals available. ~ 7920 East Osborn Road; 602-941-1585. Also open for duffers is the nine-hole public **Coronado Golf Course**. There are cart and club rentals and a driving range. Four teaching pros are available. ~ 2829 North Miller Road; 602-947-8364. **Tournament Players Club of Scottsdale** welcomes the public to its greens. The 18-hole stadium course, built specifically to host the PGA Tour Phoenix Open, features a unique island green. The club also has an 18-hole desert course. Cart and club rentals are available, as well as a golf pro for lessons. ~ 17020 North Hayden Road; 602-585-3600.

TEMPE/MESA AREA   The nine-hole **Pepperwood Golf Course** in Tempe has cart and club rentals and a golf pro available for lessons. ~ 647 West Baseline Road; 602-831-9457. Or you can bring your clubs to the **Tempe Rolling Hills Golf Course**, where you'll find two nine-hole executive courses that can be played together or separately in the hilly terrain of the Papago Buttes; there are cart and club rentals, as well as a pro shop, a bar and a restaurant. ~ 1415 North Mill Avenue; 602-350-5275. A "hidden" golfers' option, the **Karsten Golf Course** on the campus of Arizona State University is open to the public. Designed by Peter Dye, the 18-hole championship course has some of the most challenging water hazards and mounds anywhere. It hosts several major tournaments each year. Cart and club rentals available. ~ 1125 East Rio Salado Parkway; 602-921-8070.

TENNIS   Almost all of the parks in the valley's vast network have a tennis court; for information, call the **Parks and Recreation Department**. ~ Phoenix: 602-262-6861; Scottsdale: 602-994-2408.

PHOENIX   City Center Tennis Courts are open to the public. ~ 121 East Adams Street; 602-256-4120. The semi-private **Hole-in-the-Wall Racquet Club** allows nonmembers to play on its four lighted courts for a fee. ~ 7677 North 16th Street, at the Pointe at Squaw Peak Resort; 602-906-3811. The **Phoenix Tennis Center** is a large facility with 22 lighted public courts. A fee is charged and tennis pros are available. ~ 6330 North 21st Avenue; 602-249-3712. Another place to play in Phoenix is the **Watering Hole**

Racquet Club, a semiprivate club with nine lighted courts open to nonmembers for a fee. ~ 901-C East Saguaro Drive; 602-997-7237. The **Mountain View Tennis Center** is also in the Phoenix area. There are 20 lighted public courts. ~ 1104 East Grovers Avenue; 602-788-6088.

SCOTTSDALE The city of Scottsdale has no fewer than 40 public courts. All are hard-surfaced and lighted for evening play. Look for them at **Indian School Park**. ~ 4289 North Hayden Road; 602-994-2740. Or try **Chestnut Park**. ~ 4565 North Granite Reef Road; 602-994-2771. **Mountain View Park** is another option. ~ 8625 East Mountain View; 602-994-2584. And finally there's **Scottsdale Ranch Park**. ~ 10400 East Villa Linda; 602-994-7774.

TEMPE/MESA AREA Outstanding in Tempe is the city of Tempe's **Kiwanis Recreation Center**. There are 15 "cushioned" surface, lighted courts available by reservation. ~ 6111 South All-American Way; 602-350-5201.

Biking is popular as both recreation and transportation in the valley and outlying areas.

BIKING

PHOENIX A basic bikeway system was set up for Phoenix in 1987, and since then more than 100 miles of paths have been added. Unfortunately, there's a lot of traffic, so be cautious. A free *People and Places* map that also shows the Phoenix Bikeway System is available at most bike shops, or call the Parks, Recreation and Library Department. ~ 602-262-6861. For bicycling events call 602-261-8604. Also for special-event biking activities contact **Arizona Bicycle Association**. ~ 602-990-7468. Phoenix's **South Mountain Park** (10919 South Central Avenue), **Cave Creek** and **Carefree**, 30 miles northeast of town, offer great biking conditions. Also popular is **Papago Loop Bicycle Path** through the rolling hills that border the canal edging Papago Park.

SCOTTSDALE Scottsdale's **Indian Bend Wash Greenbelt** has miles of excellent bike paths.

◆◆

✔ CHECK THESE OUT—UNIQUE OUTDOOR ADVENTURES

- Ride the river wild as you take an expedition down the Verde, Salt or Gila rivers. *page 231*
- Soar through the sky and gaze at painted desert mountains from technicolor hot-air balloons. *page 232*
- Saddle up and ride the trails of cowboys past in the Tempe/Mesa area. *page 233*
- Hike up the winding Squaw Peak Summit Trail for dramatic views of Phoenix from the 2608-foot vantage point. *page 236*

Bike Rentals   Need to rent a bike or get one repaired? Try **Try Me Bicycle Shop** for both mountain and road-touring bikes. ~ 1514 West Hatcher Road, Phoenix; 602-943-1785. **Wheels 'n Gear** has just the bike for you, whether you're looking to rent a mountain bike, road bike, hybrid or children's tandem. Repairs available. ~ 7607 East McDowell Road, Scottsdale; 602-945-2881. **The Bicycle Store** sells and rents mountain bikes. It's the meeting place for a local cycling club that sponsors public rides around the city and surrounding area on weekend mornings. ~ Mill and University roads, in the Tempe Center; 602-966-7090. **Tempe Bicycle Shop** has a variety of bikes to rent. Repairs also available. ~ 330 West University Drive, Tempe; 602-966-6896.

HIKING

With all that elbow room and knockout scenery, south central Arizona is a hiker's paradise. Visitors, in fact, have been known to park their cars on the highway and impulsively hike up the side of a mountain. Note: Be sure to take water with you, and allow plenty of time to get there and back. All distances listed for hiking trails are one way unless otherwise noted.

PHOENIX AREA   The **Phoenix Mountain Preserve** has 50 miles of trails and almost pristine areas virtually in the center of Phoenix. It stretches from Lincoln Drive in Paradise Valley north to Greenway Boulevard, bordered on the west by 19th Avenue and on the east by Tatum Boulevard.

Its most popular trail is the **Squaw Peak Summit Trail** (1.2 miles) that wraps its way up Squaw Peak, offering good lookout points along the way, and from its 2608-foot summit, a dramatic view of the city. (The only drawback is the number of fellow hikers you'll meet along the way.)

A more demanding trek, for experienced hikers only, is **Circumference Trail** (3.7 miles), beginning at the parking area at the end of Squaw Peak Drive and looping around the base of the peak in a northerly direction.

SCOTTSDALE AREA   **Camelback Mountain** in the Scottsdale area is the valley's best known landmark, and serious hikers truly have not hiked Arizona until they've conquered it. Part of the Echo Canyon Recreation Area (off McDonald Drive east of Tatum Boulevard; 602-256-3220), Camelback offers sheer red cliffs that in some places rise 200 feet straight up its side. An interpretive ramada near the parking area offers information about the various trails.

A relatively easy climb (.8 mile) goes from the ramada to **Bobby's Rock**, a landmark formation of rocks set aside from the cliff and perfect for rock climbers.

Also beginning at the ramada, the **Camelback Mountain Trail** (1.2 miles) is steep and very rocky, with a 1300 foot gain in elevation. The view from the top of Camelback Mountain, 2704 feet above sea level, is spectacular, but expect a crowd on the weekends.

NORTH OF PHOENIX   A favorite at North Mountain Recreation Area is the **North Mountain National Trail** (1.6 miles) just off Seventh Street north of Peoria. The moderate to difficult paved trail climbs from 1490 feet to 2104 feet with scenic views along the way. It ends at the AK-CHIN picnic area.

The historic, 51-mile-long **Highline Trail** in the Tonto National Forest was established in the late 1800s to link various homesteads and ranches under the Mogollon Rim. In 1979, it was designated a National Recreation Trail. With 23 trailheads and spur trails, hikers can explore it in segments and loops. But a word of caution —most of the trails from the highline to the top of the rim are steep, rocky and rugged.

The main trail begins at the Pine Trailhead 15 miles north of Payson off Route 87 on Route 297, and ends at Two-Sixty Trailhead on Route 260. Shorter jaunts include **East Webber Trail** (3 miles), a difficult, little-used stretch that follows Webber Creek before ending at a spring. The most popular is **Horton Creek Trail** (4 miles), which starts at the Upper Tonto Creek Campground.

For the *Highline Trails Guide*, contact the Payson Ranger Station. ~ 1009 East Route 260; 520-474-7900.

SOUTH OF PHOENIX   One of the best trails in Phoenix's South Mountain Park is the **Mormon Loop/Hidden Valley National Trail** (6 miles) that begins at the Pima Canyon parking lot near 48th Street and Guadalupe Road and ends at the Buena Vista parking area. At the parking lot, a dirt road rambles for a quarter mile to the trailhead where you'll find a sign for Hidden Valley. The trail passes stands of saguaro, but the highlights are The Tunnel—a naturally formed rock tunnel, 50 to 60 feet long, that leads into Hidden Valley—and Fat Man's Pass, a tight squeeze between huge boulders where it is cool year-round. Here children can take turns on Slide Rock, a large, naturally polished, sleek boulder that's as smooth as a playground slide.

▼▼▼▼▼▼▼▼▼▼
Transportation

CAR

Visitors driving to Phoenix by car are in for a treat. Arizona's highways are among the best in the country, gas is traditionally cheaper and the scenery in any direction is spectacular—lofty saguaros, magnificent mountains, a cowboy here, a pickup truck there, beer signs blinking faintly in the purple glow of evening. Along the way, small Western towns unfold like storybook pop-ups. **Route 10** traverses the city from the east (El Paso) and west (Los Angeles). From the northwest, **Route 40**, once the legendary Route 66, enters Arizona near Kingman; **Route 93** continues on from there to Phoenix. **Route 17** brings you to Phoenix from the Prescott or Flagstaff area.

AIR

Sky Harbor International Airport (602-273-3300) is located four miles from downtown Phoenix and is served by Alaska Airlines, America West Airlines, American Airlines, American Trans Air, Continental Airlines, Delta Airlines, Frontier, Mesa Air, Northwest Airlines, Scenic Airlines, Skywest Airlines, Southwest Airlines, Trans World Airlines, United Airlines, Shuttle by United and USAir.

A variety of ground transportation options are available from Sky Harbor Airport. **SuperShuttle** offers airport-to-door service 24 hours a day. ~ 602-244-9000, 800-258-3826. **Courier Transportation** also provides transfers to and from the airport. ~ 602-232-2222. **Arizona Shuttle Service** has service to and from Tucson. ~ 520-795-6771, 800-888-2749.

BUS

Greyhound Bus Lines (800-231-2222) has service to Phoenix and surrounding areas from all around the country. Terminals are in Phoenix at 2115 East Buckeye Road, 602-389-4200; in Mesa at 1423 South Country Club Drive, 602-834-3360; and in Tempe at 502 South College Avenue, 602-967-4030.

CAR RENTALS

Rental companies with counters at the airport include **Advantage Rent A Car** (800-777-5500), **Alamo Rent A Car** (800-327-9633), **Avis Rent A Car** (800-331-1212), **Budget Rent A Car** (800-527-0700), **Dollar Rent A Car** (800-800-4000), **Hertz Rent A Car** (800-654-3131) and **National Car Rental** (800-328-4567). Agencies with pick-up service are **Courtesy Rent A Car** (602-273-7503), **Enterprise Leasing and Rent A Car** (800-325-8007), **Thrifty Car Rental** (800-367-2277).

PUBLIC TRANSIT

Valley Metro covers Phoenix and Scottsdale and provides express service to and from other districts within the Valley. It also serves the Phoenix airport. Express buses access Phoenix from Mesa, Tempe and other suburbs. ~ 602-253-5000. **Ollie the Trolley** offers rubber-tire trolley service from 22 Scottsdale resorts and 6 shopping areas on day-pass basis; rides are free within the downtown shopping area mid-October through April. ~ 602-941-2957. **Downtown Dash** serves the downtown Phoenix area with shuttles that depart every six to twelve minutes and loop the downtown area between the State Capitol, Arizona Center and the Civic Plaza weekdays. Rides cost thirty cents. ~ 602-253-5000.

TAXIS

Taxis are expensive in Phoenix since the city sprawls out in all directions. Going from Point A to Point B, at times, may seem like you're crossing the entire state. Some of the major companies in south central Arizona are AAA CAB (602-921-8294), ACE Taxi (602-254-1999), **Statewide Sedan, Van and Limo Service**

(602-252-1277), **Courier Cab** (602-232-2222), **Discount Cab** (602-266-1110) and **Yellow Cab** (602-252-5252). AAA, Courier and Yellow are contracted with the airport in Phoenix.

Because Arizona is big-sky country, a great way to see it is by air. **AIR TOURS** Several firms, all based out of Scottsdale's Airpark, offer tours of the Grand Canyon, Sedona, Monument Valley, Lake Powell and other scenic destinations. Among them are **Scenic Airlines** (602-991-8252) and **West Wind Aviation** (602-869-0866).

NINE

Eastern Arizona

Perhaps no other region of the state is as geographically diverse as eastern Arizona. The seemingly endless urban sprawl of Phoenix, Tempe and Mesa quickly gives way to breathtaking scenery in the form of desert gardens, jagged river canyons, rolling grasslands and deep pine forests. Venture here and you will find a wide variety of recreational opportunities, everything from fishing and hunting to hiking and skiing. There's also plenty of history—prehistoric Indian ruins and old mining towns—to be discovered along the way.

The strip of eastern Arizona stretching 203 miles east of Phoenix along Routes 89, 60 and 70 to the New Mexico state line is known as The Old West Highway. Rich in frontier history, it travels a route of the notorious—from Coronado to Geronimo to Billy the Kid.

Anchored on the west by Apache Junction, a growing suburb of the Phoenix metropolitan area and a winter retreat for thousands of snowbirds, the Old West Highway is also the starting point for a scenic detour along the Apache Trail (Route 88). Today's adventurers can wend their way along the trail through the Superstition Mountains, to the reconstructed Goldfield Ghost Town, a series of lakes originating from the Salt River, colorful Tortilla Flat, the Lost Dutchman's Mine and finally Theodore Roosevelt Dam and Lake.

Continue east on the Old West Highway and you'll come to Globe, a quiet town that retains the flavor of the late 1800s. The Old West Highway flattens out east of Globe, and the countryside becomes more arid as you descend into the lower desert. The Mescal Mountains to the south escort you into the Gila River Valley, where the mesas and buttes of the San Carlos Apache Indian Reservation stand out against the sky.

Route 70 branches off Route 60 east of Globe and crosses the southern tip of the 1.8 million-acre San Carlos Apache Indian Reservation, which stretches from the White Mountains to within two miles of Globe, north to the Mogollon Rim and south to Coronado National Forest. An estimated 10,000 Apache live on the reservation, much of it wooded forests that are home to elk, mule deer, wild turkeys, black bear and mountain lions.

On the southern horizon stands Mount Graham, at 10,720 feet one of Arizona's highest peaks. In addition to being a popular fishing, camping and hiking area, the mountain is the site of the Mount Graham International Observatory.

Route 70 continues on to the town of Safford, an important trade center for the Gila River Valley's numerous cotton farmers. From Safford, the Old West Highway cuts through the pastoral Duncan Valley, with its green alfalfa fields, grazing horses and trickling creeks at the eastern edge of Arizona. Duncan, the birthplace of Supreme Court Justice Sandra Day O'Connor, is a fertile source of fire agate, a relatively rare semiprecious stone, which can be picked up right off the ground in designated Bureau of Land Management areas.

North of Duncan on Route 191 is the historic mining town of Clifton, the southern anchor of the Coronado Trail, which climbs through the Apache-Sitgreaves National Forest on its 105-mile journey to Alpine, in the heart of Arizona's Alps.

The Coronado Trail, named for the Spanish explorer who sought the Seven Cities of Gold nearly 500 years ago, practically brushes the Arizona–New Mexico border. The trail runs north–south as Route 191 from St. Johns to Clifton via a winding and twisting paved highway, cutting through rugged mountains and magnificent forests—some of the Southwest's most spectacular scenery.

The White Mountains offer high, cool country dotted with fishing lakes and blanketed in ponderosa pine, spruce, aspen and Douglas fir. At the heart of this area are Pinetop–Lakeside, Show Low and Greer. The main reason folks venture to this part of eastern Arizona is to enjoy the outdoors, whether by fishing, skiing, hiking or simply sitting on a rock with a picnic lunch, breathing in the scent of pine and watching the breeze ripple across a lake. These towns all abound with rustic lodges, inexpensive eateries and plenty of scenic beauty.

▼▼▼▼▼▼▼▼▼▼▼▼▼▼

Apache Junction Area

At the meeting point of Routes 60, 88 and 89, Apache Junction is in an area of rough lowlands about 30 miles east of Phoenix. Once a sunburned babble of bars, motels and filling stations, it has blossomed into a rustic bedroom community for the Valley of the Sun and a popular snowbird retreat that attracts about 45,000 people each winter, causing local dude ranch operators to complain that there's no range left to ride. A metal impression in the center of the town honors the man believed to have discovered the elusive Lost Dutchman Gold Mine, who died with the secret of its location unspoken. Apache Junction is also the starting point for the 48-mile Apache Trail, Route 88, which slices its way through the Superstition Mountains.

Apache Junction was unofficially founded in 1922, when a traveling salesman named George Cleveland Curtis put up a tent and sold sandwiches and water to travelers along the highway. A year

SIGHTS

later he filed a homestead claim and built the Apache Junction Inn. Others soon followed and by 1950 there were enough residents to form a town. They chose the name Superstition City, but because it was a historical site, the Apache Junction name could not be changed.

Learn about the area's history and sights at the **Apache Junction Chamber of Commerce**, which dispenses maps and brochures. ~ P.O. Box 1747, Apache Junction, AZ 85217-1747; 602-982-3141.

For a truly spectacular view of the mountains, take a driving tour along the **Apache Trail**. It runs along Route 88 from Apache Junction to Theodore Roosevelt Lake and is about a 140-mile drive round-trip, with about 20 unpaved miles above Tortilla Flat. The Apache Trail was originally a construction road for the Theodore Roosevelt Dam, the country's first Federal Reclamation project, completed in 1911. It was named for the people who hauled materials along this road to the site of the dam. The trail starts at Tortilla Flat, an old stagecoach stop with a café, general store and a post office. Then it winds along a narrow, unpaved road through the mountains, past Canyon and Apache lakes to the dam. En route, you can pull off at certain spots for hiking, picnicking or just plain staring at the beautiful scenery.

Once past the outskirts of town, the trail enters the dacite cones of the **Superstition Mountains**, formed 20 million years ago when cataclysmic earthquakes and widespread volcanic eruptions pushed land masses thousands of feet into the air and left a depression 20 miles wide. Magma from below the earth's surface flowed in and the Superstitions were formed. The triangular-shaped mountain east of the Superstitions is Weaver's Needle, which treasure hunters say is a marking point for the Lost Dutchman Mine.

For a taste of the Old West, stop at **Goldfield Ghost Town**, which saw its heyday in the 1890s when gold was discovered at the base of the Superstitions. The weathered-wood buildings that house a restaurant, museum and antique shops look original, but they are actually re-creations, constructed in 1988. The old mining and railroad equipment scattered about are authentic, as are the museum's geology and mining exhibits and the underground mine, which you can tour. Other activities available are jeep tours, carriage rides and gold panning. ~ Route 88, four miles north of Apache Junction; 602-983-0333.

Continuing north on Route 88 you'll find a chain of lakes originating out of the Salt River. They include Saguaro, Canyon and Apache lakes. The most accessible is **Canyon Lake**, which wends its way six and a half miles upstream through one continuous deep canyon. There are boat facilities, beaches, picnic sites,

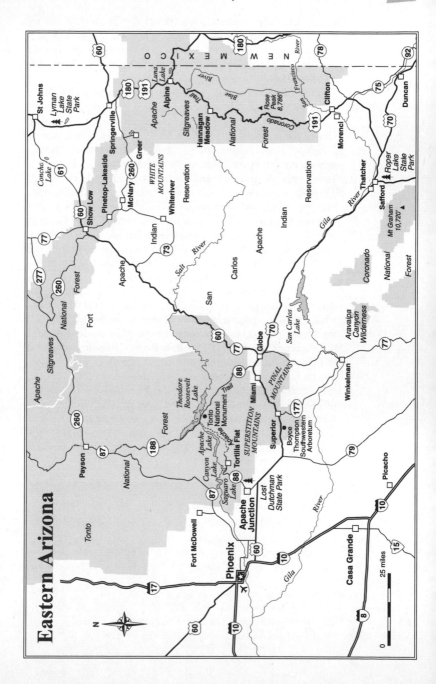

Eastern Arizona

a snack bar and campsites. Recreational activities include fishing (bass and walleye) and waterskiing. There's also a replica of a double-deck sternwheeler that plies the waters with its cargo of tourists and photographers. ~ Canyon Lake Marina, Route 88; 602-944-6504.

Proceeding upstream, you'll pass geodes imbedded in sheer rock walls, deposited by eruptions millions of years ago, on your way to **Tortilla Flat**, which boasts a population of six people. One of the last remnants of the Old West, the town was once a stagecoach stop, complete with a school, general store, restaurant/ saloon, hotel and post office, and was home to about 125 people. Today, only the general store, post office and restaurant remain. The restaurant/saloon, which looks like a wood-planked western movie set, is one of the most popular in the area and has hosted travelers from all over the country. Years of memorabilia hang from the naturalwood walls and ceiling, but most interesting are the thousands of dollar bills and foreign currency stuck to the walls with business cards from all over the world. ~ Route 88, 18 miles north of Apache Junction; 602-984-1776.

About five miles east of Tortilla Flat, the paved road surrenders to dirt and gravel and climbs to the top of Fish Creek Hill, which provides spectacular views of the canyon below. Descending the hill, the road twists through a narrow chasm along Apache Lake and finally arrives at **Theodore Roosevelt Dam**. Completed in 1911, this masonry dam, constructed entirely of quarry stone, is the world's tallest. A recent concrete addition, covering the original construction, raised the dam's height to 357 feet. A quarter-mile upstream from the dam, a 1000-foot steel arch bridge spans a portion of the reservoir, Roosevelt Lake, giving tourists—and photographers—a better view of the dam. ~ Located 45 miles east of Apache Junction on Route 88 (note: half of this distance is unpaved); 520-467-2236.

◆◆◆

✔ CHECK THESE OUT—UNIQUE SIGHTS

- Experience the Old West at **Goldfield Ghost Town**, and try your luck as you pan for those little nuggets. *page 242*
- View a piece of history as you wander through the **Besh-Ba-Gowah Archaeological Park**, home to the Salado people from 1100 A.D. to 1400 A.D. *page 251*
- Take a dip in the **Kachina Mineral Springs Spa**, set in a mix of Roman-styled tubs and rundown tack. *page 257*
- Stop by the **Little House Museum** for a glimpse into the area's history, including ranching and horse-show memorabilia. *page 268*

From Roosevelt Dam you can return to Apache Junction, or continue on Route 88 (which becomes paved again) to **Tonto National Monument**, which contains the remains of the apartment-style dwellings of the Salado people and is one of the state's better-preserved prehistoric archaeological sites. At the visitors center, you can see Salado crafts and tools and an audio-visual program. A highlight of the park itself is a paved but steep, half-mile self-guiding trail that climbs 350 feet up to the 19-room **Lower Cliff Dwelling**. The 40-room **Upper Cliff Dwelling** is open for tours from November through April (advance reservations are required). Admission. ~ Route 88, Roosevelt; 520-467-2241.

Back on Route 60, about 25 miles east of Apache Junction near the tiny mining camp of Superior, is the **Boyce Thompson Southwestern Arboretum**. This Eden-like preserve boasts over 1500 specimens, including cacti, succulents and water-efficient trees and shrubs. Home to over 200 kinds of birds and 40 wildlife species, the arboretum has walking trails that wind through 35 acres of outdoor displays and historic buildings. One long-time resident here, a red gum eucalyptus that rises more than 100 feet and boasts a trunk eight feet in diameter, was planted in 1929 as a six-foot sapling. The arboretum has an interpretive center located inside a 1920s cut-stone house listed on the National Register of Historical Places, and a visitors center with an information desk and gift store selling books, cacti and various succulents. The **Clevenger House**, a stone cabin built into a hillside and surrounded by an herb garden, is also of interest. Admission. ~ 37615 East Route 60; 520-689-2811.

Heading east from the arboretum, Route 60 gradually climbs through Gonzales Pass until the desert gives way to the Tonto National Forest. The two-lane highway cautiously winds through enchanting **Devils Canyon,** an eerie though picturesque region that seems to change its mood as the day's sunlight progresses. Near sundown, when the shadows grow long, the granite rock formations take on the shape of giant trolls and gnomes, and appear to be crouching, as if to pounce on passing motorists. The canyon and highway are narrow, but there are ample pullouts to photograph or simply enjoy the scenery.

The 121-room **Grande Hotel and Conference Center** stands at the gateway to the Superstition Mountains. The main building is red-brick tile and white stucco. The rooms, brightly colored in pink and green, have modern furnishings. The lobby is contemporary, the bar Western with copper appointments. A favorite of film crews shooting Westerns in the area, the hotel has hosted John Wayne, Ronald Reagan, Richard Boone and other Hollywood stalwarts. Rooms where they stayed bear their names. ~ 201

LODGING

West Apache Trail, Apache Junction; 602-982-3500, fax 602-983-7963; www.grand1.com. BUDGET.

The small, family-run **Palm Springs Motel** has 11 clean, well-maintained rooms, all with refrigerators, some with kitchenettes. ~ 950 South Royal Palm Road, Apache Junction; 602-982-7055. BUDGET.

In the Superstition foothills, the **Gold Canyon Golf Resort** features chalet-style guest rooms with dark-wood furniture, stone fireplaces, spa tubs, private patios and impressive views of the nearby mountain. There's also a heated pool. ~ 6100 South Kings Ranch Road, Gold Canyon; 602-982-9090, 800-624-6445, fax 602-830-5211; www.goldcanyongolfresort.com. ULTRA-DELUXE.

DINING

Lake Shore Restaurant is a rustic, casual dining facility on Saguaro Lake with a deck where you can enjoy lunch with a lake view. Shaded by a giant awning, this outdoor eatery is cooled by a mist system and ceiling fans or warmed by outdoor heaters, depending on the season. Start with a strawberry daiquiri and then order from the menu featuring burgers, salads, sandwiches and fried fish (all you can eat on Wednesday and Friday). No dinner on Monday and Tuesday. ~ 14011 North Bush Highway, Tonto National Forest; 602-984-5311. BUDGET TO MODERATE.

Down Apache Junction way, **Mining Camp Restaurant and Trading Post** is almost as famous as the Lost Dutchman Gold Mine—and it's easier to find. The long wooden tables, planked floors, tin trays and cups, and family-style, all-you-can-eat dining —chicken, beef and barbecued ribs—make it worth looking for. Closed July through September. ~ Route 88, Apache Junction; 602-982-3181. MODERATE.

There's no shortage of charm at **Tortilla Flat Restaurant**, whose weathered-wood exterior suggests a Wild West saloon. Inside, the natural-wood walls are covered with mining and cowboy artifacts, as well as business cards and currency from around the world. Home-cooked specials include oversized burgers, spicy hot chili and a few Mexican dishes. In the saloon section, you can belly up to the solid-wood bar, plant yourself on a barstool topped with a leather saddle, and pretend you're in Dodge City. Harry Connick, Jr., on the Wurlitzer jukebox will bring you back to reality. ~ Route 88, 18 miles north of Apache Junction; 602-984-1776. BUDGET TO MODERATE.

The **Barleen Family Country Music & Dinner Theatre** presents a Grand Ole Opry–style country music show performed by three generations of Barleen family members. Served at the table are hearty dinners of slow-cooked roast beef, mashed potatoes, vegetables and chocolate cake. Closed May through October. ~ 2275 Old West Highway 88, two miles east of Apache Junction; 602-982-7991. MODERATE.

The Lost Dutchman Gold Mine

With blunted peaks reaching nearly 6000 feet and razor-edged canyons plunging earthward, the Superstition Mountains comprise an area 40 miles long and 15 miles wide—some of the roughest, rockiest, most treacherous territory in the United States. It was in this rugged territory that Dutchman Jacob Waltz was believed to have discovered the Lost Dutchman Gold Mine.

Waltz supposedly found an old Spanish mine in the Superstitions near what is now Apache Junction. He was vigilant about keeping its whereabouts secret, and died in 1891 without revealing the location. Today in Apache Junction, a statue of Jacob Waltz in the center of the town honors the man believed to have discovered an elusive gold treasure. For a while people looked for the mine, then it was forgotten for about 30 years.

In the 1930s, Dr. Adolph Ruth came to the area claiming to have a map of the mine. One hot summer day he went into the area to search, and was never seen again. A few months later his skull was found with what looked like a bullet hole in it. Once again, interest in the mine was sparked and people resumed the search. To this day, the treasure has never been found, but prospectors are still looking.

To learn more about this local legend, head to the **Superstition Mountain/Lost Dutchman Museum**, which displays historical artifacts pertaining to the story of the Lost Dutchman Gold Mine. You'll also find exhibits of folk art, prehistoric Indian artifacts, Spanish and Mexican crafts and documents, pottery and relics of early cowboys, prospectors and miners. Admission. ~ Route 88, Goldfield Ghost Town, four miles north of Apache Junction; 602-983-4888.

If you'd like to try your luck in finding the legendary Lost Dutchman Gold Mine, there are a number of companies that offer three-day to seven-day—or longer—treks into the Superstitions. With the help of experienced guides, you will lash your gear to packhorses and mount up for a trip where you can pan for gold or simply ride the wilderness trails, camp, cook, bathe in icy streams and sleep out under the stars. For information, contact **Trail Horse Adventures at Superstition Stables** in Apache Junction. ~ 2151 North Warner Road; 602-982-6353. You can also try the **O.K. Corral Stables**. ~ P.O. Box 528, Apache Junction, AZ 85217; 602-982-4040.

SHOPPING   If you plan to go looking for the Lost Dutchman Gold Mine, or even if you don't, **Pro-Mack South** sells mining equipment, gold pans, lanterns, picks, rope, boots, supplies and just about everything but the treasure map. ~ 940 West Apache Trail, Apache Junction; 602-983-3484.

You'll find a few souvenirs at gift shops in the **Tortilla Flat Restaurant**. ~ Route 88, 18 miles north of Apache Junction; 602-984-1776. In **Goldfield Ghost Town**, the **Blue Nugget** (602-983-3095) sells rocks, minerals and Indian jewelry. The **Calico Corner** (602-982-2057) proffers Victorian era items. The **General Store** (602-982-3506) carries souvenirs of all kinds. ~ Route 88, four miles north of Apache Junction.

NIGHTLIFE   From Christmas to Easter, **Tortilla Flat Restaurant** features live bluegrass and country music on an outdoor barbeque patio. ~ Route 88, 18 miles north of Apache Junction; 602-984-1776.

Join the Barleen Family Band at their 500-seat **Barleen Family Country Music & Dinner Theatre** for Grand Ole Opry–style entertainment after you indulge in a gut-busting meal. Closed May through October. ~ 2275 Old West Highway 88, two miles east of Apache Junction; 602-982-7991.

PARKS   **USERY MOUNTAIN RECREATION AREA** 🚶 🚲 🐎   This 3324-acre recreational area is just northwest of the Superstition Mountains. It has an extensive hiking, mountain bike and horse trail system. Throughout the park you will find restrooms, showers and horse-staging areas. ~ It's east of Phoenix via Apache Boulevard or Superstition Freeway (Route 60). Head east to Ellsworth Road and turn north. At McKellips Road, Ellsworth becomes Usery Pass Road. Continue north to the entrance.

▲ There are 70 sites, all with RV hookups; $15 per night; 602-984-0032.

◆◆◆

ARIZONA'S RENAISSANCE FESTIVAL

Just nine miles east of Apache Junction on Route 60, you'll see a flat piece of grassland called Queen's Valley, which undergoes an interesting transformation each February and March when the **Renaissance Festival Arizona** takes place. Hundreds of costumed performers recreate the atmosphere of an Elizabethan Market Faire with jousting tournaments, strolling musicians and jugglers, medieval games and festive ceremonies. The event is staged over weekends in February and March and draws more than 100,000 visitors. For information, contact Renaissance Festival Arizona. ~ 12601 East Route 60; 602-463-2700.

LOST DUTCHMAN STATE PARK 🚶 Located in the foothills of the Superstition Mountains, this 292-acre park features eight miles of hiking trails through saguaro, palo verde and other desert flora. Interpretive tours by park rangers are conducted October through April. Facilities include a visitors center, restrooms, showers, picnic tables, drinking water and barbecue grills. Day-use fee, $4 per vehicle. ~ 6109 North Apache Trail, about five miles north of Apache Junction; 602-982-4485.

▲ There are 35 sites (no hookups); $10 per night. There is a dump station.

TONTO NATIONAL FOREST 🚶 🚴 🏇 🎣 ⛵ 🏕️ 🚣 🚤 🛥️
🐟 To explore the national forest northeast of Apache Junction, travel the famed Apache Trail (Route 88). The scenic drive follows the trail originally used by Apache Indians as a shortcut through the Superstition Mountains, eventually leading to the Salt River chain of lakes—Saguaro, Canyon, Apache and Roosevelt lakes. The lakes have been developed for fishing, boating, picnicking, hiking, biking and camping. The Salt River itself is a favorite spot for tubing. Day-use fee, $4 per carload (and $2 per water craft) at Butcher Jones Beach on Saguaro Lake.

There are several privately run marinas in the forest offering a variety of services. The **Saguaro Lake Marina** has boat rentals, storage, fuel, tours and a restaurant. There are tent-camping sites around the lake, accessible by boat only. ~ Off Bush Highway; 602-986-5546. The **Apache Lake Marina** offers boat rentals, storage and gas. Three motels, a restaurant, lounge and grocery store are also located here. There are RV sites, and tent-camping is allowed all around the lake. ~ Route 88; 520-467-2511. Also a full-service marina with a restaurant, gift shop and camping facilities, the **Canyon Lake Marina** is situated 15 miles northeast of Apache Junction. Boat tours are available. ~ Route 88; 602-944-6504.

Throughout the forest you'll find picnic areas, restrooms and hiking and riding trails. ~ The main access road from Apache Junction is Route 88 (Apache Trail). Tortilla Campground is on Route 88 about 11 miles from Apache Junction. Cholla Campground is on Route 188, eight miles north of Roosevelt Dam in Roosevelt. Mesa Ranger District: 602-610-3300. Tonto Basin Ranger District: 520-467-3200.

▲ There are 86 campgrounds (no hookups); free to $17 per night. Primitive camping is also allowed. Reservations are only needed for group sites; call USF Reservations, 800-280-2267. Located near Canyon Lake, Tortilla Campground has 70 tent/RV sites ($10 per night) and is open from October through March. Cholla Campground on Roosevelt Lake has 206 tent/RV sites ($11 to $17 per night).

THEODORE ROOSEVELT LAKE 🏃 🚲 ⛵ 🏕 🛶 ⛴ 🚤 🎣

Fed by Tonto Creek from the north and the Salt River from the east, Theodore Roosevelt Lake has more than 88 miles of shoreline, and hundreds of coves that provide excellent bass and crappie fishing, as well as hideaways for campers and picnickers. There are picnic tables, restrooms, showers and playgrounds. Roosevelt Lake Marina has a boat launch and rentals, a small grocery store (520-467-2245), a snack bar, restrooms and picnic tables. ~ Route 88 near Theodore Roosevelt Dam; 520-467-3200.

▲ There are numerous camping opportunities here. The two most developed campgrounds are Cholla and Windy Hill. Cholla Campground offers 206 sites (partial hookups) with drinking water, showers and toilets; $11 to $17 per night. Windy Hill features 347 sites with drinking water, showers, toilets and grills; $11 to $17 per night.

Globe

East of Devils Canyon, the Pinal Mountains rise to dominate the horizon, until the historic old copper-mining town of Globe wrests control of the horizon. This quiet old copper town, with its many Victorian homes dotting the hillsides, retains the flavor of the late 1800s with a turn-of-the-century main street, complete with an old-fashioned F. W. Woolworth store. Here, you'll find one of the finest American Indian archaeological sites in the state.

Globe began as a mining town in the 1860s after silver was discovered on the Apache reservation. Located at the eastern end of the Apache Trail, the town was originally called "Besh-Ba-Gowah" by the Apache, meaning "place of metal" or "metal camp." Today it is named for a spherical silver nugget with markings that resemble the continents. After the silver mines were depleted, copper was discovered, but those mines, too, were shut down by the Great Depression. The town has been dozing in the sun ever since.

SIGHTS

On your drive into **Globe** (if arriving from the west), you'll notice massive manmade hills of bleached-out dirt, a by-product of the copper mining operations here. The white mesas, which stretch for a couple of miles, are what's left after the ore has been bleached, crushed and smelted. Attempts to grow vegetation in the miniature moonscape have been all but futile, so the mountains of residue remain, perhaps to be recycled as new mining techniques allow extraction of more copper from them.

Also on the west side of town along Route 60 are five mines that you can visit on a "drive-by" tour. Among them are the Pinto Valley Mine, which produces six pounds of copper from each ton of rock; the Blue Bird Mine, which boasts the first solvent extraction electro-winning operation in the world; and the Sleeping Beauty Mine, which produced copper until 1974, when it was converted to a turquoise operation.

For local information, visit the **Greater Globe–Miami Chamber of Commerce**. Be sure to ask for the walking tour of downtown Globe, and directions to the archaeological sites. ~ 1360 North Broad Street; 520-425-4495.

Set among modern homes and paved streets, **Besh-Ba-Gowah Archaeological Park** is a prehistoric pueblo village built from rounded river cobblestone and mud walls, which surround rooms and plazas. Here, you can climb a rough wooden ladder and examine rooms with pottery and utensils that were used 600 years ago. There's also a weaver's loom, a pot over a firepit, manos and metates. A nearby museum displays artwork and utensils of the Salado, an advanced band of hunters and gatherers who lived here from 1100 to 1400 A.D. The Salado built a pueblo of more than 200 rooms (146 on the ground floor and 61 second-story rooms) around three central plazas, which housed an estimated 300 to 400 people during its peak. During their stay, they farmed along the banks of Pinal Creek, growing crops of corn, beans, squash and possibly cotton. The community was also a trade center: Archaeologists have found evidence of trade in the form of copper bells and feathers from Meso America; shells from either the coast of present-day California or the Gulf of Mexico; and pottery from various regions. There is also a botanical garden that demonstrates how the Salado utilized the surrounding vegetation.

The Salado made pottery of their own, which is on display: black-and-white designs on red clay. They also wove baskets, sandals and mats of sotol and yucca fibers, as well as fine cotton cloth. Bracelets, rings and necklaces were made from the shells they received in trade. A great drought during the 15th century is believed to have driven the Salado from the region. In addition to the partially restored pueblo, there's a museum/visitors center that displays artifacts found during early excavations. Admission. ~ Located one mile southwest of town at the Globe Community Center on Jess Hayes Road; 520-425-0320.

PINAL'S PAST

The small town of Pinal sprung up in the late 1800s after silver was discovered in the surrounding mountains. In addition to milling ore from the Silver King Mine, the town was a stopping-off place for such Old West legends as Bat Masterson, Wyatt Earp and Doc Holliday. In fact, Holliday's girlfriend, Bignose Kate, died at Pinal, and is buried there.

After leaving the archaeological park, you can get an eagle's eye view of the area by making a right turn on Jess Hayes Road, then driving to Ice House Canyon Road and Kellner Canyon, where you will circle up through the beautiful Pinal Mountains for 15 miles. At the 7850-foot level you'll pass through ponderosa pine, ferns and thick foliage. Pull out anywhere and the overlooks will give you sweeping views of Globe and Miami below.

In town, the rip-roaring days of the early miners come to life at the **Gila County Historical Museum** with exhibits of early artifacts, mining equipment and Salado Indian relics. The museum is housed in the former Globe–Miami Mine Rescue and First Aid Station. Closed weekends. ~ Route 60; 520-425-7385.

The **Old Dominion Mine**, across from the museum on Broad Street, is what's left of what was once the world's richest copper mine. In the 1930s, the depressed price of copper, coupled with increasing water seepage into the mine shafts, forced the closure of the mine. Today the mine belongs to BHP Copper Company and is a valuable source of water, which is vital to the company's other operations in the area.

In downtown Globe stands the **Historic Gila County Courthouse** built in 1906. This stately stone structure now houses the Cobre Valley Center for the Arts and a small theater. Climb the 26 stone steps and enter the carved wooden doors to find finished hardwood floors, arched passways, grand rooms with high ceilings and tall windows, and a staircase accented with copper banisters and overhead skylight. Notice that in nearly every room there's a vault. When the building served as a courthouse, various documents were stored in the building; the vaults were added for their protection. The first floor includes weaving, ceramics and stained glass studios. The entire second floor is currently a gallery for the Arts Guild. The second floor is home to the Copper Cities Community Players, who have converted the large rooms into a small theater. ~ 101 North Broad Street; 520-425-0884.

Also worth visiting is the **Globe Elks Lodge**, the world's tallest three-story building, built in 1910. ~ 155 West Mesquite Avenue; 520-425-2161. You can also check out the old **Gila County Jail** (behind the Historic Gila County Courthouse), constructed of reinforced concrete in 1909, with cell blocks transported from the Yuma Territorial Prison. The **Gila Valley Bank and Trust Building**, with its white terra-cotta facade, is an unusual example of the Beaux-Arts neoclassical style of 1909. The building was the pioneer branch of the former Valley National Bank. ~ Mesquite Avenue and Broad Street.

The **Country Corner Antique Store** was the town's grocery and mercantile when built in 1920. If the shape of the building seems odd it's because the structure was designed in the shape of the state of Arizona. Closed Sunday and Monday. ~ 383 South Hill Street; 520-425-8208. The art deco–style **Globe Theater** was built in 1918 and features copper-covered pillars under the movie marquee. ~ 141 North Broad Street; 520-425-5581. Nearby is old **Engine No. 1774**, one of only seven remaining steam locomotives in existence. Originally, 355 were built between 1899 and 1901. ~ Pine and Oak streets.

If you want more history, the city sponsors an **Historic Home and Building Tour and Antique Show** in February. Many of the structures were built by the same stonemasons who worked on nearby Roosevelt Dam. The tour usually consists of six to eight buildings. A recent one included a 1911 home built from dacite stones, a material quarried locally; a church that was hand-built by Episcopalian priests between 1900 and 1908; and a plantation-style mansion built in the late 1800s, complete with upper and lower verandas. For more information call the Globe City Chamber of Commerce, 520-425-4495.

Globe is the commercial gateway to the **San Carlos Apache Indian Reservation**, the 1.8 million-acre expanse that's home to nearly 10,000 Apache Indians. Rambling and remote, lush and rustic, the land is a natural habitat for javelina, elk, bear, mountain lions, bighorn sheep, antelope, waterfowl, grouse, quail, rabbits and a variety of freshwater fish. As you leave the San Carlos Apache Reservation, notice the telephone poles sunk into the ground near Calva Crossing. They control rain run-off and were planted there after the flood in 1983. Camping, hunting and fishing are permitted, with licenses. A recreation permit is required for off-road hiking. Tribal lakes offer boating and waterskiing. Contact the Recreation and Wildlife Department, 520-475-2343.

THE REAL GERONIMO

The San Carlos Apache Indian Reservation was where Geronimo and his Chiricahua followers were vanquished with other Apache tribes. But twice he left the reservation to resume his war with the U.S. Army. Born near Clifton, Geronimo gained notoriety in the 1870s when he and his braves terrorized southern Arizona and northern Mexico. Although there is little dispute that Geronimo participated in several massacres, recent historians are defending him as a protector of his homeland and a victim of wild stories spread by frightened settlers. Geronimo surrendered three times to the U.S. Army—the last time in 1886— before ending his personal war, and spent his final years raising watermelons and vegetables at Fort Sill, Oklahoma, where he died of pneumonia.

LODGING

In Globe you'll find the **Copper Manor Motel**, a 62-room, two-story motel with contemporary furnishing, a pool and an all-night café. ~ 637 East Ash Street; 520-425-7124. BUDGET.

Copper Hills Inn is another Globe caravansary—a 68-room Best Western with basically nondescript contemporary furnishing, a dining room, coffee shop and lounge, a gift shop, a beauty shop and a swimming pool. ~ Globe–Miami Highway; 520-425-7151, 800-825-7151, fax 520-425-2504. BUDGET.

One of the nicer motels is the **Cloud Nine Motel**, which offers ultra-clean guest rooms decorated in cool pastels, some with refrigerators and spa tubs. There is a pool and a jacuzzi. ~ 1699 East Ash Street; 520-425-5741, 800-256-8399, fax 520-402-8466. BUDGET TO MODERATE.

Globe has a small but growing number of bed-and-breakfast inns. One of the most distinctive is **Nofsger Hill Inn**, located in a former schoolhouse dating from 1906. Four large suites include four of the original classrooms, each with a fireplace, school desk and the original blackboard. No smoking. ~ 425 North Street; 520-425-2260. BUDGET TO MODERATE.

Built in 1903 for a family of 12, **Cedar Hill** is a spacious historic house with high ceilings, a backyard and a porch with swings. Its two cozy rooms are individually decorated; one is outfitted with a queen brass bed while the other has antique furniture straight from the proprietress' grandmother's dowry. Breakfast is made to order. ~ 175 East Cedar Street; 520-425-7530; e-mail 175cedar@gila.net. BUDGET.

DINING

Most locals agree some of the best food in town is at **Jerry's Restaurant**, a fast-paced, coffee-shop style eatery that dishes up hearty portions of steaks, chops, meatloaf, fish and other American stand-bys. ~ 699 East Ash Street; 520-425-5282. BUDGET.

✔ CHECK THESE OUT—UNIQUE LODGING

- *Budget:* Spend the night where the likes of John Wayne and Ronald Reagan bedded down—the **Grande Hotel and Conference Center**. *page 245*
- *Moderate:* Fish from the pond for your own dinner at the **Lakeview Lodge**, one of Arizona's oldest lodges. *page 269*
- *Deluxe:* Snooze in a true wilderness setting at **Southwest Research Station**, run by the American Museum of Natural History. *page 259*
- *Ultra-deluxe:* Retire to your chalet-style room's spa tub at the **Gold Canyon Golf Resort**, set amidst the Superstition Mountains. *page 246*

Budget: under $70   Moderate: $70–$110   Deluxe: $110–$180   Ultra-deluxe: over $180

Don't let the decor at **La Luz Del Día** fool you. Despite the old-fashioned counter, mushroom stools and vinyl booths, this isn't a 1950s burger joint; it's a Mexican bakery and coffee shop with a tasty selection of Mexican sweet rolls, buns and quesadillas. Breakfast and lunch only. ~ 304 North Broad Street; 520-425-8400. BUDGET.

El Rey Café is an authentic Mexican restaurant, small in size but big in flavor, with enchiladas, *chile rellenos*, tacos and chimichangas. Brunch is served on the weekend. Closed Tuesday. ~ Route 60/70; 520-425-6601. BUDGET.

Blue Ribbon Cafe, located in the heart of Globe's old historic district, isn't called "blue ribbon" for nothing. A popular breakfast spot, it's also busy at lunchtime serving sandwiches, salads, burgers and pasties (miner's pie). Closed weekends. Breakfast and lunch only. ~ 474 North Broad Street; 520-425-4423. BUDGET.

If you prefer Chinese cuisine, the **Jasmine Tea House** serves Mandarin and Szechuan dishes of pork, beef, chicken and seafood. ~ 1097 North Broad Street; 520-425-2503. BUDGET.

SHOPPING

The **Cobre Valley Center for the Arts**, located in the historic Gila County Courthouse, houses arts and crafts produced by local members of the Cobre Valley Fine Arts Guild (*cobre* is Spanish for copper). Media represented include stained glass, ceramics, weaving, painting (oil, acrylic, watercolors), sculpture (stone, metal, wood, plastic), photography, jewelry (silver, stone, beaded) and mixed media. There are also prints, batik silk scarfs and gift items such as Southwestern-designed soap and stationary, books and painted furniture. Climb a flight of stairs and you'll find studios of the Copper Cities Community Players. The huge room on your right is the Players' theater, but was once the old county courtroom. If you're lucky, you may happen onto a rehearsal for an upcoming play or possibly a dance recital. ~ 101 North Broad Street; 520-425-0884.

Antiques, leathercraft, dolls and jewelry by local artisans are among the offerings at **Hangin' Tree**. ~ 180 North Broad Street; 520-425-8431.

Bacon's Boots and Saddles represents the last of the great saddle makers. Owner Ed Bacon has been hand-crafting saddles for more than 50 years. His store also features a full range of Western wear. Closed Sunday. ~ 290 North Broad Street; 520-425-2681.

Pickle Barrel Antiques specializes in Fiestaware, antique lighting, primitive furniture and quilts. ~ 404 South Broad Street; 520-425-4028.

West of Globe on Route 60, **Pastime Antiques** is filled with antique furniture, paintings, western memorabilia, historic photos, old magazines, postcards, posters and other relics and remnants of the past. Even the building is a treasure. It used to be the town library. ~ 1068 Adonis Avenue, Miami; 520-473-3791.

NIGHTLIFE   Not much happens after dark, but you can see current movies at the **Globe Theater**. ~ 141 North Broad Street; 520-425-5581. Or if you prefer an evening nightcap, go to **Under the Palms Cocktails**. ~ 230 North Broad Street; 520-425-2823.

PARKS   **TONTO NATIONAL FOREST** 🚶🚵🐎⛵🚣 The Globe district, located in the southeast corner of Tonto National Forest, is a popular escape from the desert heat. The Upper Salt River boasts some of the country's best whitewater, as well as fishing at the calmer stretches. The Pinal Mountains offer endless opportunities for hiking, biking and horseback riding. The park has picnic areas, restrooms and hiking and riding trails. ~ Main access to the Globe district is Route 60. To reach Upper and Lower Pinal campgrounds from Globe head west on Route 60. Turn south on Jess Hayes Road and follow signs to the campgrounds. Oak Flat Campground is located right off of Route 60, five and a half miles east of Superior. ~ 520-402-6200.

▲ There are 86 campgrounds (no hookups); free to $17 per night. Group sites also available. Primitive camping is also allowed. Open fires are prohibited throughout the forest. Reservations are only needed for group sites in fee areas; call USFS Reservations, 800-280-2267. At a cool 7500 feet Upper Pinal Campground (4 tent sites; no fee) and Lower Pinal Campground (12 tent sites; no fee) are popular in the summer. At a lower elevation, Oak Flat Campground (18 tent/RV sites; no fee) is conveniently located four miles east of Superior.

SAN CARLOS LAKE 🚶🚣⛵ The lake, created by the construction of the Coolidge Dam, has 158 miles of shoreline when full. The fishing is good for catfish, bass and crappie. Boat rentals are available in the park. There's a general store (fishing licenses and hiking permits available here). The only other facilities are pit toilets. For information about camping and hiking on tribal lands and fishing in San Carlos Lake, call 520-475-2756. ~ Located 30 miles east of Globe.

▲ There are 11 RV sites, some with hookups; $15 per night for RVs needing hookups, otherwise wilderness camping is included with a $14 two-day fishing license, but not with the $7 one-day license, which expires at midnight.

▼▼▼▼▼▼▼▼▼▼
Safford Area

Lying low in the fertile Gila River Valley is Safford, a trade center for the valley's numerous cotton farmers, and jumping-off point for outdoor recreation in the Coronado National Forest. Just west of town are the adjoining communities of Thatcher and Pima. Named to commemorate a Christmas visit by Mormon apostle Moses Thatcher, the town is home to Eastern Arizona College; nearby Pima is the site of the Eastern Arizona Museum.

Safford's main highway is lined with modern shopping centers, but the downtown district, with its wood-frame and mason buildings, suggests a Midwestern borough. Despite the arid climate, the valley is irrigated by the Gila River and cotton is king here. The **Safford Valley Cotton Growers** has one of a handful of gins in the area that you can tour during season, typically September through January. Call ahead for reservations. ~ Route 191 and 9th Street, Safford; 520-428-0714.

Underground hot springs are another natural resource in Safford. To take a dip, stop by **Kachina Mineral Springs Spa** where you can soak in springs funneled into tiled, Roman-styled tubs. Other amenities include massages, sweat wraps and reflexology (therapeutic foot massage). Recently remodeled with a new addition that includes two large tubs for private groups, the baths are wonderful and the tubs are clean. Closed Sunday. ~ Cactus Road just off Route 191, Safford; 520-428-7212; charge for services.

A good first stop is the **Safford–Graham County Chamber of Commerce** for brochures and maps. You can also view historical dioramas and exhibits on gems, minerals and regional agriculture. ~ 1111 Thatcher Boulevard, Safford; 520-428-2511.

One of Safford's main landmarks is the **Safford Courthouse**, a neo-colonial brick building with white pillars built in 1916. ~ 8th Avenue at Main Street. Across the intersection is the 1898-vintage **city hall**, which was the town's original schoolhouse. ~ 717 Main Street, Safford.

Just outside of town, the quiet residential neighborhoods are dotted with elegant old homes. One of them is the **Olney House**, built in 1890 for George Olney, a former sheriff of Graham County. The two-story home features a plantation-style upper and lower front veranda. It is currently a bed-and-breakfast inn (see "Lodging" below for more information). ~ 1104 Central Avenue, Safford.

For a glimpse at the area's past, visit the **Graham County Historical Society Museum**, which contains a photo gallery of Graham County along with western and American Indian artifacts. Open Monday and Tuesday afternoon. ~ 808 8th Avenue, Safford; 520-348-3212.

The **Eastern Arizona Museum** has an interesting collection of pioneer and Indian relics in a turn-of-the-century building. There are also an extensive rock and mineral display and a reading room filled with historic documents. ~ Route 70 at Main Street, Pima; 520-485-9400.

If you feel like getting spaced out in Safford, stop by **Discovery Park**. This complex contains exhibits on the origins of the universe, the history and science of astronomy and radio astronomy, as well as a multimedia room where displays of real lightning are produced. There is also a 20-inch telescope for daytime and nighttime observations, and perhaps most exciting of all, a full-motion flight simulator. Open to the public Thursday, Friday and Saturday from 3 to 9 p.m. only. Admission. ~ 1651 Discovery Park Boulevard, Safford; 520-428-6260.

Nearby 10,720-foot **Mount Graham** makes for good scenic drives, and its unique ecosphere provides a succession of climate zones, each with its own ecology. The main access road to the mountain is Swift Trail, which at first passes through stands of prickly pear, mesquite, creosote and ocotillo in the lower foothills. As you rise in elevation, the dominant trees are various types of oak, alligator juniper and piñon pine. At a higher elevation (8000 feet) you'll find a profusion of ponderosa pine, Douglas fir, aspen and white fir, some of them dating to 1200 A.D. Botanists say the Douglas firs have survived because the rocky cliffs of the mountains have protected them from the harsh environment. On the drive up the mountain is an apple orchard maintained under a special use permit from the U.S. Forest Service. In late summer and early fall you can purchase fruit at roadside stands. While the orchard survived the extensive May 1996 fires, 6000 acres on Mount Graham were not as lucky; you'll pass through a number of burned out areas on your trek up the Swift Trail. The first 24 miles of Swift Trail are paved, the last 13 are gravel.

The **Mount Graham International Observatory** on Emerald Peak outside of Safford features a 1.8-meter Lennon Telescope and a Submillimeter telescope. An 8-millimeter binocular telescope is currently under construction (it will be the world's largest of its type and the most powerful, able to see deeper into space than the Hubble telescope, when completed in 2001). Further expansion of the facility will add four other telescopes including an eight-meter class infrared/optical telescope. Open to the public Thursday, Friday and Saturday from 3 to 9 p.m. All-day tours of

THE LEGACY OF BILLY THE KID

Although William Bonney—alias "Billy the Kid"—established his legend in New Mexico, local historians say he killed his first victim in Bonita, about 35 miles south of Safford on Route 266. The town's two-story general store, which was originally built in the 1870s as George Atkins' Saloon, remains a gathering place for local ranchers and farmers, who will point out bullet holes in the store's ceiling; outside, they'll show you the spot that Billy the Kid shot and killed Francis P. "Windy" Cahill on August 17, 1877.

the observatory, including a box lunch, are offered on Saturday by advance reservation. Admission. ~ 1651 Discovery Park Road, Safford; 520-428-6260.

Olney House Bed and Breakfast, a Western Colonial Revival home, has three antique-filled guest rooms, all of which share a bath and a parlor. In addition to rooms in the main house, there's a one-bedroom cottage with two twin beds and a queen-sized trundle-bed, and a circa-1890 studio cottage with a queen-sized bed. Both cottages have televisions and VCRs. Guests start the morning with a full breakfast. Before leaving, be sure to see the pecan tree, which they claim is the tallest in Arizona. ~ 1104 Central Avenue, Safford; phone/fax 520-428-5118, 800-814-5118; www.zekes.com/~olney. MODERATE.

LODGING

◄ HIDDEN

The rest of Safford's lodgings are mostly chain motels. You won't be disappointed with the **Days Inn**, which features rooms with refrigerators and microwaves, a pool and a hot tub. There's a restaurant across the street. ~ 520 East Route 70, Safford; 520-428-5000, 800-329-7466, fax 520-428-7510. BUDGET.

For beautiful scenery in the middle of true wilderness, the **Southwest Research Station,** run by the American Museum of Natural History, provides a haven for the layperson as well as the scientist. Rooms are furnished simply and three meals a day are included in the tab. Cave Creek Canyon is known for its fabulous birdwatching. A swimming pool, volleyball court and horseshoes are available for the guests. Open to the public from mid-March through October. ~ Take Route 80 to Portal, then follow Cave Creek Canyon for five miles; phone/fax 520-558-2396; www.research.amnh.org/swrs. DELUXE.

The best restaurant in town is **El Coronado,** a friendly place with blue-vinyl booths, ceiling fans and a deep narrow dining room. The tasty Mexican specialties include green chile chimichangas and quesadillas stuffed with green chile, meat, chicken, chorizo and chopped green chile. American dishes include chicken-fried steak, shrimp and sandwiches. Closed Tuesday. ~ 409 Main Street, Safford; 520-428-7755. BUDGET TO MODERATE.

DINING

El Charro Restaurant is a local hangout with formica tables and local artwork on the wall. Mexican specialties include cheese crisps with green chile con carne, green or red chile burritos and Sonora enchiladas. Closed Sunday. ~ 601 Main Street, Safford; 520-428-4134. BUDGET.

Across the street from the Ramada Spa and Resort, the **Country Manor Restaurant** is open 24 hours a day. Old farm implements hang on the walls and you're likely to see a table of old timers in here shooting the breeze and eating home-cooked meals such as Black Angus beef, Mexican dishes, homemade soups and pies, chicken fried steak, liver and onions and meatloaf. ~ 420 East Route 70, Safford; 520-428-7148. BUDGET TO DELUXE.

The **Branding Iron Restaurant** is a ranch-style building flanked by large trees. They serve Western broiled steaks, chicken, seafood, barbecued ribs in a dining room that overlooks the Gila Valley. Closed Monday. ~ 2346 North Branding Iron Lane, Safford; 520-428-6252. BUDGET TO MODERATE.

SHOPPING   The small shops on downtown's Main Street are fun to explore. In addition to thrift shops, jewelry stores and Western-wear boutiques, you'll find **Trophies n' Tees**, which has a selection of Arizona souvenirs, caps, sweatshirts and T-shirts. Closed Saturday and Sunday. ~ 513 Main Street, Safford; 520-428-0906.

Brown's Turquoise Shop Inc. carries rough and cut natural Morenci turquoise and handmade American Indian jewelry, such as kachinas and Mana pottery and black gold. Closed Sunday. ~ 2248 1st Street, Safford; 520-428-6433.

You can't miss **Pollock's Western Outfitters** with its distressed-wood exterior and horse statue on the roof. Inside, there are the latest Western fashions and accessories. Suppliers include Levi, Rocky Mountain, Justin, Tony Lama, Stetson and Resistol. You'll also find Murphy leather goods and King ropes. ~ 610 5th Street, Safford; 520-428-0093.

Behind Pollock's Western Outfitters, **Pollock's Outback Outlet** offers merchandise at discounted prices.

NIGHTLIFE   Locals converge on **Tuttie's American Club**. ~ 503 Main Street, Safford; 520-428-2727.

A mellow crowd gathers around the horseshoe-shaped bar or busies itself with pool or darts at the **Fireside Lounge**. ~ Route 666 South, three miles south of Safford; 520-428-9954.

PARKS   **MOUNT GRAHAM**   The highest peak of the Pinaleño Mountains at 10,720 feet is Mount Graham. Drive the 37-mile-long Swift Trail and you'll leave the cactus and mesquites at the base and travel to a forest of ponderosa pine, aspen and white fir, punctuated by charred areas consumed by the May 1996 forest fire. At the end of the road is 11-acre Riggs Lake, which is stocked with trout (license plus trout stamp required) and also available for boating (electric motors only). The forest's facilities are limited to water faucets, restrooms, picnic areas and a visitor station. ~ Go south from Safford for seven miles on Route 191 and turn west at the Mount Graham sign. The first 24 miles of the Swift Trail are paved; the last 13 are graded dirt. Swift Trail is closed from the end of the pavement from mid-November through mid-April. Safford Ranger District: 520-428-4150.

▲ There are six developed campgrounds; $5 per night except at Riggs Flat and Columbine Corrals ($6 per night). Primitive camping is allowed free below 9800 feet (above 9800 feet is closed to all entry).

DANKWORTH POND STATE PARK 🏃 ⚲⚲ ⛴ ⛴ ⛵ This park features two developed areas, each flanking a small artificial lake. Along the west side of the lake are picnic ramadas and restrooms. Facilities include a boat dock (electric motors only), restrooms, a picnic area and nature trails. You'll also find some mineral hot springs here. Day-use fee, $4 per vehicle. ~ Located three miles south of Roper Lake Park on Route 191; 520-348-9392.

ROPER LAKE STATE PARK ⚲ ⚲⚲ ⛴ ⛴ ⛵ In addition to swimming in a 30-acre lake with a beach, you can soak outside in a rock tub filled with hot springs bubbling up from the ground. The 240-acre park also includes a refuge for endangered fish in two ponds. The park is home to non-endangered fish as well: catfish, bass, bluegill, trout and crappie. You can fish for them from a shady dock. Boating is also allowed; electric motors only. For meals, sit out on the peninsula's grassy picnic area under a grove of shade trees. You'll find restrooms and showers. Day-use fee, $4 per vehicle. ~ Located six miles south of Safford off Route 191; 520-428-6760; 520-348-9392.

▲ There are 95 sites, 20 with RV hookups; $10 per night for standard sites and $15 per night for hookups.

ARAVAIPA CANYON WILDERNESS 🏃 Aravaipa Creek flows ◄ *HIDDEN* through an 11-mile-long canyon bordered by spectacular cliffs. Lining the creek are large sycamore, ash, cottonwood and willow trees, making it a colorful stop in fall. You may spot javelina, coyotes, mountain lions and desert bighorn sheep, as well as nearly every type of desert songbird and more than 200 other bird species. There are no facilities whatsoever. ~ To get to the West Trailhead, drive on Route 77 about 11 miles south of Winkelman. Go east on Aravaipa Road; it's 12 miles to the trailhead. To get to the East Trailhead from Globe, drive on Route 70 to Klondyke Road (eight miles east of Fort Thomas). Take this graded dirt road 45 miles. Or take Route 10 to Willcox. Take exit 340 to Fort Grant Road, then follow the signs. It's advisable to check on road conditions with the Safford District Office before setting out; high-clearance vehicles are a good idea.

▲ Primitive camping allowed. The maximum stay is three days/two nights. Permits are required and can be obtained from the Bureau of Land Management's Safford District Office. ~ 711 14th Avenue, Safford; 520-348-4400.

CLUFF RANCH WILDLIFE AREA ⌣ This area contains 1300 acres of wildlife sanctuary and recreational areas. Streams from Mount Graham feed four ponds that provide year-round fishing for trout, catfish, largemouth bass and bluegill. Birding is also excellent here. ~ Located about nine miles northwest of Safford; 520-485-9430.

▼▼▼▼▼▼▼▼▼▼▼▼▼▼

Clifton-Morenci Area

To begin the 44-mile drive from Safford to Clifton, continue east out of Safford on Route 70. The road passes along the edge of Roper Lake State Park, and parallels the Gila River for a few miles. Soon after the river parts ways with the road, take a left turn onto 191 North—otherwise, you'll promptly end up in New Mexico. The route is scenic, traveling between the Gila Mountains to the north and the Whitlocks to the south. As you pass the appropriately named Thumb Butte on your right, you'll cross from Graham County into Greenlee County; finally, the road rejoins and crosses over the Gila River, and takes you into Clifton.

The Clifton–Morenci area is a region shaped by its mining past. Today, the continent's second-largest copper mine operates in Morenci, while the copper industry's heyday is preserved along Clifton's historic Chase Creek Street.

SIGHTS

Route 191 follows the San Francisco River, much the way Francisco de Coronado and his conquistadors did, around the bend and into the historic little mining town of **Clifton**, built along the banks of the river.

All around Clifton, the red sandstone cliffs paint a brilliant contrast to the grays and tans of the shale and the tin-and-brick buildings which are reminiscent of the town's golden days at the turn of the century, when copper was king.

The town was founded around 1865, but didn't prosper until copper deposits were discovered in 1872. At first, copper ore had to be shipped to Swansea, Wales, for smelting. Then miners built their own crude adobe smelters along Chase Creek Street, and set up a narrow-gauge railroad to transport the ore from the mines on the surrounding hillsides.

Many of the remnants of early mining operations remain, along with dozens of old buildings—47 are on the National Register of Historical Places—in turn-of-the-century architecture. You'll find most of them along **Chase Creek Street**, which was once the town's main thoroughfare, lined on both sides with stores, saloons, brothels, churches and even an opera house. Today, the four-block-long street, plus a few narrow alleys, parallels Coronado Boulevard (Route 191), separated by a rudimentary brick wall. But you can still walk among the buildings, many of which have been restored or are in the process of being restored. Most retain their architectural splendor.

For instance, the **Catholic Church**, which was rebuilt in 1917 after being destroyed by flood and fire, features leaded and stained-glass windows, a marble altar and porcelain figures imported from Italy. Down the street is Clifton's first **Town Jail**, which is carved into the side of a granite cliff. Next door is the **Copper Head**, a 19th-century locomotive that once carried ore to the smelters. Across the river, the **Carmichael House** is now headquarters for mine officials. It was built in 1913 for mine president James Carmichael, who once had to flee through the home's storm sewer system to escape a mob of angry strikers.

The **Greenlee County Chamber of Commerce**, which has its offices in the old Southern Pacific train depot, dispenses maps and information about the sights and history of the area. Be sure to ask for the walking-tour map of historic Chase Creek. If you have any questions about the history of the area, ask Charles Spezia, who put together the tour. ~ 100 North Coronado Boulevard, Clifton; 520-865-3313.

You'll notice a few caves in the mountain above the south side of Chase Creek. These were built by merchants to store valuables such as whiskey, meat and vegetables. They often had rugged steel doors and sometimes were vented with a vertical shaft.

The renovated **Greenlee County Historical Museum** on the west end of Chase Creek, has assembled an impressive collection of early Clifton memorabilia, including recollections of Geronimo's birth near the Gila River about four miles from downtown. The photo gallery displays images of the region's history and paintings by Ted De Grazia, one of Arizona's most famous artists and a native of Morenci. The museum is the keeper of the baby chair and doll once belonging to Supreme Court Justice Sandra Day O'Connor, who was born in nearby Duncan. Open Tuesday, Thursday and Saturday afternoons. ~ 315 Chase Creek, Clifton; 520-865-3115.

Phelps Dodge Corporation became a major player in Clifton's development at the turn of the century, when it took over most of the local mining operations, about four miles north of town. The original mining camp was called Joy's Camp, but was later renamed **Morenci**, after a town in Michigan. Over the next 50 years, Phelps Dodge, or "PD" as the locals call it (often confused with "Petey"), became one of the largest producers of copper in the world.

Today's Morenci was built by Phelps Dodge in 1969. It consists of a motel/restaurant, a school, a library, two shopping centers, a bowling alley and the Phelps Dodge Mercantile, a combination supermarket and discount department store. Phelps Dodge operates the open-pit copper mine here, the second largest in North America and open to public tours.

The **Phelps Dodge Morenci, Inc.** mine is an awesome sight from the viewpoints along Route 191, but you can get a closer look into the depths of the mine through tours offered by Phelps Dodge. Most impressive are the earth moving equipment with tires so huge they dwarf a man, the scoop shovels that can unearth 40 cubic tons of ore with one bite, and the futuristic dump trucks with wedge-shaped bays that haul 190 tons of ore. The tour also includes the mine's crushers, concentrators and electrochemical extraction operation, which processes the copper ore into three-foot-square sheets, each weighing about 200 pounds. The tours, which last about three and a half hours, are conducted by retired miners who explain the state-of-the-art electro-winning process, which has replaced outdated smelting and refining. Closed weekends. ~ 4521 Route 191, Morenci; 520-865-4521.

Continuing north, the highway ascends a series of switchbacks into a high desert climate zone, with juniper trees seemingly growing from the red rock formations.

About halfway to Alpine, you can stop at **Rose Peak**, which offers panoramic vistas of the Escudilla Mountains. For even better views, you can hike to the forest lookout tower, about a half-mile off the highway.

LODGING

Each town has its own motel. **Rode Inn Motel** is in the traditional motel-style, with rooms decorated in a sort of modern Southwest style with antique-white walls and furnishings in pastel greens and blues. Rooms are well kept and offer in-room coffee, microwaves, refrigerators and color cable television. ~ 186 South Coronado Boulevard, Clifton; 520-865-4536, fax 520-865-2654. BUDGET.

The more modern **Morenci Motel** sits on a hill overlooking Clifton and features an adobe brick exterior, wrought-iron fixtures, adobe tiled lobby, restaurant, lounge and gift shop. The large rooms are decorated with dark-wood, Mediterranean-style furnishings. ~ Route 191, Morenci; 520-865-4111, fax 520-865-5525. BUDGET.

DINING

PJ's Restaurant, a storefront hole-in-the-wall near the old section of town, is popular with locals who feast on hamburgers, steak dishes or Mexican entrées like chile cheese crisps and green chile plates or red enchiladas. Seating is at the counter or formica dinettes, but the food is tasty and plentiful. ~ 307 South Coronado Boulevard, Clifton; 520-865-3328. BUDGET TO MODERATE.

The best place in town to eat is the **Copperroom Restaurant and Lounge**, a somewhat plain but cavernous dining room with ceiling fans, wooden tables, captain chairs and a brick fireplace used during the winter. The house specialties include steaks, prime rib, chicken, liver and onions, halibut and several Mexican dishes. ~ Morenci Motel, Route 191, Morenci; 520-865-4111. BUDGET TO DELUXE.

SHOPPING

Not much here, but if you run out of toothpaste try **Phelps Dodge Mercantile**, a combination grocery and discount department store. ~ Morenci Plant Site shopping center, Morenci; 520-865-4121.

NIGHTLIFE

For contemporary surroundings, try the **Copperroom Restaurant and Lounge**, a small but surprisingly active bar with a handful of wooden tables and copper memorabilia hanging from the ceiling. ~ Morenci Motel, Route 191, Morenci; 520-865-4111.

▼▼▼▼▼▼▼▼▼
Alpine Area

The long and winding road from Clifton up to Alpine is a beautiful one—just make sure you have plenty of gas and supplies before you begin, because there are no facilities along the 105-mile stretch. Starting from Clifton, you'll first need to make the 1300-foot climb to Morenci, then bid civilization farewell as you continue the ascent into Apache-Sitgreaves National Forest. Your progress through the Blue Range towards Alpine will be marked by the increasing height of the peaks you pass: Mitchell Peak at just under 8000 feet, Rose Peak at almost 8900 feet and Sawed Off Mountain at 9346 feet.

Be aware that this road is subject to closure during winter snow storms. If the road is closed by snow or mudslides, you can drive to Alpine via Routes 78 and 180 through western New Mexico. The detour adds only 20 miles to the trip.

SIGHTS

Twenty-two miles before you reach Alpine is **Hannagan Meadow**, a grassy clearing framed by stately ponderosa pine and blue spruce forests. In addition to excellent hiking trails, there's a rustic mountain lodge, and, in winter, cross-country skiing and snowmobiling. ~ Route 191.

The mountain village of **Alpine** is located in the heart of the Apache-Sitgreaves National Forest, or the "Arizona Alps," as it is called locally. The town was founded in 1879 by Mormon settlers who originally named it Frisco, after the San Francisco River. The name was later changed to Alpine because residents thought the area resembled the Alps. The Arizona Alps don't attract the large number of tourists who flock to the Grand Canyon, the Colorado River or other state attractions, but nature buffs will love the region's abundance of outdoor activities—hiking, camping, hunting, fishing and cross-country skiing.

Alpine has no traffic lights or video stores, just a handful of year-round residents and even fewer commercial attractions. Actually it's nothing more than an intersection of Routes 191 and

180, but there are dependable services and lodging. More important, within a 30-mile radius there are 200 miles of trout streams, 11 lakes, numerous campgrounds, plus a country club and golf course. In winter, Alpine doesn't hibernate with the black bear, but keeps busy offering cross-country skiing, sledding and ice fishing opportunities.

At an elevation of 8046 feet, Alpine is the highest town in Arizona.

The region is also a favorite with hunters because it is home to nine of Arizona's ten big game species, including mule deer, elk, black bear, bighorn sheep and mountain lion. Small-game hunters stalk blue grouse, wild turkey, Gambel's quail and a host of waterfowl. The forest is also habitat for a wide variety of rare and endangered birds, including the Mexican spotted owl, bald eagle and peregrine falcon.

From Alpine, you can strike out in any direction and discover unspoiled forests of tall pines, shimmering aspens, trickling streams, wildflower meadows and clear blue lakes. For detailed maps and descriptions of the area, stop at the **U.S. Forest Service**, where rangers can also advise on current road conditions. The office lobby is now open 24 hours, with an interactive video display giving out tourist information when rangers aren't available. ~ At the junction of Routes 180 and 191; 520-339-4384.

A picturesque spot is the pristine **Williams Valley**, located seven miles northwest of Alpine via Route 191 and Forest Road 249. Here you can explore 15 miles of hiking trails through wooded forests. Beyond Williams Valley you can drop a line in tiny Lake Sierra Blanca, which is stocked with rainbow and brook trout.

A nice scenic drive from Alpine is the **Blue River–Red Hill Loop**. Drive east three miles from Alpine on Route 180 to Forest Road 281 (the Blue Road turnoff). As you make this turnoff, you'll see the western tip of **Luna Lake**, 80 acres of crystal-clear waters surrounded by green meadows and pine forests. Facilities at the lake include a boat dock, small store and campground.

From Route 180, Blue Road winds south through ten miles of rugged hills until it descends past a few horse ranches into Box Canyon, where the road follows the **Blue River**. Continue downstream past jagged Maness Peak nine miles to the junction with Forest Route 567 (Red Hill Road). Along the way, are tributaries, such as Centerfire Creek, which are home to small schools of rainbow and brook trout. Drive west on Red Hill Road, which twists and climbs out of the valley, often following ridges with panoramic vistas back to Route 191, about 14 miles south of Alpine.

LODGING   The wood-paneled **Tal-wi-wi Lodge** offers clean, comfortable rooms featuring rustic furnishings, some with fireplaces and spa tubs. There's a seasonal outdoor sauna. The restaurant serves breakfast and dinner on the weekends only, and the lounge often has live music or karaoke. ~ Route 191, four miles north of Alpine; 520-339-4319, fax 520-339-1962. BUDGET TO MODERATE.

If you came to the mountains seeking a cozy retreat, try the **Alpine Cabins**, which feature kitchenettes and cable TV. Closed December through March. ~ On Route 180, one half block east of the intersection with Route 191, Alpine; 520-339-4440. BUDGET.

Surrounded by pine forests, the **Coronado Trail Cabins and RV Park** offers a few cozy single-room cabins fully furnished with kitchenettes and bed covers. Barbecue and picnic areas are outside the units. RV sites have full hookups. ~ 25302 Route 191, Alpine; 520-339-4772; e-mail ctcrv@cybertrails.com. BUDGET.

A pair of Alpine motels offer clean, well-maintained rooms—some with kitchenettes—at reasonable prices. One is the **Mountain Hi Lodge.** ~ 42698 Route 180; 520-339-4311. Your other choice is the **Sportsman's Lodge.** ~ 42627 Route 191, Alpine; 520-339-4576. BUDGET.

About 22 miles south of Alpine, **Hannagan Meadow Lodge** rents rustic cabins with fireplaces and antique furnishings, and has a dining room. One of the oldest inns in the state, the lodge also has a general store. ~ Route 191 at Hannagan Meadow; phone/fax 520-339-4370, 800-547-1416; www.hannaganmeadow.com. BUDGET TO MODERATE.

You'll find home cooking and a casual friendly atmosphere at the **Bear Wallow Cafe.** Traditional favorites here include T-bone steak, chicken-fried steak, homemade bread and pies. ~ 42650 Route 180, Alpine; 520-339-4310. BUDGET.

DINING

One-stop shopping is the specialty at **The Tackle Shop,** where you can fill your tank, restring your crossbow, eat lunch or rent a video. ~ Junction of Routes 180 and 191, Alpine; 520-339-4338.

SHOPPING

If you need to stock up on groceries (other than tortilla chips and bean dip), head to **Alpine Country Store** for a standard selection of meat, produce and canned goods, as well as the latest gossip circulating the mountain village. ~ 42651 Route 180, Alpine; 520-339-4914.

Where Route 60 intersects with Route 191 and the Coronado Trail, you'll come to the town of Springerville, where you can make a detour and head west to the recreation and ski area of Pinetop–Lakeside, a winter resort popular with Phoenix residents.

▼▼▼▼▼▼▼▼▼▼▼▼▼▼▼▼
Pinetop–Lakeside Area

In the Springerville area, there are two places of interest worth stopping for. Situated on a rim of volcanic rock overlooking the Little Colorado River's Round Valley is **Casa Malpais Pueblo.** Tours originate at the museum in Springerville. Here, you'll learn

SIGHTS

that the Mogollon people abandoned the pueblo in 1400 A.D., and now the archaeological dig is open to the public. For the best pueblo views, take the guided tour up a steep basalt staircase to the top of the mesa. A tour highlight is the **Great Kiva** made of volcanic rock. Admission. ~ 318 Main Street, Springerville; 520-333-5375.

Follow a dusty, bumpy road for several miles and the unlikely reward is the **Little House Museum** on the X Diamond Ranch. Inside the two-story building are exhibits relating to the area's history, including ranching and horse show memorabilia. Beside it are two restored cabins more than 100 years old. One contains antique musical instruments ranging from a player piano to a Wurlitzer circus organ.

Another building has recently been built to house the expanding instrument collection as well as an exhibit on John Wayne, who had a ranch next door. Advance reservations are suggested. Closed Tuesday and Wednesday and from mid-September to mid-May (except by appointment). Admission. ~ Located just over three miles south of Route 260 on South Fork Road, near Springerville; 520-333-2286.

Climbing the steep incline of the Mogollon Rim leads to Show Low, Pinetop and Lakeside, forested hamlets of cabins, motels, resorts and campgrounds in a pine woods setting. Most of the commercial activity takes place in Show Low along Route 60.

There is actually a fascinating story behind **Show Low**'s name. Government scout Croydon E. Cooley and partner Marion Clark had a ranch here in the 1870s, but decided that it wasn't big enough for both of them. So they played a card game of Seven-Up to decide who would move. On the last hand, Cooley only needed one point to win. Clark said, "If you can show low, you win." Cooley threw down his hand and said "Show low it is," and pulled out an unbeatable deuce of clubs. He took the ranch, and it has been called Show Low ever since. In fact, the main street through town is called Deuce of Clubs after the winning hand.

SALT RIVER CANYON

Nicknamed the miniature Grand Canyon, the **Salt River Canyon** is a spectacular sight that you can drive right through on Route 60 about 50 miles south of Show Low. There's a bridge where Route 60 crosses the Salt River, which carved the canyon millions of years ago. Seven miles downstream from the bridge via a paved road are fascinating salt banks sacred to the Apache and colored with green, red and orange minerals and algae.

The population of Show Low swells from about 5500 year-round residents to more than 13,000 during the summer, when the big attractions are excellent trout fishing and big game hunting in the Mogollon Rim country and White Mountains. Also popular are hiking, horseback riding, golf and scenic drives. Many Arizonians also keep summer homes at the 6400-foot-elevation town to escape the blistering summer temperatures in Phoenix and other "flatlander" communities. During winter, the Sunrise ski resort on the White Mountain Apache Reservation is famous for its downhill runs and cross-country trails.

Southeast of Show Low lie the mountain resort twins of **Pinetop** and **Lakeside**, and beyond, the Indian towns of Whiteriver and Fort Apache. Lakeside is a starting point for hiking, fishing, camping and backpacking in and near the three resort communities, which are connected by a highway lined with motels, restaurants, gas stations and small businesses.

Built in 1916, the **Lakeview Lodge** is one of the oldest lodges in Arizona. The rustic lounge has a fireplace, high-beamed ceilings and Indian rugs hanging from the second-story railing. The nine rooms and cabins are simply furnished and come with a complimentary bottle of wine. Fishermen can use the private pond, then grill their catch on the premises. ~ 2251 Route 260, Pinetop–Lakeside; phone/fax 520-368-5253. MODERATE.

LODGING

A nice alternative to camping out is staying at the **Lake of the Woods Resort**. Twenty-nine log cabins are scattered amidst pine trees beside a private lake. All of the cabins have fireplaces, TVs, microwaves, kitchen and dining areas and outdoor barbecues. Although some cabins are geared toward honeymooners, most are more family oriented. Amenities include shuffleboard, horseshoes, spas, a sauna, playground, ping-pong, pool tables and boats for rent. ~ 2244 West White Mountain Boulevard, Pinetop–Lakeside; 520-368-5353; www.wmonline.com. BUDGET TO MODERATE.

Located on Sunrise Lake near the ski resort four miles south of Route 260 is **Sunrise Park Resort**, owned and operated by the White Mountain Apache Tribe. Guests come to fish in summer and ski in winter, staying at one of the 94 modern, nicely furnished hotel rooms. Amenities include a heated indoor pool, indoor and outdoor spas and restaurant and lounge. Closed April and May. ~ Route 273, 20 miles east of McNary; 520-735-7669, 800-554-6835, fax 520-735-7315; www.sunriseskipark.com. MODERATE TO DELUXE.

A beautiful setting amidst pine, spruce and aspen trees, rather than luxurious accommodations, are what you pay for at **Hawley Lake Resort**. The resort is remote—12 long, winding miles off Route 260—and situated on a lake in one of the highest points in the White Mountains. In the summer, this area is 40° cooler than the flatlands of Phoenix. The resort has twelve motel rooms and eight cabins overlooking the lake. If you get lucky fishing, grills are available outside and cabins have kitchenettes. The resort is located on the White Mountain Apache Indian Reservation. Amenities include a café, boat rentals, gas and a store. Closed from December through April. ~ Route 473, 19 miles east of McNary; 520-335-7511, fax 520-335-7434. MODERATE.

Pastoral is the only word for the setting at **Greer Lodge**, located on the Little Colorado River with a view of meadows and mountains. To many, it is *the* place to stay. Built by hand as a church retreat in 1948 out of ponderosa pine and aspen, it now is a charming getaway with eight rooms in the main lodge and nine cabins. The lounge/restaurant area has comfy couches, a huge fireplace, vaulted ceilings and almost floor-to-ceiling windows where guests can look out at the snow falling in winter. Country furnishings warm up the rooms, along with cozy rocking chairs and quilts on the beds. Horse-drawn sleigh rides and ice skating also available in winter; flyfishing in stocked ponds in summer. ~ Route 373, Greer; 520-735-7216, 888-475-6343, fax 520-735-7720. DELUXE.

Molly Butler Lodge is the oldest lodge in Arizona, built in 1910. Rooms are small and very basic, but prices are inexpensive. A nice touch are the plaques on each door with the name and information about a local pioneer. The on-site restaurant serves dinner only in winter and lunch and dinner in summer. ~ 109 Main Street, Greer; 520-735-7226. BUDGET.

Snowy Mountain Inn is a bed and breakfast nestled in the forest near a trout-stocked pond. Accommodations consist of seven separate log cabins and four knotty-pine bedrooms with private baths located inside the main building of the inn. Four of the cabins have private spas and all the cabins have fireplaces (gas-log) in the living room, housekeeping kitchens and lofts with queen

---

✔ CHECK THESE OUT—UNIQUE DINING

- *Budget:* Stroll through Globe's historic district and stop for breakfast at the **Blue Ribbon Cafe**, a celebrated eatery. *page 255*
- *Budget to moderate:* Dine on Mexican or American cuisine at **El Coronado**, a friendly place with the best eats in Safford. *page 259*
- *Moderate:* Look for **Mining Camp Restaurant and Trading Post** and its all-you-can-eat dining in Apache Junction. *page 246*
- *Moderate to deluxe:* Feast on New Zealand lamb or marinated quail at the intimate **Snowy Mountain Inn**. *page 270*

Budget: under $8   Moderate: $8–$16   Deluxe: $16–$24   Ultra-deluxe: over $24

beds and a sitting area. Three of the inn rooms have fireplaces and two have jacuzzi tubs. There is also a spacious common room furnished with soft, red leather couches and artifacts from the owner's travels. The gourmet restaurant has a high vaulted ceiling and a large rock fireplace. Hiking trails can be accessed from the property, which borders on National Forest land. ~ 38721 Route 373, Greer; 520-735-7576, fax 520-735-7705; www.snowy mountain.net. MODERATE TO DELUXE.

Charlie Clark's Steak House has been around since 1938. A Western theme predominates, with stuffed bear and deer and wildlife paintings. Prime rib, steak and seafood are the primary offerings, but vegetarian dishes are available upon request. ~ 1701 East White Mountain Boulevard, Pinetop; 520-367-4900. MODERATE TO ULTRA-DELUXE.

DINING

Coyote's Grill & Cantina has salads, sandwiches and hamburgers. Breakfast and lunch only Monday through Thursday; breakfast, lunch and dinner on Friday, Saturday and Sunday. ~ Lakeview Lodge, 2251 Route 260, Pinetop–Lakeside; 520-368-5253. BUDGET TO MODERATE.

Catch your own rainbow trout in Fred's Lake, just outside the door at **Farmer Dunn's Vittles**, and they'll cook it for you! An adjoining concession rents fishing equipment. Every night is fish fry night; otherwise, the fare is steak, chops, prime rib, burgers, sandwiches and chicken. Inside the cheery, barnlike building, farm implements hang on the walls. A clawfoot bathtub holds the salad bar, while soup warms on a wood-burning stove. Call ahead for hours. ~ 1543 East Fir Lane, Pinetop–Lakeside; 520-367-3866. BUDGET TO MODERATE.

For gourmet dining, try the **Snowy Mountain Inn**. Cuisine includes spinach ricotta flan, New Zealand lamb, roast duck and even kangaroo. The knotty pine walls adorned with creative artifacts give this elegant restaurant a cozy, intimate aura. ~ 38721 Route 373, Greer; 520-735-7576. MODERATE TO ULTRA-DELUXE.

Antiquing is popular in this area. Choices include **The Orchard Antiques** with quality furniture, Nippon china, vintage clothing and primitives; the shop is located in an old house. ~ 1664 West White Mountain Boulevard, Lakeside; 520-368-6563.

SHOPPING

Sherry's Jewelry & Antiques has gold and silver estate jewelry, Depression ware, glass and furniture. ~ Route 260, Ponderosa Plaza, Pinetop–Lakeside; 520-367-5184.

Primitives, pine and oak furniture, quilts, gifts and gourmet coffee beans are what you'll find at **Billings Country Pine Antiques and General Store**. ~ 103 West Yaeger Street, Pinetop–Lakeside; 520-367-1709.

PARKS

WOODLAND LAKE PARK 🚶🚴🏇🚤⛵ This 580-acre scenic park located in the middle of Pinetop–Lakeside, offers hiking, equestrian and mountain biking trails, volleyball courts, softball fields, boating and playgrounds. People can fish for trout from the shore and pier; a second newly constructed pier is wheelchair accessible. Tall, thin pine trees surround the lake and a one-mile paved loop trail encircles it. The park is also connected with the White Mountain Trailsystem (see "Hiking" at the end of the chapter). Other facilities you'll find in the park are restrooms, picnic tables, barbecues and ramadas ($10 reservation fee). ~ Located a quarter-mile south of Route 260 off Woodland Lake Road; 520-368-6700.

▼▼▼▼▼▼▼▼▼▼
St. Johns Area

From Show Low, head east on Route 60 and northeast on Route 61 to arrive at St. Johns. Built along the banks of the Little Colorado River, St. Johns, with a population of about 3500, serves as the Apache County seat. The Coronado Trail (Route 180/191), named after the Spanish explorer who first sojourned here, begins innocently enough in the high desert area near St. Johns.

SIGHTS

St. Johns has few sights, except for the **St. Johns Equestrian Center**, which is rapidly becoming one of the premier equestrian facilities in the Southwest, attracting horses and riders from New Mexico, Colorado and Utah, as well as throughout Arizona. Surrounded by rolling hills and juniper-studded deserts, amenities include an 80-acre cross-country course, rodeo arena, show and dressage rings, six-furlong race track, stables and RV sites. In spring and summer, the center hosts local and regional events, both Western and English, rodeos and other horse competitions. ~ Adjacent to St. Johns Airport; call City Hall at 520-337-4517 for more information.

You can find out about the area's history at the **Apache County Historical Society Museum**, which houses displays that include pioneer memorabilia and a log cabin, as well as a set of prehistoric woolly mammoth tusks and a camel's leg bone, both estimated to be about 24,000 years old. Closed weekends. ~ 180 West Cleveland Avenue, St. Johns; 520-337-4737.

If you need additional information, contact **St. Johns Regional Chamber of Commerce**. Closed Saturday and Sunday. ~ P.O. Box 178, St. Johns, AZ 85936; 520-337-2000.

The northern part of the **Coronado Trail** meanders through a region of juniper-dotted hillsides, alfalfa pastures, grazing cattle and a few sandy-topped buttes about 44 miles southeast of Petrified Forest National Park. The trail then heads south through Apache-Sitgreaves National Forest to Clifton.

As the Coronado Trail climbs on its journey south, chaparral gives way to pine and aspen, and you pass **Nelson Reservoir**, a 60-acre lake stocked with rainbow, brown and brook trout. If you are ready for a break, there are picnic grounds, restrooms and a boat ramp, but no overnight camping.

South of the reservoir are the rolling **Escudilla Mountains**, a 5000-acre wilderness area with forests of spruce, fir, pine and aspen, and nature trails where hikers are often rewarded with raspberries, elderberries and gooseberries, and glimpses of elk and deer in their natural habitat.

LODGING

St. Johns' lodging scene is unexceptional, but you'll find well-maintained rooms at **Days Inn**, a trailer-court type of motel with old-fashioned casement windows and adobe-like walls. A restaurant and lounge adjoin the motel. ~ 125 East Commercial Street, St. Johns; 520-337-4422, fax 520-337-4126. BUDGET.

The newly remodeled **Super 8 Motel** offers all the standard amenities including phones, coffee and cable color TV. ~ 75 East Commercial Street, St. Johns; 520-337-4126, 800-800-8000, fax 520-337-4478. BUDGET.

DINING

For a varied menu, try the **Rhino's Horn**, which orchestrates a good rendition of several Italian dishes including lasagna, pizza and calzones. You can also feast on frisbee-sized burgers, a slab of barbecue ribs or fresh catfish. ~ 855 West Cleveland Street, St. Johns; 520-337-2223. BUDGET TO MODERATE.

If you're craving something spicier, **El Camino** serves a traditional Mexican menu of tacos, enchiladas and tostadas. Closed Sunday. ~ 277 White Mountain Drive, St. Johns; 520-337-4700. BUDGET.

PARKS

CONCHO LAKE 🏊 ⛵ 🚤 ⛴ This lake, stocked with rainbow and brook trout, is a peaceful spot to drop a line. Non-motorized boating is allowed. Or you may choose to play a round of golf at the neighboring public course. The only facilities in the park are restrooms. ~ The lake is ten miles west of St. Johns off of Route 61; 520-337-2266.

▲ Free camping permitted.

LYMAN LAKE STATE PARK 🚶 🐎 🏊 🛶 🎣 🚣 ⛵ 🚤 ⛴ A small herd of buffalo greets visitors at the entrance to the park. Farther on, a 1500-acre lake lures both fishing and boating enthusiasts. In fact, it is the only lake in the White Mountains where powerboating is allowed, so waterskiers and jetskiers flock to Lyman Lake. This is also a good place to swim as there's a cove especially marked off for swimming. Anglers fish offshore for rainbow trout, catfish, bluegill and widemouth bass. The lake was formed by damming the Little Colorado River and is fed by snow-melt from the slopes of Mount Baldy and Escudilla Mountain. Other attractions include hiking the three trails, which range from a half a mile to one mile in length, and are dotted with Indian petroglyphs. From May through September, guided tours take hikers to petroglyph sites and a pueblo ruin. This 1180-acre park was the first recreational state park in Arizona and sits at an elevation of 6000 feet. Facilities include restrooms, a store and hot showers. Day-use fee, $4 per vehicle. ~ Eleven miles south of St. Johns off Route 180/191; 520-337-4441.

▲ There are 40 RV sites with electrical and water hookups and 21 developed sites for tents, complete with picnic tables and barbecue grills. Beach and wilderness camping are allowed. Fees are $10 per night for tents, $15 per night for RV hookups.

▼▼▼▼▼▼▼▼▼▼▼▼▼▼
Outdoor Adventures

FISHING

Eastern Arizona boasts numerous lakes that dot the area around Pinetop–Lakeside and Greer. Anglers will find plenty of challenge—and game fish—along the Old West Highway.

APACHE JUNCTION AREA   Saguaro, Canyon, Apache and Roosevelt lakes are popular year-round fishing meccas.

GLOBE   San Carlos Lake near Globe is the biggest fishing draw in this area.

SAFFORD AREA   Roper Lake in Safford attracts anglers from all over Arizona.

ALPINE AREA   Bear Wallow Creek, a tributary of the Black River, is famous for Arizona Native trout. Also on the **Black River** at different stops you can try for rainbow trout, while trout and catfish can be found in **Eagle Creek**. East of Alpine and dropping off into the Blue Primitive Area, rainbow trout can be found in **Luna Lake** and the ruggedly remote **Blue River**. North of Alpine you'll find rainbow, brown and brook trout in **Nelson Reservoir**. More casual anglers can seek catfish in the **San Francisco River** near Clifton. You can buy bait, tackle and a license at **The Tackle Shop**. ~ At the intersection of Routes 180 and 191, Alpine; 520-339-4338.

PINETOP–LAKESIDE AREA   To fish at the lakes on the White Mountain Apache Indian Reservation, which are stocked with rainbow and brown trout, contact the **Game and Fish Department**. ~ South Route 73, Whiteriver; 520-338-4385. For general fishing information in the White Mountains, stop by the **Arizona Game and Fish Department**. ~ 2878 East White Mountain Boulevard, Pinetop; 520-367-4281.

For private fly-fishing, catch and release, try **X Diamond Ranch**. ~ South Fork; 520-333-2286. There are quality waters with rainbow, brown and Apache trout as well as boat rentals and camping May through October at **Hawley Lake**. ~ Route 473, 19 miles from McNary; 520-335-7511. For fishing and camping supplies or a license, check with **Western Drug**. ~ 105 East Main Street, Springerville; 520-333-4321.

ST. JOHNS AREA   In the St. Johns area, 60-acre **Concho Lake** is a good spot for rainbow and brook trout (shore fishing only). **Lyman Lake State Park** has a lake stocked with trout, bass, catfish and bluegill. ~ Located 11 miles south of St. Johns off of Route 180/191; 520-337-4441.

RIVER RAFTING

During the spring runoff, the Upper Salt River offers some of the country's best whitewater rafting opportunities. **Sun Country Rafting** operates out of Globe and runs single- and multiday whitewater paddle trips from one to three days through the spectacular canyons of the Upper Salt River. ~ 520-425-8842, 800-272-3353.

WINTER SPORTS

Eastern Arizona increasingly attracts recreationally minded tourists, and not just in the summer. Locals are somewhat stunned by the growing number of winter visitors here in recent years.

ALPINE AREA   Cross-country skiing, sledding and snowmobiling are popular at **Hannagan Meadow**, 22 miles south of Alpine on Route 191, where there are over 11 miles of machine-packed trails, which are serviced after each storm. The snowmobiles in the area are prohibited from designated ski trails. Another good spot for cross-country skiers is **Williams Valley**, which features nine miles of groomed ski trails, plus an additional five and a half miles of marked trails. From Alpine, drive one and a half miles north on Route 191 to the Williams Valley turnoff, Forest Road 249, and continue for five miles.

PINETOP-LAKESIDE AREA   **Sunrise Park Resort** on the White Mountain Apache Indian Reservation has 800 acres of skiable area on three mountains and ten lifts. There's a base elevation of 9200 and a vertical drop of 1800 feet. Facilities include a snowboard park and a children's ski school, as well as groomed cross-country trails. ~ Located 20 miles east of McNary on Route 273; 520-735-7669.

HUNTING

Hunters love the forests around Alpine because of the abundance of both big and small game—such as mule deer, whitetail deer, elk, javelina, black bear, mountain lion, Merriam's turkey, bighorn sheep, pronghorn antelope, blue grouse, Albert's squirrels, cottontail rabbits, mourning doves, Gambel's quail and many waterfowl.

You can buy a license and supplies at **The Tackle Shop**. ~ Intersection of Routes 180 and 191, Alpine; 520-339-4338. For maps and information about the area, as well as a list of hunting guides, check at the **U.S. Forest Service Office.** ~ Intersection of Routes 191 and 180, Alpine; 520-339-4384.

GOLF   If you feel the need to tee off in the mountains, greens are scattered throughout the region. Most are nine-hole courses; keep in mind that many are closed in the winter.

APACHE JUNCTION AREA   In Apache Junction, try one of two 18-hole courses at the semiprivate **Gold Canyon Golf Club.** Cart and club rentals are available, as well as a golf pro for lessons. ~ 6100 South Kings Ranch Road; 602-982-9449.

GLOBE   **Cobre Valley Country Club** has a nine-hole course with lush greens, subtle breaks and slopes, club and cart rentals, a bar and a pro shop. ~ Route 88 north of Globe; 520-473-2542.

SAFFORD AREA   The **Mount Graham Country Club** offers an 18-hole course for year-round play, a pro shop, club and cart rentals and a lounge. ~ Two miles south of Safford at Daley Estates; 520-348-3140.

ALPINE AREA   You can tee off at the semiprivate **Alpine Country Club,** which features an 18-hole course, a restaurant and a lounge. Closed in winter. ~ 58 North County Road 2122; 520-339-4944.

PINETOP–LAKESIDE AREA   The Pinetop–Lakeside area offers **Silver Creek Golf Club,** an 18-hole course with club rentals, a clubhouse and a pro shop. ~ 2051 Silver Lake Boulevard, White Mountain; 520-537-2744. Also in the area is the 18-hole **Pinetop Lakes Golf & Country Club.** ~ 4643 Bucksprings Road; 520-369-4531. North of Pinetop–Lakeside, the **Show Low Country Club** offers a dramatic contrast between the front nine holes, lined with ponderosa pines, and the back nine in open high-desert terrain. Cart and club rentals are available as well as a golf pro for lessons. ~ 860 North 36th Drive, Show Low; 520-537-4564.

RIDING STABLES   This is the real Wild West; there's no better place to saddle up and take to the hills. If you're lucky, you may even find the legendary Lost Dutchman Mine and strike it rich—but if you don't, a ride in this beautiful backcountry is its own reward. Giddyup!

APACHE JUNCTION AREA   **Don Donnelly Stables at Gold Canyon** takes you on two- to four-hour and overnight rides to the foot of the Superstition Mountains and through the Sonoran desert. ~ 6010 South Kings Ranch Road, Gold Canyon; 602-982-7822. For trips into the Superstition Mountains, contact **O.K. Corral Stables.** They offer half-day, full-day (lunch provided) and longer rides into the wilderness. On the longer trips, all gear and food are provided (except sleeping bags). ~ P.O. Box 528, Apache Junction, AZ 85217; 602-982-4040.

PINETOP-LAKESIDE AREA   Between Pinetop and Greer at the Sunrise Ski Resort Park on the White Mountain Apache Reservation, you can saddle up at **Lee Valley Outfitters** for one-hour to overnight trips through the White Mountains, one of the most scenic areas in Arizona. There are also wagon rides in the summer and sleigh rides in the winter. ~ P.O. Box 207, Greer, AZ 89527; 520-735-7454.

If you don't get a chance to go horseback riding, at least take the opportunity to hoof it along some of Eastern Arizona's wilderness trails. Bird and animal enthusiasts should keep an eye peeled for samples of western wildlife; everyone should keep an eye on the panoramic views. All distances for hiking trails are one way unless otherwise noted.

HIKING

APACHE JUNCTION AREA   Usery Mountain Recreation Area offers the well-maintained **Wind Cave Trail** (1.5 miles), which is moderately challenging and popular with local climbers. The moderate-to-difficult **Pass Mountain Trail** (7 miles) takes about four hours to complete.

SAFFORD AREA   Arcadia Trail (5.1 miles), located in the Pinaleño Mountains, passes through a forest of Douglas fir, aspen and pine trees, along with wild raspberry vines. As the highest range in southern Arizona, hikers will see a panoramic view of the area.

ALPINE AREA   The 450,000-acre Apache-Sitgreaves National Forest is a hiker's paradise, with terrain ranging from piñon and juniper woodlands to high-elevation forests of spruce and fir, meadows and alpine lakes.

About 14 miles south of Alpine, hikers can explore the **Red Hill Trail No. 56** (9.7 miles), a trek along a dirt road that leads into the Blue Range Primitive Area. From the upper trailhead at the Right Fork of Foote Creek, just off Forest Route 567 a mile east of Route 191, the trail traces the ridges of the Red Hill mountains, then descends along Bush Creek on its way to the Blue River. About seven and a half miles from the upper trailhead, the trail

✔ **CHECK THESE OUT—UNIQUE OUTDOOR ADVENTURES**

- Sleep close to the stars at 10,720 feet atop Mount Graham, the highest point in the Pinaleño Mountains. *page 260*
- Escape the desert heat and try your luck at landing a rainbow trout at Hawley Lake. *page 274*
- Cross-country ski through Hannagan Meadow with its 11 miles of machine-packed trails. *page 275*
- Get back in the saddle and ride the trails through spectacular Gold Canyon. *page 276*

joins Tutt Creek Trail (#105) for the last two miles of the journey. The lower trailhead is at Tutt Creek near Blue Crossing Campground, off Forest Road 567 (Red Hill Road).

Swimming is ideal at Canyon, Apache and Roosevelt lakes.

If you like to do your hiking by horseback, corrals have recently been built at the upper and lower trailheads.

In the **Blue Range Primitive Area**, you'll find spectacular rock formations with steep escarpments, along with thick forests of spruce, fir and ponderosa pine. Keep a sharp watch for black bear, Rocky Mountain elk, bighorn sheep, javelina, mule deer, mountain lions and bobcats. The area is excellent for birdwatching; keep your binoculars trained for the Arizona woodpecker, American peregrine falcon and southern bald eagle.

West of the Coronado Trail (Route 191), the **Bear Wallow Wilderness** contains 11,000 acres including one of the largest stands of virgin ponderosa pine in the Southwest. **Bear Wallow Trail No. 63** (7.6 miles), which begins off of Forest Road 25, traces Bear Wallow Creek downstream from the trailhead (about 31 miles south of Alpine) through jagged canyons of spruce, fir, Ponderosa pine and aspen west to the San Carlos Apache Indian Reservation's eastern boundary. Two shorter trails connect with the main trail and creek from the north: **Reno Trail No. 62** (1.9 miles) and **Gobbler Point Trail No. 59** (2.7 miles).

There's excellent hiking in the **Escudilla Wilderness Area**, an alpine forest with peaks over 10,000 feet, ten miles north of Alpine. The **Escudilla National Recreation Trail** (3 miles) from Terry Flat takes you to the summit of Escudilla Mountain through aspen groves, pine forests and grassy meadows. The trailhead is along Forest Route 56, four and a half miles east of Route 191. Rangers at the **U.S. Forest Service** (intersection of Routes 180 and 191, Alpine; 520-339-4384) will provide detailed trail maps and advice on current conditions.

There area many guides and outfitters in the Alpine area. Operating out of Alpine is the **Neal Reidhead Alpine Guide Service**. Hikes through Blue River Unit 27 and Unit 1 offer ample opportunities to view bear, elk and bald eagles. ~ P.O. Box 596, Alpine, AZ 85920; 520-339-1936. For a complete list of current outfitters call the **Alpine Ranger District**. ~ 520-339-4338. Also in Alpine is **The Tackle Shop**. ~ P.O. Box 125, Alpine, AZ 85920; 520-339-4338.

PINETOP-LAKESIDE AREA The **White Mountains Trailsystem** contains about 180 miles of trails from Vernon in the east to Pinedale in the west. For a map of trails, stop by the **Lakeside Ranger District**. ~ 2202 South White Mountain Boulevard (Route 260); 520-368-5111. The Trailsystem has recently been completed and consists of ten loop trails. Some highlights are **Blue Ridge Trail** (8.7 miles roundtrip) in Pinetop–Lakeside, which is easy to moderate. It passes Billy Creek and climbs through tall pines to the top of Blue Ridge with vistas along the way. The newly completed **Ghost-of-the-Coyote Trail** (14-mile loop) begins near Pinedale. The fairly flat trail winds through juniper and pine forests.

The **Mogollon Rim Overlook** (1 mile roundtrip) is an easy hike with interpretive placards along the way and beautiful views of the valley below the Mogollon Rim. It's two miles north of Pinetop–Lakeside off Route 260.

ST. JOHNS AREA There are a couple of short trails that pass by ancient petroglyphs in **Lyman Lake State Park**. Along the way, you'll be able to enjoy views of the lake below.

▼▼▼▼▼▼▼▼▼▼
Transportation

CAR

The western anchor of the Old West Highway, Apache Junction, is about 30 miles east of Phoenix via **Route 60**. On its eastern end you can join the Highway at Safford via **Route 191** from Clifton, or **Route 70**, which crosses to Lordsburg, New Mexico. **Route 180/191** links the Coronado Trail towns of St. Johns, Alpine and Clifton. You can get to the Pinetop–Lakeside area from the west via Route 60, turning onto **Route 260** at Show Low. From the east, Route 260 connects to Route 180 at Springerville.

BUS

The closest **Greyhound Bus Lines** (800-231-2222) terminal to Coronado Trail towns is in Safford about 30 miles southwest of Clifton. ~ 404 5th Street, Safford; 520-428-2150.

CAR RENTALS

Along the Old West Highway, you can rent a car or van at **Cobre Valley Motors**. ~ Route 60, Globe; 520-425-4487. There is also **Hatch Brothers Auto Center**. ~ 1623 Thatcher Boulevard, Safford; 520-428-6000.

TEN

Southern Arizona

Southern Arizona is a vast region of grasslands and desert punctuated by some of the state's most beautiful mountains. Four ranges have peaks higher than 9000 feet—the Santa Catalinas, Santa Ritas, Huachucas and Chiricahuas. At the heart of the region is Tucson, an urban metropolis rising out of the Sonoran Desert. A rich cultural tradition ranging from the Pima tribe to the Jesuits reflects this community's close ties to neighboring Mexico.

Scattered east of Tucson are portions of the Coronado National Forest. To the southeast, the rolling grasslands and woodland hills around Patagonia are some of the state's best cattle and horse ranchland, while the Elgin area has acres of green vineyards where local wines are produced. Farther east is Sierra Vista, whose claim to fame is Fort Huachuca, a historic military base whose troops defeated Apache leader Geronimo. Some 11,400 soldiers and civilians are still based here. Nearby Tombstone and Bisbee are old mining towns. Tombstone, the town "too tough to die," survives by selling its history. There are museums and exhibits on every corner—each, of course, charging for the pleasure of your company. Visitors flock here to relive the rowdy life of the Old West, from the shootout at O.K. Corral to the gambling at Birdcage Theater. Bisbee has become a quiet artists' colony with a more bohemian flavor. Here, visitors can shop in historic buildings along Main Street, tour old mines and walk along the narrow, hilly streets dotted with Victorian architecture. Up around Willcox are orchards teeming with fruit and vegetables. In autumn, you can pick your own or stop at one of the many roadside stands.

South of Tucson is the most populated portion of southern Arizona. Off Route 19 is Tubac, an artists' community with about 100 studios and galleries. Farther south is the border town of Nogales, where you can bargain for Mexican crafts and sample authentic cuisine. Southwest of Tucson is a large, scarcely populated area containing the Tohono O'odham Indian Reservation, Cabeza Prieta National Wildlife Refuge and Organ Pipe Cactus National Monument. In the westernmost corner of the state is Yuma, a historic town on the Colorado River that attracts residents with its lush, subtropical climate, farmlands fertile with vegetables, citrus trees and groves of date palms.

Although Tucson and southern Arizona abound with history, the real reason people visit is for the natural beauty—for the meditative solitude of a desert that seemingly rolls on endlessly, creating vast spaces for the imagination.

▼▼▼▼▼▼▼▼▼▼

Tucson

The ultimate insult to a Tucson resident is to say his town is just like Phoenix. Like bickering siblings, the two cities have never gotten along well and each is proud of its unique personality. While Phoenix is a vast, sprawling city that welcomes booming development, Tucson would just as soon stay the same size and keep developers out—especially those who would alter the environment. Phoenix thrives on a fast pace; Tucson is informal, easygoing and in no great rush to get anywhere.

Surrounded by five mountain ranges and sitting in a cactus-roughened desert, Tucson is an arid, starkly beautiful place with wide-open skies and night silences broken only by the howling of coyotes. The highest mountains are powdered with snow in winter; the desert is ablaze with cactus blooms in spring.

Most of Tucson's 12 inches of annual precipitation arrives during the late summer monsoon season when afternoon thunderstorms roll through the desert with high winds and dramatic lightning shows. During summer, the average high temperature hovers around 98°. In winter, average highs are about 65°, making the city a popular spot for winter visitors, who come to golf and relax in the balmy weather.

Basically, Tucson is an affable, unpretentious town that feels comfortable with itself. There's no need to impress anyone here with high fashion—blue jeans are good enough for most places. Nor do wealth and conspicuous consumption have a large following. Most Tucsonians don't come here to make lots of money, but rather to live in a beautiful, natural area that's within driving distance of more of the same.

The cultural heritage of Tucson is a mix of Spanish, Mexican and American Indian. The city is only 60 miles from Nogales and the Mexican border, but you don't have to go that far to find Mexican food, artwork and culture. The red-tiled adobe homes spread across the valley reflect the residents' love of Spanish and American Indian architecture.

The Hohokam people were the first in the area. Father Eusebio Francisco Kino, a Jesuit priest, came to work with them and established a chain of missions, including Tucson's famous Mission San Xavier del Bac.

Later, the Spanish flag flew over the city, as did the Mexican, Confederate and United States flags. In 1867, Tucson was the capital of the Arizona Territory. But when the capital moved north, disgruntled Tucson was given the University of Arizona as compensation. This increased the population, and it jumped again just before World War II when nearby Davis-Monthan Air Force Base began training pilots to fly B-17 bombers. Today 750,000 people call Tucson home and live within the metro area's 500 square miles. The university has grown to 35,000 students, and Davis-Monthan is still an active military base with more than 7767 military personnel and civilians.

SIGHTS

Nine miles southwest of Tucson is the **Mission San Xavier del Bac** on the Tohono O'Odham Indian Reservation. Known as the White Dove of the Desert, this stunning white adobe church rises from the open desert floor and is picturesquely framed by blue sky and the mountains beyond. Although the Jesuits founded the mission in the 1600s, the present building was built between 1783 and 1797. It is a combination of Spanish, Byzantine and Moorish architecture. Visitors can walk in through weathered mesquite doors, sit on the worn wooden pews, and feast their eyes on the ornate statues, carvings, painted designs and frescoes. In addition to touring the facility, you can attend mass Tuesday through Friday, which is open to the public, or visit during one of the celebrations. ~ Signs appear as you drive south on Route 19; 520-294-2624.

Across the square in the **San Xavier Plaza**, American Indians sell fry bread and crafts.

Drive north to Speedway Boulevard, turn left and you'll reach Gates Pass, where the road begins to twist and you'll have splendid panoramic views of Tucson and the saguaro-dotted landscape of Tucson Mountain Park. This is where you'll find **Old Tucson Studios**, a re-creation of an old Western frontier town. Columbia Pictures created Old Tucson Studios in 1939 as a movie location for the film *Arizona*, and since then more than 300 films and television episodes have been shot here including *Rio Bravo*, *Gunfight at the O.K. Corral* and *El Dorado*. If a film crew is in town, you can watch them film. Otherwise, ride the narrow-gauge railroad, watch shootouts on the wide dirt streets, enter the adobe and slatboard buildings and listen to dance-hall music, or indulge in shopping. Closed Thanksgiving and Christmas. Call ahead for information. Admission. ~ 201 South Kinney Road; 520-883-0100.

Just a few minutes down Kinney Road is the **Arizona-Sonora Desert Museum**. A cross between a zoo and a botanical garden with more than 300 different animals and 1400 plant species indigenous to the Sonoran Desert, this facility has been ranked among the world's ten best zoos. Visitors can inspect the aquatic exhibits and the animals in their desert habitats, or walk inside an aviary and a re-created limestone cave (all exhibits are wheelchair accessible). Definitely worth a visit. Admission. ~ 2021 North Kinney Road; 520-883-2702.

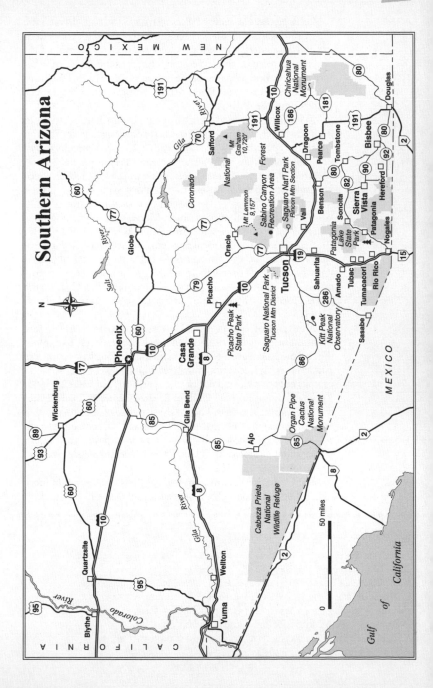

Southern Arizona

For a panoramic view of Tucson from 3100 feet, drive to the top of **A Mountain**. Settlers of territorial days used it as a lookout for Apache raiders. The latest raiders are students from the University of Arizona, who have been whitewashing the A on it before the first football game of the season since 1915. ~ Take Congress Street exit west off Route 10 to Cuesta Street, then go south onto Sentinel Peak Road.

El Presidio Historic District, running from Church Avenue to Alameda Street, was once the Presidio of San Augustin del Tucson, which the Spanish army enclosed with a 12-foot-high adobe wall in 1783. Today, the main attraction in El Presidio is the **Tucson Museum of Art**, a complex specializing in pre-Columbian, modern American and Southwestern art, along with several historic houses and the Plaza of the Pioneers—a showplace for the museum's sculpture collection. Closed Monday in summer. Admission (free on Tuesday). ~ 140 North Main Avenue; 520-624-2333.

Arizona's oldest historical museum, the **Arizona Historical Society Museum**, has everything from a full-scale reproduction of an underground mine tunnel to an exhibit on the history of transportation. Also at the museum is a special exhibit called "Life on the Edge: History of Medicine in Arizona." ~ 949 East 2nd Street; 520-628-5774

A big part of Tucson is the **University of Arizona**, a 350-acre campus dotted with red-brick buildings. If you decide to explore the campus, there are a few worthwhile stops. Student volunteers take visitors on free tours of the sprawling University of Arizona campus once or twice a day. For tour schedules, call 520-621-3641.

One definite stop is **Flandrau Science Center & Planetarium** with its laser light shows, science store, public observatory with a 16-inch telescope available for public use and science exhibits such as a mineral exhibit, a walk-through model asteroid and a night skies exhibit. Admission. ~ Corner of University Boulevard and Cherry Avenue; 520-621-7827.

The **Center for Creative Photography** has a collection of more than 50,000 photographs, along with galleries, a library and re-

---

✔ CHECK THESE OUT—UNIQUE SIGHTS

- Bask in the beauty of **Mission San Xavier del Bac**'s ornate statues, carvings and frescoes. *page 282*
- See Georgia O'Keeffe originals and 3000 other pieces of European and American art at the **University of Arizona Museum of Art**. *page 285*
- Bring your binoculars when you visit the **Ramsey Canyon Preserve**—the birdlife is colorful and plentiful. *page 303*
- Wander the ruins and cemeteries of **Duquesne** and other **ghost towns** off Route 82. *page 315*

search facilities. Photography exhibitions from the permanent collection and traveling exhibitions are displayed in the galleries. ~ 1030 North Olive Street; 520-621-7968.

The **University of Arizona Museum of Art** has Renaissance and later European and American art, including works by Rembrandt, Picasso, Rothko and O'Keeffe. The collection includes more than 3000 paintings, sculptures, drawings and prints. Closed Saturday. ~ Southeast corner of Park Avenue and Speedway Boulevard; 520-621-7567.

Tucson Botanical Gardens contains a small field of American Indian crops, a cactus and succulent garden, a tropical greenhouse, an herb garden, a sensory garden, a backyard bird garden and a xeriscape (arid landscaping) demonstration garden. Perhaps most unusual is the historic garden—lush foliage and flowers that surround and reflect the era of the 1920s Porter House. Two new gardens are the Plants of the Tohono O'Odham Path and *Nuestro Jardin* (a Mexican-American Garden). Admission. ~ 2150 North Alvernon Way; 520-326-9255.

The late Ted De Grazia gained fame painting impressionistic-style portrayals of the Southwest and its people. Today his home and galleries, the **De Grazia Gallery in the Sun**, are open to the public. Skylights in the adobe structures bathe his paintings in light. Walking through, you pass underneath brick archways and go through landscaped courtyards that he so lovingly tended when he lived here. The unusual architecture, including an iron gate inspired by the historic Yuma Prison, is worth a visit in itself. ~ 6300 North Swan Road; 520-299-9191.

Fort Lowell Museum is a reconstructed commanding officers'   ◀ HIDDEN
quarters from the days when it was a key military post during the Apache Indian wars of the 1870s and 1880s. Life on a military post in frontier Arizona is revealed through furnishings, artifacts and displays of military equipment. Closed Sunday through Tuesday. ~ 2900 North Craycroft Road; 520-885-3832.

Pima Air and Space Museum contains one of the largest collections of historic aircraft in the world. Among the 200 aircraft are the Boeing B-29 Superfortress, the type of plane that dropped the first atomic bomb on Japan, and the SR-71 Blackbird, the world's fastest aircraft. Admission. ~ 6000 East Valencia Road; 520-574-0462.

For a truly unusual experience, stop by **Columbia University's Biosphere 2 Center**, a controversial three-acre miniature replica of the earth with a tropical rainforest, savannah, marsh and desert. There are small greenhouses where different ecosystems are displayed. Research focus has shifted from sustainable agriculture to global climate changes. Although you can't go inside most of the airtight structure, you can visit the living quarters and the command room. You can also see the outside of this high-tech, space-age glass and steel monolith, look through its glass walls and stop by the visitors center. Tours are offered every day on the hour. Admission. ~ Route 77 Mile Marker 96.5, Oracle; 520-896-6200.

LODGING   Although Tucson is known for its upscale, full-service resorts—a haven for those escaping cold winters elsewhere—it also has a number of budget and mid-range accommodations.

Located across the street from the train and bus stations, the **Hotel Congress** is a piece of Tucson's history. The block-long classical brick and marble structure was built in 1919 to serve Southern Pacific railroad passengers, and John Dillinger's gang were among its guests. Geometric Indian designs add character to the lobby, which also provides seating for the Cup Café and overflow from the nightclubs. The renovated hotel rooms are decorated with black-and-white-tile bathrooms, black headboards and salmon-colored walls. Of the hotel's 40 rooms, seven are hostels with bunk or single beds and private baths. None of the rooms have televisions, but they *do* have a rarity nowadays—windows that open. Gay-friendly. ~ 311 East Congress Street; 520-622-8848, 800-722-8848, fax 520-792-6366; www.hotcong.com. BUDGET.

Originally built as a market in the 1920s, **Elysian Grove Market Bed & Breakfast Inn** now stands as a stunning abode with high ceilings, hardwood floors and two fireplaces. Folk art, rugs and antiques enliven both the house and its four colorful rooms. Two of the rooms were converted from wine cellars; two others have French doors that open onto a garden teeming with cactus, flowers and mesquite trees. Continental breakfast features Mexican pastries. ~ 400 West Simpson Street; 520-628-1522; www bbonline.com/az/elysiangrove. MODERATE.

Built in the 1930s, the **Arizona Inn** is a historic gem. Although it's in the middle of town, it feels like a lush oasis with 14 acres of lawns and gardens thick with orange trees, native cypress and date palms. No two of the resort's 86 rooms are alike, but all are decorated in the manner of the 1930s period and some have antiques. The inn also has a swimming pool, tennis courts, a restaurant and a cocktail lounge decorated with 19th-century Audubons. ~ 2200 East Elm Street; 520-325-1541, 800-933-1093, fax 520-881-5830. ULTRA-DELUXE.

The lobby of the **Sheraton Tucson** has a mural of Mexican village life and waterfalls. The 216 suites and rooms are Southwestern in style, but lean toward darker shades rather than pastels. The suites feature a couch, table, wet bar, coffeemaker, fridge, a television in an armoire, and a tiny balcony. The rooms have all of the above except the couch, armoire and balcony. Amenities include a swimming pool, restaurant, jacuzzi, exercise room, sauna and steam room. ~ 5151 East Grant Road; 520-323-6262, 800-257-7275, fax 520-325-2989. DELUXE.

For an assortment of affordably priced motels, drive down Miracle Mile, once the main thoroughfare through the city. The area is a bit seedy with several strip joints, but there are a few decent places. One is the **Best Western Ghost Ranch Lodge**. The property has 83 rooms housed in brick buildings surrounded by grassy lawns, palm trees and cactus gardens. The theme is Western, with a cow skull over the lobby fireplace and Western memorabilia throughout. There's also a restaurant, bar, pool and whirlpool. ~ 801 West Miracle Mile; 520-791-7565, 800-456-7565, fax 520-791-3898; www.ghostranchlodge.com. MODERATE TO DELUXE.

Bed and breakfasts are proliferating in Tucson. Built in 1905, the **Peppertrees Bed and Breakfast Inn** is a red-brick Territorial home. There are two Southwest-style, two-room guest houses, a one bedroom Mexican casita, and three main rooms furnished with period pieces from England. French doors lead outside to a beautifully landscaped patio. Room rate includes a full breakfast. ~ 724 East University Boulevard; phone/fax 520-622-7167, 800-348-5763; www.bbonline.com/az/peppertrees. MODERATE TO DELUXE.

La Posada del Valle is a stucco-and-adobe inn built in 1929. A novelty is afternoon tea, served in a living room furnished with art deco antiques from the '20s and '30s. The 1920s theme carries over to the five guest rooms, and each is named after famous women of that era. Sophie's Room is a favorite with an 1818 king-size Victorian bedroom set. Karen's Cottage, separate from the main house, is an early 1900s suite with an African motif. Full breakfast is included. ~ 1640 North Campbell Avenue; phone/fax 520-795-3840, 888-404-7113; www.bbhost.com/laposadadelvalle. MODERATE TO DELUXE.

Centrally located, **North Campbell Suites Hotel** offers four-room suites with kitchens. The 11 suites aren't fancy, but are homey and functional with adequate furnishings and a hide-a-bed

▲▲

✔ CHECK THESE OUT—UNIQUE LODGING

- *Budget:* Absorb some of Tucson's history at the 1919 **Hotel Congress**, built to accommodate Southern Pacific railroad passengers. *page 286*
- *Moderate:* Perch on Ajo's highest hill at **The Mine Manager's House Inn** for a view of the mine that was run by this abode's original residents in 1919. *page 317*
- *Deluxe:* Enjoy serene mountain scapes from your **Rio Rico Resort & Country Club** roost. *page 317*
- *Ultra-deluxe:* Pretend you're in paradise at the **Arizona Inn**, where 14 acres of lush gardens surround you. *page 286*

Budget: under $70   Moderate: $70–$110   Deluxe: $110–$180   Ultra-deluxe: over $180

in the living room for extra sleeping space. A swimming pool and trees help soften the look of the motor court. ~ 2925 North Campbell Avenue; phone/fax 520-323-7378. DELUXE.

Located on five acres of Sonoran desert, surrounded by saguaro cacti, is **Casa Tierra Adobe Bed and Breakfast Inn**. With a central courtyard and fountain, it is an elegant hacienda-style inn with vaulted brick ceilings, Mexican-style furnishings and four guest rooms with private patios overlooking the desert. There is a jacuzzi, a workout gym and a large common room with games, stereo and VCR. Full breakfast included. ~ 11155 West Calle Pima; 520-578-3058, fax 520-578-8445; e-mail casatier@azstarnet.com. DELUXE.

The Lodge on the Desert is a garden resort hotel with 39 adobe rooms grouped around patios that open to lawns and gardens. Rooms have beamed ceilings, handpainted Mexican tile accents, Monterey furniture, and many have mesquite-burning beehive fireplaces. Other amenities include a restaurant and a pool with mountain views. ~ 306 North Alvernon Way; 520-325-3366, 800-456-5634, fax 520-327-5834; www.lodgeonthedesert.com. DELUXE TO ULTRA-DELUXE.

Hawthorn Suites is a hacienda-style inn with rooms overlooking a lush courtyard dotted with Mexican fountains. The 90 guest rooms are clean and comfortable; some have kitchenettes. There is a pool and complimentary breakfast. ~ 7007 East Tanque Verde Road; 520-298-2300, 800-527-1133, fax 520-298-6756; www. hawthorn.com. DELUXE.

The resorts are expensive during winter high season, but most slash prices during the hot summer months. Among the best resorts is the **Westin La Paloma**. The 487 Southwest-style rooms have private balconies or patios, a sitting area, oversized closet and a stocked fridge. Many of the suites have wood-burning fireplaces and sunken spa tubs. There are three swimming pools including one with swim-up bar, Jack Nicklaus golf course, tennis and racquetball courts, a health center and, for tired parents, day care for the small fry! ~ 3800 East Sunrise Drive; 520-742-6000, 800-677-6338, fax 520-577-5877; www.westin.com. ULTRA-DELUXE.

Spread on 80 acres in the foothills of the Santa Catalina Mountains, the **Westward Look Resort** is a scenic getaway. The 244 rooms here are actually worth spending time in with their beamed ceilings, couches, refrigerator and wet bar, skylights, balconies and Mexican tile trim on the extra-long bathroom sinks. If you ever leave the room, check out the tennis courts, fitness center, pools, spas, restaurant or lounge. ~ 245 East Ina Road; 520-297-1151, 800-722-2500, fax 520-297-9023; www.westwardlook.com. DELUXE TO ULTRA-DELUXE.

Located in the foothills of the Santa Catalina Mountains, **Loews Ventana Canyon** is another 93-acre, luxury resort. Highlights are an 80-foot waterfall cascading down into a pond, and secluded paths lined with mesquite, squawbush and blue palo verde. Many of the 398 Southwest-style rooms have original artwork, burnished-pine furnishings, private balconies and bathrooms with marble floors. Amenities include five restaurants and lounges, tennis, golf, fitness trails, pools, a health club and shops. ~ 7000 North Resort Drive; 520-299-2020, 800-234-5117, fax 520-299-6832; www.arizonaguide.com/loews-ventana. ULTRA-DELUXE.

Looking for a little pampering? Then check out the **Omni Tucson National Golf Resort & Spa** where you can relax in the European spa with a massage, facial, herbal wrap and other treatments. Located on the northern edge of town, away from the city's hustle and bustle, the resort offers quiet and mountain views. The 167 rooms have wet bars and refrigerators, and most have private patios overlooking the championship 27-hole golf course. Other amenities include a gift shop, restaurant, beauty salon, pool, tennis and basketball. ~ 2727 West Club Drive; 520-297-2271, 800-

POINTS OF INTEREST
- **A** A Mountain
- **B** El Presidio Historic District
- **C** Fort Lowell Park
- **D** Gene C. Reid Park
- **E** Mission San Xavier del Bac
- **F** Tucson Botanical Gardens
- **G** Tucson Mountain Park
- **H** University of Arizona

Tucson

528-4856, fax 520-297-7544; www.tucsonnational.com. ULTRA-
DELUXE.

Just north of town is **The Triangle L Ranch Bed & Breakfast**,
an 1880s homestead on an 80-acre ranch. The four private cottages include an ivy-covered adobe cottage with a clawfoot tub in
the bathroom and screened sleeping porch, and one with a stone
fireplace, rose arbor entry and private patio. Two of the cottages
have kitchens and multiple bedrooms. A wood-burning stove
warms the kitchen for breakfast, which consists of eggs from the
owner's chickens and other homemade treats. The ranch rents the
cottages September through June. Closed in summer. ~ 2805 Triangle L Ranch Road, Oracle; 520-896-2804, 888-782-9572;
www.triangle/ranch.com. MODERATE TO DELUXE.

Northeast of town on Mount Lemmon is the **Alpine Lodge**.
It's part pub, part six-room inn. Rooms are plainly furnished with
light-brown carpet, table and chairs, a dresser and shower/
bathroom. No televisions or phones. ~ 12925 North Sabino Canyon Road, Summerhaven; 520-576-1544; www.mtlemmon.com/
alpine. htm. MODERATE.

Picacho Motel & Apartments has been around since the
1930s. Just outside the 26 rooms are palm and fruit trees, while
inside is somewhat worn wood paneling hung with country pictures, along with bureaus and desks. ~ 6698 Eisenhower Street,
Picacho; phone/fax 520-466-7500. BUDGET.

For information on bed and breakfasts throughout Arizona,
contact the **Arizona Association of Bed & Breakfast Inns**. ~ P.O.
Box 36656, Tucson, AZ 85740-6656; 800-284-2589; www.
bbonline.com/az/aabbi/index.html.

DINING   **Mi Nidito** is a tiny, tacky, crowded Mexican joint with great food,
from enchiladas to menudo. Portions are generous and there are
always plenty of locals lining up to fatten their waistlines. Walls
are covered with murals of palm trees. Closed Monday and Tuesday. ~ 1813 South 4th Avenue; 520-622-5081. BUDGET.

Micha's is a larger restaurant owned by the Mariscal family for
many years and whose portrait is just inside the door. You won't
leave here hungry—even the flour tortillas are about a foot in
length. Don't miss the chimichangas, topopo salad or grilled
shrimp fantasia. ~ 2908 South 4th Avenue; 520-623-5307. BUD-
GET TO MODERATE.

HIDDEN ►   Located in the warehouse district, **Tooley's** has good, inexpensive food. Customers order food at the counter, then sit in the
dining room or patio. The menu boasts that Tooley's is home of
the turkey taco, and turkey is used instead of chicken in all their
entrées. If you're watching your wallet, you can't beat the super
low prices. Lunch only. Closed Sunday. ~ 299 South Park Avenue;
520-882-9758. BUDGET.

Delectables is decorated with brass chandeliers and turn-of-the-century oak antiques. Inside are wood tables, wood-beamed ceilings and curving tinted windows that look out onto 4th Avenue, while outside are green metal tables covered in floral tablecloths, with matching chairs. This eatery offers fresh ruby trout and New York strip steak plus salads and sandwiches. ~ 533 North 4th Avenue; 520-884-9289. BUDGET TO MODERATE.

For the innovative in pizza, try **Magpies Pizza**. Examples of their fare include The Greek with spinach, basil, garlic, piñon nuts, feta cheese, cheese and sun-dried tomatoes, or Cathy's with garlic, stewed tomatoes, mushrooms, artichokes, roasted red peppers and Romano cheese. Located in a small strip center, Magpies has a contemporary look with a black-and-white-tile floor, wooden chairs and modern art on the walls. ~ 605 North 4th Avenue; 520-628-1661. BUDGET TO DELUXE.

There is an eclectic mix of cuisine in Tucson—but Southwest- and Sonoran-style Mexican fare are the specialties. Walk into **Café Poca Cosa** and you're bombarded with festive color. Green paint covers the ceilings, red chile peppers dot the walls, lights hang on indoor trees, and purple, green and red tiles cover the tables. The menu changes two or three times daily, and is written on a blackboard that's brought to the table. Dishes are homestyle Mexican. Specialties include chicken breast in mango sauce, *pollo en chipotle* (chile) sauce and pork marinated in beer. Closed Sunday. ~ 88 East Broadway; 520-622-6400. MODERATE.

Bentley's House of Coffee & Tea has wooden tables and chairs and the walls display rotating art shows. Food is typical café fare—soups, sandwiches, quiches—while beverages include espresso, gourmet coffee and a wide range of Italian cream sodas. ~ 1730 East Speedway Boulevard; 520-795-0338. BUDGET.

At the **Arizona Inn,** you choose the ambience: formal dining room, casual patio or courtyard ablaze with tiny lights in the trees. The fare includes Continental, Southwestern, nouvelle and traditional selections. One treat is the fresh steamed fish, enhanced with ginger and leeks, and served at your table from a bamboo steamer. ~ 2200 East Elm Street; 520-325-1541. DELUXE TO ULTRA-DELUXE.

Tork's Too is a family-run place with only a handful of tables and delicious Middle Eastern and North African food. The *shawerma* plate with beef, chicken or lamb contains strips of meat cooked with onions and bell peppers. Other choices are the vegetarian falafel plate, hummus dip, tabouleh and kabobs. Closed Sunday. ~ 3502 East Grant Road; 520-325-3737. BUDGET.

Buddy's Grill is a white-collar hangout. The narrow, blue-and-white room consists mainly of booths. Here, you'll find fajita salads, sandwiches, burgers cooked on a mesquite-wood grill and delicious baked French onion soup. You might also take a peek at the exhibition kitchen. ~ 4821 East Grant Road; 520-795-2226. BUDGET TO MODERATE.

At the **Blue Willow Restaurant,** you can either dine inside the house with its light peach walls and artsy posters, or opt for the brick, vine covered courtyard. Either choice is a winner. Although they serve sandwiches and salads at lunch and dinner, breakfast is the most popular meal here with 24 omelettes, including one with avocados, jack cheese and green chiles. ~ 2616 North Campbell Avenue; 520-795-8736. MODERATE.

Two minutes away is **Coffee Etc.,** where it's best to skip the entrée and go straight for the dessert and coffee. Favorites are the Snicker cheesecake served with Danish nutcream or cocoa almandine coffee. Resembling an open air café, the restaurant has umbrellas over the tables and clouds painted on the ceilings. ~ 2830 North Campbell Avenue; 520-881-8070. BUDGET TO MODERATE.

For Southwestern food, try **Café Terra Cotta.** The outdoor patio is lit by miniature white lights at night, while the indoor section is decorated in turquoise and terra cotta colors. Entrées include large prawns stuffed with herbed goat cheese and Southwestern tomato coulis, stuffed red and green chiles, and pizzas that are cooked in the woodburning oven and topped with ingredients such as herbed mozzarella, lime and cilantro. ~ 4310 North Campbell Avenue; 520-577-8100. BUDGET TO DELUXE.

In St. Philips Plaza, the casually elegant **Daniel's Restaurant** has received national acclaim for its Northern Italian cuisine since opening several years ago. Inventive appetizers such as sweet-potato chips layered with housemade gravlax, red-onion capers and chive oil lead the way for traditional pasta dishes and an array of lamb, veal and fresh fish entrées. The menu also boasts an extensive wine, grappa, beer and single malt scotch list. ~ 4340 North Campbell Avenue, Suite 107; 520-742-3200. DELUXE TO ULTRA-DELUXE.

It's hard to beat dining at **Anthony's in the Catalinas** with its top-notch views and ambience. The almost floor-to-ceiling windows look over the city lights in this hacienda-style building. Dinner is served on elegant china with pale pink linens, fresh flowers and classical music playing in the background. Chandeliers hang from the vaulted, beamed ceiling and a large fireplace warms the room in winter. The Continental specialties include veal sonoita with sun-dried tomatoes and roasted garlic, lamb Wellington and chateaubriand. Wash it down with a bottle from the extensive selection of about 1300 wines. Closed Saturday and Sunday for lunch only. ~ 6440 North Campbell Avenue; 520-299-1771. DELUXE TO ULTRA-DELUXE.

Szechuan Omei Restaurant is a Chinese restaurant where you can choose from more than 135 entrées, including lunch specials. Decor is nothing fancy, just red tablecloths and chairs and the usual Chinese lanterns and paintings. ~ 2601 East Speedway Boulevard; 520-325-7204. BUDGET.

The **Presidio Grill** offers dishes with a Southwestern flavor. Try an appetizer of roasted whole garlic and brie with marinated peppers, followed by Presidio chicken pasta prepared with browned garlic, poblano chiles, prosciutto, fresh basil, roma tomatoes and olive oil. Decor here is "architectural fantasy" with a variety of colors accenting the walls. And for those booth aficionados among us, it's nice to find a place with more booths than tables. The Silver Room offers a more formal setting with white tablecloths and metal accents. ~ 3352 East Speedway Boulevard; 520-327-4667. DELUXE.

The two boulevards boasting the largest concentration of restaurants in Tucson are Broadway and Speedway.

Jamaica Bay Café has, as one would expect, a tropical setting with high ceilings, plants and colorful carpeting. They serve breakfast only, an all-American buffet. ~ 6350 East Speedway Boulevard; 520-296-6111. MODERATE.

Classical music, fresh flowers and candles—all help set a romantic mood at **Le Rendezvous**, a French restaurant where the specials change daily depending on the market. Sample the Grand Marnier soufflé, which takes 45 minutes to make, the duck à l'orange, or veal medallions with apple and calvados. ~ 3844 East Fort Lowell Road; 520-323-7373. MODERATE TO ULTRA-DELUXE.

The Sonoran-style dining room of the **Tanque Verde Ranch** has picture windows facing the desert mountains, a corner fireplace and elegant mahogany tables with carved Mexican chairs. Entrées change, but often include such choices as mesquite-barbecued pork loin ribs with poblano chile hushpuppies, duckling glazed with prickly pear cactus syrup, pecan fried chicken or broiled salmon with bérnaise sauce. ~ 14301 East Speedway Boulevard; 520-296-6275. DELUXE.

Webb's Old Spanish Trail Steak House specializes in delicious barbecue ribs and chicken, as well as steaks. At night, settle down by the picture window. There's also outdoor patio dining. Closed Monday and Tuesday. ~ 5400 South Old Spanish Trail; 520-885-7782. MODERATE.

An old-fashioned pancake house with a European feel, **Millie's Pancake Haus** is a welcoming spot for breakfast or lunch with its cozy brick and wood interior, tied-back lace curtains, displays of bric-a-brac and pleasant staff. Along with pancake choices, the menu features Russian blintzes, corn cakes, omelets and daily specials. Breakfast and lunch only. Closed Monday. Millie's has two locations. ~ 6530 Tanque Verde Road; 520-298-4250 and 7053 North Oracle Road; 520-797-8997. BUDGET.

◄ HIDDEN

For something special you can't beat **Janos**, which serves French-inspired Southwestern cuisine created by award-winning chef Janos Wilder. Menus are seasonal, but typical entrées are pepito-roasted lamb loin with wild mushroom spoon bread and ancho-chile sauce, or sesame-crusted ahi with stir-fried Napa cabbage and mango sauce. Closed Sunday. ~ 3770 East Sunrise Drive; 520-615-6100. ULTRA-DELUXE.

In a landscape full of cactus and mesquite you'll find **The Tack Room**, a truly Western dining experience. Inside the Italianate villa, the feel is rustic with horse saddles, a deer head above the fireplace, rough-hewn beamed ceilings and a stone fireplace. But instead of Western wear, waiters sport tuxedos and the food, adorned with a twist of Southwest flavor, is anything but casual. Try the rack of lamb with mesquite honey, which comes with chile-cheese corn muffin, the northern Pacific salmon with sun-dried tomato pesto and chives, ginger-lime butter and sautéed red chard, or other steak and seafood entrées. ~ 7300 Vactor Ranch Trail; 520-722-2800. ULTRA-DELUXE.

HIDDEN ▶

Walk through antique, hacienda-style doors and you're inside **Tohono Chul Tearoom**, located in a rustic, 52-year-old house in the midst of Tohono Chul Park. Unless the weather is bad, opt for outdoor dining in the lush courtyard or on a patio that sits amid a wildflower landscape and offers free entertainment from the birds and other critters that come to nibble. For lunch, innovative sandwiches, soups and salads are served. Other choices are breakfast, Sunday brunch and afternoon tea. No dinner. ~ 7366 North Paseo Del Norte; 520-797-1222. MODERATE.

SHOPPING

If you want anything with a Southwestern flair, Tucson is where you'll find it. You'll also find shops catering to almost every need, with the majority of the artsy and antique shops downtown and various specialty shopping plazas scattered throughout the town.

For shopping mixed with entertainment, head for the **Tucson Arts District** on the first and third Saturday of the month when "Downtown Saturday Night" is held. During this event, stores, restaurants and galleries stay open late, musicians perform in the streets, and the area becomes a hot night spot for entertainment-seekers and shopaholics. There are over 40 galleries and artists' studios, in addition to antique, novelty and specialty shops. Every Thursday an "Artwalk" is held in the district, making stops at exhibit rooms, galleries and artists' studios. Programs are available at the information booth on the corner of 6th Avenue and Congress Street. ~ Located downtown roughly between Congress Street and Broadway, and Stone and 4th avenues; 520-624-9977.

Built in 1939, **Broadway Village** was one of the first shopping centers in Arizona. It houses a variety of shops in whitewashed red-brick buildings. ~ Corner of Broadway and Country Club Road. The more unusual includes a tiny mystery bookshop called

HIDDEN ▶

Clues Unlimited. ~ 123 South Eastbourne; 520-326-8533. There's also an expensive, fashionable children's boutique called **Angel Threads**. ~ 3050 East Broadway; 520-326-1170.

In the Broadway Village area there's **Yikes!**, a toy store with unusual gifts, small toys and books. Connected to Yikes! and sharing the same phone number, **Picante** sells various imported gift items, T-shirts, ethnic clothing and jewelry. ~ 2930-2932 East Broadway; 520-622-8807.

A worthwhile stop in El Presidio Historic District is the **Tucson Museum of Art gift shop** with contemporary pottery and other artistic gifts. ~ 140 North Main Avenue; 520-624-2333.

Nearby is **4th Avenue** with over 100 shops and restaurants. Shops in this older neighborhood contain vintage clothing, unique fashions, jewelry, books and art. Don't be surprised to find touches such as incense burning in the shops.

Antigone Books specializes in books by and about women as well as gay and lesbian literature. ~ 411 North 4th Avenue; 520-792-3715. For clothing, try **Jasmine** with its natural fiber clothing, some handwoven in Morocco. ~ 423 North 4th Avenue; 520-629-0706. **Del Sol** carries Southwestern clothes, scarves and jewelry, and a huge selection of rugs made by the Zapotecs of Mexico. ~ 435 North 4th Avenue; 520-628-8765. **The Jewel Thief** offers a huge selection of earrings, with most hanging on large boards around the shop and many priced at under $10. ~ 557 North 4th Avenue; 520-623-7554.

On the vintage side, stop by the **Tucson Thrift Shop**, which specializes in vintage clothing from the 1960s. ~ 319 North 4th Avenue; 520-623-8736. Another thrift store is **Loose Change**, a funky place with used vintage and contemporary clothing that you try on in rooms closed off with refrigerator doors. ~ 417 North 4th Avenue; 520-622-5579.

For Mexican imports, check out what is unofficially called the Lost Barrio Warehouse District—a group of shops located in old, red-brick warehouses. **Rustica** sells Southwestern and Mexican furnishings and accessories. ~ 200 South Park Avenue; 520-   ◄ *HIDDEN*

TED DE GRAZIA

One of Arizona's most renowned artists was Ted De Grazia, who depicted the Southwest in paintings, prints, bronzes and collector's plates. His distinctive, impressionistic-style works, with their signature bright colors and featureless faces, hang in Tucson's De Grazia Gallery in the Sun. Born in Morenci, Arizona, in 1909, De Grazia spent his life traveling through Mexico and the Southwest, learning the lore of the Apache, Navajo, Yaqui and Papago tribes and collecting three art degrees. One of his most surprising moves came in 1976. To protest the severe taxes on heirs of artists, he burned 150 of his paintings—valued at $1.5 million. He was irate that his wife would have to sell most of these paintings to pay the inheritance tax on their value whenever he died. In 1982, De Grazia died of cancer.

HIDDEN ▶   623-4435. **Magellan Trading Company** has great buys on Mexican glassware as well as handicrafts, artifacts and furniture from Mexico, New Guinea, Indonesia and Africa. ~ 228 South Park Avenue; 520-622-4968.

Among the many notable downtown galleries is the **Kaibab Courtyard of Shops**, which for over 50 years has been a source of collector-quality Hopi Kachina dolls, Zuni fetishes, Navajo and Zapotec weavings, Mexican folk art and more. ~ 2841 North Campbell Avenue; 520-795-6905. Offering a wide choice of contemporary arts and crafts in a variety of media is **Obsidian Gallery**. ~ 4340 North Campbell Avenue; 520-577-3598. Another good stop is **Milagro Art Gallery**, which presents traditional and unique works in all media by regional, national and internationally established artists. ~ 2920 North Swan Road, Suite 119; 520-323-1138.

St. Philips Plaza is a cluster of Southwest-style shops with red-tile roofs that include art galleries, clothing stores and restaurants. ~ Corner of River Street and Campbell Avenue. **Bahti Indian Arts** offers American Indian crafts such as drums, jewelry, rugs, pottery and kachina dolls. ~ 4300 North Campbell Avenue; 520-577-0290. **El Presidio Gallery Inc.**, a large fine-arts gallery with original Southwestern art in a variety of media, has two locations. ~ 4340 North Campbell Avenue, Suite 62, and 7000 East Tanque Verde Road; 520-529-1220.

One of the most popular shopping venues, judging by the ever-crowded parking lot, is **Bookman's**—*the* place for bibliophiles to browse. The owner claims the largest selection of used books and magazines in the Southwest. Bookman's also has a rare-book room and sells used magazines, records, tapes, video games, computer software and CDs. ~ 1930 East Grant Road; 520-325-5767.

Drive down River Street and you will see **River Center**, a Southwest-style shopping plaza. The stores surround a brick courtyard with a fountain and waterway. **The West** (520-299-1044) has cookbooks, cards, kids gifts and needlework supplies, with proceeds going to local women's and children's charities. ~ River Center: corner of River Street and Craycroft Road.

For a fun, unusual children's toy store, stop by a place called **Mrs. Tiggy–Winkle's**. ~ 4811 East Grant Road, Suite 151; 520-326-0188.

For antiques outside of the downtown area, browse through **Unique Antique**, a 90-dealer antique mall that owners claim is the largest in Southern Arizona. ~ 5000 East Speedway Boulevard; 520-323-0319.

In the Plaza Palomino, **Orient East** specializes in Asian imports including lamps, furnishings, artifacts and jewelry. ~ At Swan and Fort Lowell streets; 520-323-6250.

Casas Adobes Shopping Center is yet *another* Southwest-style shopping plaza with a variety of specialty shops. ~ 7051 North Oracle Road. A favorite is **Antigua de Mexico**, a Latin American import store with Mexican Colonial and Southwestern furniture, folk art, pottery, glassware, tinware and sterling silver from Taxco. ~ 7037 North Oracle Road; 520-742-7114.

Bargain shopping in a beautiful setting describes **Foothills Mall**. Painted clouds cover the ceiling between skylights, and a waterfall tumbles down steps from ceiling to floor. Stroll through the toy train museum, then stop by the specialty shops. For marked-down designer clothing, there's **Sak's Fifth Avenue** (520-544-0449). Other outlets include **Donna Karan**, **Bali**, **Samsonite**, **Black & Decker**, **Mikasa**, **Nike** and **Adidas**. With only about 40 stores and restaurants, shopping here tends to be more relaxed than at the megamalls in town. ~ 7401 North La Cholla Boulevard; 520-742-7191.

NIGHTLIFE

For alternative music—and alternative crowds—peek into **Club Congress** adjoining the Hotel Congress. Tucson's unconventional set mixes with the college crowd at this cavernlike place with a red-and-brown-tile floor and dark walls. There's live music on Monday and Friday; a deejay spins tunes the rest of the week. Cover. ~ 311 East Congress Street; 520-622-8848.

Once a blacksmith shop, store and nightclub in the 1930s, today **Cushing Street Bar and Restaurant** is a popular bar. Patrons here enjoy drinks at turn-of-the-century tables and chairs amid antiques such as a floor-to-ceiling, 1880s legal bookcase and a circa-1850 cut-glass globe above the bar. There's also an outdoor patio. ~ 343 South Meyer Avenue; 520-622-7984.

The **Outback** offers a whole complex for evening entertainment—cocktails in an outdoor patio, dancing in the Thunderdome, light dining in the Down-under Cafe, and billiards in the Boomerang Bar. Always open Tuesday, Wednesday, Friday and Saturday. Open other days for special events. Cover. ~ 296 North Stone Avenue; 520-622-4700.

Bum Steer is a casual place in a large, barnlike building containing a restaurant, several bars, a video arcade, volleyball court and small dancefloor. Inside, everything from cannons to airplanes hang from the vaulted roof. Entertainment includes live rock bands on Thursday and a deejay spinning dance music on Friday and Saturday. Cover on Thursday and Friday. ~ 1910 North Stone Avenue; 520-884-7377.

For traditional jazz Thursday, Friday and Saturday night, stop by **Café Sweetwater**, a narrow bar squeezed next door to the restaurant of the same name. ~ 340 East 6th Street; 520-622-6464.

Graffiti on the tables and walls is the decor at **Bob Dobbs' Bar & Grill**, a local hangout for the college and older crowd. A bright, noisy place, it has indoor and outdoor seating and plenty of televisions for catching the latest sports coverage. ~ 2501 East 6th Street; 520-325-3767.

Gentle Ben's Brewing Co. is a microbrewery near campus with delicious European-style ales. If you're there at the right time of the day, you can actually see workers brewing. This two-story building is furnished with recycled tables and chairs, and there's outdoor seating where you can see and be seen. On Wednesday, Paul Elia sings Sinatra, backed by a four-piece band, on Thursday there is a live disco band and on Saturday a deejay plays dance tunes. Cover for live bands. ~ 865 East University Boulevard; 520-624-4177.

Trophies is a popular sports bar offering pool, darts, satellite TV and casual fare. ~ Sheraton Tucson, 5151 East Grant Road; 520-323-6262.

Laffs Comedy Café hosts everything from national to local acts. Saturday, starting at 5 p.m., is open mike night, Wednesday is ladies night and Thursday is college and military I.D. night. The schedule can change, so call ahead. Cover. ~ 2900 East Broadway; 520-323-8669.

Decorated with lots of oak and brass, **Suite 102** is where lawyers and other professionals meet. There's an outdoor dining area and background contemporary tunes. ~ 5350 East Broadway; 520-745-9555.

Follow the cowboy hats and neon lights and you'll find **Cactus Moon**, a huge place specializing in country music. Western artwork hangs on the walls and rodeos roll on movie screens. A glittering, colored light shines on the dancefloor, which is big enough for two-steppers not to be toe-steppers. Closed Monday and Tuesday. Weekend cover. ~ 5470 East Broadway; 520-748-0049.

Berkey's Bar is a good place to hear the blues with live music. A mixed crowd hangs out here, ordering drinks from the glass block bar, dancing and shooting pool. Cover on Friday and Saturday. ~ 5769 East Speedway Boulevard; 520-296-1981.

The Chicago Bar and Grill offers a heady mix of music. There is rock-and-roll on Monday and Tuesday, reggae on Thursday and Saturday, and blues on Sunday, Wednesday and Friday. Chicago memorabilia covers the walls, from White Sox parking signs to hometown banners. Cover Wednesday through Saturday. ~ 5954 East Speedway Boulevard; 520-748-8169.

Tucson McGraws is bar and dining room serving steaks and ribs. Step outside, walk down the steps and you'll land on the terrace ramada that looks toward the Santa Rita Mountains and Tucson's beautiful sunsets. An outdoor fireplace warms customers on cold evenings. ~ 4110 South Houghton Road; 520-885-3088.

THEATER Arizona Theater Company has been unofficially called the State Theater of Arizona and performs six varied productions in Phoenix and Tucson from September to May. ~ 330 South Scott Avenue; 520-622-2823. Plays by the Arizona Theater Company and other groups are performed in the restored Spanish Colonial revival **Temple of Music and Art** in Tucson and the **Herberger Theater Center** in Phoenix.

Tucson has more sunshine than any other city in the United States—about 350 days each year.

Gaslight Theatre offers corny musical melodramas. Patrons eat free popcorn while hissing at the villain and cheering for the hero or heroine. Many of the comedies are original, written especially for the theater. ~ 7010 East Broadway; 520-886-9428.

Invisible Theatre has classics, musicals and Off-Broadway plays by Arizona playwrights and contemporary dramatists from September through June. ~ 1400 North 1st Avenue; 520-882-9721.

OPERA, SYMPHONY AND DANCE Ballet Arizona is the state's professional ballet company that performs in both Tucson and Phoenix. They perform a repertoire of classical and contemporary works including world and national premieres from September through April. ~ 888-322-5538.

Arizona Opera serves both Tucson and Phoenix and produces Grand Opera. The season runs from October through March, and productions have included *Don Giovanni, Otello* and *Madame Butterfly*. ~ 260 South Church Avenue, Tucson; 520-293-4336.

For classical, pops and chamber concerts there is the **Tucson Symphony Orchestra**. Performances run from September through May. ~ 2175 North 6th Avenue; 520-792-9155.

Centennial Hall hosts a full lineup on an international scale, from Chinese acrobatics to African dances to Broadway shows. Past performers include Itzhak Perlman, the Prague Symphony Orchestra and George Winston. ~ University of Arizona, Building 29; 520-621-3341.

A professional modern dance company, **Tenth Street Danceworks** performs about four times a year. ~ 3400 East Speedway Boulevard, Suite 118-262; 520-795-6980.

GENE C. REID PARK This 131-acre park is a lush oasis in the desert with grassy expanses dotted with mature trees. There are a wide variety of recreational facilities here, including a recreation center, two golf courses, a swimming pool, pond, paddle boat rentals, tennis and racquetball courts and Hi-Corbett field where major league baseball teams come for spring training. Other attractions are Reid Park Zoo and a rose garden with more than 2000 plants. The park has restrooms, picnic tables and ramadas. ~ Located between Broadway and 22nd Street, Country Club Road and Alvernon Way; 520-791-4873.

PARKS

TUCSON MOUNTAIN PARK 🏃 🚵 🐎   Winding, hilly roads take you through this 20,000-acre, high-desert area brimming with ocotillo, palo verde, mesquite and saguaros and punctuated by mountains with rugged volcanic peaks. A popular spot is the Gates Pass overlook just past Speedway where you can pull off the road and get a panoramic view of Tucson, Avra Valley, Kitt Peak and watch Arizona's renowned sunsets. The park also includes the Arizona-Sonora Desert Museum and Old Tucson; there is an admission fee to both sites. There are established picnic areas throughout the park. The park also features archery and rifle ranges. (Archery hunting is allowed in season with proper permit.) ~ Located about ten miles west of the city limits off Gates Pass Road (no recreational vehicles are allowed on the road). Another entrance is on Kinney Road off Ajo Way; 520-740-2690.

▲ Gilbert Ray Campground has 160 sites, all with electric hookups; $6 per night for tents and $9.50 per night for RVs; information, 520-883-4200, 520-740-2690.

FORT LOWELL PARK 🏃 ⛵   With its blend of history and recreation, Fort Lowell Park is an ideal family getaway. Fort Lowell was once a major military post and supply depot. Stroll between the trees on Cottonwood Lane, and you'll see a number of ruins, including that of the adobe post hospital built in 1875. Farther down is a museum in the reconstructed officers' quarters. The 59-acre park also has a pond with a fountain and plenty of hungry ducks around the perimeter, and a trail with marked exercise stops along the way. The park also includes tennis and racquetball courts, pool, picnic areas, lighted ball fields and shade ramadas. ~ Located at 2900 North Craycroft Road; 520-791-4873.

SAGUARO NATIONAL PARK   Established to protect the saguaro cactus, found mainly in Arizona, the park is divided into two segments on opposite sides of Tucson. For general information, call 520-733-5100.

Rincon Mountain District 🏃 🚵 🐎   A popular segment of Saguaro National Park is the Rincon Mountain District east of town, a 67,293-acre chunk established in 1933. Begin your tour at the visitors center, with dioramas and other exhibits of the geological and botanical history of the park. Then drive along Cactus Forest Drive, a scenic eight-mile-loop showing off tall saguaro cacti with their splayed arms. This district has more than 100 miles of hiking and equestrian trails. You'll also find picnic areas, restrooms and barbecue grills. ~ Drive east on Old Spanish Trail about three miles beyond city limits; visitors center: 520-733-5153.

Tucson Mountain District 🏃 🚵 🐎   The 24,034-acre Tucson Mountain District to the west has a visitors center with orientations to the park, exhibits, maps and books, and features the six-mile-long Bajada Loop Drive that passes dense saguaro forests and American Indian petroglyphs. There are 40 miles of hiking and equestrian trails. Bicycling is limited to the roads. Amenities include picnic areas, restrooms and barbecue grills. ~ Located two miles beyond the Arizona-Sonora Desert Museum off Kinney Road; visitors center: 520-733-5158.

SABINO CANYON RECREATION AREA 🏃🚴 One of the most scenic spots in the region is a route that cuts through the Santa Catalina Mountains in the Coronado National Forest. You can either hike, bike or take the shuttle on a seven-and-a-half-mile round trip that climbs a road lined with cottonwoods, sycamores, ash and willow trees. Along the route flows Sabino Creek with its pools and waterfalls that tumble underneath arched stone bridges. The shuttle makes nine stops along the way, so you can jump on or off as you go. For the romantically inclined, the shuttle has moonlight rides during the full moon from April to June and September to December. The shuttle will also take you on the two-and-a-half-mile trip to Bear Canyon Trail, where you then hike two more miles to Seven Falls, which cascade almost 500 feet down the side of a hill. Bicycling is restricted to before 9 a.m. or after 5 p.m. and is not allowed at all on Wednesday or Saturday. Facilities in the park are limited to restrooms and a visitors center. ~ Located at the north end of Sabino Canyon Road shortly before it dead-ends near the intersection with Sunrise Drive; general information, 520-749-8700 or shuttle information, 520-749-2327.

> In May and June, if rainfall has been sufficient, saguaro cacti by the thousands burst forth with their creamy blossoms—the state flower of Arizona.

MOUNT LEMMON 🏃🚴⛷🛶 In the hour's drive from Tucson to the top of Mount Lemmon, you travel from a lower Sonoran Desert zone to a Canadian zone forest, or from cacti to pine forests. For this reason, Tucsonians flock there in summer to escape the heat, and in winter to ski at Mount Lemmon Ski Valley, the southernmost ski area in the United States. If you take Catalina Highway to the top, the steep and winding mountain road will pass Rose Canyon Lake stocked with trout, and the town of Summerhaven with its handful of shops and restaurants. Once on Mount Lemmon, you can hike on 150 miles of trails. There are restrooms and picnic areas. ~ Mount Lemmon is within the Coronado National Forest. Drive east on Tanque Verde Road to Catalina Highway, then head north 25 miles to Summerhaven; 520-749-8700.

▲ There are tent and RV sites (no hookups) with toilets and drinking water at Rose (74 sites) and Spencer (62 sites) canyons; $8 per night. Molina Basin has 37 tent sites; $8 per night. General Hitchcock campground also has 12 tent sites; $5. Rose and Spencer canyons are closed in winter.

HIDDEN ▶ **TOHONO CHUL PARK** Few tourists know about this treasure hidden in northwest Tucson. But walk down the winding paths of the 49-acre park and you'll discover about 400 species of arid climate plants, many of which are labeled, along with water fountains, grotto pond areas and a greenhouse with plants for sale. In addition, you'll find an exhibit hall, two gift shops and a tea room as well as picnic tables, ramadas and restrooms. ~ Located off Oracle Road at 7366 North Paseo del Norte, about six miles north of the Tucson city limits; 520-742-6455.

CATALINA STATE PARK 🚶 🚲 🐎 This 5500-acre preserve sits in the Santa Catalina foothills. Highlights include Romero Canyon, a beautiful area with pools shaded by sycamore and oak trees, and adjacent Pusch Ridge Wilderness, home to desert bighorn sheep. The Hohokam once farmed the area, and as you walk through the park you can still see some of the pit houses and ball court ruins. Facilities include restrooms, showers, picnic tables and grills. Day-use fee, $4. ~ Off Route 77, about nine miles north of the city limits at 11570 North Oracle Road; 520-628-5798.

▲ Catalina State Park Campground has 48 tent and RV sites; $10 per night without hookups, $15 with hookups.

PICACHO PEAK STATE PARK 🚶 The most dramatic part of the park is Picacho Peak, a landmark formation that rises 1500 feet above the desert floor and can be seen for miles around. The peak is believed to be 22 million years old—or four times as old as the Grand Canyon—and was used as a landmark by early explorers. It was also the site of the battle of Picacho Pass during the Civil War. The 4000-acre park has seven miles of developed hiking trails that wind past saguaro cacti as well. Facilities include picnic areas, ramadas, restrooms and showers. Day-use fee, $4. ~ Located 40 miles north of Tucson just off Route 10 (exit 219); 520-466-3183.

▲ There are 83 sites ($10 per night) and 12 RV hookups ($13 per night).

▼▼▼▼▼▼▼▼▼▼▼
East of Tucson The Wild West comes to life in this area of Arizona where murder and lynching were once considered leisure activities, poker was more popular than Sunday church services and whiskey was king. While this region is best known for infamous spots like Boot Hill and the O.K. Corral, it's also the home of historic mining towns like Bisbee, mineral spas and a cowboy hall of fame.

SIGHTS Get on Route 10 heading east and one of the first attractions you'll pass is **Colossal Cave**, one of the largest dry caverns in the world. Set in the Rincon Mountains, it was once home for Indians and outlaws. During 50-minute tours, hidden lights illuminate for-

mations such as the Silent Waterfall and Kingdom of the Elves.
Admission. ~ Off Old Spanish Trail, Vail; 520-647-7275.

Farther east on Route 10 is Benson, where the **Arts & His-**   ◄ HIDDEN
torical Society tells the story about how Benson grew along with
the arrival of the railroad. Inside are antiques, artifacts and an old
grocery store. A gift shop offers local arts and crafts. Closed Sunday and Monday and the month of August. ~ 180 South San Pedro
Street, Benson; 520-586-3070.

On your way to the Old West towns of Bisbee and Tombstone,
take a detour toward Elgin. You will enter what at first seems an
oxymoron—Arizona **wine country**. But there are several wineries
out here, and it's a pretty drive through the vineyards.

One of four buildings in the town of Elgin is **The Chapel of**   ◄ HIDDEN
the Blessed Mother, Consoler of the Afflicted. It's a small chapel
set amid grasslands, vineyards and cottonwood trees. ~ Elgin.

Head south on Route 90 and you can't miss **Fort Huachuca**,
a National Historic Landmark founded in 1877 to protect settlers from Apache raiders. The Fort Huachuca soldiers eventually tracked down and defeated Apache leader Geronimo. Today,
this 73,000-acre installation is home to the U.S. Army Intelligence
Center and School. One highlight is the Fort Huachuca Museum,
located in a turn-of-the-century building first used as a bachelor
officers' quarters. Inside are military artifacts, dioramas and the
history of the fort. The museum annex is across the street, and
down the road is the Army Intelligence Museum. For a panoramic
view of the fort and town, drive up Reservoir Hill Road. If you'd
prefer picnicking, there are plenty of scenic spots amid large, old
trees. ~ Sierra Vista; 520-533-3638.

Take Route 92 south and you'll find a place known to birders worldwide. **Ramsey Canyon Preserve** is home to a variety of
birds, including 14 species of hummingbirds from April to mid-
September. Also commonly spotted here are white-tailed deer,

A DOC GOODFELLOW

In the early 1880s, Tombstone was full of colorful characters, one of
whom was Doc Goodfellow—a man much needed during those rowdy,
dangerous frontier days. Nicknamed the "gunshot physician," he had
an office over the Crystal Palace Saloon. Some of his exploits included
commandeering and driving a steam locomotive in order to expedite
getting a gunshot victim to a Tucson hospital, crawling into a mine
shaft filled with smoke to save some miners, and riding his horse
to a remote region in the mountains to doctor a cattle rustler sick
with lead poisoning.

gray squirrels and coati. The Nature Conservancy owns this 300-acre wooded gorge set in the Huachuca Mountains. The preserve is often full so call in advance for reservations. ~ Route 92, five miles south of Sierra Vista; 520-378-2785.

Hop on Route 90 again for the quick trip to **Bisbee** near the Mexican border. An old mining town and now an artists' enclave, the town is full of Victorian architecture perched on hillsides, along with funky shops and restaurants. For the full history of the town, start at the **Bisbee Mining & Historical Museum**, located in the former General Office Building of the Copper Queen Consolidated Mining Co. This is the first rural museum to become a Smithsonian affiliate. On the front lawn is old mining equipment, while inside the 1897 red-brick building are photo murals, artifacts and walk-in environments that highlight Bisbee's history. By the year 2001, the museum will have a large display of rocks and precious minerals currently housed at the Smithsonian Institute. Admission. ~ 5 Copper Queen Plaza, Bisbee; 520-432-7071.

For a firsthand view of mining history, put on a slicker, hard hat and battery-pack light and hop on the underground train at the **Queen Mine Underground Tour**. An ex-miner narrates as he takes you through the Copper Queen Mine, which prospered for more than 60 years before it closed in 1944. The journey is a cool one, so bring a jacket. From here you can also take the **Lavender Open Pit Mine Tour**, a narrated, 13-mile bus tour around a 300-acre hole where more than 380 million tons of ore and tailings have been removed. In conjunction with this, the **Historic District Tour** travels through the old section of Bisbee spotlighting such buildings as the Copper Queen Hotel and the Phythian Castle. Admission. ~ 478 North Dart Road, Bisbee; 520-432-2071.

Continue your time travel to the Old West at **Slaughter Ranch**, located near the Mexican border. Now a National Historic Landmark, it was once the home of John Slaughter, a former Texas Ranger, sheriff of Cochise County and one of the founders of Douglas. He bought the fertile grassland in 1884 and developed it into a cattle ranch. Slaughter's house and half a dozen other buildings furnished to reflect the era are still on the 140-acre site. Closed Monday and Tuesday. Admission. ~ Geronimo Trail, 15 miles east of Douglas; 520-558-2474.

The **Gadsden Hotel** in Douglas is a National Historic Monument that opened in 1907 as a hotel for cattlemen, miners and ranchers. Step into the magnificent lobby for a look at a solid white Italian-marble staircase, four marble columns with capitals decorated in 14K gold leaf, and vaulted stained-glass skylights that run its length. Several Hollywood movies have been filmed here. ~ 1046 G Avenue, Douglas; 520-364-4481.

Northwest of Douglas is **Tombstone**, the town too tough to die. When prospector Ed Schieffelin headed to what is now Tombstone in hopes of staking a silver claim in 1877, he was warned by friends that all he'd find was his own tombstone. Instead, he got rich and named the town after their warning—Tombstone. When he discovered silver, Ed's brother Al commented, "You're a lucky cuss," and the profitable mine was named "Lucky Cuss." Names for other Tombstone area mines were equally colorful, including Goodenough (which is open for tours), Tough Nut and Contention, named after a claims dispute between several men. Early residents of Tombstone included Wyatt Earp, Doc Holliday and Bat Masterson. Unfortunately, today the town is extremely touristy and every attraction is out to make a buck, but there are a few worthwhile stops.

The **Tombstone Courthouse** has a restored courtroom and two floors of historic exhibits that reflect the ups and downs of this once rowdy town. Now part of the Arizona State Park system, the red-brick building was the town's courthouse from 1882 until 1929. Admission. ~ 3rd and Toughnut streets, Tombstone; 520-457-3311.

A huge rosebush that spreads across 8600 feet of supports is the main attraction at the **Rose Tree Inn Museum**. Planted in 1885, the bush is an especially awesome sight if you come in April when it's covered with white blossoms. You can also tour the historic adobe home with local artifacts and period rooms. Admission. ~ 4th and Toughnut streets, Tombstone; 520-457-3326.

Allen Street is the heart of Tombstone. At one end is the **Bird Cage Theatre**, a famous night spot in the late 1800s that is now a National Historic Landmark. Overlooking the gambling casino and dance hall are birdcage-like compartments where prostitutes plied their trade. Never a dull place, the theater was the site of 16 gunfights. If you bother to count you'll find 140 bullet holes riddling the walls and ceilings. Also, the longest poker game in the history of the West reputedly unfolded here . . . it lasted eight years, five months and three days. Is this an ace attraction or what? Admission. ~ 6th and Allen streets, Tombstone; 520-457-3421.

◆◆

GADSDEN HOTEL

Built in 1907, with no expenses spared, the Gadsden Hotel in Douglas was the social and financial center for cattlemen and rich miners. Cattlemen would frequent the hotel's Saddle and Spur Saloon where, for a fee, they could have their ranch brands painted on walls. And a favorite gathering place for Douglas residents during the Mexican Revolution was, of all places, the hotel roof! This gave them ringside views of General Francisco "Pancho" Villa's army battling the Federales at Agua Prieta. The only drawback—stray bullets sometimes sent the spectators running for cover.

The most famous of Tombstone's many gunfights occurred in 1881 at **O.K. Corral** down the street from the Bird Cage. Life-size figures stand in the corral as a narrator describes the shootout. There is also a live show every day at 2 p.m. An adjacent building showcases old Tombstone photos and other historic items. Admission. ~ Allen Street, Tombstone; 520-457-3456.

The losers of the shootout and other gunslingers lay buried at **Boot Hill Graveyard**. Enter the graveyard through the gift shop to see rows of graves—little more than piles of rocks with white metal crosses to mark them—as well as a spectacular view of the area. ~ Route 80 West, Tombstone; 520-457-9344.

Founded in 1880, the **Tombstone Epitaph** is the oldest continuously published newspaper in Arizona. In one corner of the newspaper office is the original press and other printing equipment. As residents say, every Tombstone should have an Epitaph. ~ 9 South 5th Street, Tombstone; 520-457-2211.

After looping off Route 10 to see Sierra Vista, Bisbee and Tombstone, get back to Route 10 and go east to Dragoon, home of the **Amerind Foundation** (an archaeological research facility) and little else. This is a real treasure tucked away amidst the rock formations of Texas Canyon. The research facility and museum have been devoted to American Indian culture and history since they opened in 1937. Visitors walk through the Spanish Colonial revival–style buildings to see American Indian pieces, such as beadwork, costumes, ritual masks and weapons, as well as Western artwork, including works by Frederic Remington and William Leigh. Closed Monday and Tuesday in summer. Admission. ~ Dragoon Road, Dragoon; 520-586-3666.

More Western history is found farther east on Route 10 in Willcox at the **Museum of the Southwest**. There's a bust of Chief Cochise, Indian and mining artifacts and a mineral and rock collection. ~ 127 East Maley Avenue, Willcox; 520-384-2272.

The most famous cowboy of the area was Rex Allen, born in Willcox in 1920. **The Rex Allen Arizona Cowboy Museum** features mementos of Rex Allen's life, from his homesteading and ranch life in Willcox to his movies and television shows. Another section features the pioneer settlers and ranchers of the West. Admission. ~ 155 North Railroad Avenue, Willcox; 520-384-4583.

LODGING   A good motel choice in Benson is the **Best Western Quail Hollow Inn** which has 89 spacious, white-walled guest rooms with oak-finished furniture, green and mauve fabrics and artwork depicting the native quail. Amenities include refrigerators, TVs and a heated pool. ~ 699 North Ocotillo Street, Benson; 520-586-3646, 800-322-1850, fax 520-586-7035. BUDGET.

The majority of accommodations in Sierra Vista are along Fry Boulevard—the main commercial thoroughfare through town—

and on South Route 92. **Sierra Suites** is a two-story, red-brick hotel that lures guests with complimentary breakfast. The 100 rooms face courtyards, and inside are mirrored sliding glass closet doors, glass tables, a chest of drawers, refrigerators, coffeemakers, microwaves and hairdryers. The price includes use of the pool and whirlpool. ~ 391 East Fry Boulevard, Sierra Vista; 520-459-4221, fax 520-459-8449. BUDGET TO MODERATE.

Thunder Mountain Inn is a two-story, beige-colored brick building with 102 rooms, a dining room, café and lounge. Lower-level guest rooms facing the pool have sliding-glass doors. Most accommodations have double beds and a desk. ~ 1631 South Route 92, Sierra Vista; 520-458-7900, 800-222-5811, fax 520-458-7900. BUDGET.

For a really secluded getaway, venture out to **Ramsey Canyon Inn** located in the Huachuca Mountains along a winding mountain stream and adjacent to the Nature Conservancy's Mile Hi/Ramsey Canyon Preserve and the Coronado National Forest. Accommodations consist of two fully equipped apartments decorated with antiques. There is also a six-room bed-and-breakfast inn run by the Nature Conservancy, with a private bath in each room. The rates for the inn include a full breakfast and homemade pies in the afternoon. ~ 29 Ramsey Canyon Road, Hereford; phone/fax 520-378-3010; e-mail lodging@theriver.com. MODERATE TO DELUXE.

◄ HIDDEN

Built in 1917, **The Bisbee Inn** overlooks Brewery Gulch, once one of the Southwest's wildest streets. Each of the 19 rooms has handmade quilts on the beds, antique dressers with mirrors, and its own sink. Four guest rooms share bathrooms in the hall; the rest have bathrooms with showers. There are also two suites behind the inn. This red-brick inn offers an all-you-can-eat breakfast, included in the price of the room. ~ 45 OK Street, Bisbee; 520-432-5131, 888-432-5131, fax 520-432-5343; e-mail BisbeeInn@aol.com. BUDGET TO DELUXE.

School House Inn Bed & Breakfast is a large, restored, 1917 red-brick schoolhouse just above Garfield Park. The nine rooms are fairly large, and each has a private bath with a large tub. A full breakfast is served. ~ 818 Tombstone Canyon, Bisbee; phone/fax 520-432-2996, 800-537-4333. BUDGET TO MODERATE.

The Copper Queen Mining Co. built the **Copper Queen Hotel** just after the turn of the century when it was a gathering place for politicians, mining officials and travelers, including the young Teddy Roosevelt. A plaque on one door marks the room where John Wayne stayed. The hotel is in the midst of an ongoing restoration, so ask for the restored rooms when you go. These are decorated Victorian style with floral wallpaper and tile bathrooms. The four-story building contains 45 guest rooms, along with the

Text continued on page 310.

Calling All City Slickers!

Fueled by romantic images of Western heroes and desert sunsets and indulging in the fantasy of an escape to simpler times, more people than ever are opting to hang their saddles at dude ranches. In Southern Arizona, cowpokes have more than their fair share of choices. Guest ranches here range from resorts where you're more likely to overheat in the jacuzzi than the saddle, to working ranches where wranglers round 'em up and dine on beans and burgers. Whatever the orientation, most have horseback riding, a whole range of outdoor activities, and a casual, secluded atmosphere. Some are closed during the hot summer months, so call ahead.

One of the most luxurious getaways is **Tanque Verde Guest Ranch**, which has been around since the 1880s. It comes complete with indoor and outdoor swimming pools, tennis courts, an exercise room and, of course, horseback riding. Guests stay in one of 70 *casitas* and patio lodges, some with beehive fireplaces, antiques and Indian bedspreads. Sliding glass doors offer stunning desert views. To relax, cozy up in the lobby with a good Western novel by the stone fireplace. ~ 14301 East Speedway Boulevard, Tucson; 520-296-6275, 800-234-3833, fax 520-721-9426; www.tvgr.com. ULTRA-DELUXE.

White Stallion Ranch sprawls across 3000 acres—grazing land for their herd of Longhorn. Guests take breakfast rides, watch rodeos every Saturday afternoon, and pet miniature horses, donkeys, pot-bellied pigs, pygmy goats and a llama at the on-site zoo. Rooms at this ranch are rustic with Western decor. Rates include all meals and activities. Closed June through August. ~ 9251 West Twin Peaks Road, Tucson; 520-297-0252, 888-977-2624, fax 520-744-2786; www.wsranch.com. ULTRA-DELUXE.

Don't look for televisions or telephones inside the 23-room **Lazy K Bar Ranch**, because here you're meant to leave the outside world behind. Ranch-style meals are served in a dining room, and Saturday night is set aside for steak cookouts beside a waterfall. Afterward, you can relax in the comfortable library with wood paneling and beams, bookshelves, a fireplace and card table. Rooms are comfortable, carpeted and decorated in a Southwestern motif. ~ 8401 North Scenic Drive, Tucson; 520-744-3050, 800-321-7018, fax 520-744-7628; www.lazykbar.com. ULTRA-DELUXE.

Price Canyon Ranch in the Chiricahua Mountains is a working cattle ranch with one- and two-room bunk houses with baths. Meals are served in the 113-year-old main ranch house. Visitors can hike or ride horses in the surrounding national forest, or cool off in the swimming pool. Accommodations include meals, horseback riding and other ranch activities. Visitors are welcome to participate in the spring and fall roundups. ~ Off of Route 80 between the 400- and 401-mile markers. Turn onto Price Ranch Road and drive seven miles, Douglas; 520-558-2383; e-mail pcranch@gateway.net. ULTRA-DELUXE.

Grapevine Canyon Ranch offers accommodations in guest rooms with country-ranch furnishings and American Indian touches and include three meals. Visitors also lounge in the sitting room, a cozy place with a wood-beamed ceiling, Indian-design rugs and steer horns over the fireplace. At this working cattle ranch, horseback riding is the main attraction. ~ Highland Road, Pearce; 520-826-3185, 800-245-9202, fax 520-826-3636; www.beadude.com. ULTRA-DELUXE.

Circle Z Ranch in the foothills of the Santa Rita Mountains is a colorful, unpretentious place built in the mid-1920s. It accommodates no more than 45 people at a time. The ranch's adobe cottages are decorated with brightly painted wicker furniture and Mexican crafts, but don't have TVs or telephones. Instead, recreation centers around horseback riding. There is also a heated pool and a tennis court. The lodge has a massive stone fireplace and bookshelves filled with classics, including Zane Grey titles. All meals are included in the price of a room. The ranch has a three-night minimum, and is open from November 1 through May 15. ~ P.O. Box 194, Patagonia 85624; 520-394-2525; www.circlez.com. ULTRA-DELUXE.

Sitting in the foothills of Baboquivari Peak on the Mexican border, **Rancho De La Osa** is a 200-year-old Territorial-style ranch. Constructed with handmade adobe block, rooms have fireplaces and Indian and Spanish furnishings. Activities include riding, biking, hiking and swimming. The Cantina, an old Spanish/Indian mission, features gourmet Southwestern cooking. Meals are included in the room rate. Closed in August. ~ 28201 West La Osa Ranch Road, Sasabe; 520-823-4257, 800-872-6240, fax 520-823-4238; www.guestranches.com/ranchodelaosa. ULTRA-DELUXE.

Another ranch of note is **Triangle T Guest Ranch**, with ten cabins, a restaurant, a saloon, nature trails and horseback riding. ~ Route 10, exit 318 Dragoon Road, Dragoon; phone/fax 520-586-7533. BUDGET TO MODERATE. The 26-room **Rex Guest Ranch** is also worth checking out. Along with horseback riding, biking and hiking, you can enjoy the outdoor spa and junior Olympic–size pool. ~ 131 East Mado Montoso Road, Amado; 520-398-2914, 800-547-2696, fax 520-398-8229; www.rexranch.com. DELUXE TO ULTRA-DELUXE.

Copper Queen Saloon and Dining Room. ~ 11 Howell Avenue, Bisbee; 520-432-2216, 800-247-5829, fax 520-432-4298. MODERATE TO DELUXE.

The **Bisbee Grand Hotel** is ideally located in the main shopping area in town. The original hotel was built in 1906. There are three suites with private baths and eight rooms. The adjacent Captain's Suite, which sleeps up to six people, has a kitchenette. All rooms reflect the era with period wallpaper, red carpeting, brass beds and antiques. They also have sinks and ceiling fans. The rooms are upstairs, while downstairs is the Grand Western Saloon and Billiards Room. All rates include breakfast, except the Captain's Suite. ~ 61 Main Street, Bisbee; 520-432-5900, 800-421-1909. BUDGET TO ULTRA-DELUXE.

The **Jonquil Motel** is a small motor court with seven clean, comfortable rooms. The rooms have televisions but no telephones. ~ 317 Tombstone Canyon, Bisbee; 520-432-7371. BUDGET.

The seven-room **Tombstone Boarding House Bed and Breakfast Inn** is housed in an adobe building constructed around 1879. Rooms are tastefully decorated in pastel colors with lacy curtains and Victorian-era furnishings. A full breakfast is served in the country kitchen. ~ 108 North 4th Street, Tombstone; 520-457-3716, fax 520-457-3038. MODERATE.

The **Buford House** is an authentic 1880 adobe house with bed-and-breakfast accommodations, a wraparound porch and a barbecue grill. Most of the five rooms have private baths; the Garden Room has a sunken tub and private entrance. The grounds include a delightful garden and fish pond. Full breakfast included. ~ 113 East Safford Street, Tombstone; 520-457-3969, 800-263-6762. MODERATE.

DINING

HIDDEN ►

Horseshoe Cafe is a family-owned restaurant that has been around for more than 50 years. On the walls are Western murals by artist Vern Parker, and the posts in the café display cattle brands of Southern Arizona. A neon horseshoe on the ceiling helps light the room. Entrées include chili, sandwiches, omelettes, burgers, steaks and Mexican specialties. ~ 154 East 4th Street, Benson; 520-586-3303. BUDGET.

Peking Chinese Cuisine is located in a small strip center with neon signs in the windows. The best deal here is an all-you-can-eat lunch buffet. The place is casual with red booths and tables, and Chinese lanterns and fans hanging from the ceiling. ~ 1481 East Fry Boulevard, Sierra Vista; 520-459-0404. BUDGET TO MODERATE.

Speaking in relative terms, the **Thunder Mountain Inn Restaurant** is one of the more expensive places in town. Diners eat prime rib and seafood atop white tablecloths in booths divided by etched glass. ~ 1631 South Route 92, Sierra Vista; 520-458-7900. MODERATE TO DELUXE.

Fine Continental cuisine is the last thing you'd expect to find out here, but **Karen's** fits the bill. The menu changes weekly, but typical entrées are grilled chicken breast stuffed with mozzarella and herbs, then covered with a sun-dried tomato sauce, or New York strip steak topped with blackberry barbecue sauce. Lunch served daily; dinner served Thursday through Saturday. ~ Route 82, Sonoita; 520-455-5282. MODERATE TO ULTRA-DELUXE.

A sleek bistro-style restaurant designed to please urban cowboys, **Café Roka** offers a wide variety of flavorful pastas and house specialties such as smoked salmon with gorgonzola. Open weekends only in the summer and Tuesday through Saturday the rest of the year. ~ 35 Main Street, Bisbee; 520-432-5153. MODERATE.

The **Renaissance Cafe** is a tiny, no-frills place where the locals hang out. Local artists' works hang on the walls, bulletins paper the front window, and a radio station plays in the background. There are a few tables inside, and a few out on the sidewalk. Offerings include sandwiches, pizza, quiche, crêpes, salads and desserts as well as tasty coffee, espresso and herbal teas. ~ 10-A Lyric Plaza, Bisbee; 520-432-4020. BUDGET.

Enjoy Mexican or American favorites under the watchful eye of Marilyn Monroe at **Grand Cafe & Gallery**; the blonde bombshell appears in paintings, drawings and photographs exhibited throughout the eatery. Burritos, fajitas and flautas are some of the Mexican dishes while T-bone steaks and shrimp scampi are featured on the American menu. Breakfast, lunch and dinner. ~ 1119 G Avenue, Douglas; 520-364-2344. BUDGET TO MODERATE.

The **Nellie Cashman Restaurant** is housed in an 1879 building with decor to reflect the era including a stone fireplace, high wood ceilings and photos of bygone years. Although they serve sandwiches, burgers, steaks, chicken and pasta, they're best known for their homemade berry pies. ~ 117 South 5th Street, Tombstone; 520-457-2212. BUDGET TO DELUXE.

If you're in the mood for the biggest hot dog in Cochise County, weighing in at half-pound and measuring a foot long, then saunter over to the **Longhorn Restaurant** and order a Longhorn Dog. If that's not what you crave, they offer other big food, including a 40-ounce steak. The decor is Western with longhorns hanging over the door and yellowing wanted posters of characters such as Billy the Kid laminated on the tables. ~ 501 East Allen Street, Tombstone; 520-457-3405. MODERATE TO ULTRA-DELUXE

Singing Wind Bookshop is in the *really hidden* category. From Route 10, turn north on Ocotillo Road, then go for two and a quarter miles and turn right on West Singing Wind Road until you see the chained green gate. Don't let it stop you—just open it and drive on in and down to the ranch house. Here, there are two huge rooms full of new books about the Southwest, Western Americana

SHOPPING

◄ *HIDDEN*

and other categories. In addition, there is a room full of children's books. ~ West Singing Wind Road and North Ocotillo Road, two and a quarter miles north of Route 10, Benson; 520-586-2425.

Head south to Sierra Vista and you'll discover **Misty's Gift Gallery**, one of the largest collectors' galleries in the Southwest with names that include Goebel, Hummel, Gorham, De Grazia and Perillo. There is also a gallery with original artwork, lithographs and bronzes. Closed Sunday and Monday most of the year; closed Sunday in December. ~ 228 West Fry Boulevard, Sierra Vista; 520-458-7208.

The Gold Shop features innovative, contemporary jewelry created by local and regional artists. ~ 24 Main Street, Bisbee; 520-432-4557. The **Johnson Gallery** carries American Indian arts and crafts and Quezada family pottery. ~ 28 Main Street, Bisbee; 520-432-2126.

Poco Loco features striking hand-painted dinnerware and other pottery plus Western collectibles, furniture and jewelry. ~ 81 Main Street, Bisbee; 520-432-7020.

Allen Street is the heart of shopping in Tombstone, where you will find lots of souvenir shops mixed in with higher-quality jewelry and clothing stores. **Arlene's Southwest Silver & Gold** is a large place with American Indian jewelry and artwork including pottery, baskets, kachina dolls and rugs. ~ 404 Allen Street, Tombstone; 520-457-3344.

Gabe's Victorian Shop and Doll Museum is one of the oldest shops in Tombstone. The place is crammed full of dolls, dollhouse pieces, Victorian cards, collectibles and more than 250 paper dolls. In the back of the shop is a museum with dolls dating back to the 1830s. Admission to museum. ~ 312 Allen Street, Tombstone; 520-457-3419.

The **Territorial Book Trader** has a huge selection of titles on Wyatt Earp and the Old West. ~ 401 Allen Street, Tombstone; 520-457-3170.

Looking for antique African clamshell discs, camel bone beads or yak bone beads handcarved in Pakistan? Even if you aren't, the **Tombstone Bead Co.** has them, and one of the largest selections of beads in the country. They import from all over the world and also make their own beads. ~ 416 Allen Street, Tombstone; 520-457-2323.

Medicine Bow has leathers and Western wear including handmade belts, hats, buckles and knives. ~ 509 Allen Street, Tombstone; 520-457-3805.

Near the tiny ghost town of Gleeson, you'll find rattlesnake regalia galore at **John & Sandy's Rattlesnake Crafts**. Hatbands and belts made from the hide, and jewelry made from the vertebrae are just a few of the items created from the rattler that this amazing little store carries. The owners do all the hunting and craftwork themselves. ~ Gleeson Road, 12 miles east of Tombstone; 520-642-9207.

The time to travel out to the Willcox area is fall, when farms and roadside stands are selling their produce. The Willcox Chamber of Commerce has a brochure listing 27 orchards and mills where you can stop. One is **Stout's Cider Mill**, where you can buy apples, cider, dried fruit, nuts, peaches, apple pies, chile peppers and Arizona desert preserves. ~ 1510 North Circle I Road, Willcox; 520-384-3696.

Pardners Arena Saloon & Rodeo Grounds overlooks the rodeo grounds, where events are staged five nights a week. Inside a Western theme dominates. A lasso hangs on the door, cow skulls decorate walls, and you can warm yourself by the big rock fireplace. There are also a pool table and dancefloor, along with outdoor picnic benches. Closed Monday. ~ 250 North Prickly Pear Street, Benson; 520-586-9983.

NIGHTLIFE

◄ HIDDEN

Established in 1902, **St. Elmo Bar and Grill** in historic Bisbee is a tradition around here. Memorabilia such as old maps hang on the walls, and seating is mainly stools at the counter. On weekends there's live music and dancing. Entertainment during the week is supplied by the CD jukebox or pool tables and dart board. ~ 36 Brewery Avenue, Bisbee; 520-432-5578.

Adjoining the Copper Queen Hotel, the **Copper Queen Saloon** is a small, dark, intimate place with some turn-of-the-century furnishings and live jazz on Friday and Saturday nights. ~ 11 Howell Avenue, Bisbee; 520-432-2216.

At the **Stock Exchange Bar,** almost one whole wall is covered with an original board from the New York stock exchange. This historic building has a pressed tin roof and worn wooden floors. There's live rock and blues some weekends and karaoke at other times. Downstairs is the Brewery Restaurant. ~ 15 Brewery Avenue, Bisbee; 520-432-9924.

At one time, Tombstone reputedly had saloons and gambling halls making up two of every three buildings.

Walk through the swinging doors of **Big Nose Kate's Saloon** and you're back in the Old West. Waitresses dressed as saloon gals serve drinks in the same place where Lily Langtry and Wyatt Earp once drank. Lighted, stained-glass panels depict Tombstone's characters, and old photographs hang on the walls. On weekends you'll find live country-and-western music and skits of Western brawls. ~ 417 East Allen Street, Tombstone; 520-457-3107.

The Crystal Palace Saloon has been restored to look like it did when it was built in the 1880s. The long, narrow room has old wood tables and red drapes underneath a copper ceiling. Live music is performed every day except Monday. ~ 420 East Allen Street, Tombstone; 520-457-3611.

Johnny Ringo's Saloon is a historic, intimate bar where the main attraction is the collection of more than 600 military patches on the walls. ~ 404 Allen Street, Tombstone; 520-457-3961.

PARKS   **CHIRICAHUA NATIONAL MONUMENT** 🏃 The Chiricahua Apaches called this area the Land of the Standing-Up Rocks because throughout the park are huge rock spires, stone columns and massive rocks perched on small pedestals. Geologists believe that these formations were created as a result of explosive volcanic eruptions. For an overview of the park, drive up the winding, eight-mile-long Bonita Canyon Drive. You'll pass pine and oak-juniper forests before reaching Massai Point at the top of the Chiricahua Mountains where you can see the park, valleys and the peaks of Sugarloaf Mountain and Cochise Head. You can also explore the park on foot via about 20 miles of trails. Other attractions include historic Faraway Ranch and Stafford Cabin. There are picnic tables, restrooms and a visitors center with exhibits. Day-use fee, $6. ~ From Willcox, go southeast on Route 186 for 37 miles; 520-824-3560.

▲ There are 24 sites; $8 per night. No backcountry camping is allowed within the monument.

▼▼▼▼▼▼▼▼▼▼▼▼▼▼▼
South/West of Tucson

Far off the beaten track, southwestern Arizona is home to the world's leading astronomical center, remote ghost towns, wildlife preserves and a sanctuary dedicated to the unusual organ pipe cactus. This is also where civilization disappears and the desert blooms.

SIGHTS   Heading south on Route 19, you will pass the retirement community of Green Valley and arrive at the **Titan Missile Museum**, the only intercontinental ballistic missile complex in the world that's open to the public. Here you'll be taken on a one-hour guided tour into the bowels of the earth, experience a countdown launch of a Titan missile and view a silo. It's an eerie excursion. Closed Monday and Tuesday in summer. Admission. ~ 1580 West Duval Mine Road, Green Valley; 520-625-4759.

To get away from the high-tech missiles and delve deeper into the area's history, continue farther south on Route 19 to Tubac. Here, the Spanish founded a presidio in 1752 to protect settlers from the Indians. At **Tubac Presidio State Historic Park** visitors can see the remains of the original presidio foundation, the foundation of the Spanish captain's house from the military garrison in 1750, an 1885 schoolhouse, a 1914 community hall and a museum detailing the history of Tubac. Admission. ~ Route 19, Tubac; 520-398-2252.

A few more minutes down Route 19 are the adobe ruins of a Spanish frontier mission church at the **Tumacacori National**

Historical Park. Along with the museum, visitors walk through the baroque church, completed in 1828, and the nearby ruins, such as a circular mortuary chapel and graveyard. Since little has been built in the vicinity, walking across the grounds feels like a walk back in time. Admission. ~ Route 19, Exit 29, Tumacacori; 520-398-2341.

Continuing south, Route 19 hits the Mexican border. **Nogales, Mexico,** is a border town offering bargain shopping, restaurants and some sightseeing. On the other side is Nogales, Arizona. Photographs and artifacts detail the town's history at the **Pimeria Alta Historical Society Museum,** a 1914 mission-style building that once housed the city hall, police and fire departments. Open on Saturday or by appointment. ~ 136 North Grand Avenue, Nogales; 520-287-4621.

Just off of Route 82 you'll pass by some **ghost towns,** including Harshaw and Duquesne. **Duquesne** was a mining center established around the turn of the century with a peak population of 1000 residents, including Westinghouse of Westinghouse Electric. **Harshaw** was settled around 1875 and operated about 100 mines. Today all that's left are ruins and graveyards. Some of the roads en route are extremely rugged and bumpy, so be prepared.

Tucson and the surrounding area is known as the Astronomy Capital of the World with more astronomical observatories than anywhere else. One of the most famous is the **Kitt Peak National Observatory.** Drive up a mountain road and you'll come across the observatory's gleaming white domes and its 24 telescopes. During tours you can step inside some of the telescopes, including the 18-story-high four-meter telescope. There's also a museum with exhibits on the observatory, as well as star-gazing programs (520-318-8726 for schedule). Serious astronomy buffs can spend the night on top for a steep fee. If you're planning on staying awhile, bring food—it's a long haul up the mountain and there's nothing to nibble on at the top. ~ Located 56 miles southwest of Tucson off Route 386; 520-318-8600.

Continuing to the west about 100 miles on Route 85 you'll come to **Ajo,** a small scenic town whose center is a green plaza surrounded by Spanish Colonial–style buildings. It is also an old copper mining town and as such shows its scars. The **Phelps Dodge Ajo Incorporated Copper Mine** is one of the largest open-pit copper mines in the world, stretching a full mile in diameter. Although operations ceased in 1984, you can go to the pit lookout and learn about mining operations at the adjacent visitors center. Closed Saturday and Sunday. ~ South Route 85, Ajo; 520-387-7451.

From the mine you can see the **Ajo Historical Society Museum** located in what was once St. Catherine's Indian Mission, a stucco church built in 1942. Inside are artifacts from Ajo's history, including a blacksmith shop, dentist's office, printing shop and American Indian artifacts such as old saddles found on graves. ~ 160 Mission Street, Ajo; 520-387-7105.

HIDDEN ►

From Ajo, drive north on Route 85 until you reach Route 8; proceed west and you'll eventually hit Wellton. Don't blink, or you'll miss the **McElhaney Cattle Company Museum** with its amusing collection of antiquities including buggies, carriages, a popcorn wagon, an old hearse, several stagecoaches, a fire wagon and antique cars. Closed Sunday. ~ County Road 9, Wellton; 520-785-3384.

Much farther west, near the California border, is **Yuma**. Once a steamboat stop and major crossing on the Colorado River, today it's a bustling city that supports farming and basks in a subtropical climate. The first major construction here was the **Yuma Territorial Prison**, a penitentiary built between 1876 and 1909 and now a state historic park. Despite its infamous reputation, written evidence indicates that the prison was humanely administered and was a model institution for its time. Prisoners received regular medical attention and schooling was available to the convicts. Those who escaped were faced with hostile deserts and the currents of the Colorado River. The prison was closed in 1909 because of overcrowding. Today visitors walk through the gloomy cells and climb the guard tower, where one can see the Colorado River and surrounding area. Admission. ~ 1 Prison Hill Road, Yuma; 520-783-4771.

For an excursion on the Colorado River, try a jetboat tour. Yuma River Tours offers rides past petroglyphs, homesteads, steamboat landings and mining camps. ~ 1920 Arizona Avenue, Yuma; 520-783-4400.

The military supply hub for the Arizona Territory is now the **Yuma Crossing State Historic Park Quartermaster Depot**, which served the Southwest until it closed in 1883. Several of the original buildings remain, including the commanding officer's quarters and Office of the Quartermaster. Admission. ~ 201 North 4th Avenue, Yuma; 520-329-0471.

More of Yuma's history comes to light in the **Arizona Historical Society Century House Museum**. Once the home of pioneer merchant E. F. Sanguinetti, it now has artifacts, photographs and furnishings of Arizona's territorial period. Just outside are colorful gardens and aviaries with exotic birds. Closed Sunday and Monday. ~ 240 South Madison Avenue, Yuma; 520-782-1841.

Old Town Art Gallery features the work of many local and regional artists, including paintings, ceramics, fine woodworking and hand-crafted furniture. Closed Sunday. ~ 297 South Main Street, Yuma; 520-782-1148.

LODGING

Located in Madera Canyon, **Santa Rita Lodge Nature Resort** is a perfect birders' getaway. Just outside the large windows in each of the 12 rooms are feeders that attract a number of bird species.

Inside the rooms, charts hang with pictures of different types of hummingbirds. The lodge also offers nature programs that meet in the patio area, and staff birders will take guests on birding walks. All rooms have kitchens. ~ Located 13 miles southeast of Green Valley in the Coronado National Forest; 520-625-8746, fax 520-648-1186; e-mail lcollister@theriver.com. MODERATE.

Bing Crosby founded the **Tubac Golf Resort** back in 1959. The 45 rooms and suites are decorated in a Western motif and have tiled bathrooms and patios facing the mountains. Some have woodburning fireplaces. The resort has a golf course, tennis court, pool and spa, hiking trails and a full service restaurant and bar. ~ 1 Avenida de Otero, Tubac; 520-398-2211, 800-848-7893, fax 520-398-9261; www.arizonaguide.com/tubac. DELUXE.

Rio Rico Resort & Country Club is a beautiful resort in the Cayetano Mountain range. Many of the rooms have wood-beamed ceilings, sliding glass doors overlooking the pool or mountains, and contemporary Southwestern decor in pastel colors. Amenities include a golf course, tennis courts, horse stables, jacuzzi, exercise room, restaurant and lounge. ~ 1069 Camino Caralampi, Rio Rico; 520-281-1901, 800-288-4746, fax 520-281-7132; www.arizonaguide.com/riorico. DELUXE.

The Stage Stop Inn is a 43-room hotel with a restaurant and clean, comfortable rooms (some with kitchenettes) facing the pool in the middle. Movie casts and crew often stay here while filming in the area. The Western lobby showcases an antelope head above the fireplace, cattle brands on the tile floor and Western paintings on the walls. ~ 303 McKeown Avenue, Patagonia; phone/fax 520-394-2211, 800-923-2211. BUDGET.

A charming old adobe that was once a boarding house for miners, **Duquesne House Bed and Breakfast Gallery** offers four comfortable suites with brick floors and Mission-style architectural details. The upstairs suite has a private balcony. The common room features a woodstove and TV. A pleasant back porch overlooks a garden and fish pond. A full breakfast is served. ~ 357 Duquesne Street, Patagonia; 520-394-2732, fax 520-394-0054. MODERATE.

Looking like a miniature dollhouse, **The Guest House Inn** is a charming white house with blue trim and a long front porch dotted with white-cushioned wicker furniture for lazing away the hours. Phelps Dodge once entertained dignitaries here; breakfast is now served on the 20-foot-long walnut dining table where these guests once ate. Inside the setup is unusual, with a living room in the middle and guest rooms lining either side. Each of the four bedrooms has a private bath and its own decorating scheme. ~ 700 Guest House Road, Ajo; 520-387-6133. MODERATE.

Located atop the highest hill in Ajo, **The Mine Manager's House Inn** was built in 1919 for the mine manager's family. You can see the mine from the house, and inside old photos of the mine hang in the cozy living room. The room furnishings are a mixture of modern and antique. Breakfast is served at the huge pecan table original to the house. During free time, stop in the reading room or soak in the outdoor hot tub. ~ 601 West Greenway Drive, Ajo; 520-387-6505, fax 520-387-6508. MODERATE.

Built during the space races with the Russians, the theme at the **Best Western Space Age Lodge** is obvious. Guest rooms have pictures of rockets blasting off into space and contain whitewashed wood furniture, pastel colors and large, well-lighted mirrors above the counter. There's also a pool and coffee shop. ~ 401 East Pima Street, Gila Bend; phone/fax 520-683-2273, 800-528-1234. BUDGET.

La Fuente Inn has 96 Southwest-style rooms decorated in pastels. Rooms face the grassy interior courtyard and pool. Prices include a complimentary continental breakfast, happy hour and use of the fitness room. ~ 1513 East 16th Street, Yuma; 520-329-1814, 800-841-1814, fax 520-343-2671. MODERATE.

Shilo Inn Hotel offers 134 rooms decorated in pastel colors, some with couches, patios and tile bathrooms. Suites with kitchenettes are also available. A three-story-high lobby with marble floors and mirrored columns welcomes guests. Amenities include a swimming pool, whirlpool bath, exercise rooms, sauna and steam room. ~ 1550 South Castle Dome Avenue, Yuma; 520-782-9511, 800-222-2244, fax 520-783-1538. MODERATE.

DINING

HIDDEN ▶

Even though there's not much in Amado, it's worth a stop to eat at **The Cow Palace**, a local landmark that has been around since the 1920s. While in town to shoot movies, Western stars have frequented the place, and their photos hang on the walls. Decor is rustic Western, with a wagon wheel for a chandelier and red tablecloths, carpet and curtains. Entrées carry on the theme with names such as The Trail Boss porterhouse steak and Chuck Wagon barbecue beef sandwich. ~ Off Route 19 (Exit 48), 28802 South Nogales Highway, Amado; 520-398-2201. BUDGET TO DELUXE.

If you've never dined in a 150-year-old horse stable, stop in at **The Stables** restaurant at The Tubac Golf Resort. Actually, the place is quite nice. Inside are arched windows, cobblestone floors and pottery made by Mexicans and American Indians. Look closely and you might find Apache Indian arrowheads embedded in the restaurant's adobe walls. Dinner focuses on steak, pasta, seafood and Mexican specialties with a Southwestern twist. ~ 1 Avenida de Otero, Tubac; 520-398-2678. MODERATE TO DELUXE.

Opened in the 1940s as a coffee shop in someone's home, **Wisdom's Café** is now a restaurant crammed with old photographs, farming tools, velvet paintings, patchwork rugs and other odds and ends. You can spot it on the road by the two gigantic imitation chickens in front. If you can get by the chickens, try some of their Mexican food. Closed Sunday. ~ Route 19 frontage road, Tumacacori; 520-398-2397. BUDGET.

San Cayetano in the Rio Rico Resort & Country Club offers Southwestern cuisine as well as a Sunday champagne brunch. Two walls have floor-to-ceiling windows with panoramic views of the mountains. The interior has tables and booths decorated in blue, tan and maroon to fit a casual Southwestern look. ~ 1069 Camino Caralampi, Rio Rico; 520-281-1901. MODERATE TO DELUXE.

Home Plate is a greasy spoon where the locals meet to chow ◀ HIDDEN
down on burgers and hot and cold sandwiches. Civic-club banners circle the room and partially cover the brick walls. Open for breakfast and lunch only. ~ 277 McKeown Avenue, Patagonia; 520-394-2344. BUDGET.

The dining room at the **Stage Stop Inn** has the hotel's Western theme with cattle brands on the floors and a chuckwagon containing a wine display. Offerings include sandwiches, hamburgers, steaks, Mexican food and homemade desserts. ~ 303 McKeown Avenue, Patagonia; 520-394-2211. BUDGET.

Although the exterior of **Dago Joe's** is rather plain, the owners have livened up the interior with contemporary decor—framed posters, plants, a peach-accented wall and white and red tablecloths. The menu is varied, but they're known for steaks. Closed Tuesday. ~ 2055-A North Route 85, Ajo; 520-387-6904. BUDGET TO MODERATE.

A Yuma tradition for more than a decade, **Hensley's Beef Beans and Beer** is the place for prime rib and hamburgers. Food is served amid walls covered with cowboy pictures and cow horns. ~ 2855 South 4th Avenue, Yuma; 520-344-1345. MODERATE.

For satisfying burgers and a variety of sandwiches on the cheap try **Lutes Casino**. The history adds ambience, as this large, dark

✔ **CHECK THESE OUT—UNIQUE DINING**

- *Budget:* Step past two enormous chickens into **Wisdom's Café** for Mexican food amidst farming tools and velvet paintings. *page 318*
- *Moderate:* Sample tantalizing *pollo en chipotle* and beer-marinated pork in **Café Poca Cosa's** technicolor environment. *page 291*
- *Deluxe:* Indulge in duckling glazed with prickly pear cactus sauce served with a mountain view at the elegant **Tanque Verde Ranch**. *page 293*
- *Ultra-deluxe:* Admire the Tucson Museum of Art's collection, then dine at neighboring **Janos**, where pepito-roasted lamb loin is among the offerings. *page 293*

Budget: under $8   Moderate: $8–$16   Deluxe: $16–$24   Ultra-deluxe: over $24

pool hall, domino parlor and restaurant was a casino back in 1920s. ~ 221 Main Street, Yuma; 520-782-2192. BUDGET.

A ladies luncheon kind of place, **Garden Café** in back of the Century House Museum offers sandwiches, salads and quiche. The setting is charming amidst gardens and aviaries full of birds. An added perk is outdoor misters that help keep diners cool on hot days. The Garden Café serves breakfast, lunch and Sunday brunch. ~ 250 South Madison Avenue, Yuma; 520-783-1491. BUDGET TO MODERATE.

SHOPPING   About 80 shops and restaurants make up the town of **Tubac**. Although it's geared to tourists, they've managed to avoid the rubber-tomahawk syndrome and you'll find high-quality artwork. All of the shops are within walking distance and are evenly distributed along Tubac Road, Plaza Road and Calle Otero.

Tortuga Books, known throughout the Southwest, specializes in philosophy, psychology, children's books, Southwestern literature, greeting cards, CDs and cassettes. ~ 19 Tubac Road, Tubac; 520-398-2807. **The Pot Shop Gallery** features signed lithographs by R. C. Gorman, as well as prints, pottery and clay artwork created by Arizona artisans. ~ 16 Tubac Road, Tubac; 520-398-2898. The **Chile Pepper** and **Chile Pepper, Too!** offer Southwestern gourmet foods, chile food products, chile wreaths, coffees, teas, clothing and jewelry. ~ 201 Tubac Road, Tubac; 520-398-2921. For handcrafted American Indian jewelry, kachinas, sandpaintings, baskets and pottery, stop in **Old Presidio Traders**. ~ 27 Tubac Road, Tubac; 520-398-9333.

Owned and operated by American Indians, **Cloud Dancer Jewelry Studio** is a fine art gallery that has the largest Hopi kachina collection in the Southwest. Cloud Dancer also offers custom-designed jewelry with turquoise and precious gems in gold, silver and platinum settings, as well as paintings, pottery and sculpture. ~ 4 Tubac Road, Tubac; 520-398-2546.

To shop in the older, more historic section of town, go to Calle Iglesia. In this area you'll find **Hugh Cabot Studios & Gallery** housed in a 250-year-old adobe building that used to be a hostelry for Spanish soldiers. This internationally known artist creates Southwestern and general-interest works in several mediums and makes his home in Tubac. Closed Sunday and the month of July. ~ Calle Iglesia, Tubac; 520398-2721.

The **Tubac Country Shop** sells Mexican pottery, glassware, dried flowers and children's gifts. ~ Rodgers Lane, Tubac; 520-398-2121.

The **Ajo Art Gallery** has contemporary paintings by artists from across the United States. Closed Monday and from May through September. ~ 661 North 2nd Avenue, Ajo; 520-387-7525.

Colorado River Pottery has quite a selection of ceramics made on-site. Open on Saturday by appointment; closed Sunday. ~ 67 West 2nd Street, Yuma; 520-343-0413. At the **One Percent Gallery**, George Tomkins creates decorative clay pieces while wife Neely fashions sculpture from clay and other media. Call for hours. ~ 78 West 2nd Street, Yuma; 520-782-1934.

Scenic mountain views from picture windows draw people to **Calabasas Lounge** at the Rio Rico Resort & Country Club. The contemporary, Southwest-style bar has live Top-40, jazz and dance music on weekends. ~ 1069 Camino Caralampi, Rio Rico; 520-281-1901.

NIGHTLIFE

Lutes Casino is one of the oldest continually owned and operated pool and domino parlors in the state. Open since 1920, the place is crammed full of farm implements, paintings and historic memorabilia. ~ 221 Main Street, Yuma; 520-782-2192.

For live alternative and rock bands, head on over to **Jimmie Dee's**. Antique signs and assorted knickknacks give this bar an old-timey feel. ~ 38 West 2nd Street, Yuma; 520-783-5647.

PATAGONIA LAKE STATE PARK   **PARKS**
The largest recreational lake in Southern Arizona (265 acres) is located in this park. Patagonia Lake, nestled amid rolling hills, was created by the damming of Sonoita Creek in 1968. It's stocked with bass, crappie, catfish, bluegill and, in the winter, trout. A small, sandy beach lures swimmers. You can windsurf and waterski here, but waterskiing is not allowed on weekends or holidays from May through October. Because of its elevation of 3750 feet, the 645-acre park sometimes has temperatures cooler than Tucson. The park provides picnic areas, restrooms, showers and a marina with boat rentals. Pontoon birding tours are offered on Saturday or by request. Day-use fee, $5. ~ Located off Route 82 about 12 miles north of Nogales. Follow the signs to the park; 520-287-6965.

▲ There are 119 sites, including 34 RV hookups and 13 accessible by boat only; hookups are $15 per vehicle, all other sites $10 per vehicle.

PATAGONIA SONOITA CREEK PRESERVE Nine miles north of Patagonia Lake State Park is a 312-acre sanctuary in a narrow flood plain between the Santa Rita and the Patagonia mountains. This preserve encompasses a one-and-a-half-mile stretch of Sonoita Creek lined with large stands of cottonwoods—some a hundred feet tall—as well as Arizona walnut, velvet ash, willows and Texas mulberry. Birdwatchers from all over the world come here because more than 200 species of birds have been seen. It is also home to white-tailed deer, bobcat, javelina, coyotes and the most endangered fish in the Southwest, the Gila Topminnow. There are restrooms and water in the preserve. Closed Monday and Tuesday. ~

From Patagonia, turn northwest off Route 82 onto 4th Avenue, then go left on Pennsylvania Avenue. When the pavement ends, cross the creek and follow the dirt road for two miles. There will be an entrance with the visitors center on your left; 520-394-2400.

CORONADO NATIONAL FOREST The Coronado National Forest in Arizona has 1.7 million acres of public land in 12 sky islands, or mountain ranges that jut above the surrounding desert. Following are three of the highlights:

Madera Canyon 🧍 🚲 🐎 This spot is a great place for birdwatching, with more than 200 species including several varieties of woodpeckers, hawks, wrens and vultures. Driving up through the canyon the desert changes from grassland to forest. Trees on the lower slopes of the Santa Rita Mountains are mesquite, and farther up are live oaks, alligator junipers, cottonwoods and sycamores along Madera Creek. There are more than 70 miles of trails. You'll find restrooms, picnic areas and grills. The $5 day-use fee covers both Madera Canyon and Pena Blanca Lake. ~ Take Route 19 south from Tucson to Green Valley's Continental Road, then go southeast for 13 miles; 520-281-2296.

▲ There are 13 sites at Bog Springs Campground; $10 per night per vehicle.

Pena Blanca Lake 🧍 🐎 🚤 🛥 This is a 49-acre lake surrounded by oak, cottonwood and mesquite trees and light-colored bluffs. The lake is situated at 4000 feet—making it higher and somewhat cooler than Tucson. Fishing is good for bass, bluegill, crappie, catfish and rainbow trout but because of high mercury levels, the Fish and Wildlife Department recommends that you catch and release all but trout. A trail leads around the lake. Also here are picnic areas, pit toilets and picnic tables. ~ Located five miles north of the Mexican border. Take Route 19 south from Tucson to Ruby Road, then go west for about nine miles; 520-281-2296.

▲ There are 15 sites at White Rock Campground (a quarter-mile from the lake), although there are no lake views; $5 per night per vehicle.

Parker Canyon Lake 🚤 🛥 Parker Canyon Lake is an 130-acre fishing lake west of the Huachuca Mountains and surrounded by grassy, rolling hills. Bluegill, bass, perch, trout and catfish are the common catches. To assist with the fishing there are boat rentals, bait and a fishing dock. There are also restrooms, picnic areas and a grocery store. Day-use fee, $5. ~ From Sonoita, take Route 83 south for 30 miles until it runs into the park; 520-378-0311.

▲ There are 64 sites and an overflow area in the summer that accommodates 50 to 75 self-contained vehicles; $10 per night.

ORGAN PIPE CACTUS NATIONAL MONUMENT 🧍 🚲 This 330,000-acre refuge became a national monument in 1937 to protect the Sonoran desert plants and animals and the unique organ pipe cactus. Start at the visitors center 17 miles south of the northern entrance. Here you can see exhibits and pick up a self-guided tour pamphlet. A good tour is the **Puerto Blanco Scenic Drive**, a 53-mile graded dirt loop with numbered stops described on the tour. The only paved road through the park is Route 85. While exploring the monument, you'll pass mountains, plains, canyons, dry washes and a pond surrounded by cottonwood trees. Picnic areas and restrooms are the only facilities in the park. Day-use fee, $4. ~ The monument is located 35 miles south of Ajo, and the visitors center is at the 75-mile marker on Route 85; 520-387-6849.

An innocent-looking cactus can fool you. If you get stuck, use tweezers or two sticks to remove the thorn.

▲ There are 208 sites in the main campground; $8 per night. Fresh water is available at the dump station and at the visitors center. Primitive camping is allowed at four sites in the Alamo campground and anywhere in the backcountry as long as you're a half mile from the road; you can pick up the free permits for backcountry camping at the visitors center. No campfires.

CABEZA PRIETA NATIONAL WILDLIFE REFUGE Established in 1939 to protect wildlife and wildlife habitat, the 860,000-acre refuge is an arid wilderness rife with cactus and mountains. Passing through the refuge is the 250-mile El Camino del Diablo (Highway of the Devil) that was pioneered by Spanish Conquistador Captain de Anza in 1774—and stretches from Mexico to California. Along the way you pass Cabeza Prieta Mountain with its lava-topped granite peak, and Mohawk Valley with sand dunes and lava flows. Since roads here are rugged and unimproved, four-wheel-drive vehicles are required. Also, beware of the six species of rattlesnakes. There are no facilities in the refuge; the closest groceries are in Ajo, seven miles east. The refuge is sometimes closed for inclement weather; call ahead to see if it's open. ~ You'll need explicit directions, which you can get when you pick up the Refuge Entry Permit at the refuge office in Ajo (1611 North 2nd Avenue). It's advisable to call ahead; 520-387-6483.

▲ There are three primitive campgrounds with no facilities; no wood fires allowed; no water. Permit required.

Outdoor Adventures

Although water isn't plentiful in Southern Arizona, there are a few lakes where boats are available to rent.

BOATING

TUCSON You can rent paddle boats in Tucson and cruise around the duck island in Gene C. Reid Park's **Reid Lake**. ~ Between Broadway and 22nd Street, Country Club and Alvernon Way, Tucson; 520-791-4873; rentals, 520-791-4088.

EAST OF TUCSON   Boat rentals are available at **Parker Canyon Lake,** nestled among the foothills of the Huachuca Mountains. ~ Off Route 83, 30 miles southwest of Sierra Vista; 520-455-5847.

SOUTH/WEST OF TUCSON   **Patagonia Lake State Park** rents rowboats, canoes and paddleboats. ~ Patagonia; 520-287-6063.

SWIMMING   For a retreat from the heat take a plunge at Tucson's public pools. **Fort Lowell Park** has an Olympic-size pool. ~ 2900 North Craycroft Road; 520-791-2585. Dive in at **Himmel Park.** Closed in winter. ~ 1000 North Tucson Boulevard; 520-791-4157. Get wet at **Morris K. Udall Park.** ~ 7200 East Tanque Verde Road; 520-791-4004. **Joaquin Murieta Park** has a public pool. Summer only. ~ 1400 North Silverbell Road; 520-791-4752. Cool yourself down in **Jacobs Park'**s pool. Summer only. ~ 1010 West Lind; 520-791-4358.

BALLOON RIDES   For those without a fear of heights, there's nothing like floating above it all. Ballooning is a great way to escape the heat and get a magnificent view at the same time.

TUCSON   A **Southern Arizona Balloon Excursion** ascends from the Tucson area. Sunrise trips fly high enough for great views of Tucson and the Catalina Mountains and low enough to see wildlife along the Santa Cruz River. ~ 537 West Grant, Tucson; 520-624-3599. Another company hovering above is **Balloon America,** which offers sunrise flights over the Sonoran desert, the Catalina Mountains and the Grand Canyon. ~ Located near Speedway Boulevard and Houghton Road; 520-299-7744.

SKIING   There's only one place to ski and snowboard in these parts—the **Mount Lemmon Ski Valley.** The southernmost ski-area in North America, Mount Lemmon offers 18 runs, equipment rentals, a ski school and a restaurant. ~ 10300 East Ski Run Road, Mount Lemmon; 520-576-1321.

RIDING STABLES   If you prefer to let someone else do the walking, there are several horseback riding outfitters in the area.

TUCSON   A Western town like Tucson wouldn't be the same without opportunities to go riding. Dudes and dudettes can saddle up at **Walking Winds and El Conquistador Stables.** They offer rides in the Catalina Mountains as well as hayrides. ~ 10811 North Oracle Road; 520-742-4200. **Pusch Ridge Stables** leads one-hour to overnight excursions; all meals and equipment are provided on overnight trips. ~ 13700 North Oracle Road; 520-825-1664. Saddle up at **Pantano Riding Stables** for a guided trip into Coronado National Forest and the foothills of the Catalina Mountains. ~ 4450 South Houghton Road; 520-298-9076. **Wild Horse Ranch Resort** has pony rides for kids along with trail rides into the Sonoran desert and the foothills of the Tucson mountains. ~ 6801 North Camino Verde; 520-744-1012.

Mild winters make this region ideal for golfers, and aficionados can choose between a wide range of private and public courses. Most courses listed have club and cart rentals, pro shops and golf pros available for lessons.

GOLF

TUCSON The semiprivate **Tucson National Golf Club** has 27 holes—three 9-hole courses that can be played in different combinations—and hosts many tournaments. ~ 2727 West Club Drive; 520-575-7540. **Starr Pass Golf Club**, an 18-hole mountain course, sports long fairways, rolling greens and many elevation changes. Carts are mandatory. ~ 3645 West Starr Pass Boulevard; 520-670-0400. **Randolph Municipal Golf Course**'s 18-holes have long fairways and water hazards on six holes. The adjacent 18-hole **Del Urich Municipal Golf Course** has tall trees, lush fairways, straight holes and rolling terrain, with elevated tees and greens. Both courses share a pro shop, practice area, driving range and putting green. ~ 600 South Alvernon Way; 520-791-4161.

Be the best that you can be at the 18-hole executive **Dorado Golf Course**. ~ 6601 East Speedway Boulevard; 520-885-6751. Go for a hole in one at the public 18-hole **Arthur Pack Desert Golf Course**. ~ 9101 North Thornydale Road; 520-744-3322. Play the manicured greens at the semiprivate **Ventana Canyon Golf & Racquet Club**, an 18-hole PGA resort course that runs through rocky canyons, arroyos and foothills. ~ 6200 North Club House Lane; 520-577-1400. Beware the hazards at the 18-hole **Cliff Valley Golf Course**. ~ 5910 North Oracle Road; 520-887-6161. Tee off at the 18-hole, public **El Rio Golf Course**. ~ 1400 West Speedway Boulevard; 520-791-4229. **Fred Enke Golf Course** is an 18-hole desert course. ~ 8251 East Irvington Road; 520-296-8607. Situated on the bank of the Santa Cruz River, 18-hole **Silverbell Golf Course** sports flat fairways, large greens and nine lakes. ~ 3600 North Silverbell Road; 520-791-5235.

EAST OF TUCSON A golfing spot east of Tucson is the 18-hole **Turquoise Valley Golf Course**. ~ 1741 Newell Road, Bisbee; 520-432-3091. In Douglas, the 18-hole **Douglas Municipal Golf Course** has a a lounge and an adjacent RV park under the same ownership, all in a desert setting surrounded by mountains. Cart rentals only. ~ Leslie Canyon Road North, Douglas; 520-364-3722.

SOUTH/WEST OF TUCSON **Canoa Hills Golf Course** is an 18-hole public facility. ~ 1401 West Calle Urbano, Green Valley; 520-648-1880. **Pueblo Del Sol Golf Course**, an 18-hole green, rents clubs and carts. ~ 2770 St. Andrews Drive, Sierra Vista; 520-378-6444. At the Resort Rio Rico, play the greens at the private, 18-hole **Rio Rico Golf Course**. ~ 1069 Camino Caralampi, Rio Rico; 520-281-8567. **Tubac Valley Country Club**, an 18-hole course with lots of trees as well as a restaurant and bar, is the premier spot in Tubac. ~ 1 Otero Road; 520-398-2211. If passing through Safford, check out the 18-hole **Mount Graham Golf Course**. ~ Golf Course Road, Safford; 520-348-3140. In Yuma you can tee off at the 18-hole **Mesa Del Sol Golf Club**. ~ 12213 Calle del Cid; 520-342-1817.

TENNIS

The dry, hot climate provides excellent court conditions all year.

TUCSON   When it's not too hot to serve, try the public tennis courts in Tucson. **Fort Lowell Park** has eight lighted courts as well as racquetball courts and a tennis pro. Fee. ~ 2900 North Craycroft Road; 520-791-2584. **Himmel Park** also has eight lighted courts. Fee. ~ 1000 North Tucson Boulevard; 520-791-3276. All 25 courts at the **Randolph Tennis Center** are lighted for night play. Fee. ~ 50 South Alvernon Way; 520-791-4896. **Pima Community College** has eight lighted courts for public use on a first-come, first-served basis; classes have priority. ~ 2202 West Anklam Road; 520-206-6619.

BIKING

In the mountains or along a river, on asphalt or dirt, through residential areas or among the mighty saguaro, Tucson is bicycle-friendly. If you haven't brought one, rent one in town and take to the road or trail.

TUCSON   Tucson is a very popular area for bicycling. Some favorite routes include riding on **Oracle Road** north of Ina Road where cyclists find wide shoulders and beautiful mountain views. On the way back turn into Sun City Vistoso, a large retirement community where the roads are wide and the scenery pretty.

Another popular ride is parallel to the Santa Catalina Mountain foothills along **Sunrise Drive** to Sabino Canyon, where you can climb up a challenging, four-mile road through the mountains. Because of the tour shuttles, Sabino Canyon is only open to bicyclists before 9 a.m. and after 5 p.m., except Wednesday and Saturday when it is closed to bicyclists entirely. For more information, call 520749-8700.

Starting on North Campbell Avenue and running along the banks of the dry Rillito River is a multi-use **asphalt trail**. Currently it's about four miles long, and more trails are added annually. The **Santa Cruz River Park** has another trail that runs about four miles along a riverbank, on both sides of the river

The **Saguaro National Monument**, both east and west, also offers a number of good trails, both for mountain and road bikes, as does the hilly **Tucson Mountain Park**. Both are in scenic areas studded with cactus and mountains. Another enjoyable route is along the **Old Spanish Trail** from Broadway to Colossal Cave.

For more information and maps on bicycling in the area, contact the **City of Tucson bicycling coordinator** at 520-791-4372.

EAST OF TUCSON Good areas for bicycling can also be found outside of Tucson. Bikeable roads east of the city are **Route 90**, which you can take to Sierra Vista and then on to Bisbee, and **Route 80** through Tombstone.

SOUTH/WEST OF TUCSON A good ride is to take **Route 83** from Colossal Cave, past Sonoita and Patagonia to Nogales. This road has little traffic and wide shoulders.

Bike Rentals There are a handful of places in Tucson where you can rent bicycles, including **University Bicycles**, which provides mountain bikes for rides in Tucson Mountain Park and Catalina State Park. Repairs available. ~ 940 East University Boulevard; 520-624-3663. You can also rent a mountain bike and buy a trail map at **Broadway Bicycles**. ~ 140 South Sarnoff Drive; 520-296-7819. Equipment and mountain-bike rentals are available at **Tucson Bicycles**, where they also organize bicycle tours. ~ 4743 East Sunrise Drive; 520-577-7374. **Full Cycle** will help you get set up with mountain bike rentals. Repairs available. ~ 3232 East Speedway Boulevard; 520-327-3232.

HIKING

With trails lacing its many national monuments, recreation areas and state parks, Southern Arizona is built for hiking. You can view old adobe ruins, lime kilns, ancient petroglyphs and geological marvels, or scale one of the many peaks, for a stellar view of your surroundings. All distances for hiking trails are one way unless otherwise noted.

TUCSON In the Rincon Mountain District in Saguaro National Park is the **Freeman Homestead Nature Trail** (1 mile), a loop that starts off the spur road to the Javelina picnic area and descends from a saguaro forest to a small wash filled with mesquite trees. Along the way you pass the ruins of an adobe house built in the 1920s.

The **Cactus Forest Trail** (7 miles) takes you though a saguaro forest between Broadway and Old Spanish Trail. You also pass

✔ **CHECK THESE OUT—OUTDOOR ADVENTURES**
- Pack a picnic lunch, then spend the day at Patagonia Lake State Park fishing, boating and swimming. *page 318*
- Check out the 15 ski runs at the southernmost ski-area in North America—Mount Lemmon Ski Valley. *page 321*
- Cool your feet in refreshing Sabino Creek after cycling Sabino Canyon in the foothills of the Santa Catalina Mountains. *page 323*
- Breathe the pine-filled air as you hike Heart of Rocks Trail and pass rock formations called Totem Pole and Big Balanced Rock. *page 325*

the remains of the first ranger station built in the park and two kilns used to process lime around the turn of the century.

For a trek on **Mount Lemmon** follow the **Wilderness of Rocks Trail** (4 miles). The trailhead is a mile and a half past Ski Valley. On the way are pools along Lemmon Creek and thousands of eroded and balanced rocks.

Pima Canyon Trail (7.6 miles) in the Santa Catalina Mountains is a difficult trail that climbs from 2900 to 7255 feet through a bighorn-sheep management area. Along the way you'll pass Pima Canyon Spring and good views of Tucson and A Mountain. Beyond the spring, the trail becomes steeper and harder to follow. At the top, you'll find good views of Cathedral and Window rocks. To get there, follow Christie Drive north until it dead-ends at Magee Road. Go right and park. Carry lots of water.

In the **Tucson Mountain District** the **King Canyon Trail** (3.5 miles) begins off of Kinney Road across from the Arizona-Sonora Desert Museum, then climbs up to a picnic area and beyond to the top of Wasson Peak (elevation 4687), the highest point in the area.

The short **Signal Hill Petroglyphs Trail** (.13 mile) goes up a winding path along a small hill off Golden Gate Road. At the top are rocks with ancient Indian petroglyphs on them.

The **Valley View Overlook Trail** (.75 mile) on the Bajada Loop Drive descends into two washes and ends on a scenic ridge overlooking most of Avra Valley.

Hunter Trail (2 miles) in **Picacho Peak State Park** offers scenic views as it climbs from 2000 to 3374 feet in elevation. It was named for Captain Sherod Hunter, a Confederate officer who placed lookouts at Picacho pass and was involved in the battle that occurred here in 1862.

EAST OF TUCSON   To find **Lutz Canyon Trail** (2.9 miles), drive 12 miles south of Sierra Vista on Route 92 to Ash Canyon Road. Hikers walk past old mine workings in a narrow, deep canyon with oak, juniper and Douglas fir. ~ Sierra Vista Ranger District: 520-378-0311.

Crest Trail (12 miles) in the **Coronado National Memorial** runs along the crest of the Huachuca Mountains which affords a great view of northern Mexico on clear days. ~ 520-366-5515.

Within the **Chiricahua National Monument** you'll find **Massai Point Nature Trail** (.5 mile), which starts at the geology exhibit at Massai Point and takes you past a large balanced rock, a board with a description of the park's geologic story and views across Rhyolite Canyon.

The **Sugarloaf Trail** (.9 mile) takes you to a fire lookout at the top of Sugarloaf Mountain, the highest point within the monument.

Natural Bridge Trail (2.5 miles) begins at the Bonita Canyon scenic drive, then passes a natural rock bridge and climbs through oak and juniper woodlands to a pine forest.

Heart of Rocks Loop Trail (8-mile loop) winds through pine and fir forests and some of the park's most impressive rock formations, including Big Balanced Rock, Punch and Judy and Totem Pole.

Built as a supply artery for fire fighters stationed in the high Chiricahuas, **Greenhouse Trail** (3.75 miles) ascends 1500 feet. Along the way you'll pass Cima Cabin, the fire fighters' headquarters, and Winn Falls, which flows at a peak during the summer. To get there, go north off Cave Creek Spur Road onto Greenhouse Road and drive half a mile.

The **Coronado National Forest** offers the **South Fork Trail** (6.8 miles). Beginning off Cave Creek Road at the road end in South Fork Forest Camp 3.5 miles above Portal, Arizona, it passes South Fork Cave Creek, one of the most famous birdwatching canyons in the Chiricahua Mountains, and a 70-foot-tall finger of red rhyolite called Pinnacle Rock. It starts in a forest of sycamores, cypress and black walnut trees and leads to huge Douglas fir trees and the small bluffs above the South Fork Cave Creek. ~ Douglas Ranger District: 520-364-3468.

SOUTH/WEST OF TUCSON Kent Springs–Bog Springs Trail Loop (4.3 miles) within the Santa Rita Mountains climbs from 4820 feet to 6620 feet. Along the way are three seasonal springs, which create an unusually lush area with large sycamore, silver-leaf oak, Arizona bamboo and walnut trees alive with birds. Exit off of Route 19 at Madera Canyon and park near the Bog Springs campground.

▼▼▼▼▼▼▼▼▼▼
Transportation

CAR

From Tucson, **Route 10** runs north toward Phoenix, then crosses **Route 8** which heads west toward Gila Bend and Yuma. **Route 85** from Gila Bend goes south, turns into **Route 86**, cuts through the Papago Indian Reservation and goes to Tucson. South of Tucson is **Route 19** to Nogales, while the main thoroughfare east from Tucson is Route 10 toward New Mexico. Jutting south off Route 10 are **Route 83** to Sonoita, **Route 90** to Sierra Vista, **Route 191** to Douglas and **Route 186** to Chiricahua National Monument.

AIR

AeroCalifornia, Aeroliteral, America West Airlines, American Airlines, Continental, Delta Air Lines, Northwest Airlines, Reno Air, Southwest and United Airlines fly into **Tucson International Airport** (520-573-8000).

Yuma International Airport (520-726-5882) is served by America West Express and United Express, while **Sierra Vista Municipal Airport** (520-452-7091) is served by America West Express.

TRAIN

Amtrak (800-872-7245) services the area with the "Texas Eagle" and the "Sunset Limited." Stations are in Tucson at 400 East

Toole Street, in Benson at 4th and Patagonia streets, and in Yuma at 281 Gila Street.

BUS

Greyhound Bus Lines (800-231-2222) services Tucson and the surrounding area from around the country. Stations are in Tucson at 2 South 4th Avenue, 520-792-3475; in Nogales at 35 North Terrace Avenue, 520-287-5628; in Yuma at 170 East 17th Place, 520-783-4403; in Benson at 242 East 4th Street, 520-586-3141; and in Willcox at 622 North Haskell Avenue, 520-384-2183.

CAR RENTALS

At Tucson International Airport are **Avis Rent A Car** (800-331-1212), **Dollar Rent A Car** (800-800-4000), **Hertz Rent A Car** (800-654-3131) and **National Car Rental** (800-227-7368).

Car-rental agencies at the Yuma International Airport are **Avis Rent A Car** (800-331-1212), **Budget Rent A Car** (800-227-3678) and **Hertz Rent A Car** (800-654-3131).

Enterprise Rent A Car (800-325-8007) serves the Sierra Vista Municipal Airport.

PUBLIC TRANSIT

For extensive bus service throughout Tucson, call **Sun Tran** (520-792-9222). Local bus service in Nogales is **Dabdoub Bus Service** (520-287-7810).

TAXIS

Leading cab companies in Tucson include **Allstate Cab Co.** (520-888-2999), **Checker Cab Co.** (520-623-1133) and **Yellow Cab Co.** (520-624-6611).

In Sierra Vista try **Angel Transport** (520-452-9976).

Index

Lodging Index

Dining Index

HIDDEN GUIDES

Adventure travel or a relaxing vacation?—"Hidden" guidebooks are the only travel books in the business to provide detailed information on both. Aimed at environmentally aware travelers, our motto is "Adventure Travel Plus." These books combine details on unique hotels, restaurants and sightseeing with information on camping, sports and hiking for the outdoor enthusiast.

THE NEW KEY GUIDES

Based on the concept of ecotourism, The New Key Guides are dedicated to the preservation of Central America's rare and endangered species, architecture and archaeology. Filled with helpful tips, they give travelers everything they need to know about these exotic destinations.

ULTIMATE FAMILY GUIDES

These innovative guides present the best and most unique features of a family destination. Quality is the keynote. In addition to thoroughly covering each destination, they feature short articles and one-line "teasers" that are both fun and informative.

Ulysses Press books are available at bookstores everywhere. If any of the following titles are unavailable at your local bookstore, ask the bookseller to order them.

You can also order books directly from Ulysses Press
P.O. Box 3440, Berkeley, CA 94703
800-377-2542 or 510-601-8301
fax: 510-601-8307
e-mail: ulysses@ulyssespress.com

Order Form

HIDDEN GUIDEBOOKS

____ Hidden Arizona, $14.95
____ Hidden Bahamas, $12.95
____ Hidden Baja, $14.95
____ Hidden Boston and Cape Cod, $13.95
____ Hidden Cancún & the Yucatán, $16.95
____ Hidden Carolinas, $17.95
____ Hidden Coast of California, $17.95
____ Hidden Colorado, $13.95
____ Hidden Florida, $17.95
____ Hidden Florida Keys & Everglades, $11.95
____ Hidden Georgia, $14.95
____ Hidden Hawaii, $17.95
____ Hidden Idaho, $13.95
____ Hidden Maui, $12.95

____ Hidden Montana, $14.95
____ Hidden New England, $17.95
____ Hidden New Mexico, $14.95
____ Hidden Oahu, $12.95
____ Hidden Oregon, $14.95
____ Hidden Pacific Northwest, $17.95
____ Hidden Rockies, $16.95
____ Hidden San Francisco and Northern California, $17.95
____ Hidden Southern California, $17.95
____ Hidden Southwest, $17.95
____ Hidden Tahiti, $17.95
____ Hidden Tennessee, $15.95
____ Hidden Washington, $14.95
____ Hidden Wyoming, $14.95

THE NEW KEY GUIDEBOOKS

____ The New Key to Belize, $14.95
____ The New Key to Costa Rica, $17.95
____ The New Key to Guatemala, $14.95

____ The New Key to Ecuador and the Galápagos, $16.95

ULTIMATE FAMILY GUIDEBOOKS

____ Disneyland and Beyond, $12.95

____ Disney World and Beyond, $13.95

Mark the book(s) you're ordering and enter the total cost here ⟹ [   ]

California residents add 8% sales tax here ⟹ [   ]

Shipping, check box for your preferred method and enter cost here ⟹ [   ]

☐ BOOK RATE   **FREE! FREE! FREE!**

☐ PRIORITY MAIL $3.00 First book, $1.00/each additional book

☐ UPS 2-DAY AIR $7.00 First book, $1.00/each additional book

[   ]

Billing, enter total amount due here and check method of payment ⟹

☐ CHECK   ☐ MONEY ORDER

☐ VISA/MASTERCARD_____EXP. DATE _____

NAME _____PHONE _____

ADDRESS_____

_____

CITY_____ STATE _____ ZIP_____

MONEY-BACK GUARANTEE ON DIRECT ORDERS PLACED THROUGH ULYSSES PRESS.

ABOUT THE AUTHOR

STEPHEN DOLAINSKI, former editor-in-chief of *Guest Informant* and a regular contributor to *Westways* and *Avenues*, is a freelance travel editor and writer living in Southern California. He has written about travel, culture, the arts, entertainment and business for magazines, and has contributed to several travel guidebooks, including *Hidden Pacific Northwest* and *Disneyland and Beyond*. He is presently writing the guide *Romantic Days and Nights in Los Angeles* for Globe-Pequot Press.

ABOUT THE ILLUSTRATOR

GLENN KIM is a freelance illustrator residing in San Francisco. His work appears in numerous Ulysses Press titles including *Hidden Southwest*, *Hidden New Mexico* and *The New to Key Belize*. He has also illustrated for the National Forest Service, several Bay Area magazines, book covers and greeting cards, as well as for advertising agencies that include Foote Cone and Belding, Hal Riney and Jacobs Fulton Design Group.